volume
7

on
the
Tracks

Shuzo
Oshimi

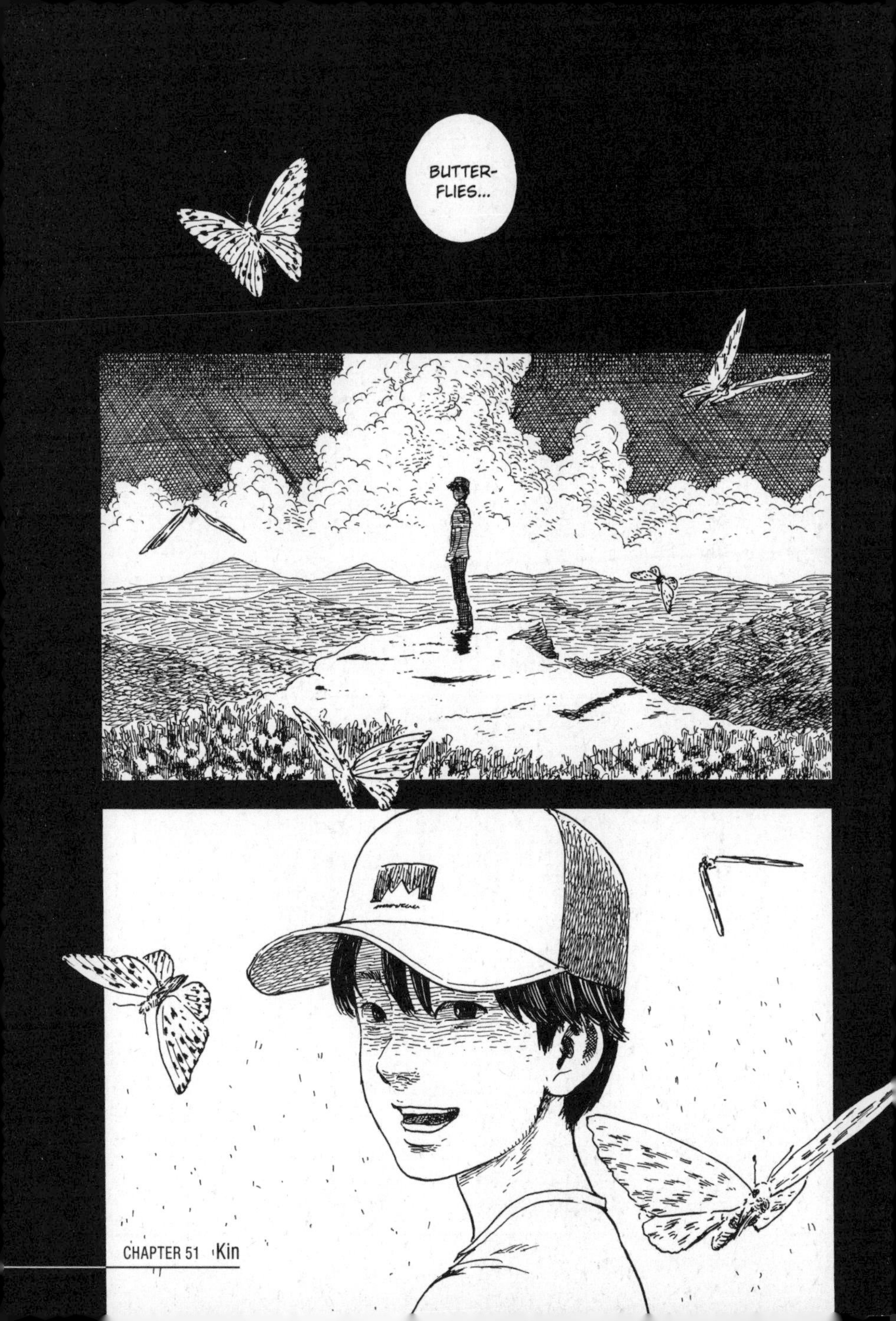
BUTTER-
FLIES...

CHAPTER 51 Kin

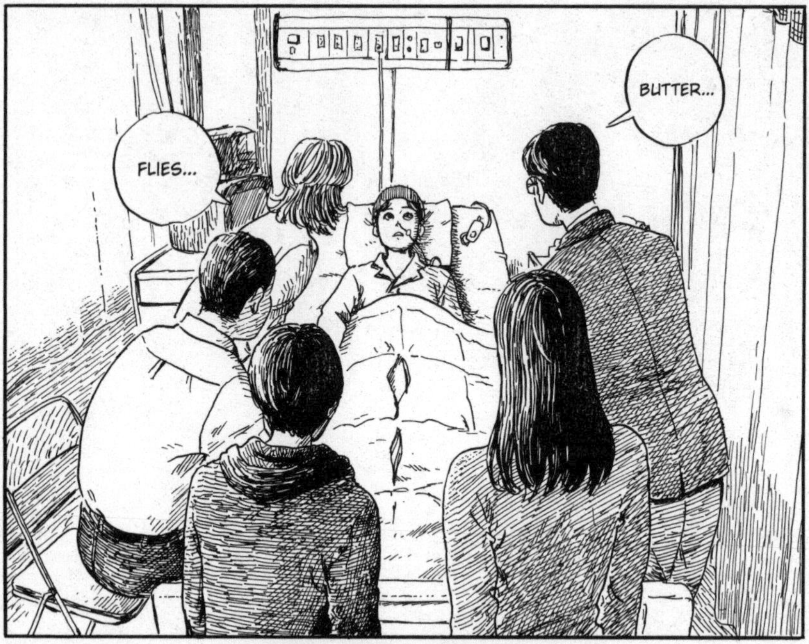
BUTTER...
FLIES...

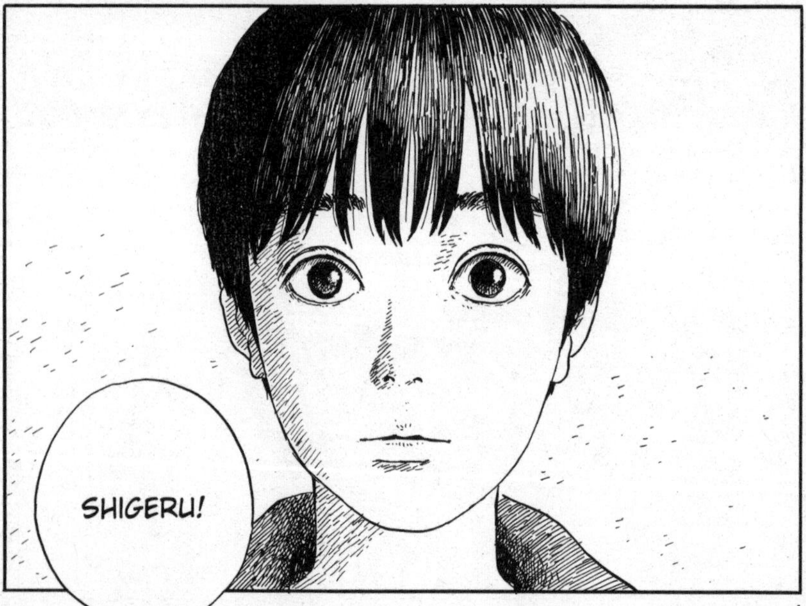
SHIGERU!

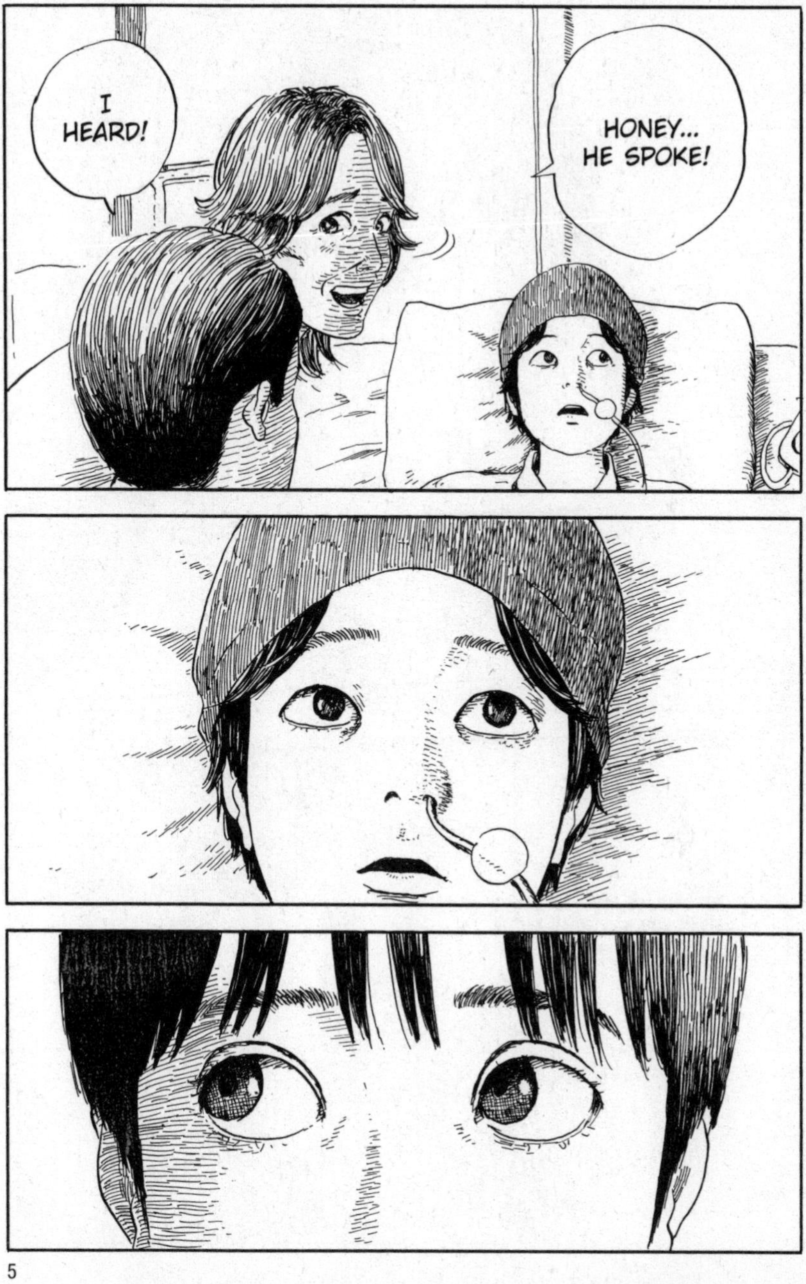
HONEY... HE SPOKE!
I HEARD!

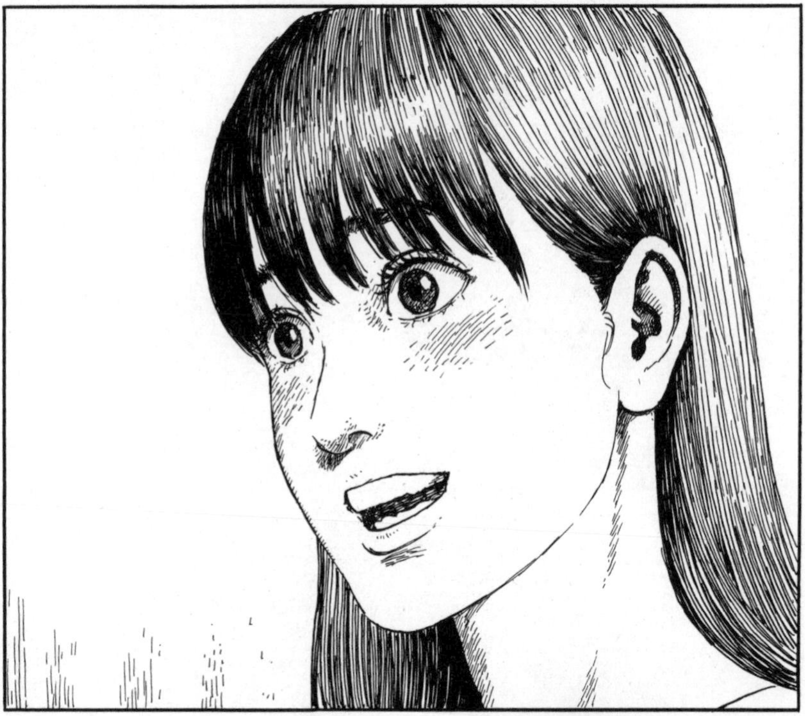

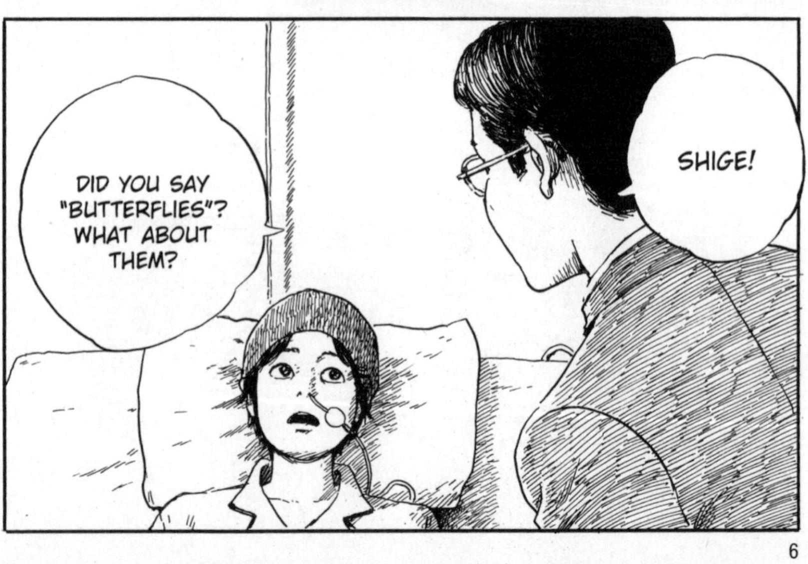
SHIGE!
DID YOU SAY "BUTTERFLIES"? WHAT ABOUT THEM?

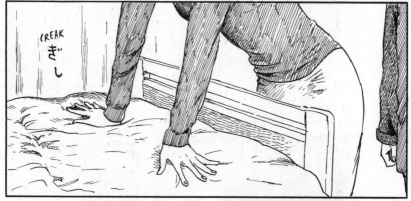

CREAK
ぎし

SHIGE.

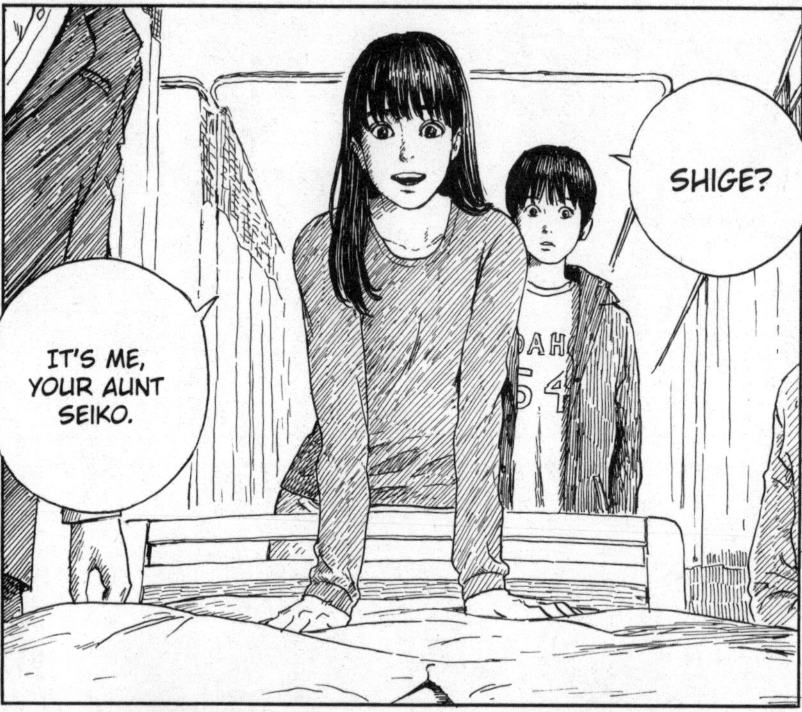
SHIGE?
IT'S ME, YOUR AUNT SEIKO.
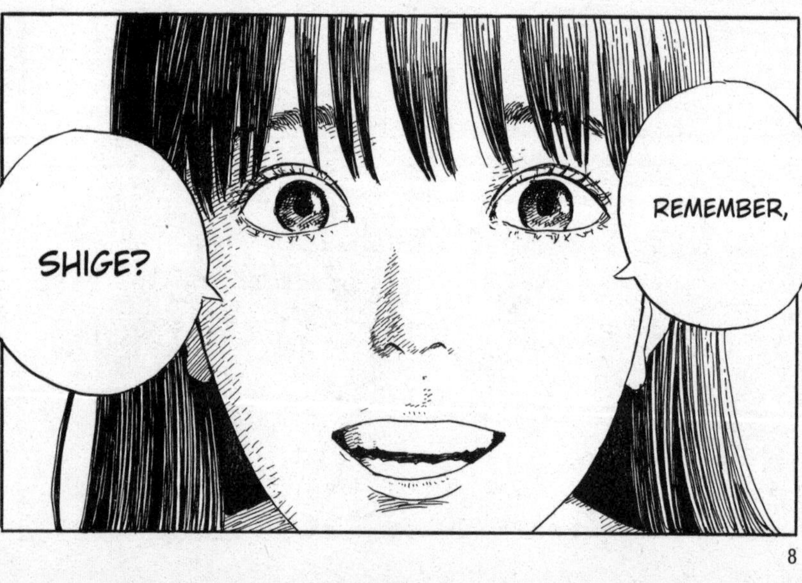
REMEMBER,
SHIGE?

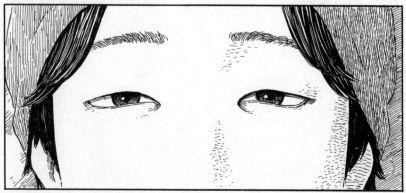

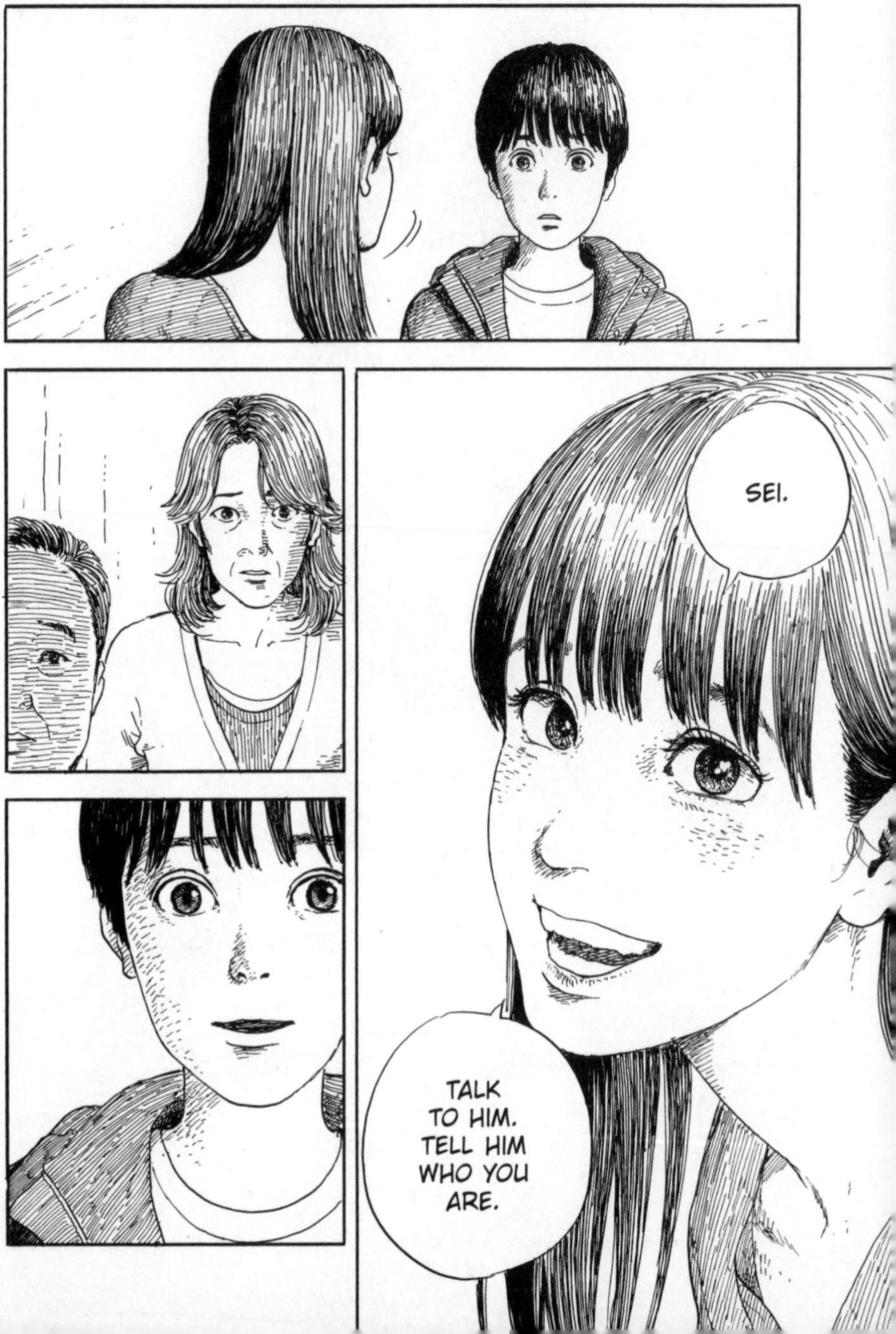
SEI.
TALK TO HIM. TELL HIM WHO YOU ARE.

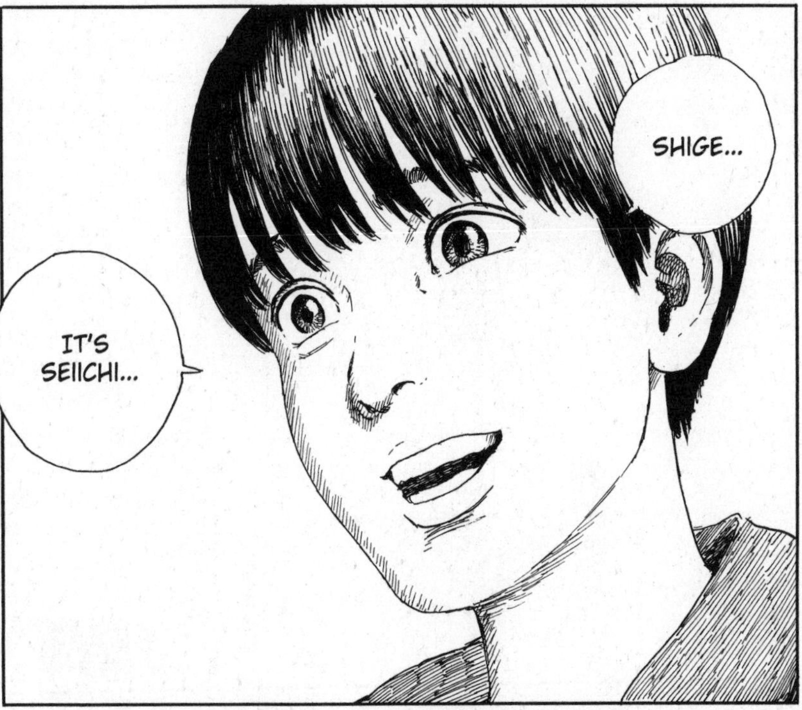
SHIGE...
IT'S SEIICHI...
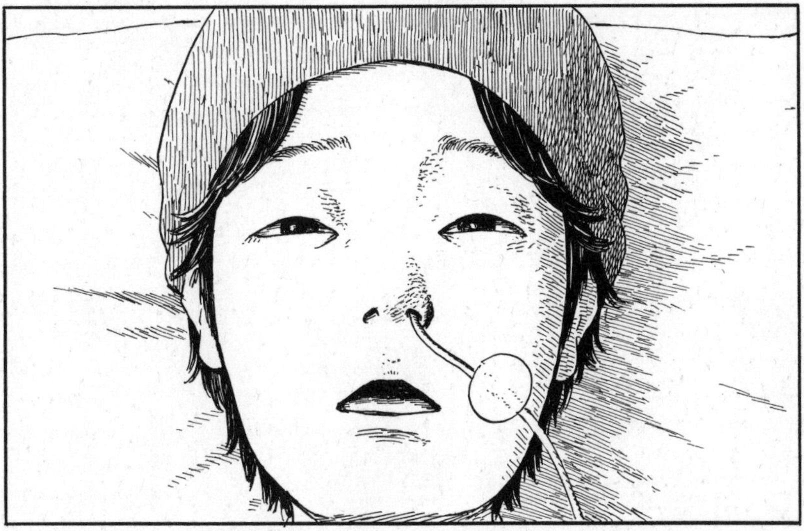

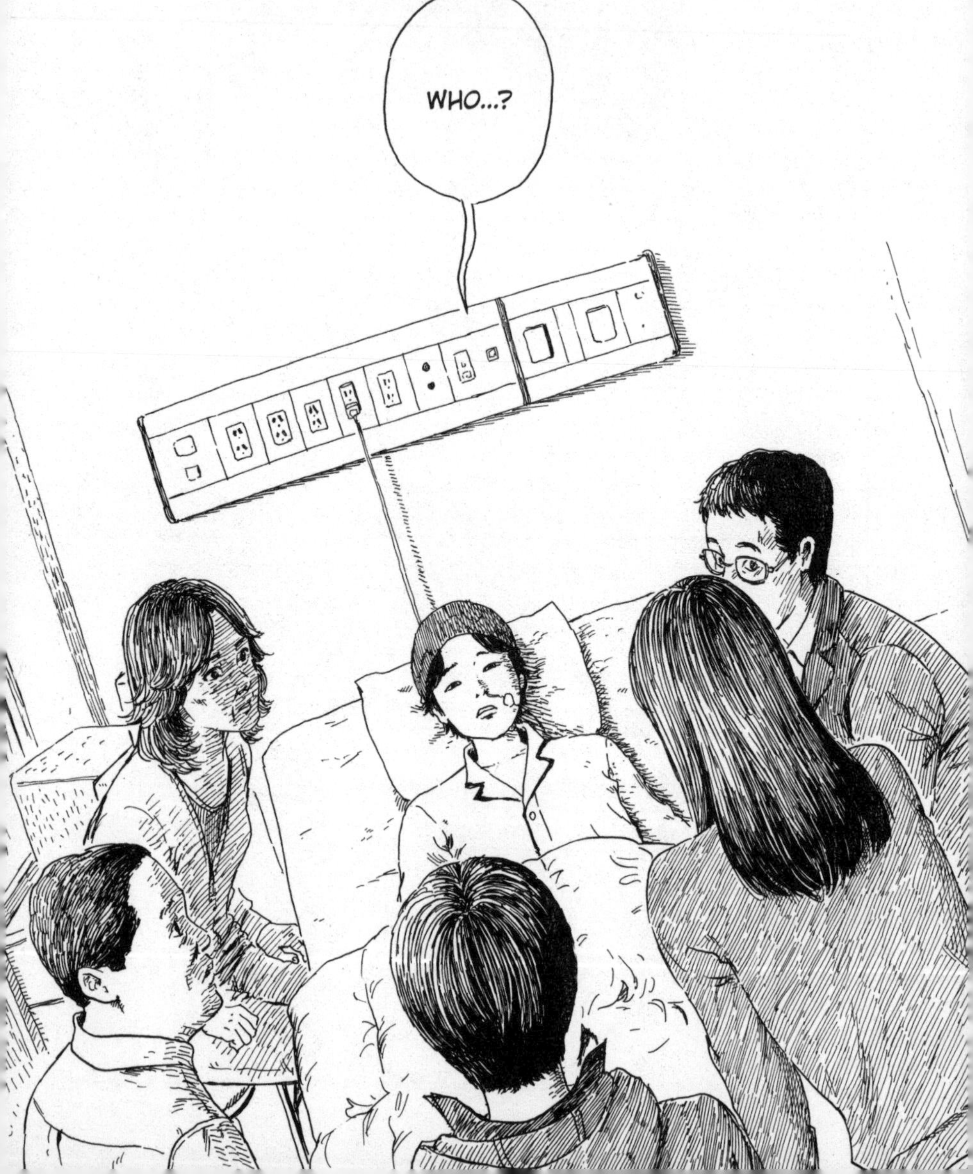
WHO...?

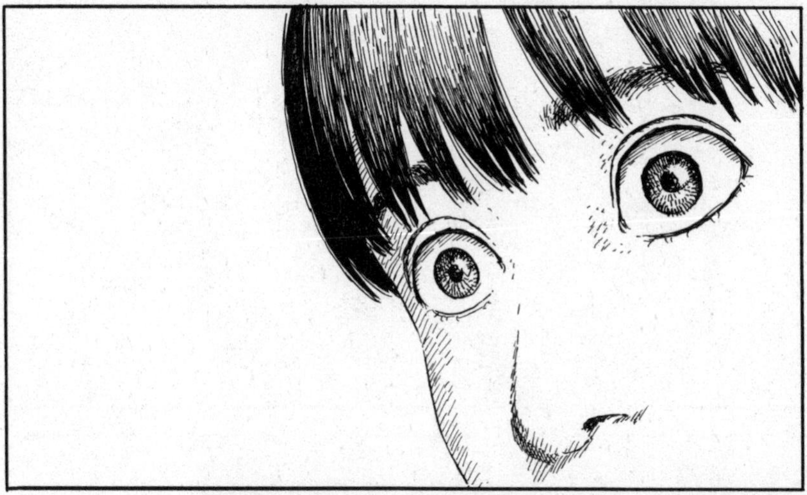

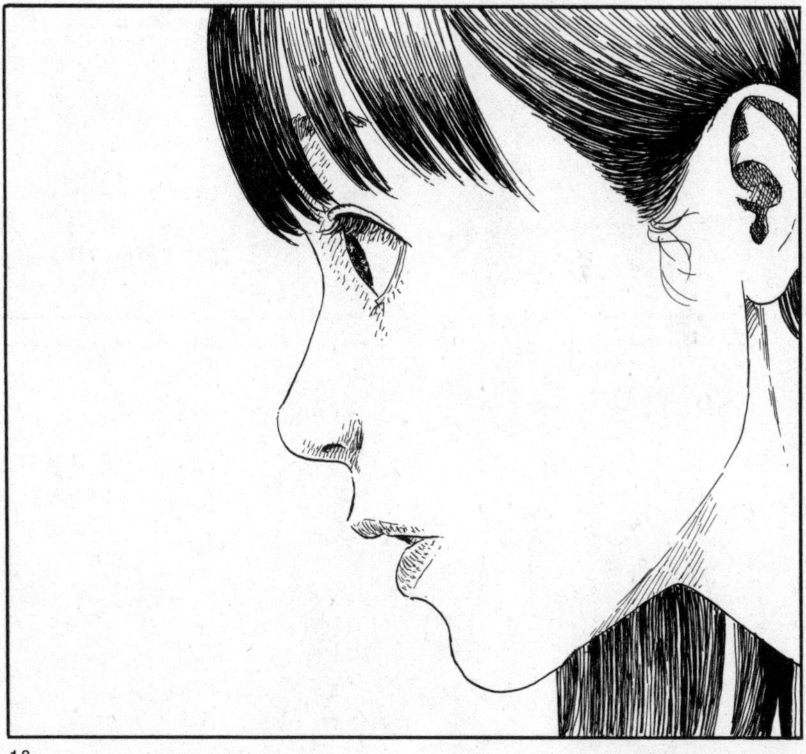

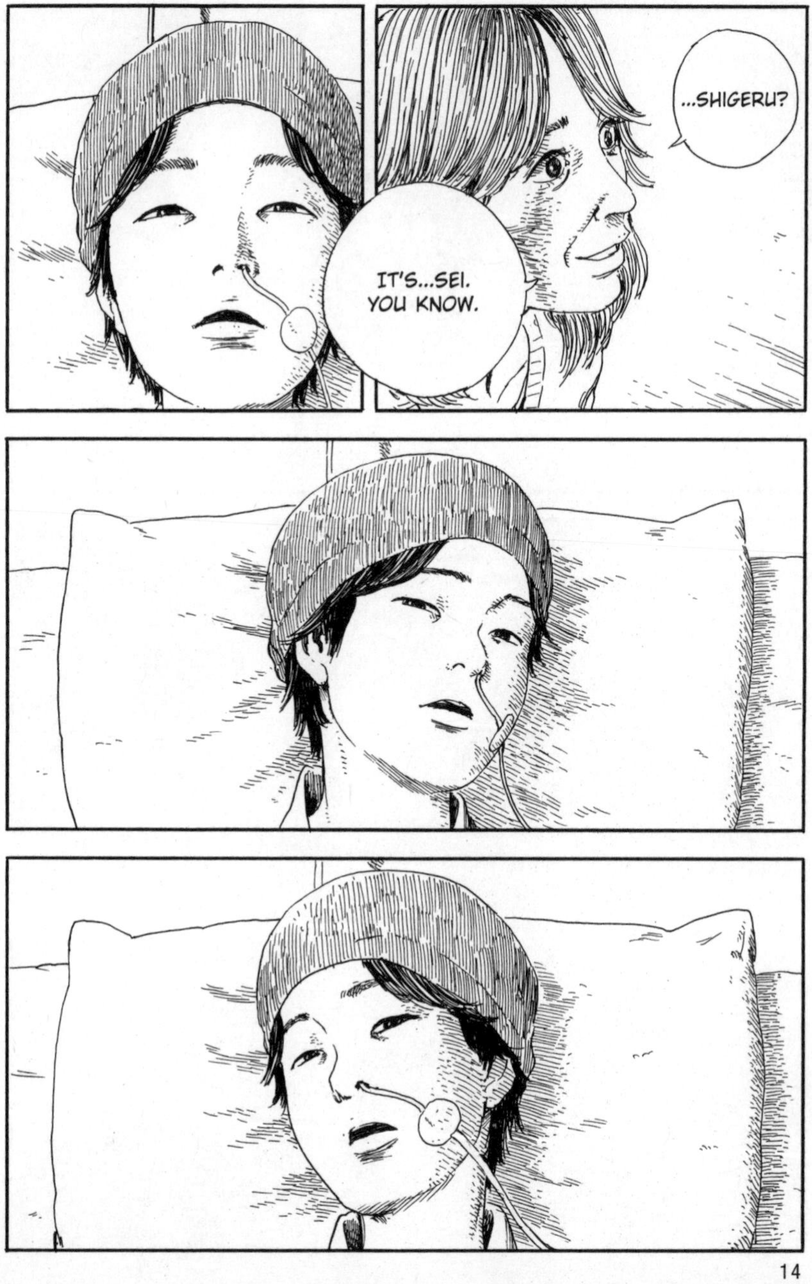
...SHIGERU?
IT'S...SEI. YOU KNOW.

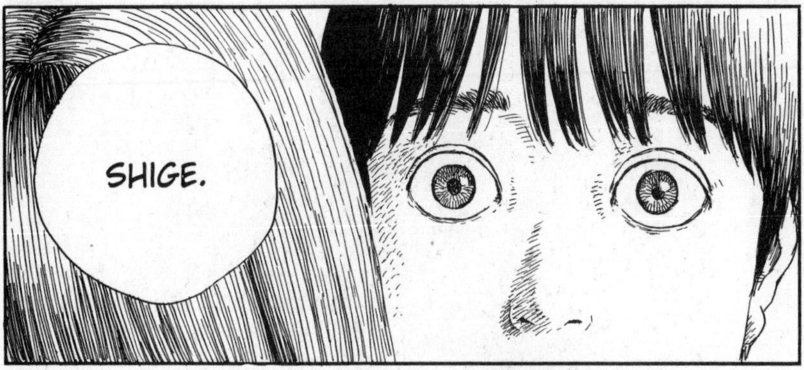
SHIGE.

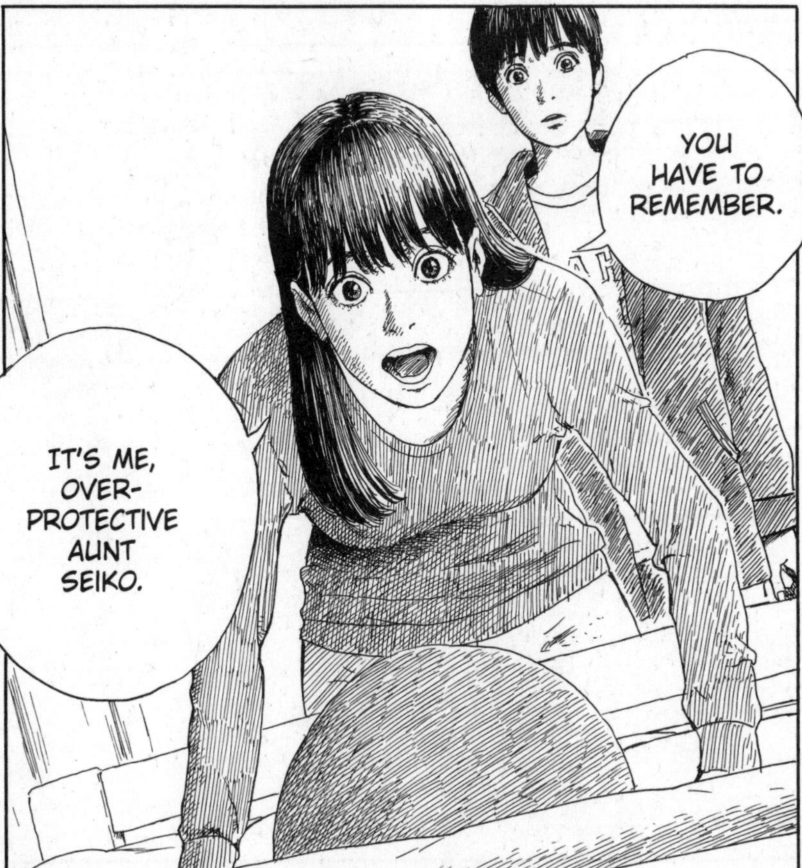
YOU HAVE TO REMEMBER.
IT'S ME, OVER-PROTECTIVE AUNT SEIKO.

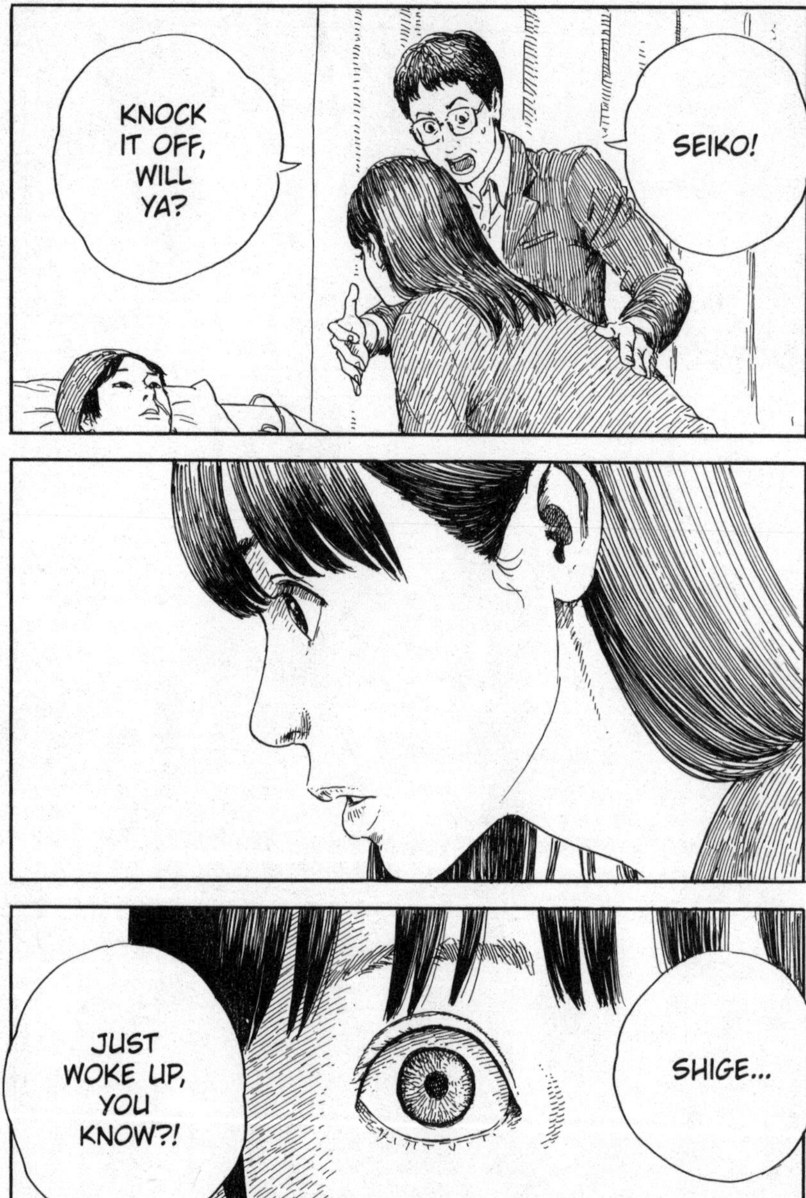
SEIKO!
KNOCK IT OFF, WILL YA?
SHIGE...
JUST WOKE UP, YOU KNOW?!

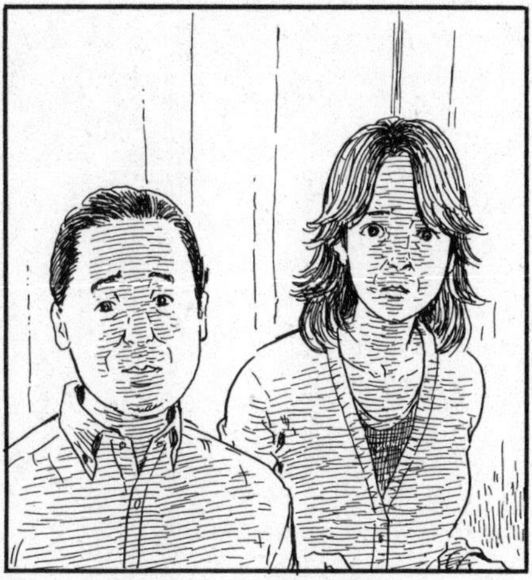

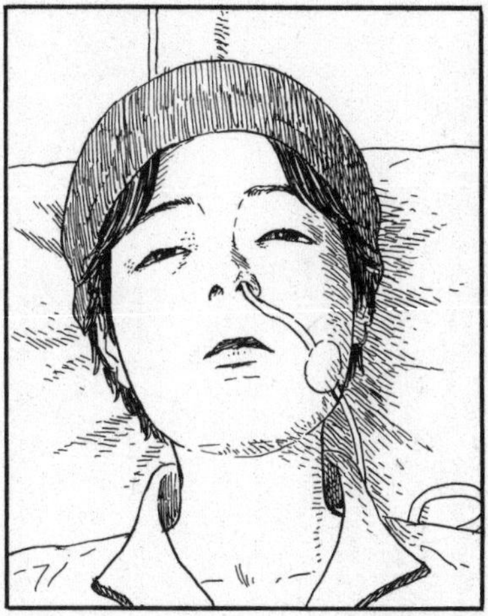

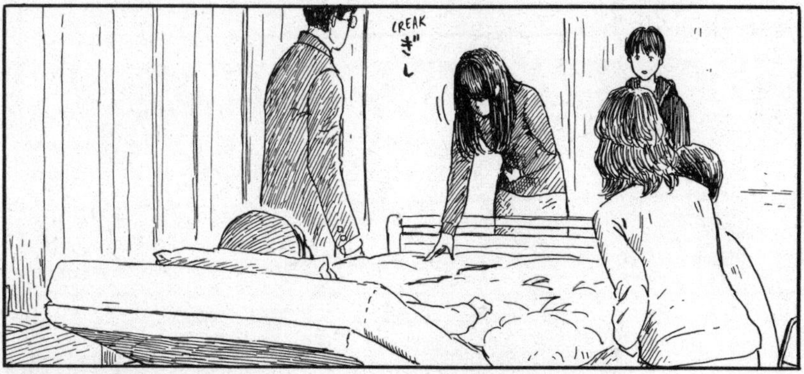
CREAK
ぎし

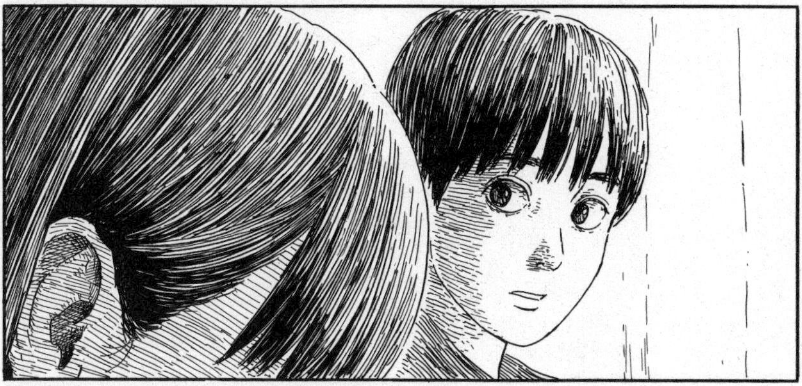

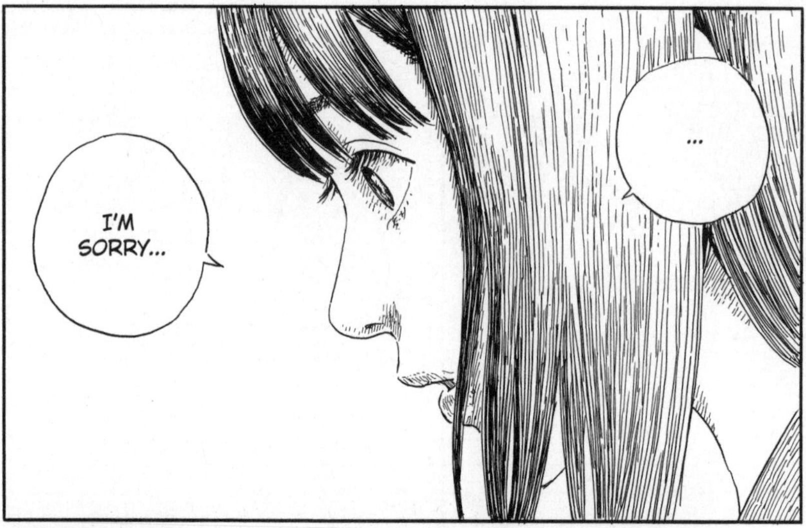
...
I'M SORRY...
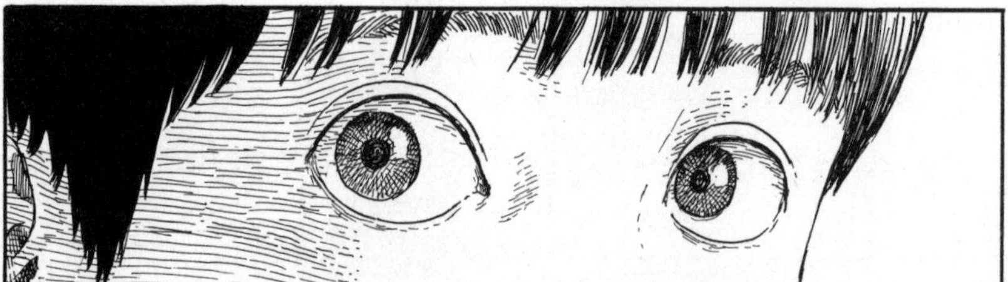
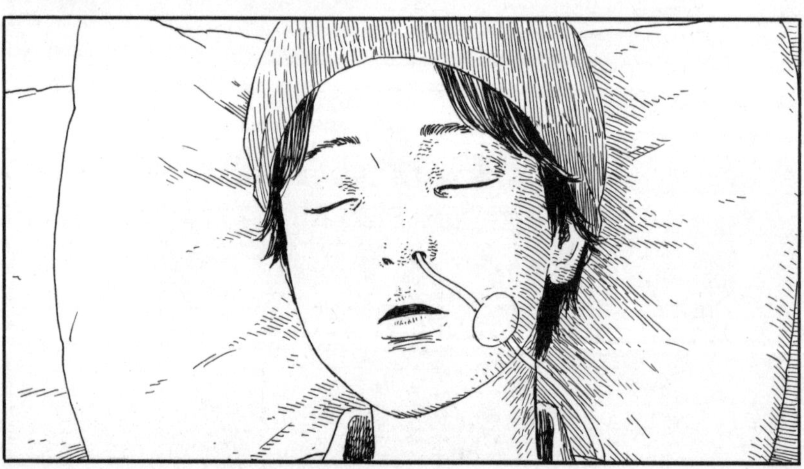

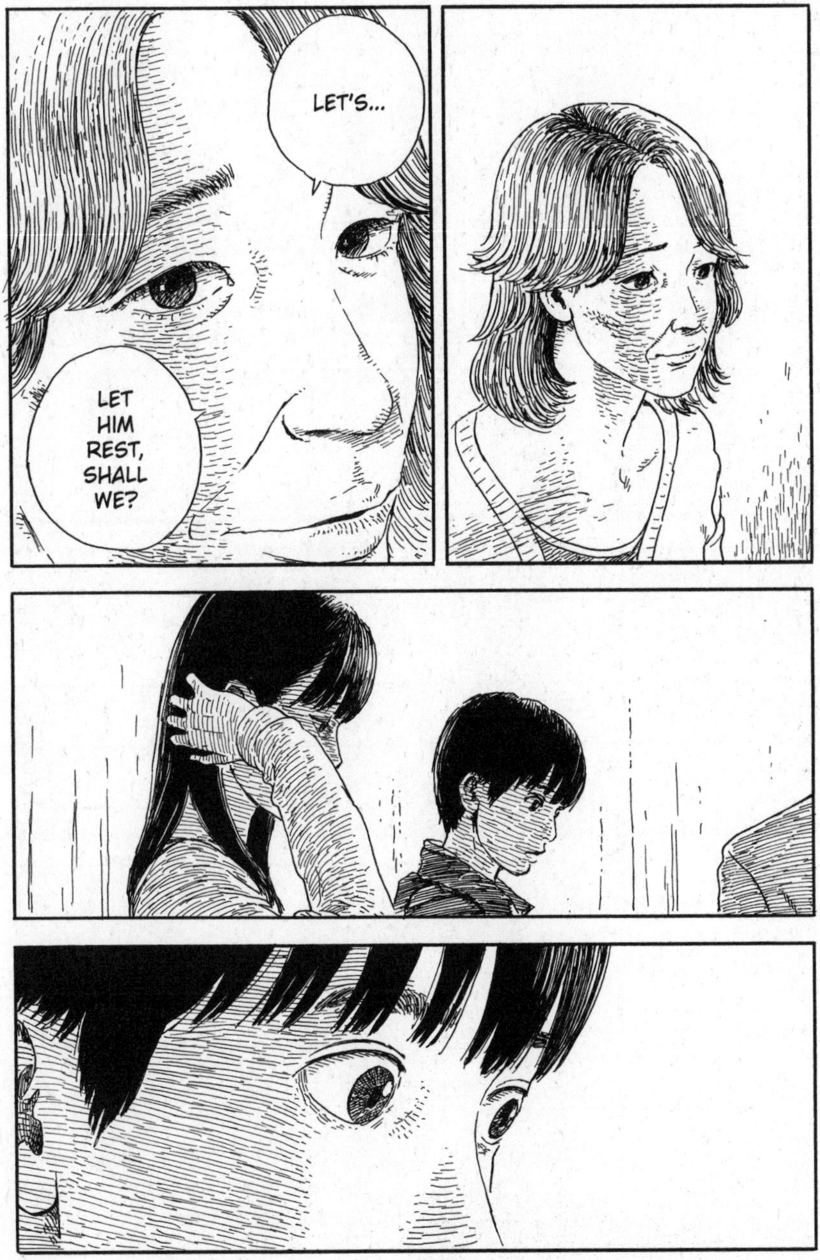
LET'S...
LET HIM REST, SHALL WE?

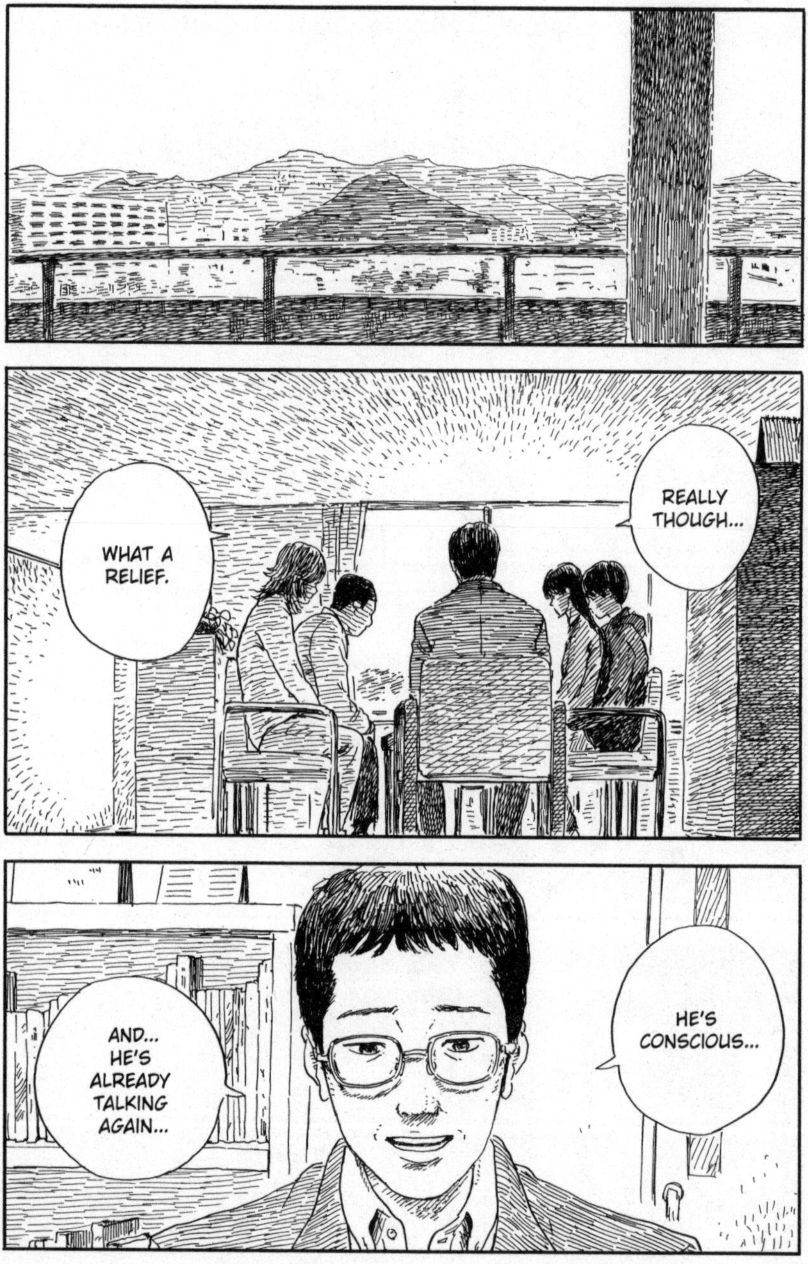
REALLY THOUGH...
WHAT A RELIEF.
HE'S CONSCIOUS...
AND... HE'S ALREADY TALKING AGAIN...

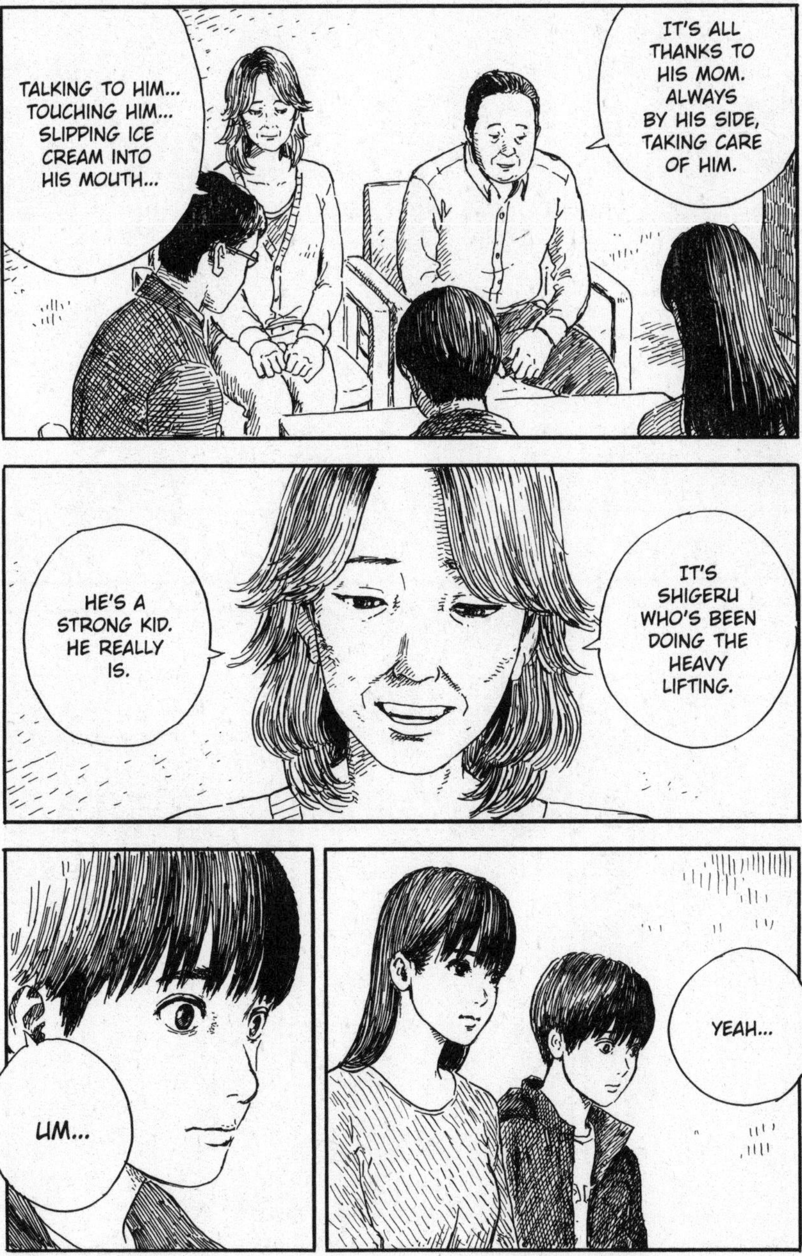
IT'S ALL THANKS TO HIS MOM. ALWAYS BY HIS SIDE, TAKING CARE OF HIM.
TALKING TO HIM... TOUCHING HIM... SLIPPING ICE CREAM INTO HIS MOUTH...
IT'S SHIGERU WHO'S BEEN DOING THE HEAVY LIFTING.
HE'S A STRONG KID. HE REALLY IS.
YEAH...
UM...

I'M SORRY.
FOR NEVER... COMING TO VISIT...

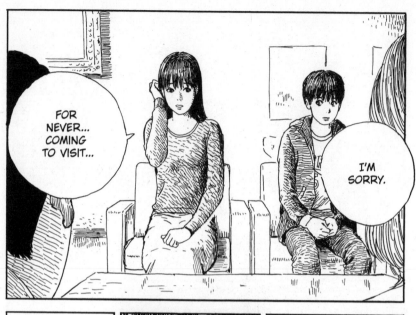

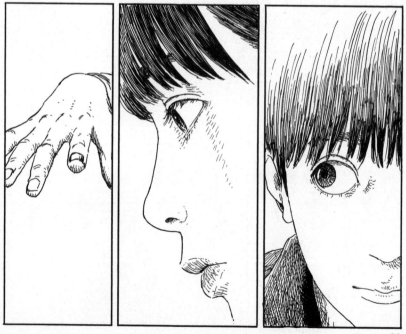

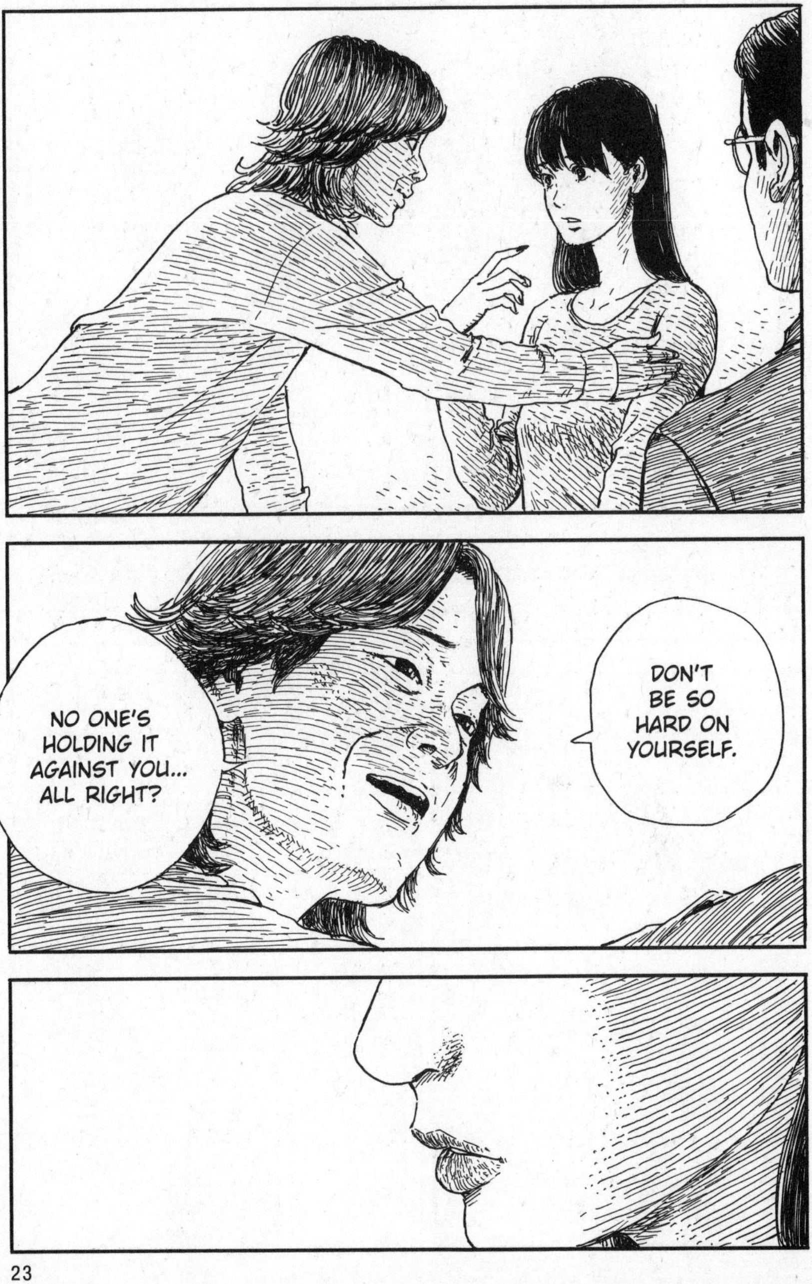
DON'T BE SO HARD ON YOURSELF.
NO ONE'S HOLDING IT AGAINST YOU... ALL RIGHT?

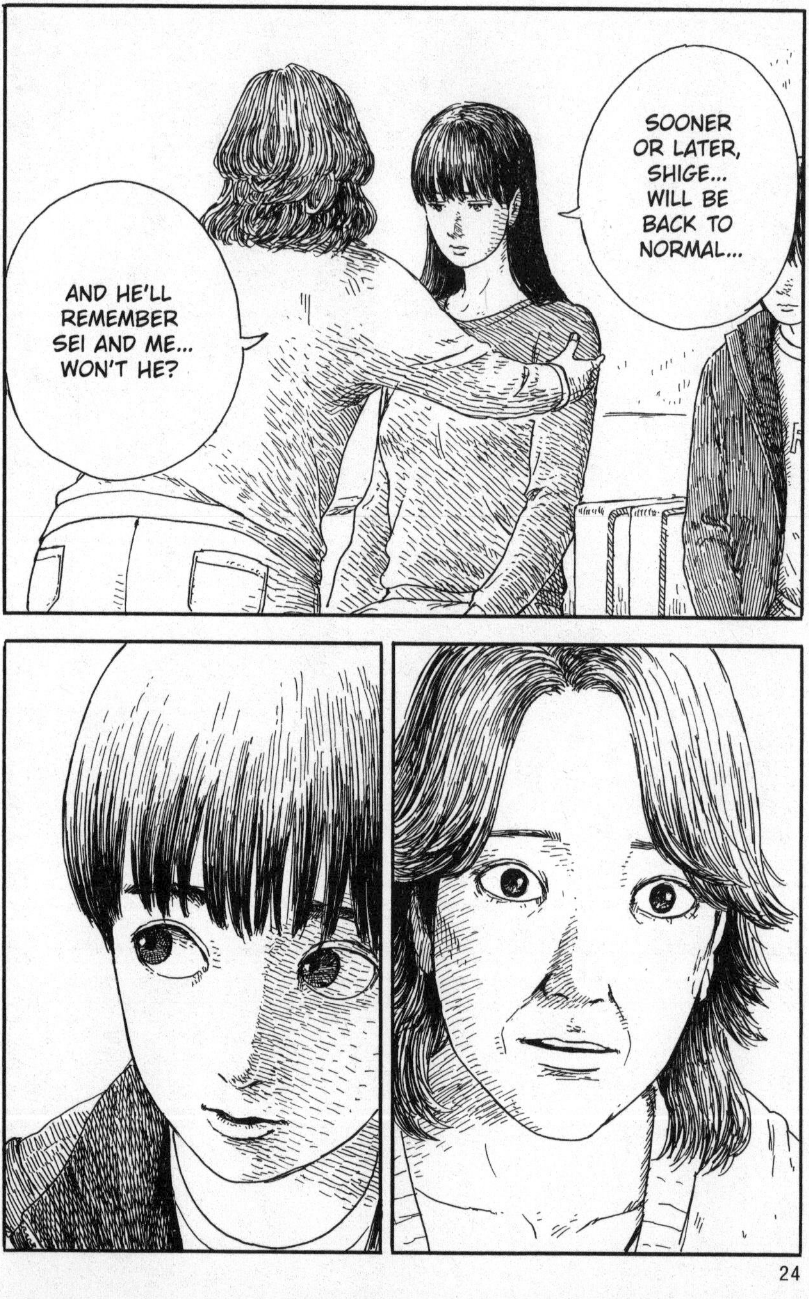
SOONER OR LATER, SHIGE... WILL BE BACK TO NORMAL...
AND HE'LL REMEMBER SEI AND ME... WON'T HE?

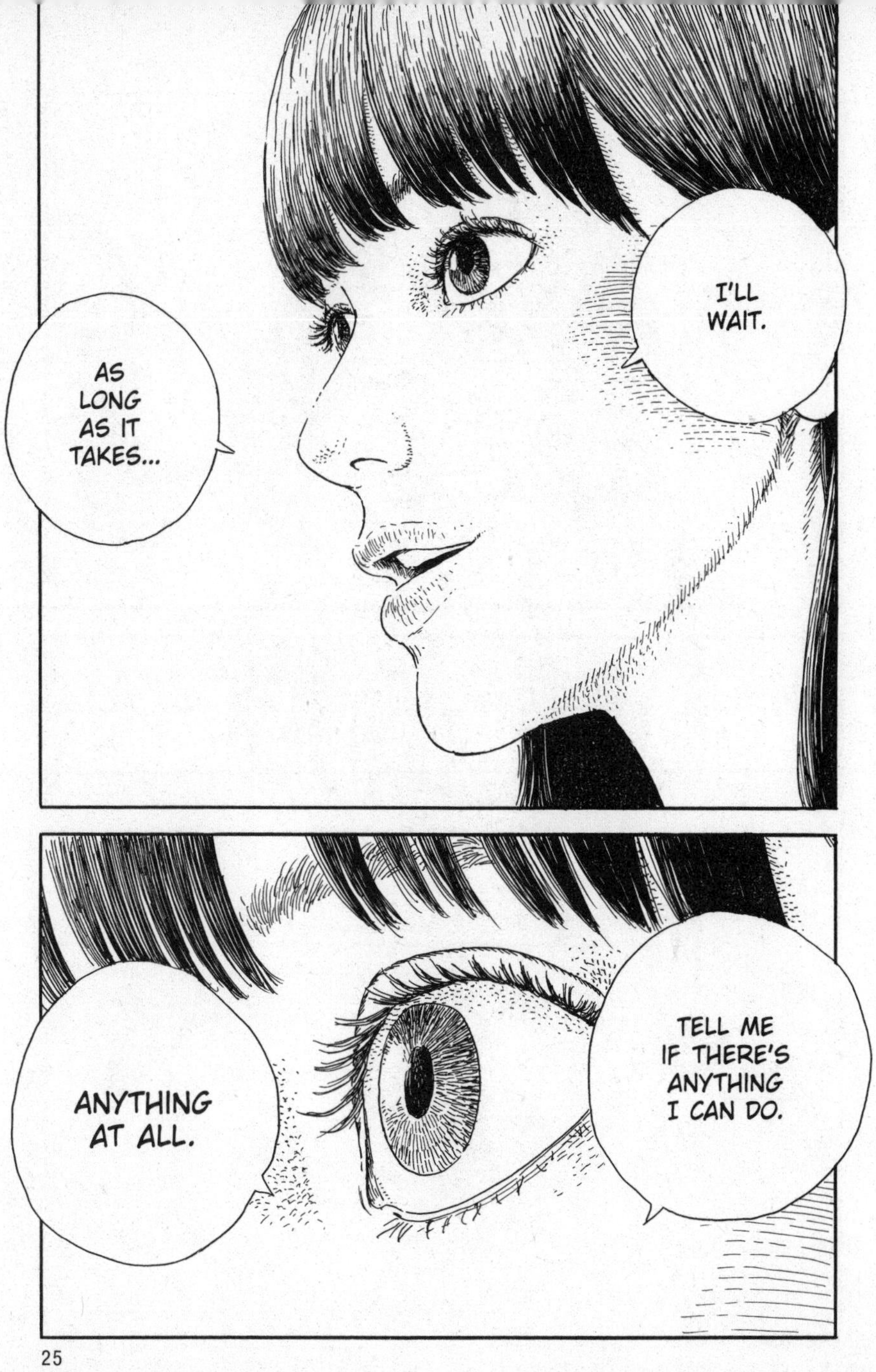
I'LL WAIT.
AS LONG AS IT TAKES...
TELL ME IF THERE'S ANYTHING I CAN DO.
ANYTHING AT ALL.

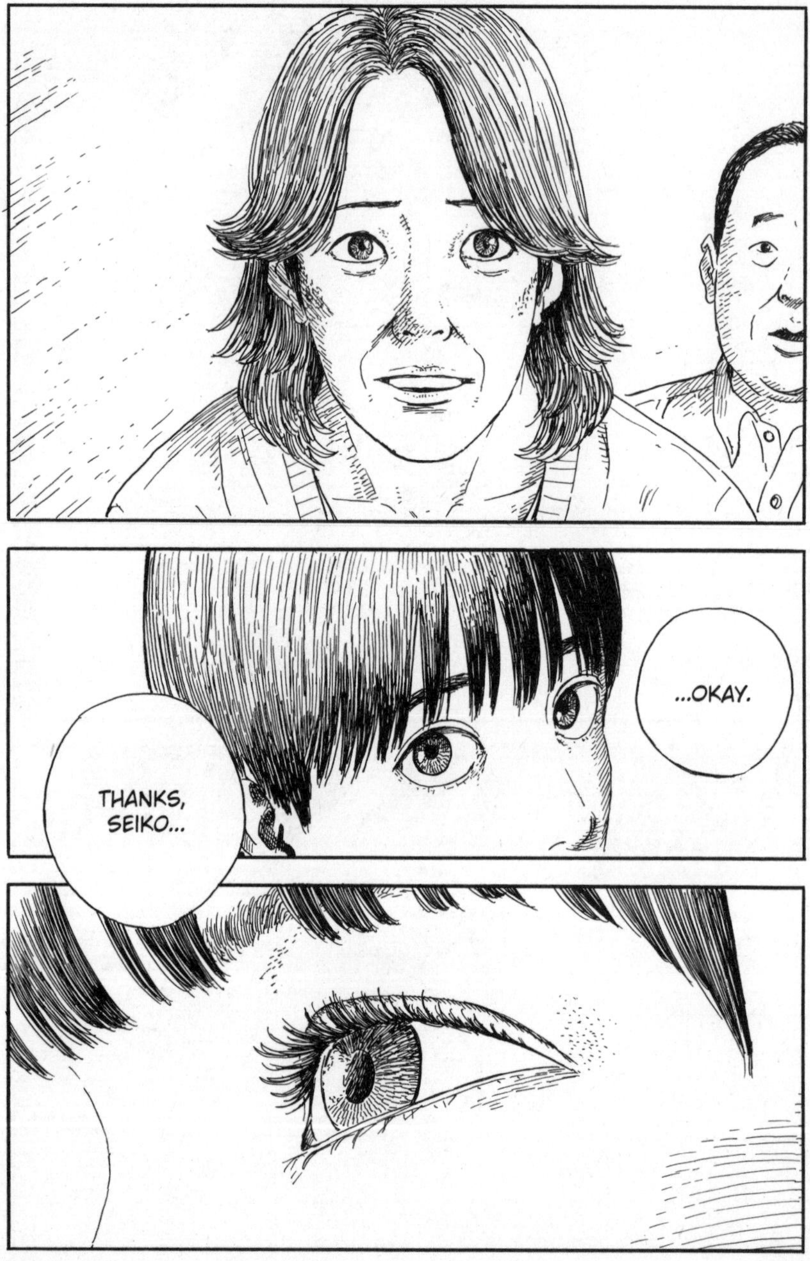
...OKAY.
THANKS, SEIKO...

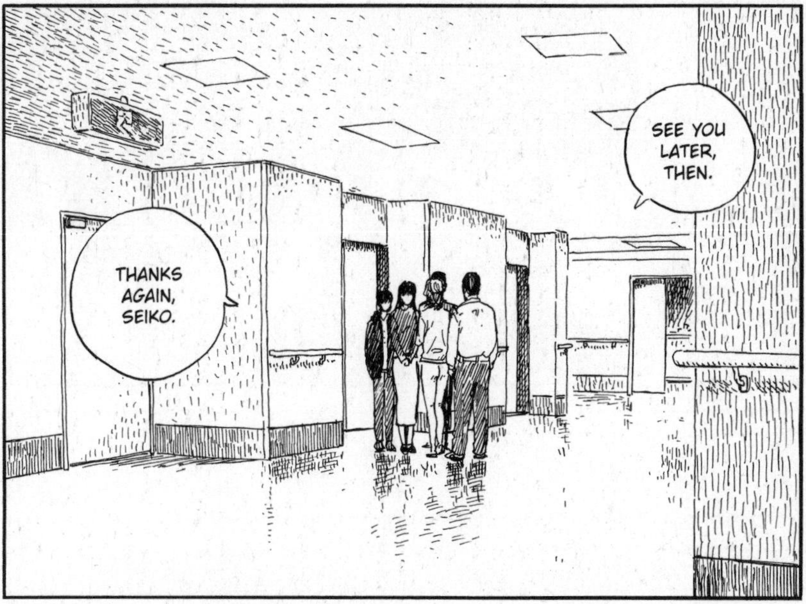
SEE YOU LATER, THEN.
THANKS AGAIN, SEIKO.

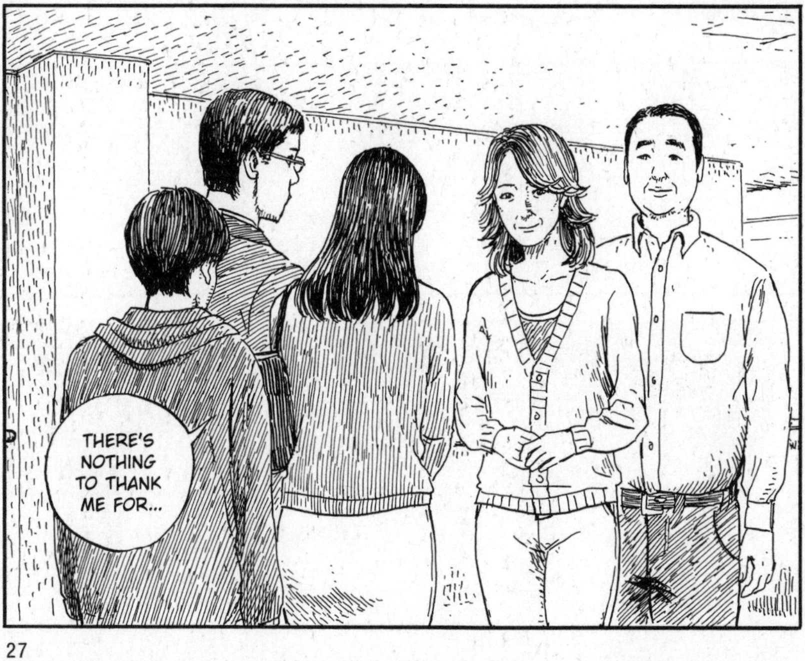
THERE'S NOTHING TO THANK ME FOR...

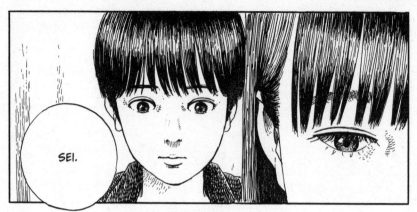

SEI.
I GOTTA THANK YOU TOO.
COME SEE SHIGERU AGAIN, OKAY?

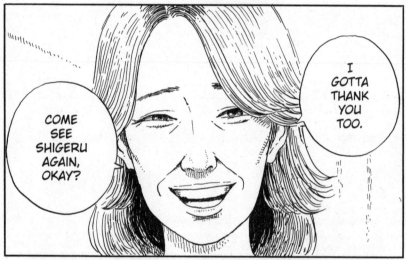

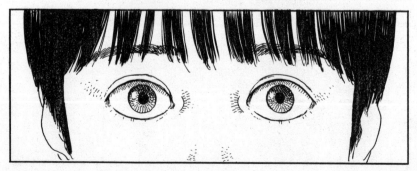

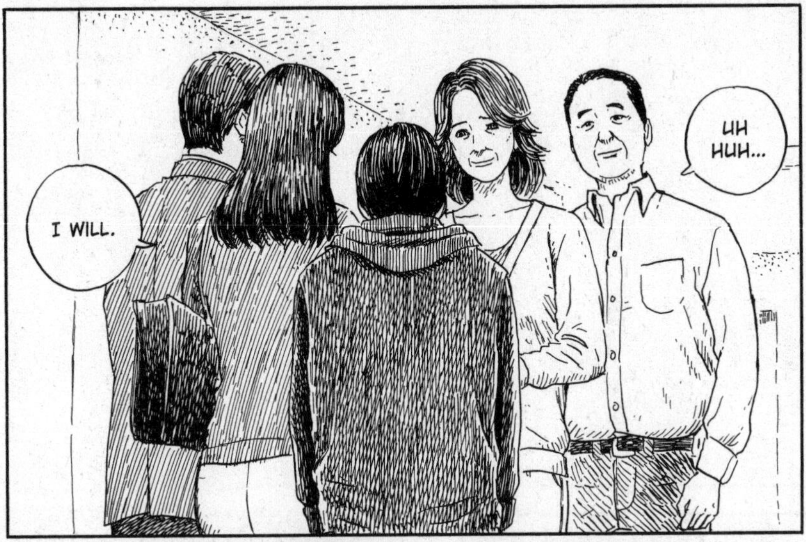
UH HUH...
I WILL.
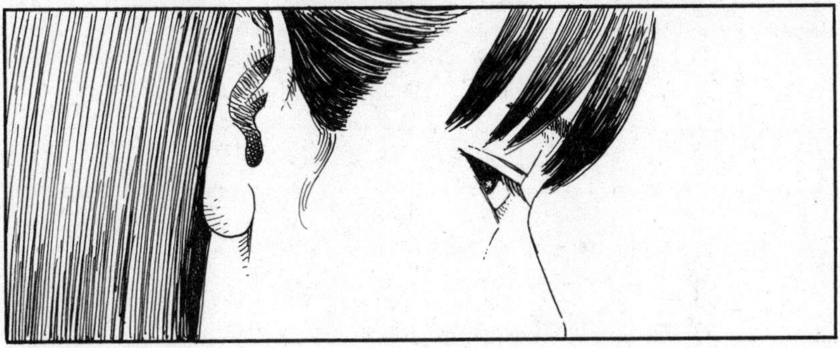
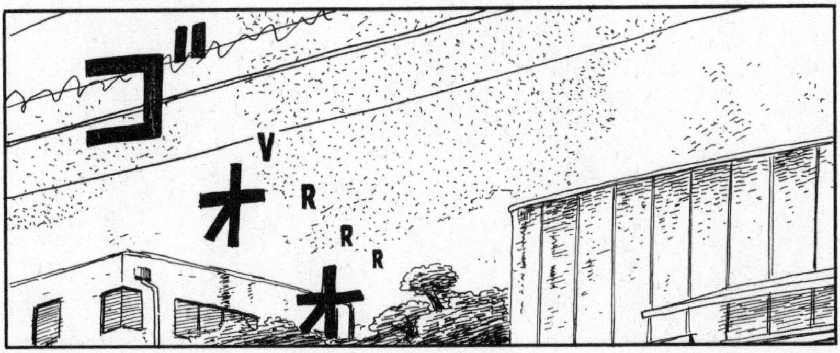
ゴオオ
VRRRR

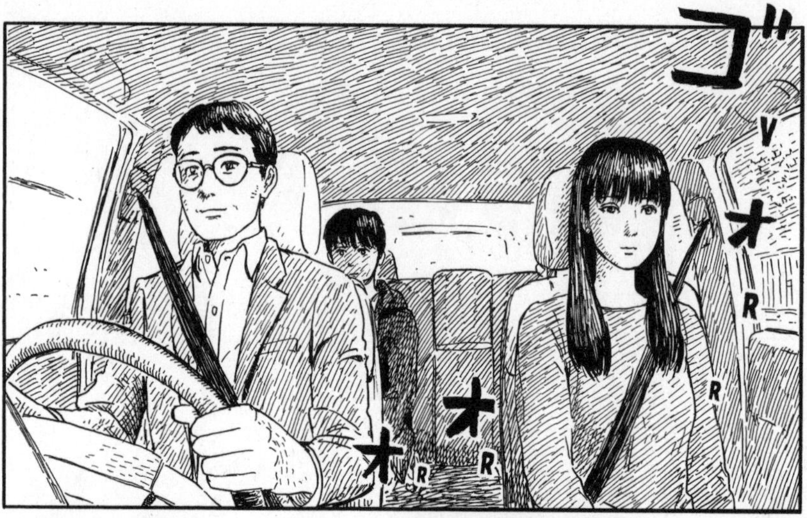
ゴオオオ
VRRRR

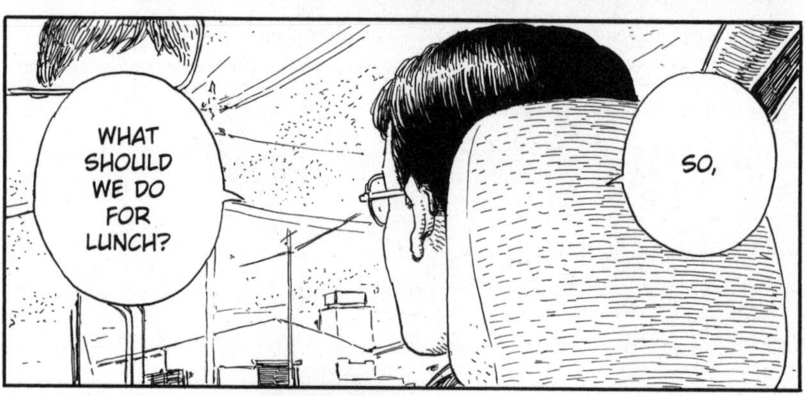
SO,
WHAT SHOULD WE DO FOR LUNCH?

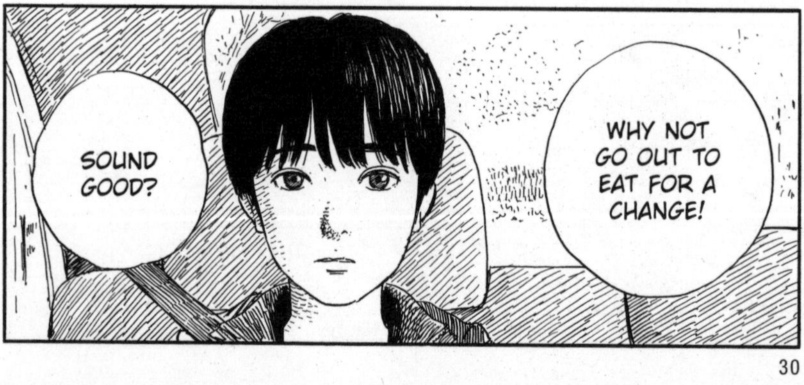
WHY NOT GO OUT TO EAT FOR A CHANGE!
SOUND GOOD?

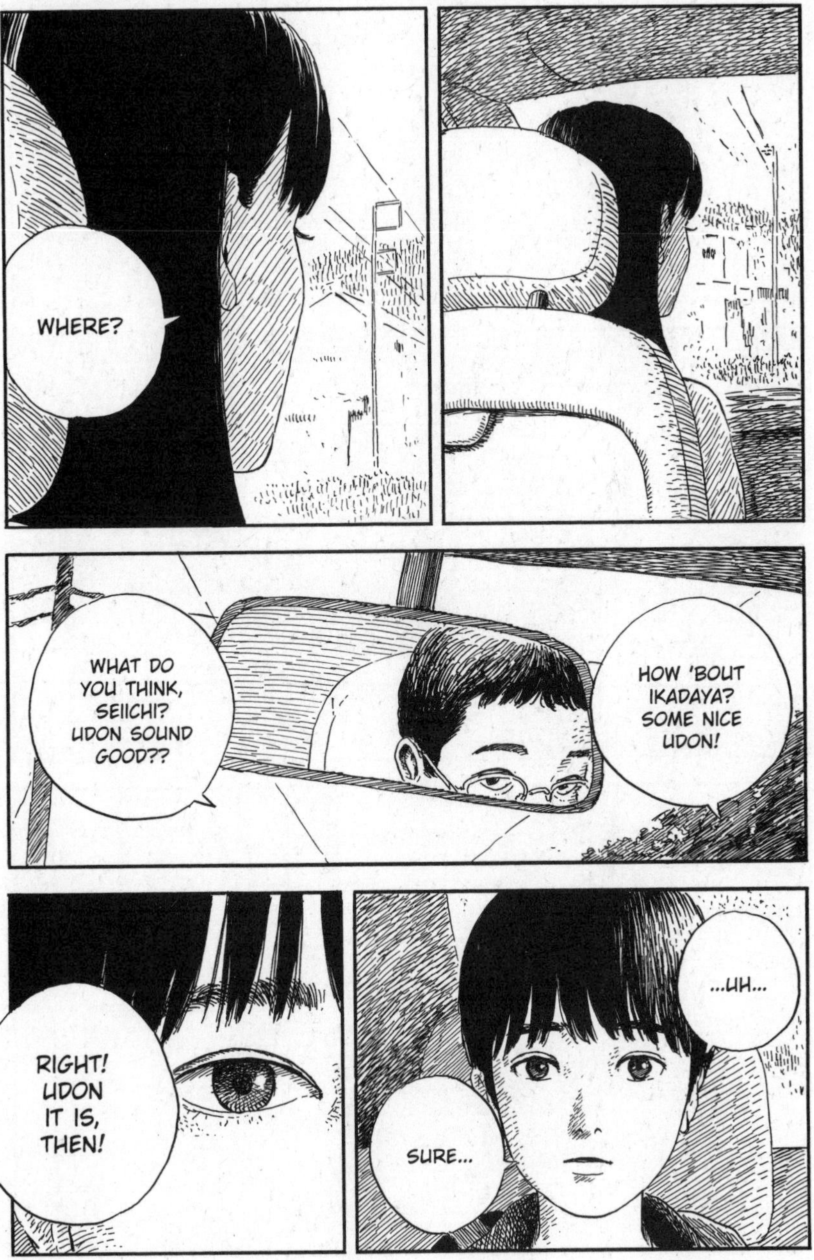
WHERE?
HOW 'BOUT IKADAYA? SOME NICE UDON!
WHAT DO YOU THINK, SEIICHI? UDON SOUND GOOD??
...UH...
SURE...
RIGHT! UDON IT IS, THEN!

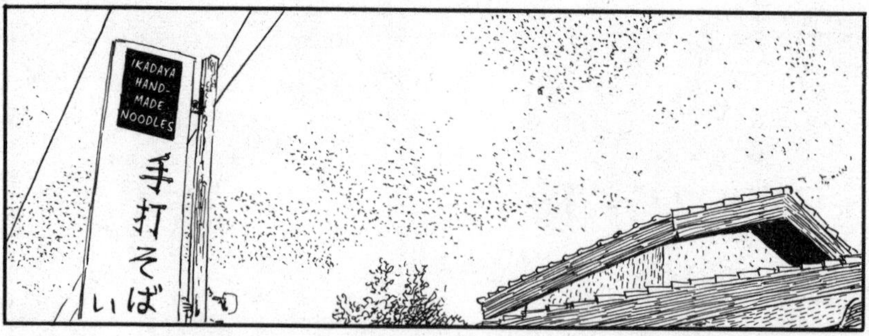
IKADAYA HAND-MADE NOODLES
手打そば
い
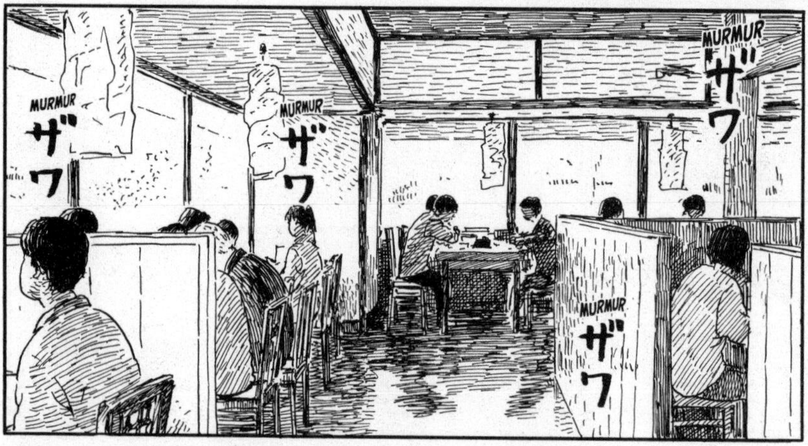
MURMUR
ザワ
MURMUR
ザワ
MURMUR
ザワ
MURMUR
ザワ
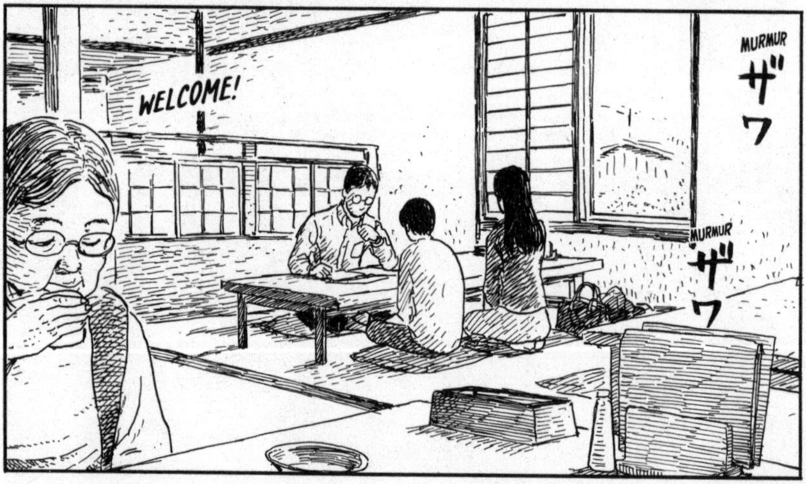
MURMUR
ザワ
WELCOME!
MURMUR
ザワ

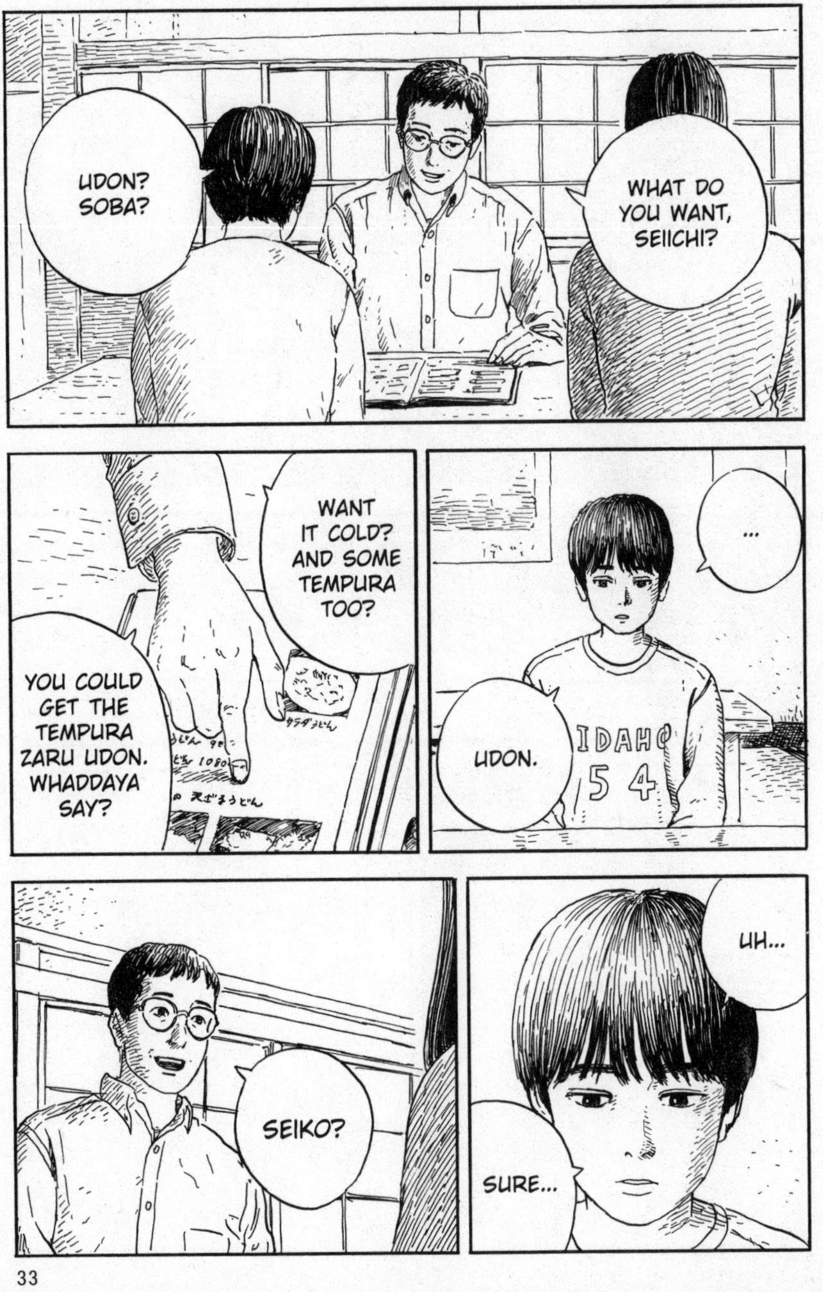
WHAT DO YOU WANT, SEIICHI?
UDON? SOBA?
...
UDON.
WANT IT COLD? AND SOME TEMPURA TOO?
YOU COULD GET THE TEMPURA ZARU UDON. WHADDAYA SAY?
UH...
SURE...
SEIKO?

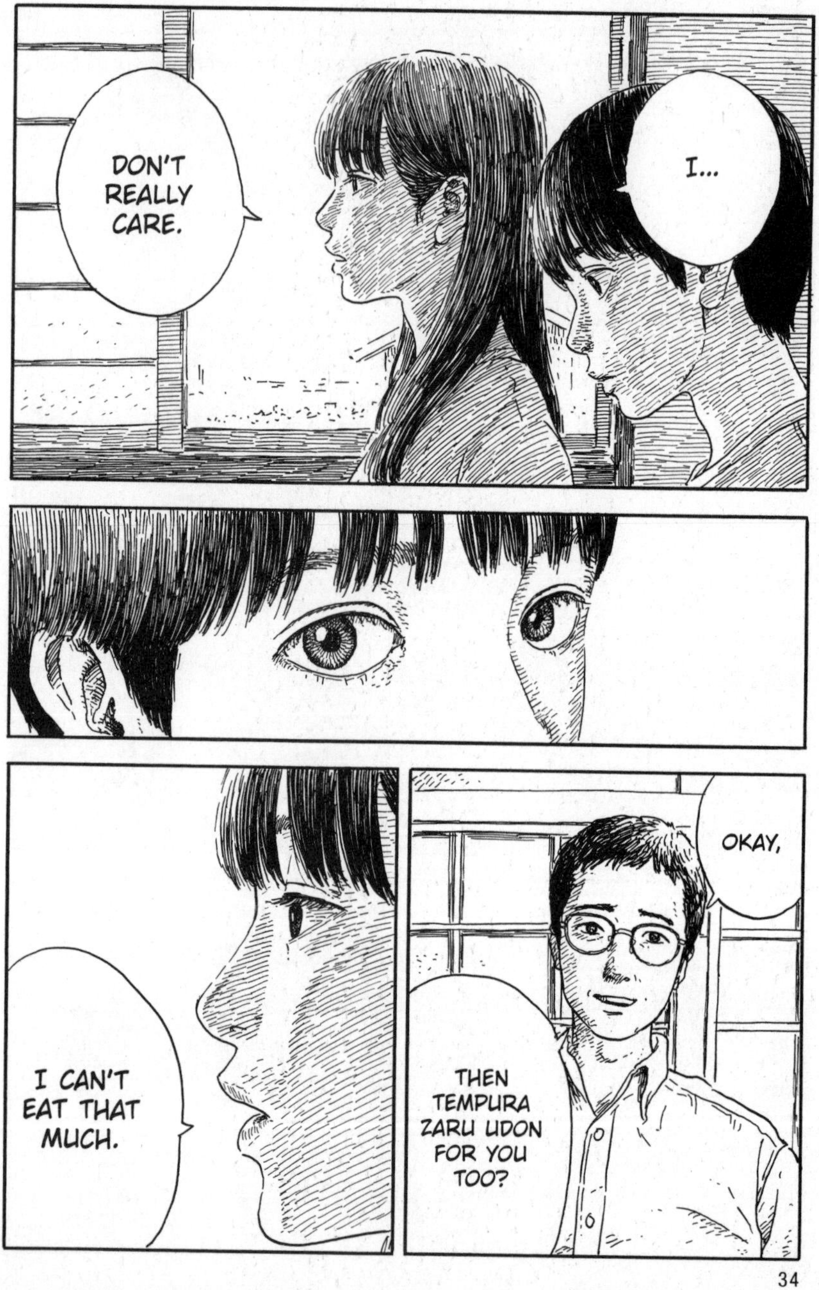
I...
DON'T REALLY CARE.
OKAY,
THEN TEMPURA ZARU UDON FOR YOU TOO?
I CAN'T EAT THAT MUCH.

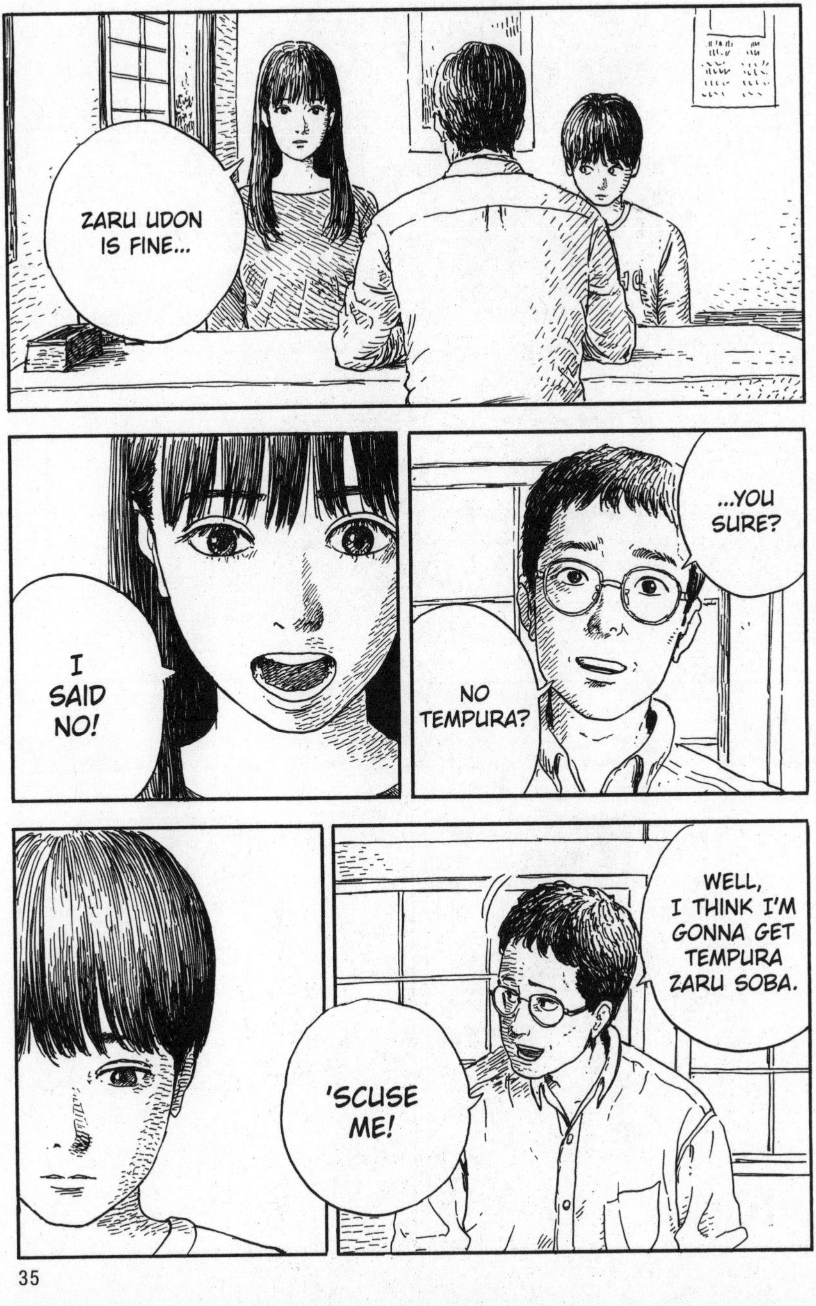
ZARU UDON IS FINE...
...YOU SURE?
NO TEMPURA?
I SAID NO!
WELL, I THINK I'M GONNA GET TEMPURA ZARU SOBA.
'SCUSE ME!

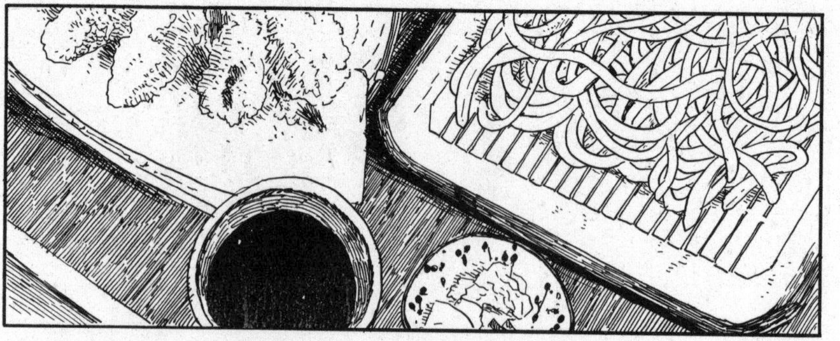

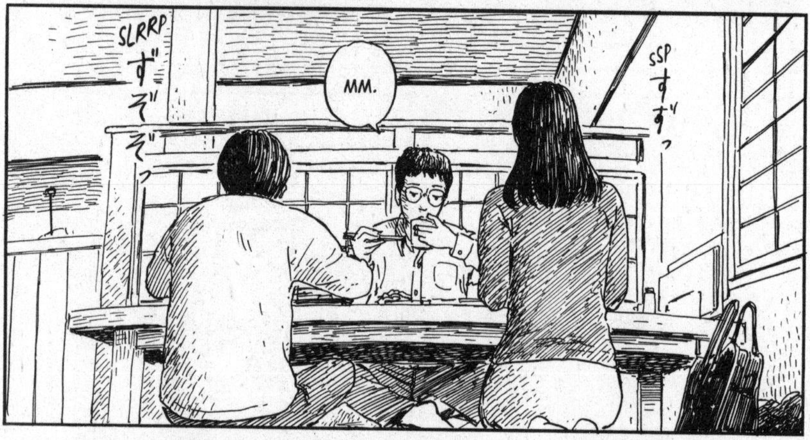
SSP
すずっ
MM.
SLRRP
ずぞぞっ

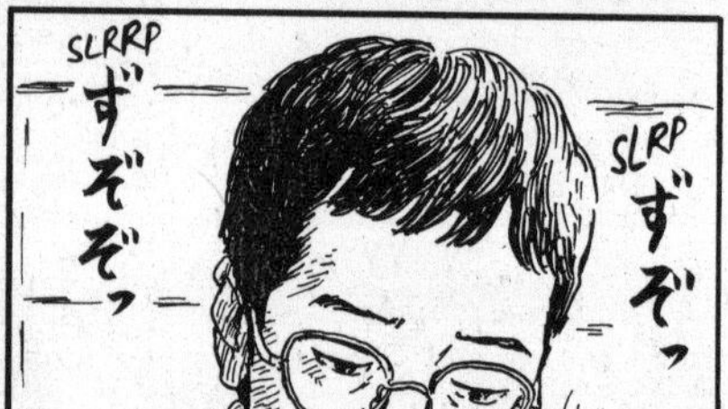
SLRP
ずぞっ
SLRRP
ずぞぞっ

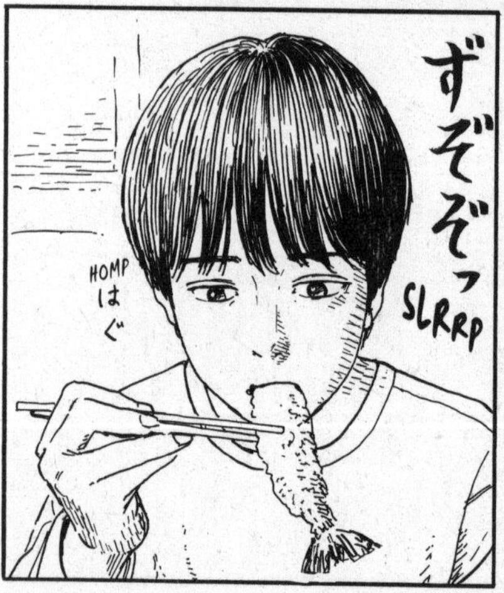
ずぞぞっ
SLRRP
HOMP
はぐ

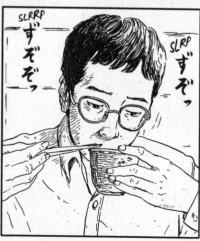

HFFFFF...

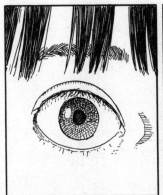

WHAT'S WRONG?

SEIKO,

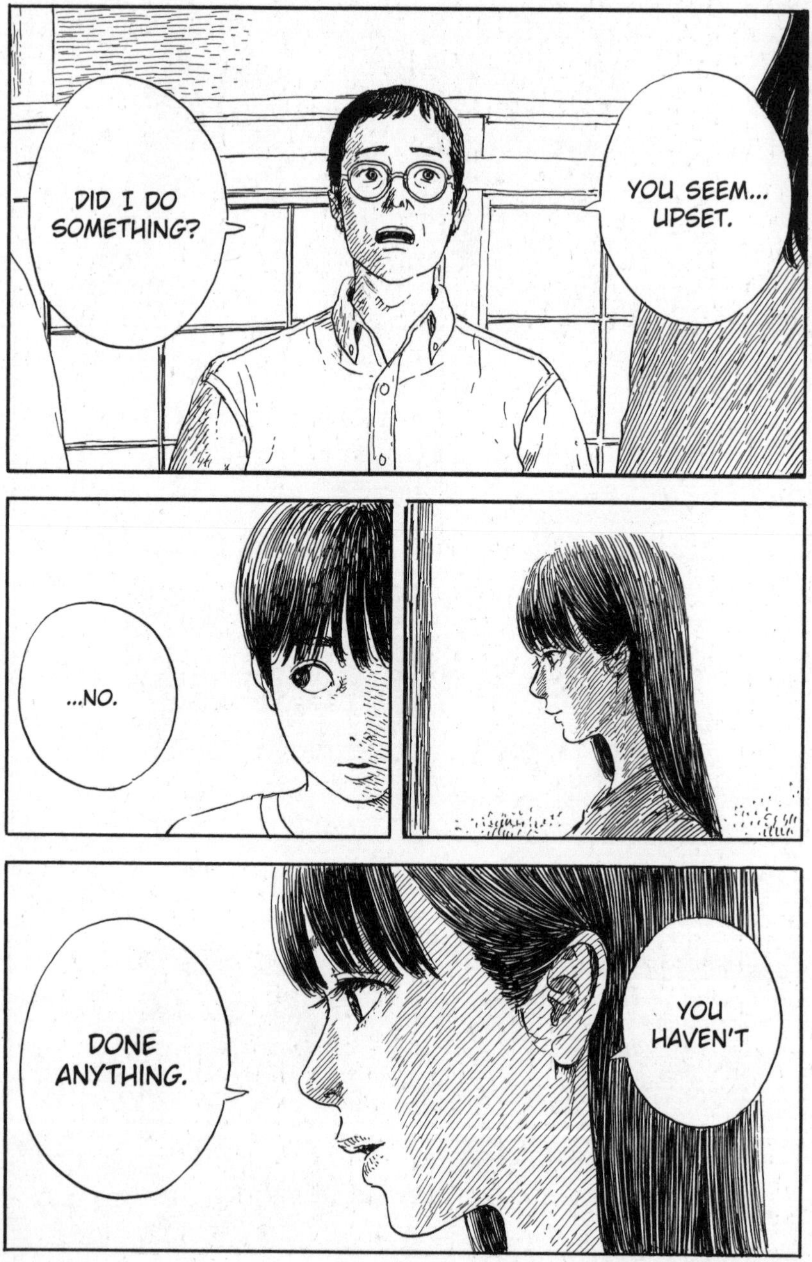
YOU SEEM... UPSET.
DID I DO SOMETHING?
...NO.
YOU HAVEN'T
DONE ANYTHING.

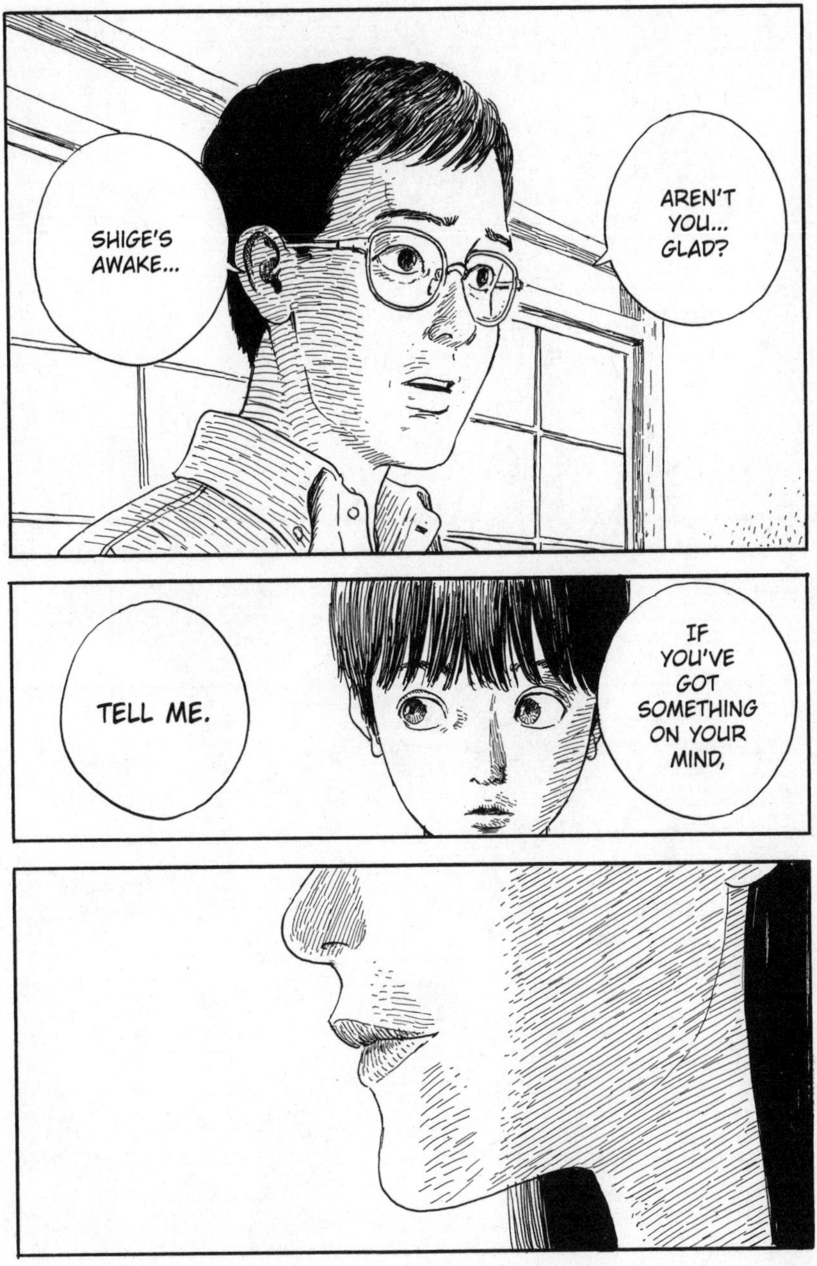
AREN'T YOU... GLAD?
SHIGE'S AWAKE...
IF YOU'VE GOT SOMETHING ON YOUR MIND,
TELL ME.

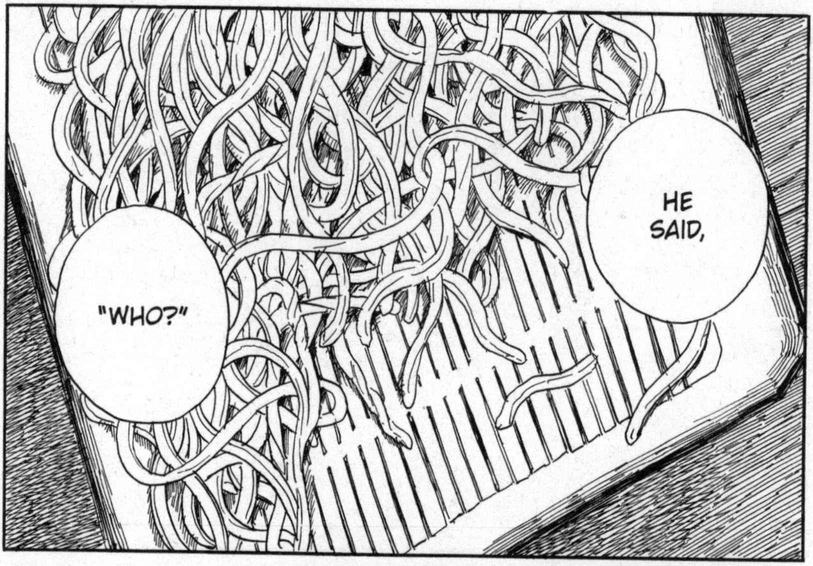
HE SAID,
"WHO?"

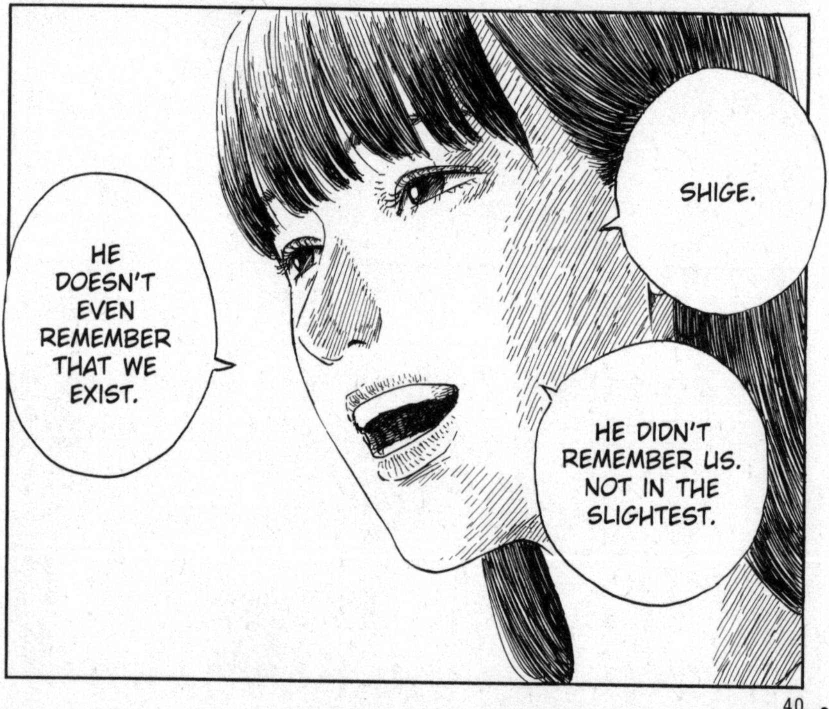
SHIGE.
HE DIDN'T REMEMBER US. NOT IN THE SLIGHTEST.
HE DOESN'T EVEN REMEMBER THAT WE EXIST.

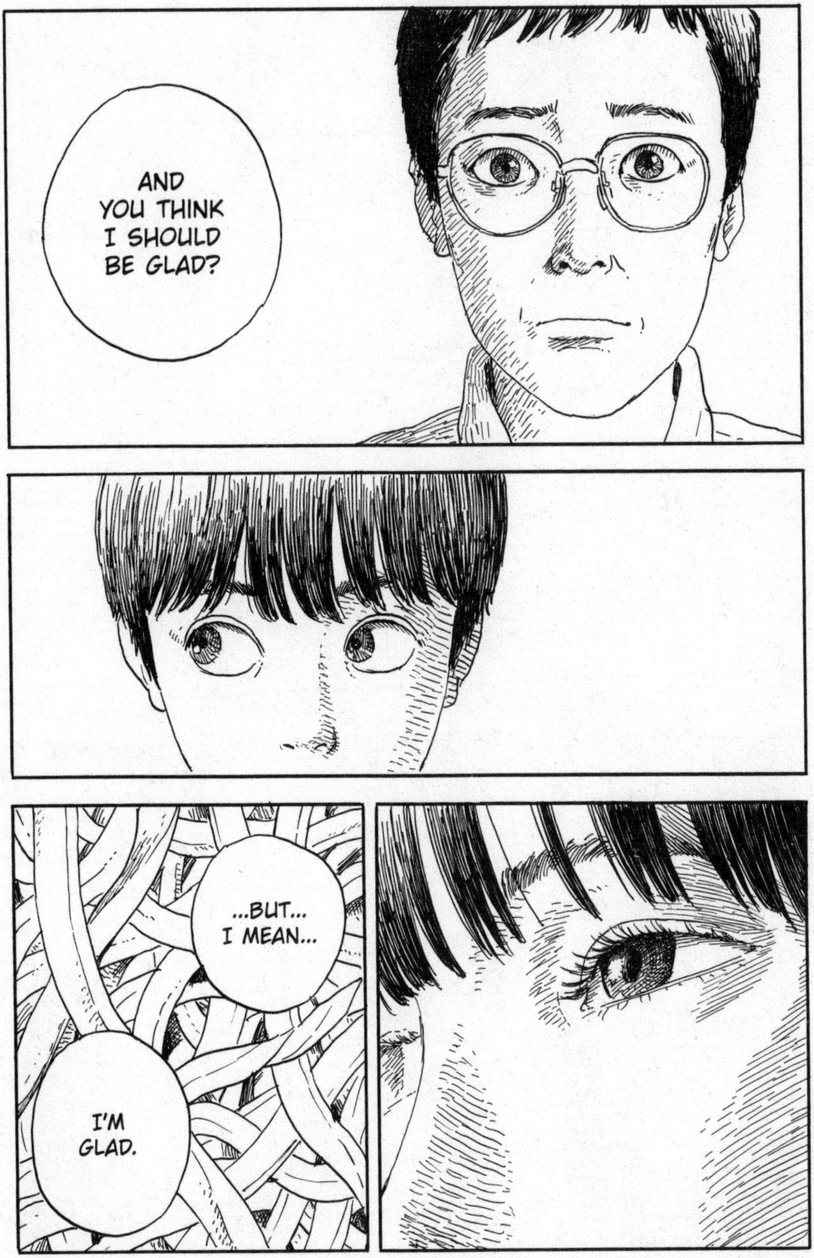
AND YOU THINK I SHOULD BE GLAD?
...BUT... I MEAN...
I'M GLAD.

HE'S... FINALLY REGAINED CONSCIOUS-NESS.
I'M SURE IT'LL COME BACK TO HIM, LITTLE BY LITTLE.
WILL IT?
WILL IT REALLY?
BASED ON WHAT ?!

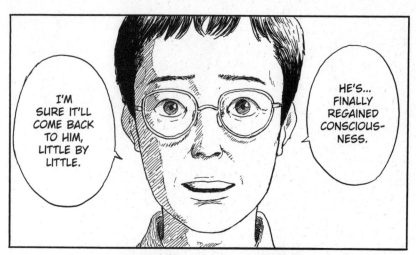

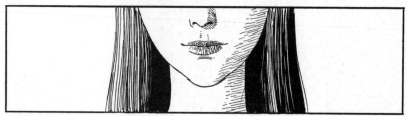

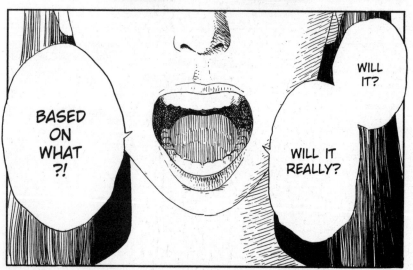

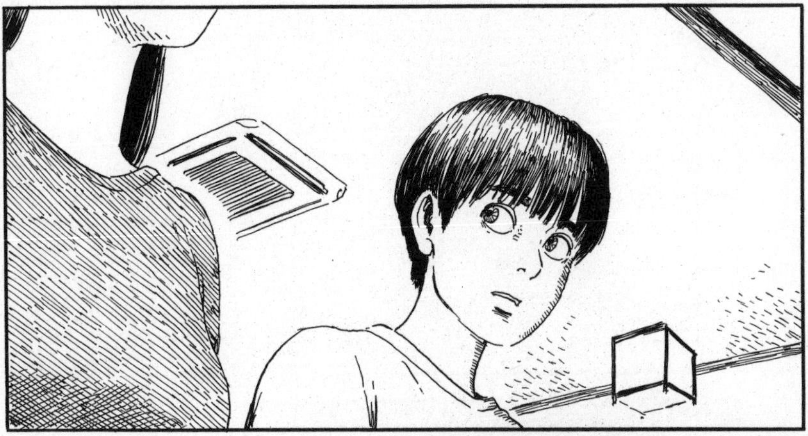

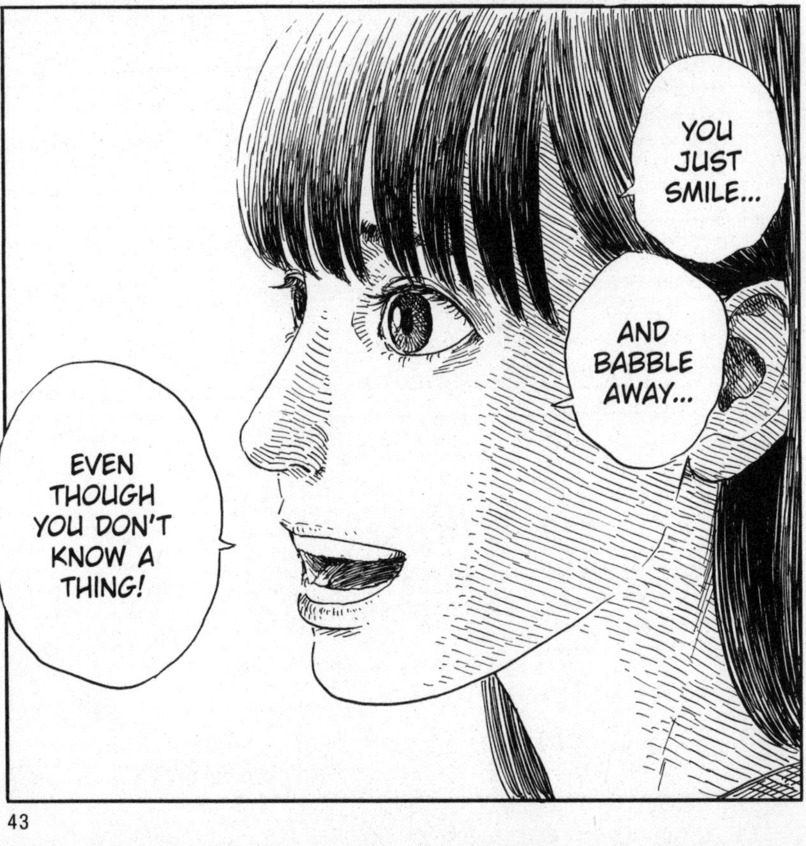
YOU JUST SMILE...
AND BABBLE AWAY...
EVEN THOUGH YOU DON'T KNOW A THING!

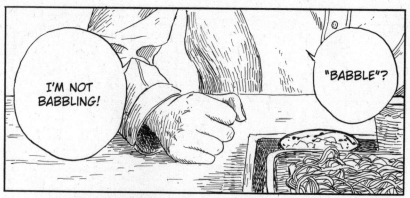

"BABBLE"?
I'M NOT BABBLING!
I'M... HONESTLY GLAD...
I MEAN, COME ON... HAVEN'T YOU BEEN WORRIED TOO? HASN'T IT BEEN EATING YOU UP INSIDE?
BUT NOW SHIGE'S CONDITION HAS... IMPROVED...
SO I THOUGHT YOU'D BE HAPPY...

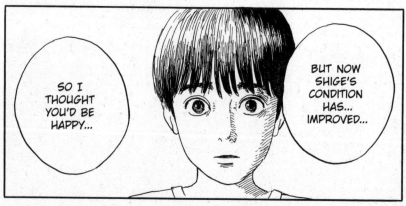

WELCOME!

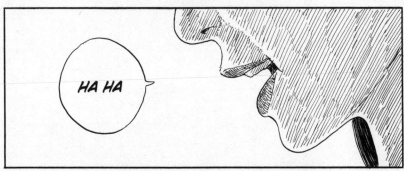

HA HA

...IF SHIGE... DOESN'T REMEMBER...

HOW... HOW... AM I...

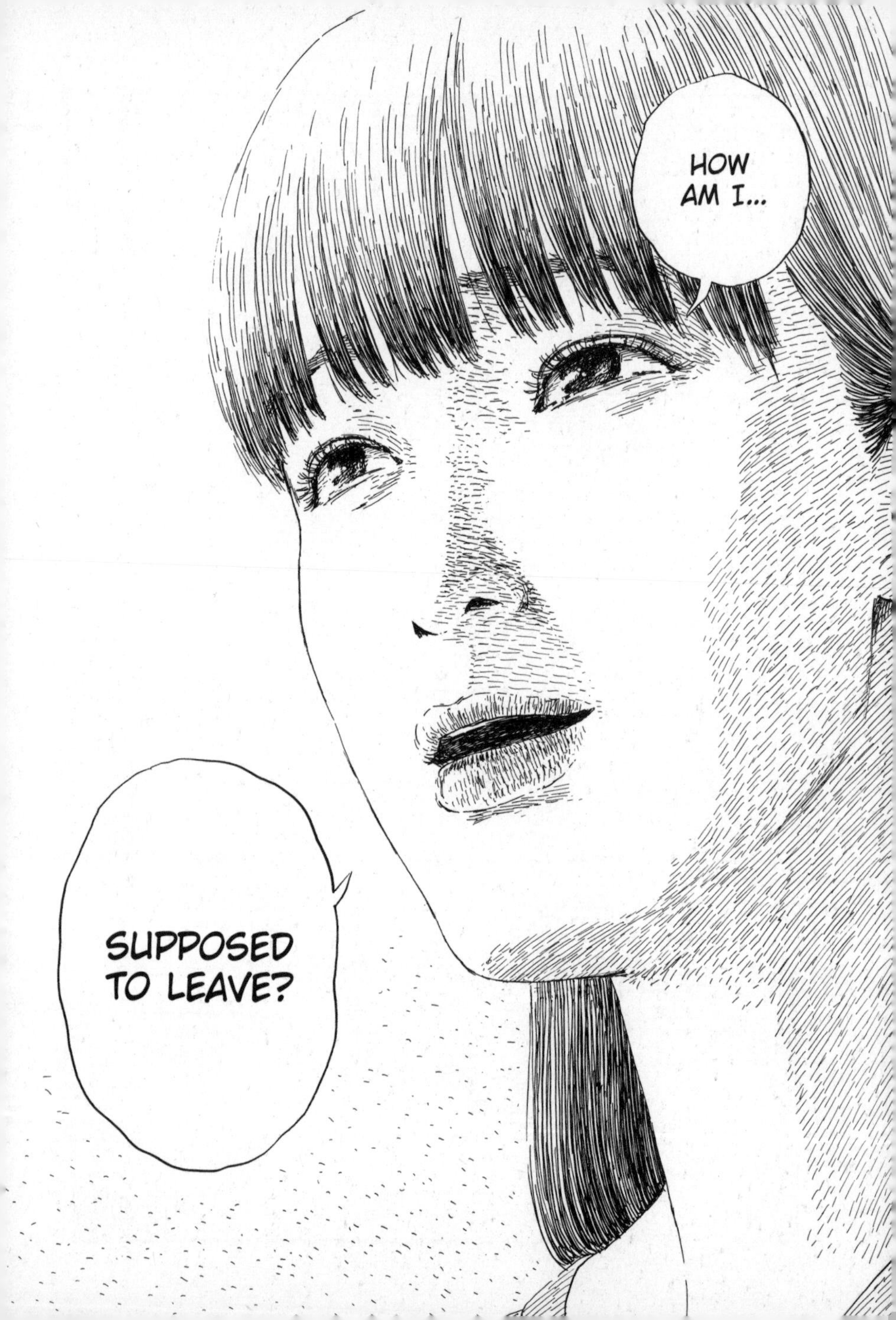
HOW AM I...
SUPPOSED TO LEAVE?

TO LEAVE...

I THOUGHT... I'D FINALLY GET...

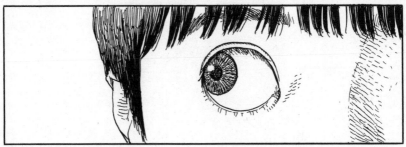

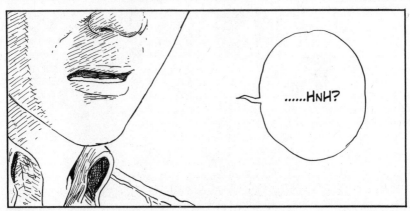

......HNH?

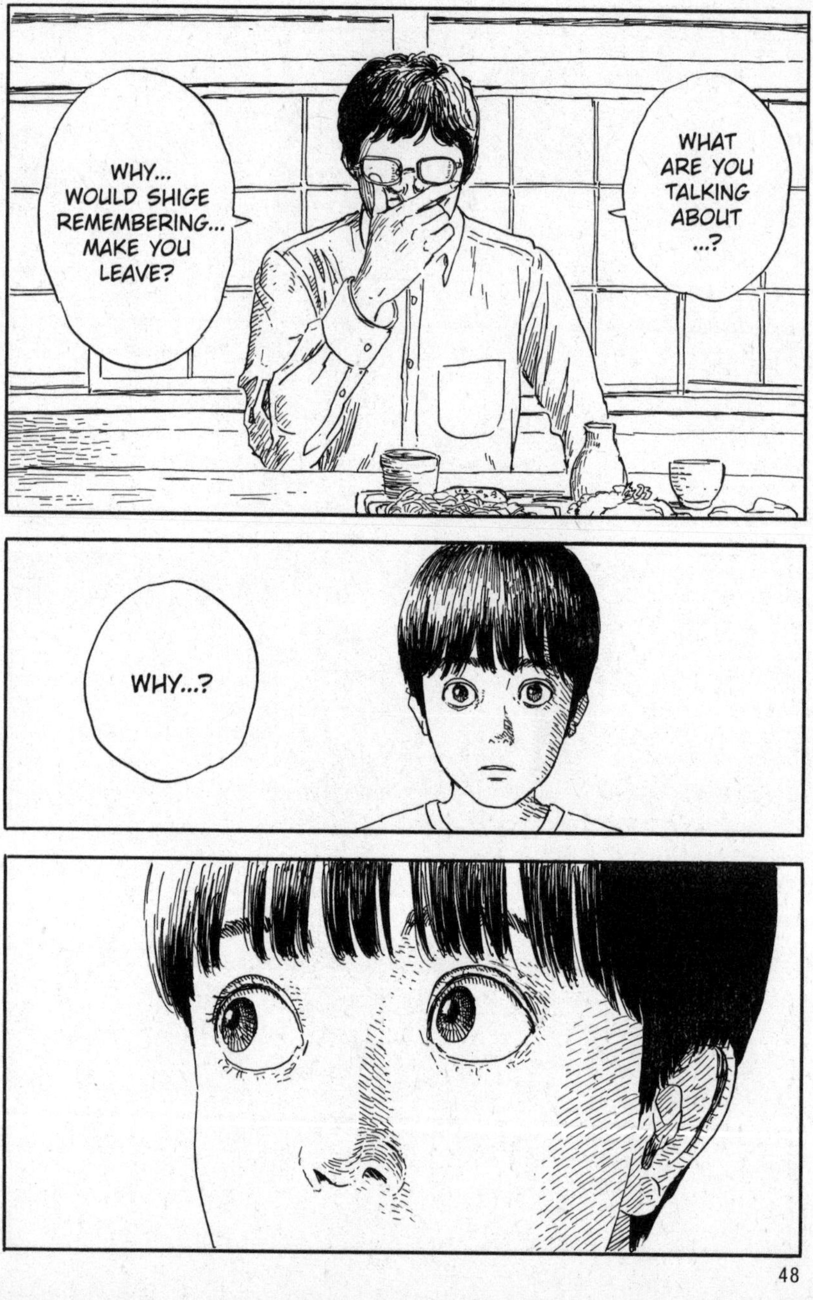
WHAT ARE YOU TALKING ABOUT ...?
WHY... WOULD SHIGE REMEMBERING... MAKE YOU LEAVE?
WHY...?

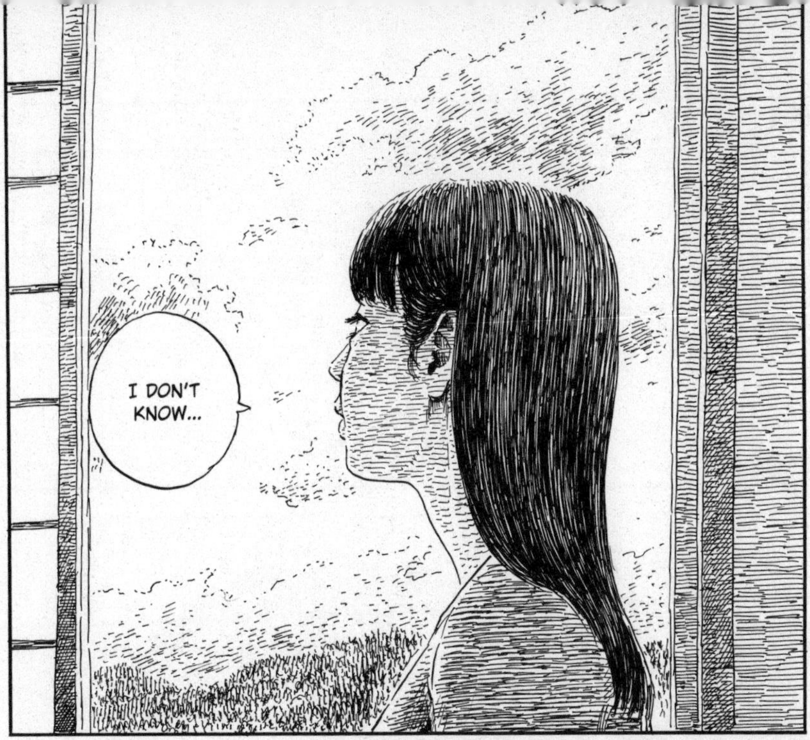
I DON'T KNOW...

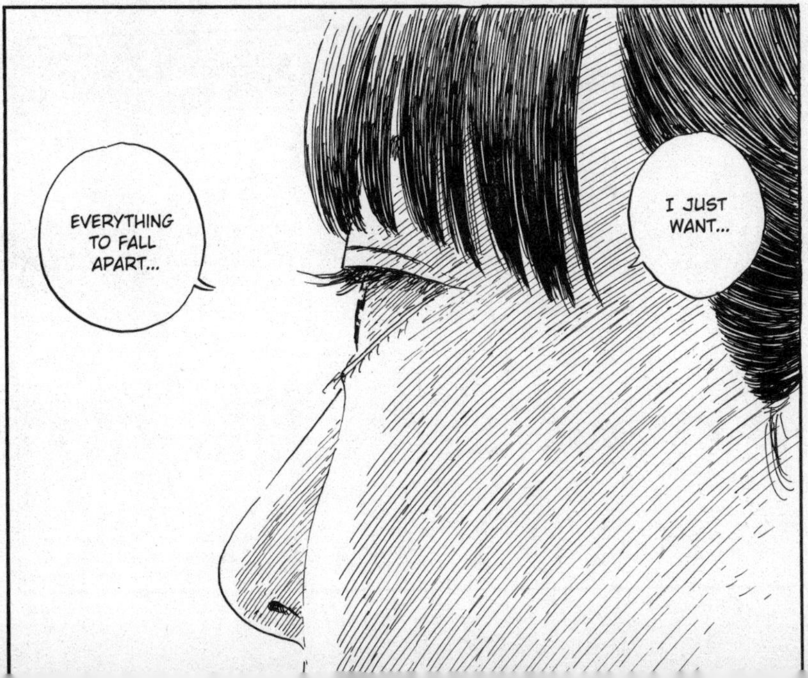
I JUST WANT...
EVERYTHING TO FALL APART...

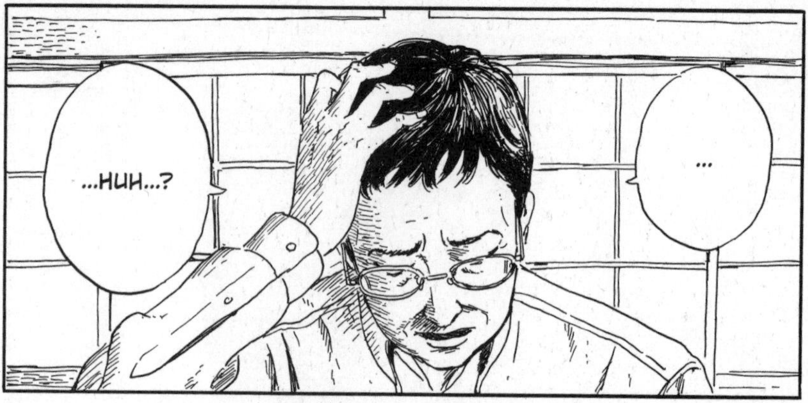
...
...HUH...?
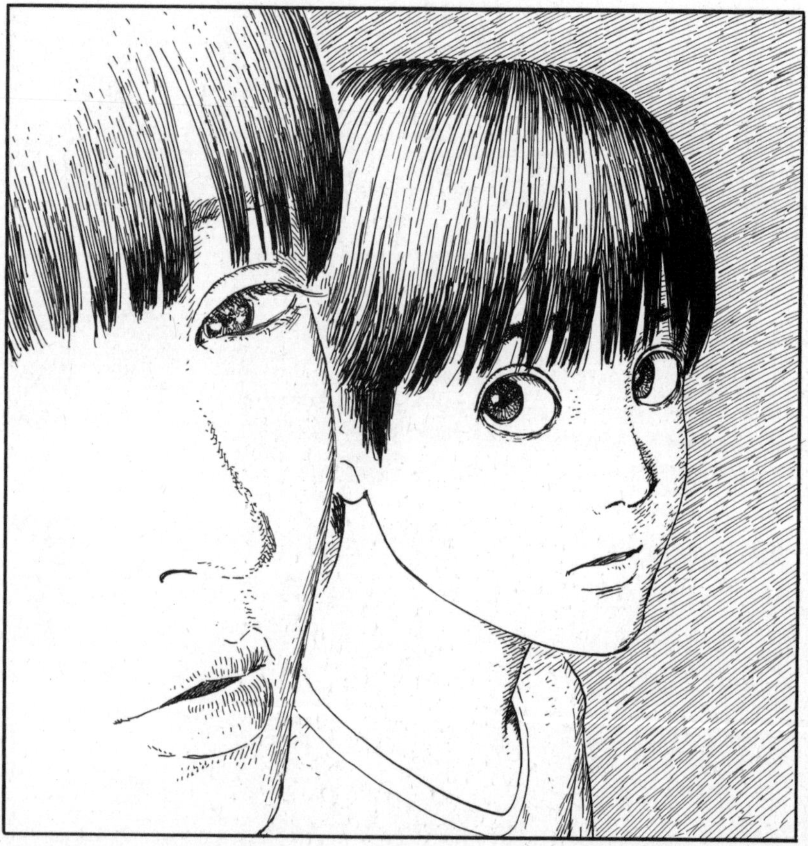

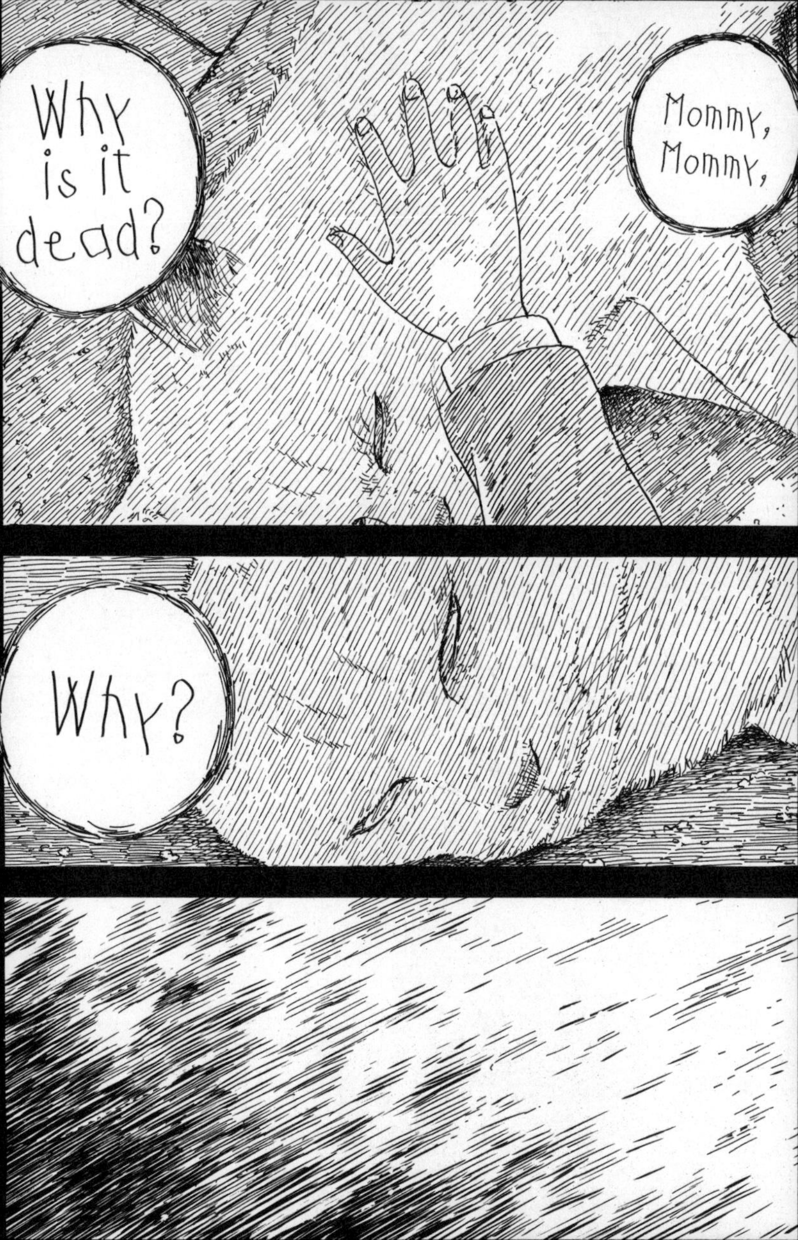
Mommy, Mommy,
Why is it dead?
Why?

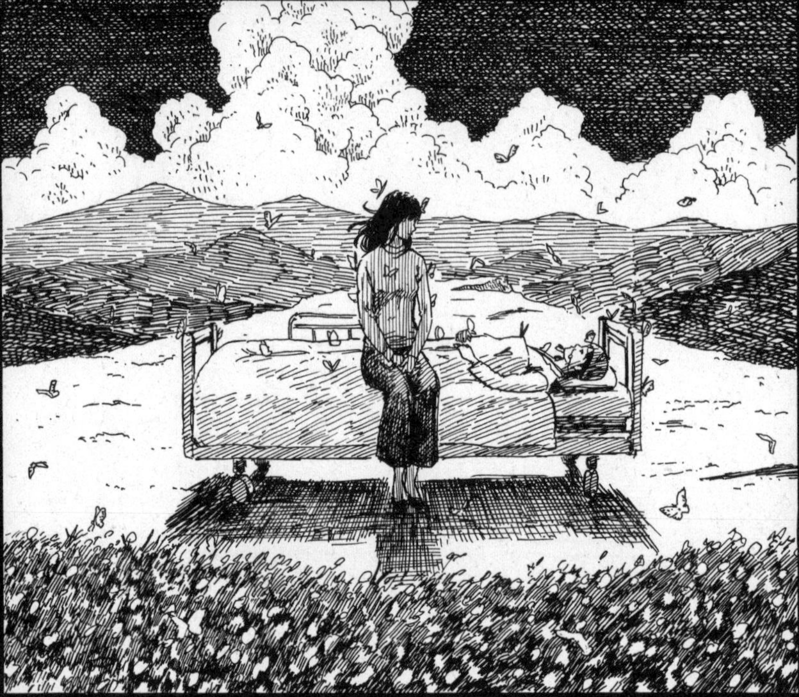

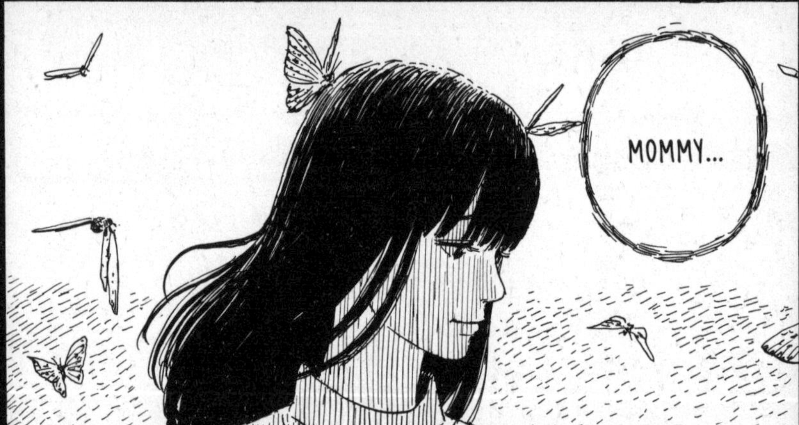
MOMMY...

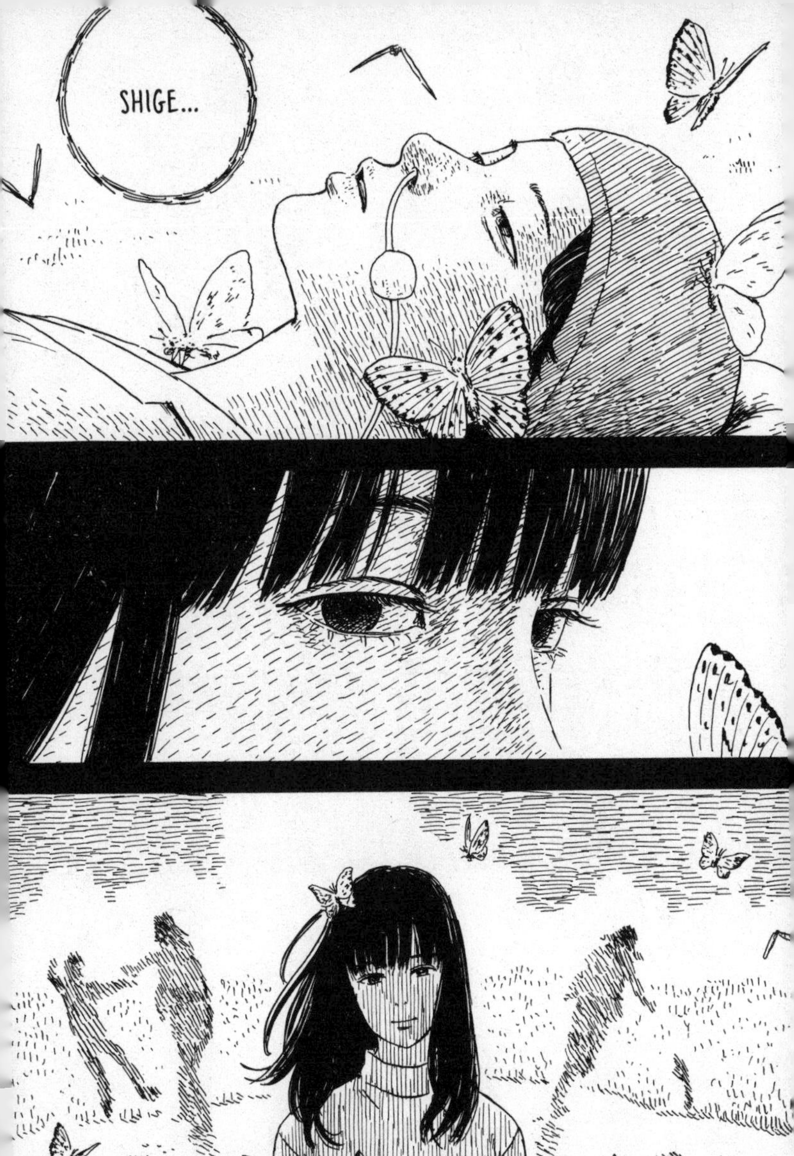
SHIGE...

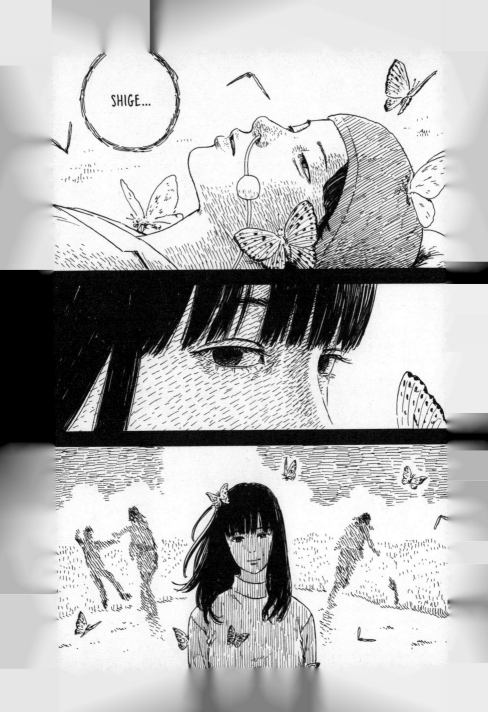

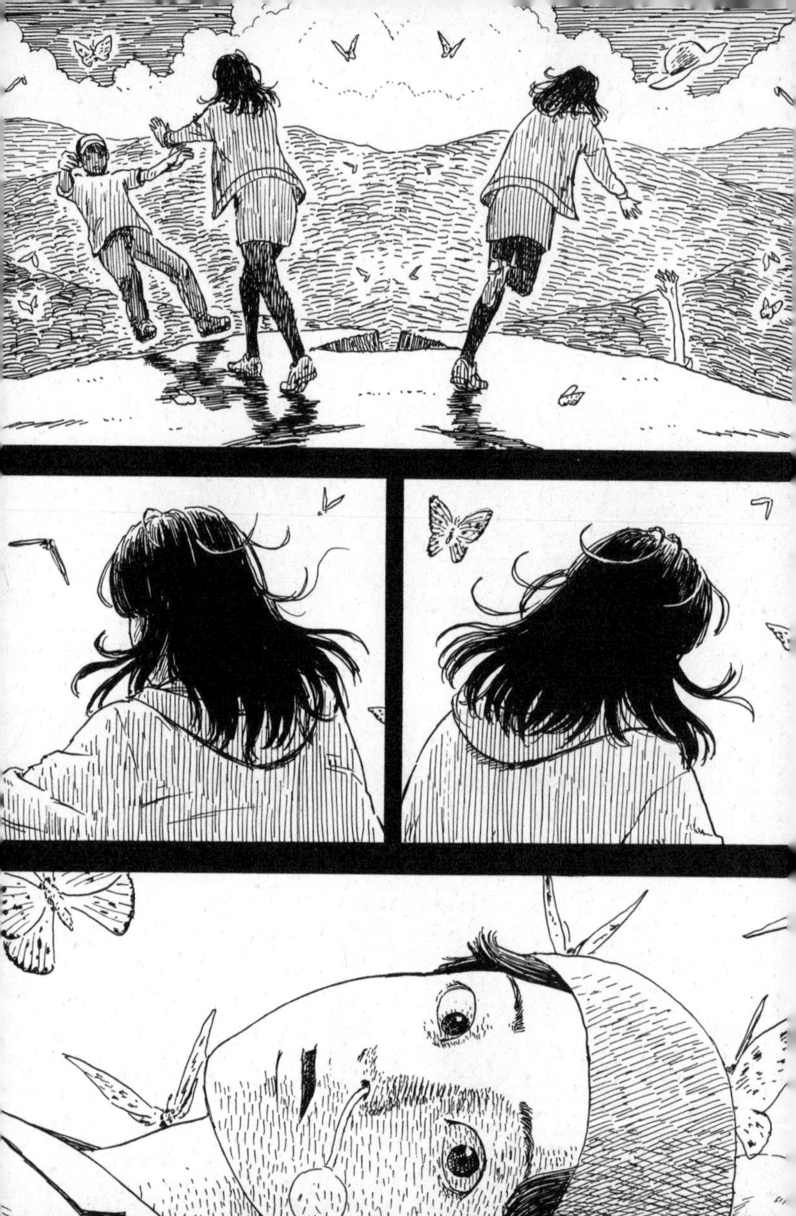

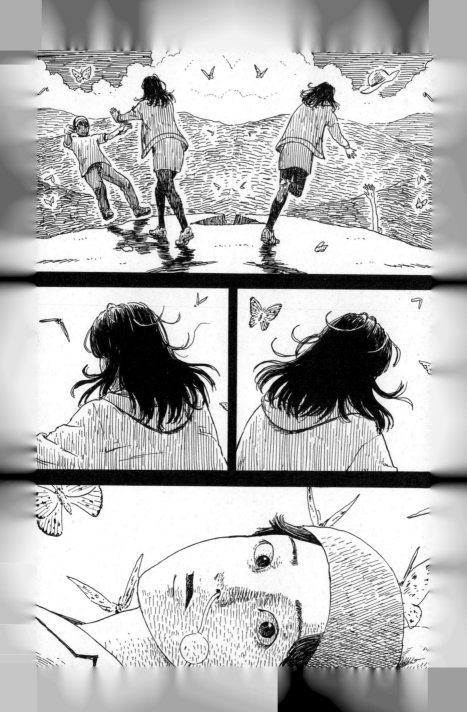

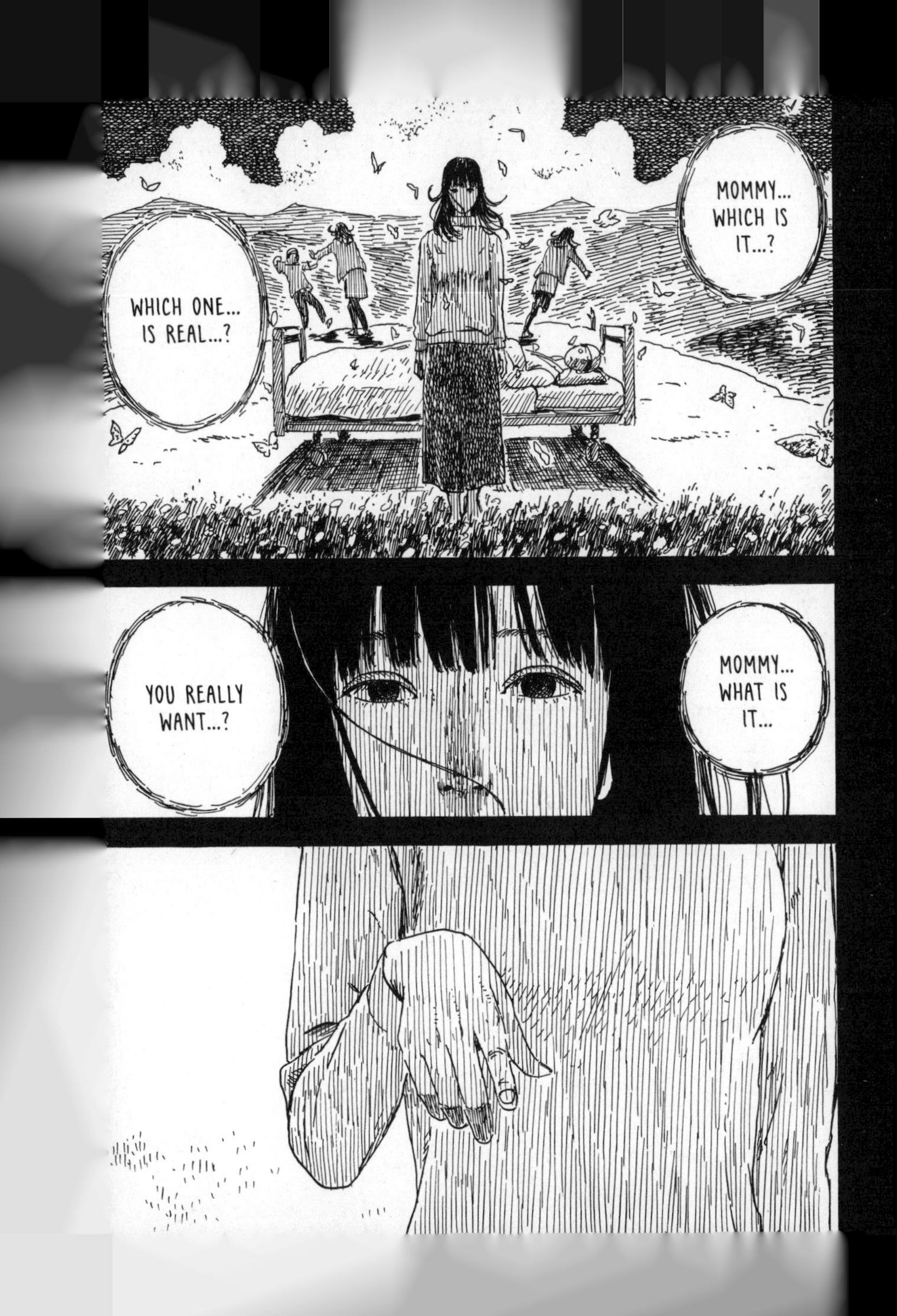
MOMMY... WHICH IS IT...?
WHICH ONE... IS REAL...?
MOMMY... WHAT IS IT...
YOU REALLY WANT...?

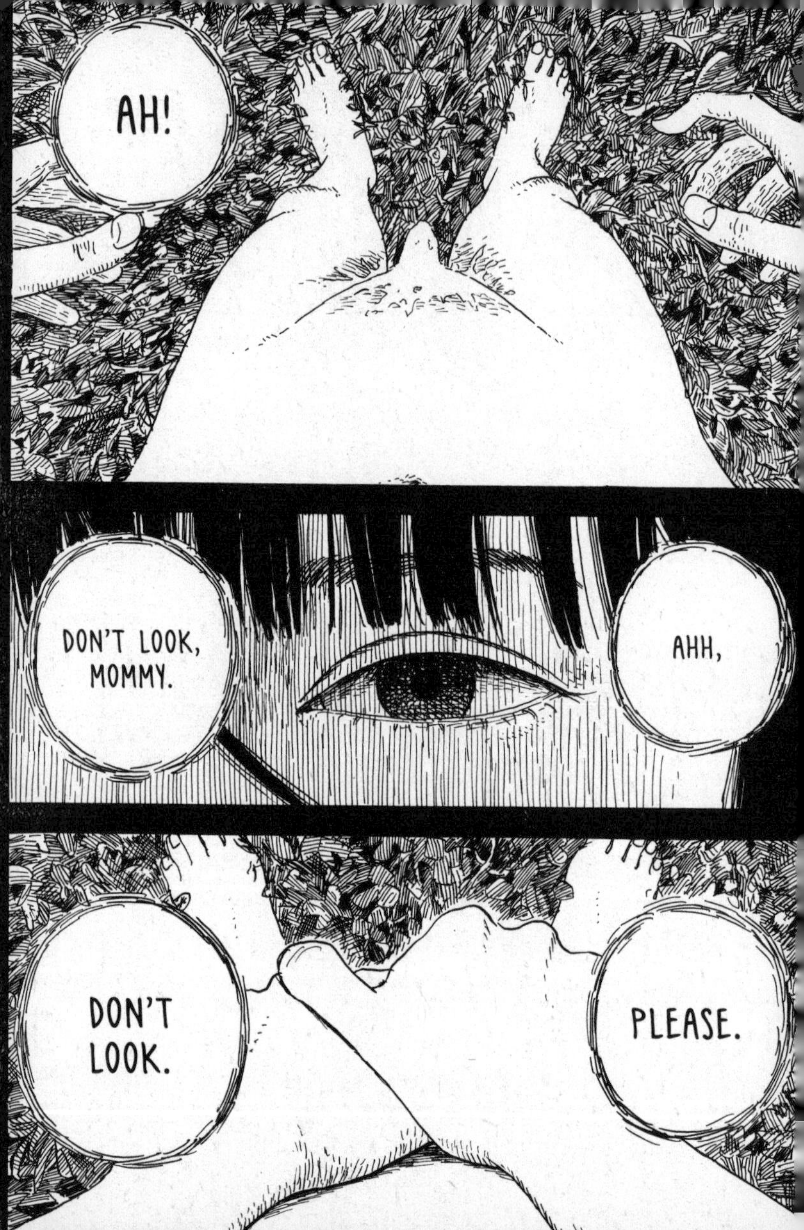
AH!
AHH,
DON'T LOOK, MOMMY.
PLEASE.
DON'T LOOK.

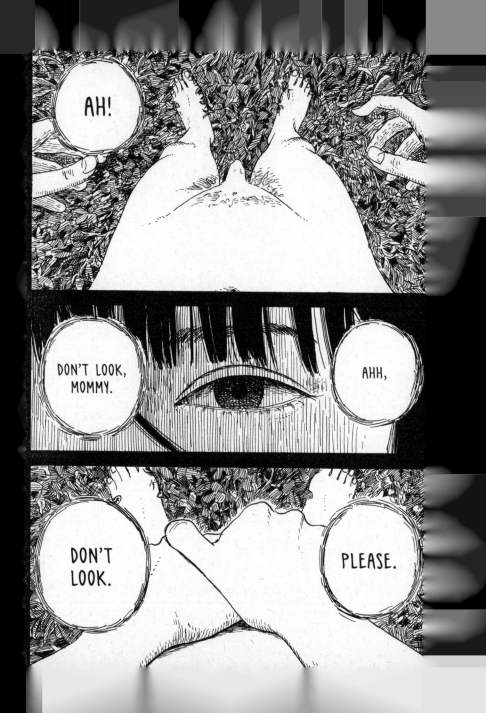

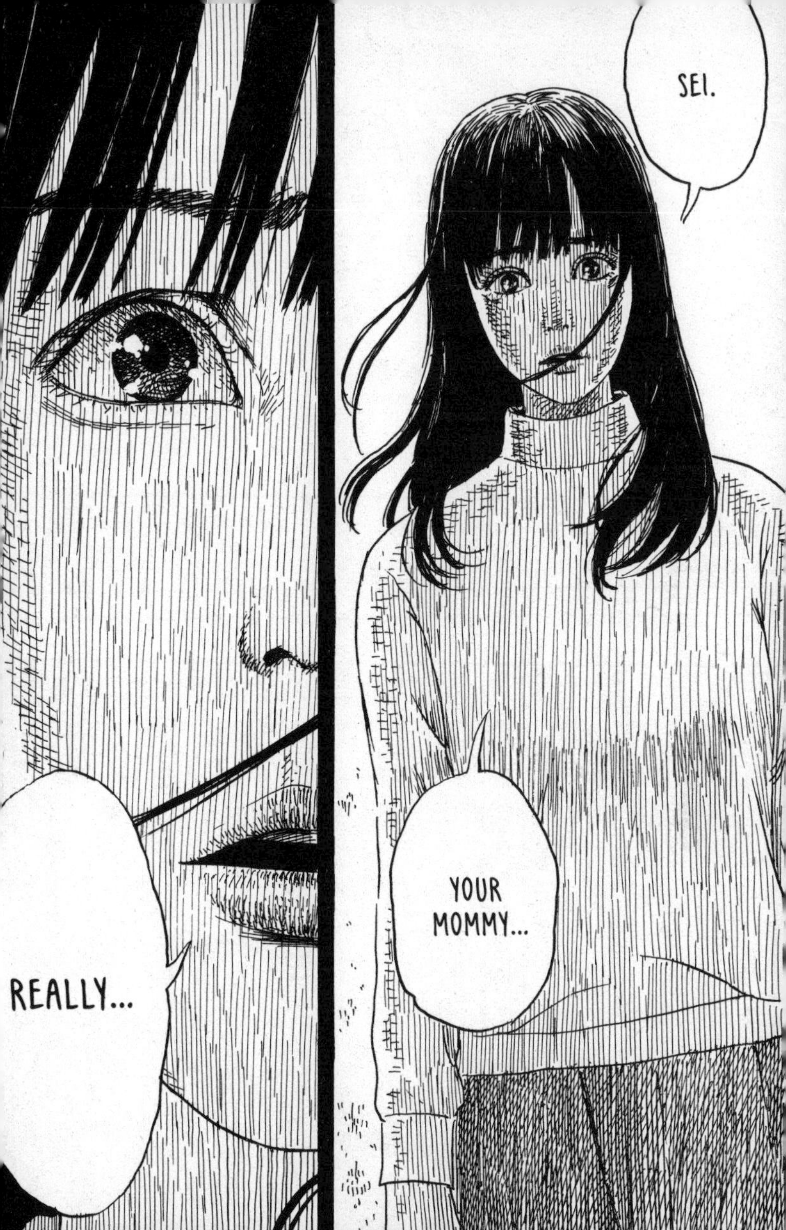
SEI.
YOUR MOMMY...
REALLY...

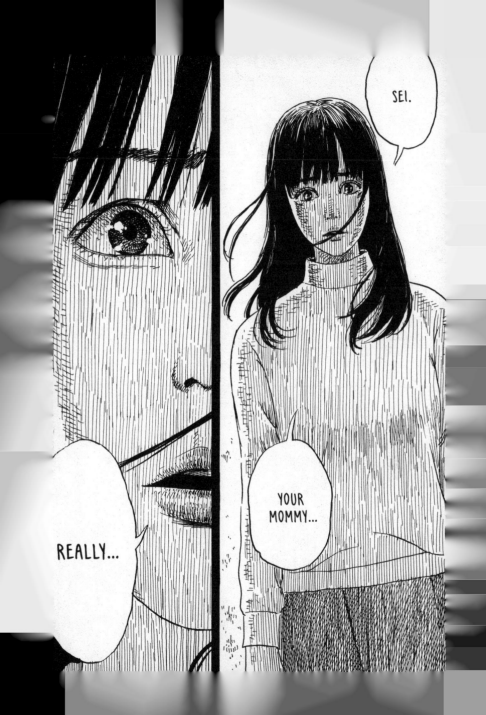

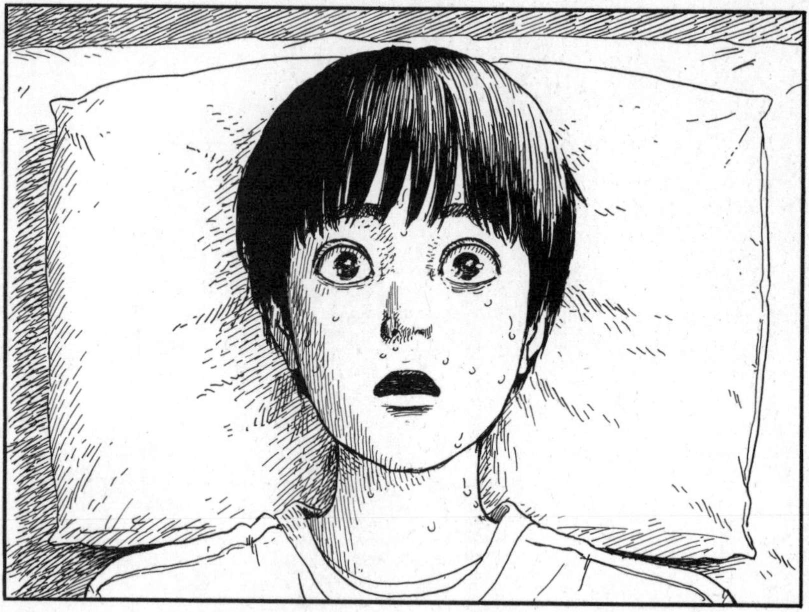

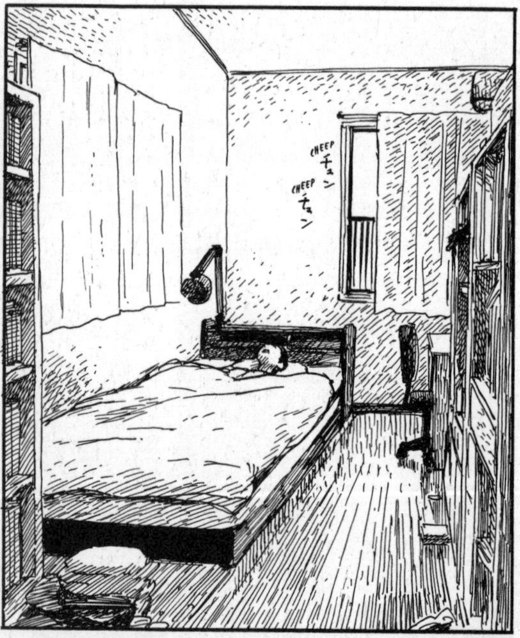
CHEEP チュン
CHEEP チュン

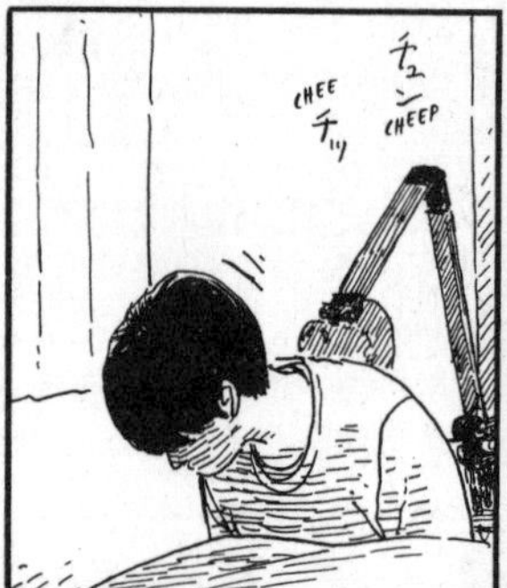
チュン CHEEP
CHEE チッ

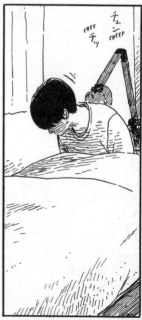

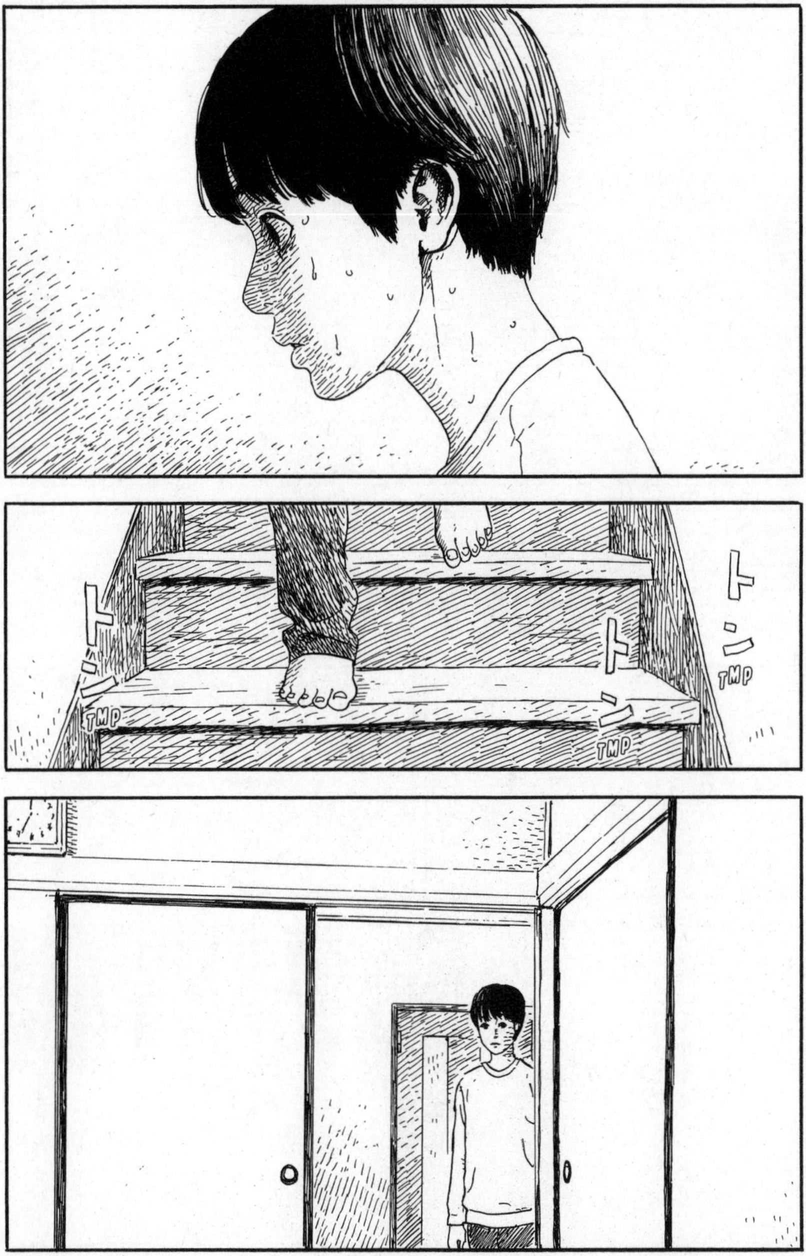
トン
TMP
トン
TMP
トン
TMP

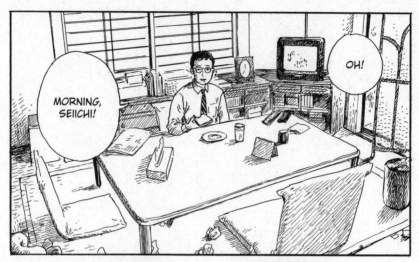

OH!
MORNING, SEIICHI!
WHAT DO YOU WANT FOR BREAK-FAST?
I'M HAVING TOAST, YOU WANT SOME?
...HUH?

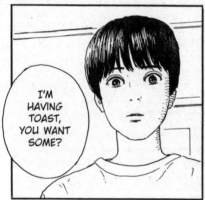

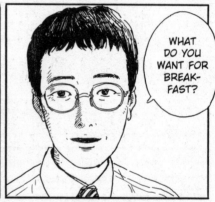

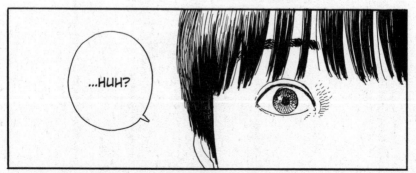

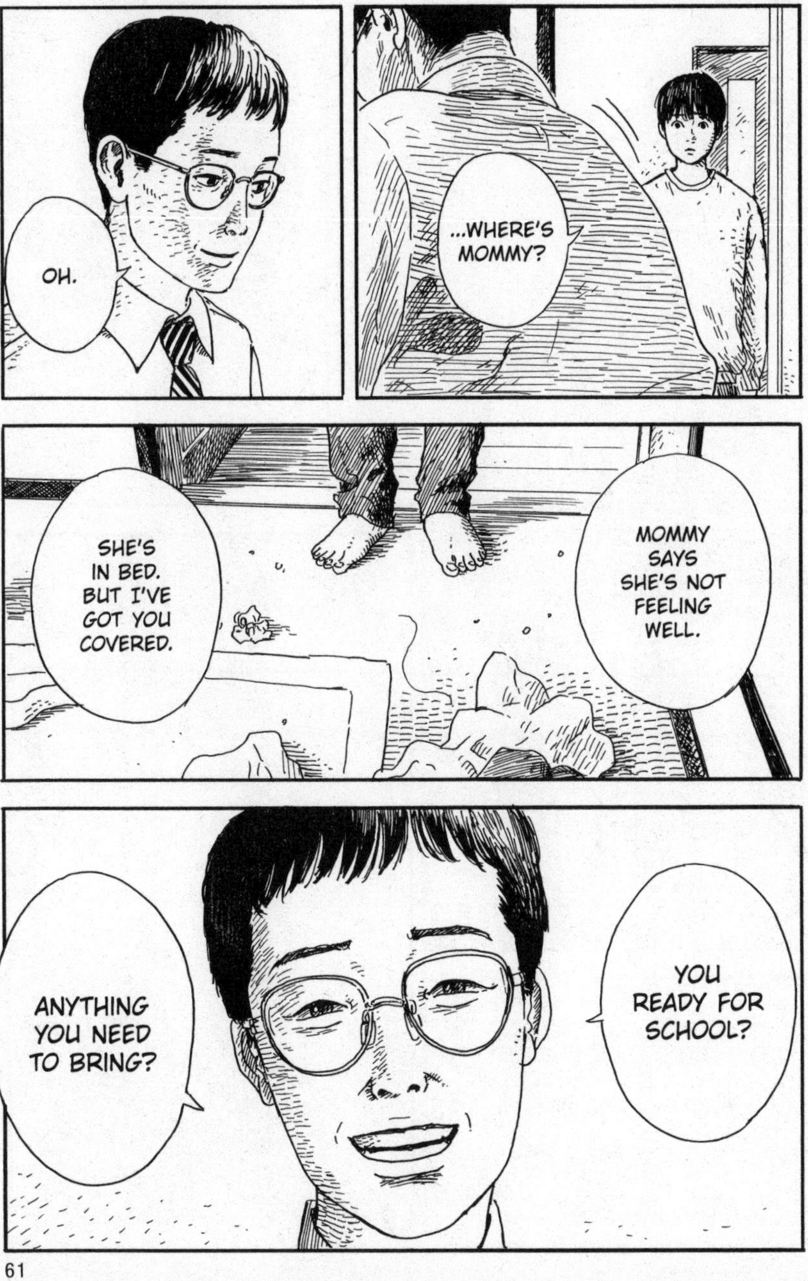
...WHERE'S MOMMY?
OH.
MOMMY SAYS SHE'S NOT FEELING WELL.
SHE'S IN BED. BUT I'VE GOT YOU COVERED.
YOU READY FOR SCHOOL?
ANYTHING YOU NEED TO BRING?

トン
TMP
トン
TMP

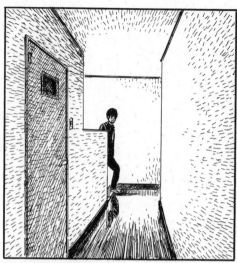

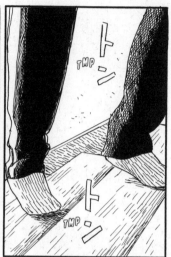

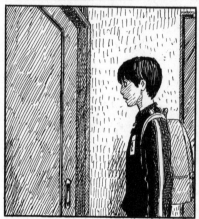

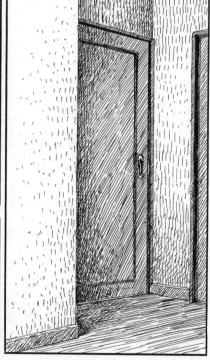

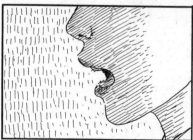

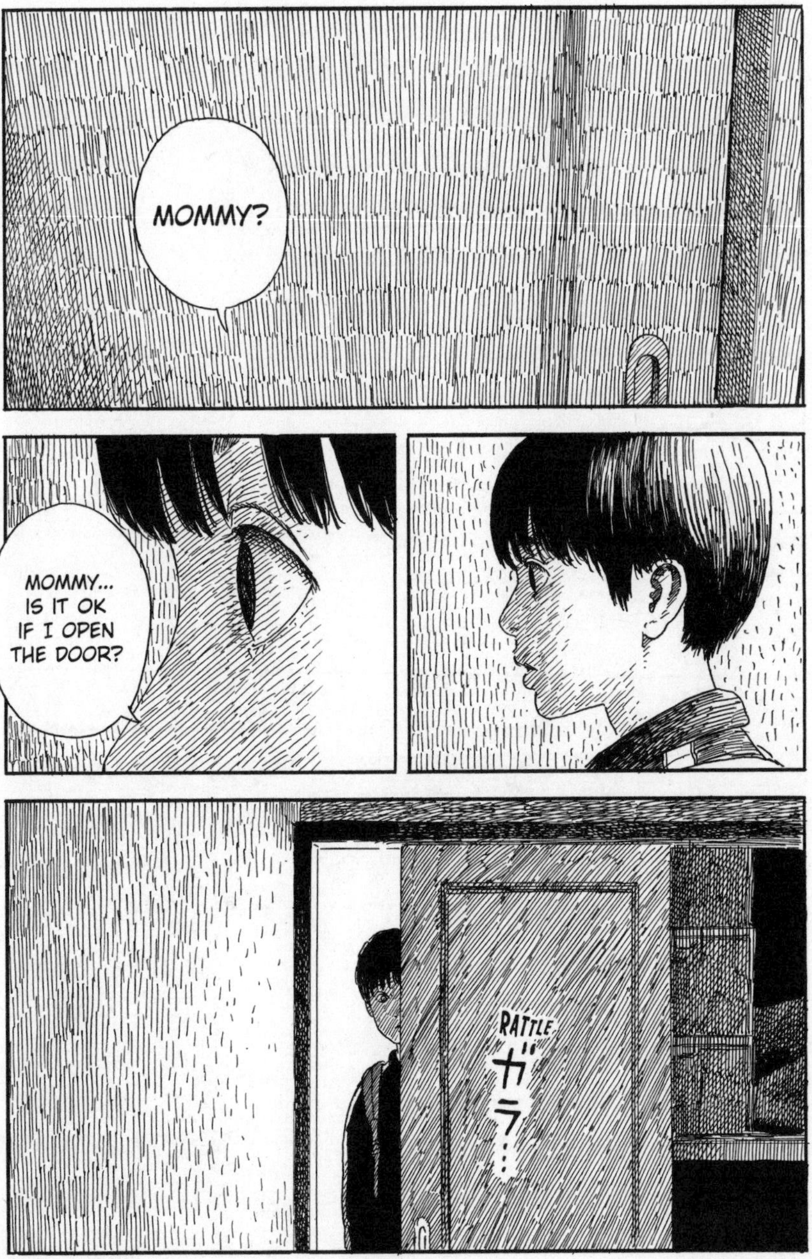
MOMMY?
MOMMY... IS IT OK IF I OPEN THE DOOR?
RATTLE
ガラ…

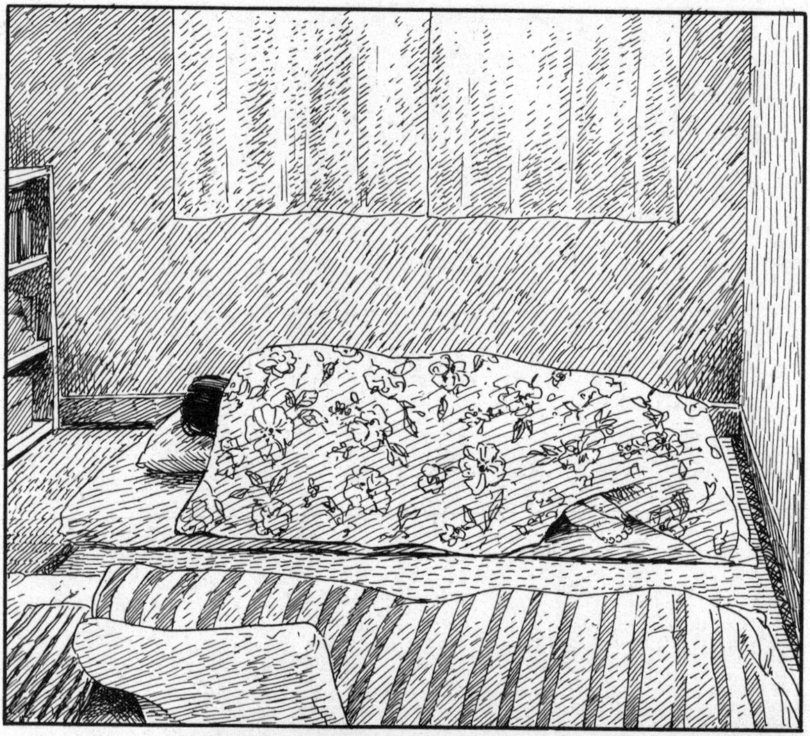

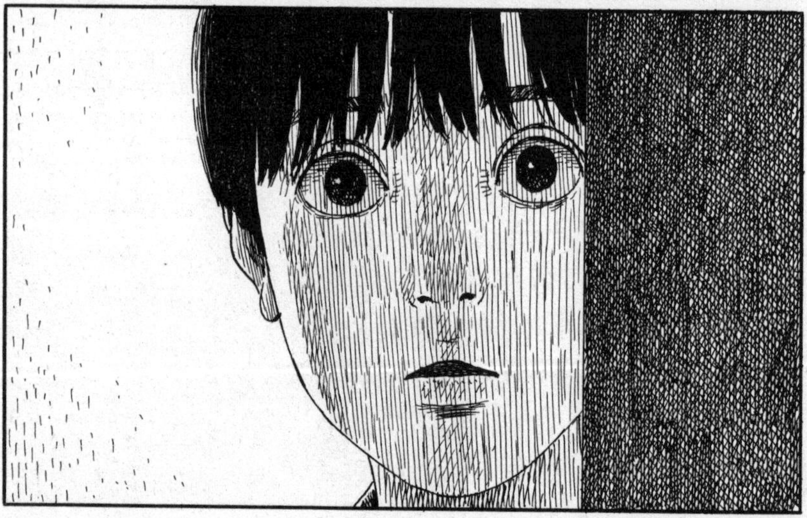

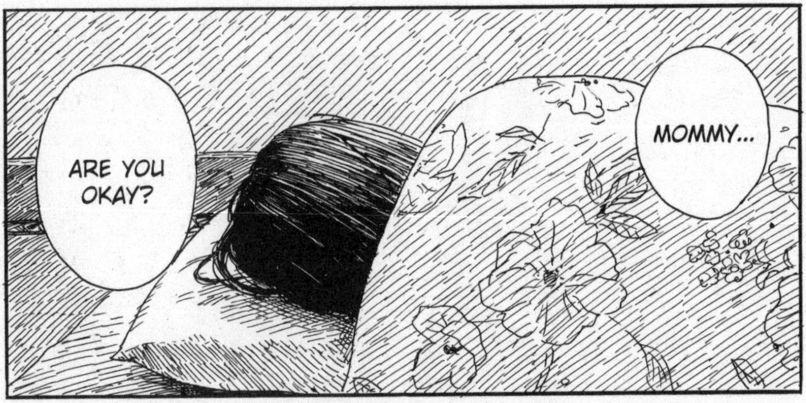
MOMMY...
ARE YOU OKAY?
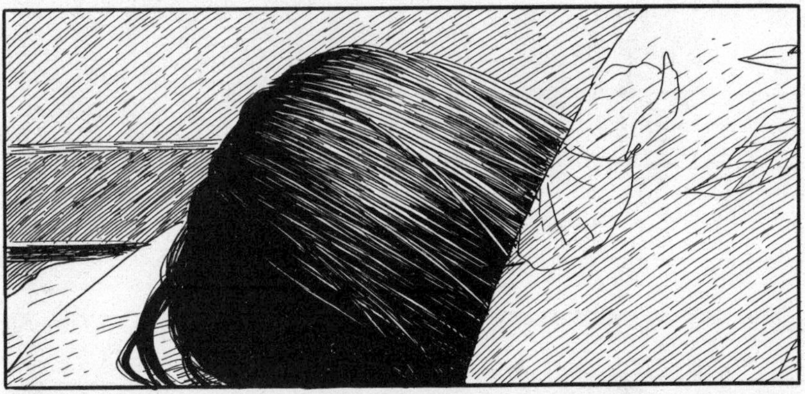
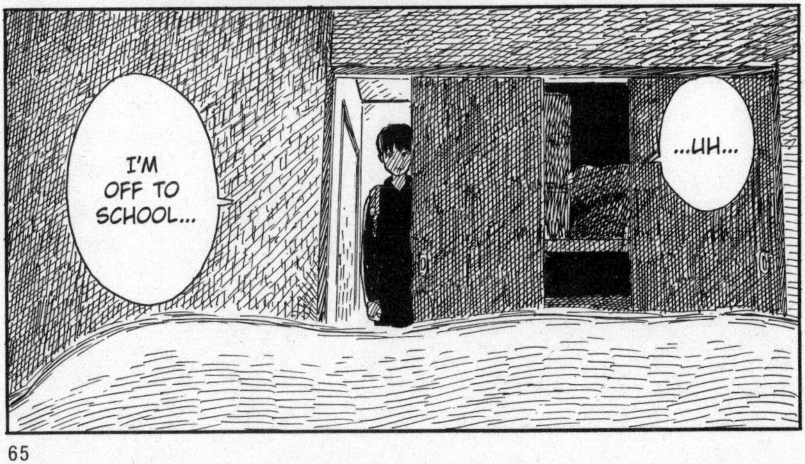
...UH...
I'M OFF TO SCHOOL...

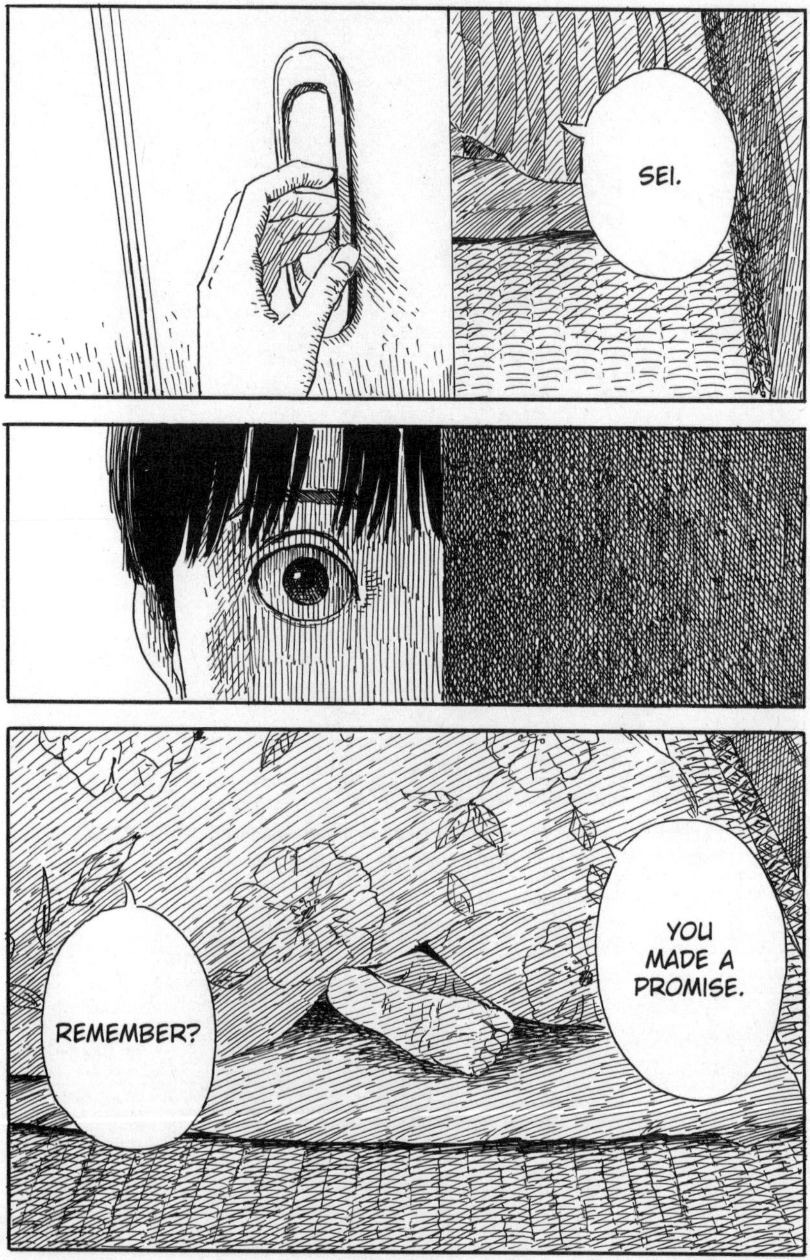
SEI.
YOU MADE A PROMISE.
REMEMBER?

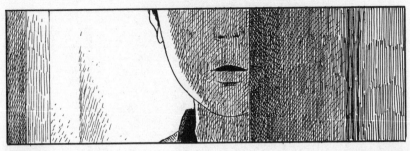

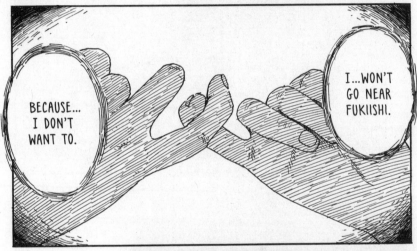

I...WON'T GO NEAR FUKIISHI.
BECAUSE... I DON'T WANT TO.
...
YES.

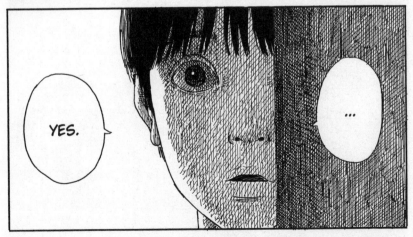

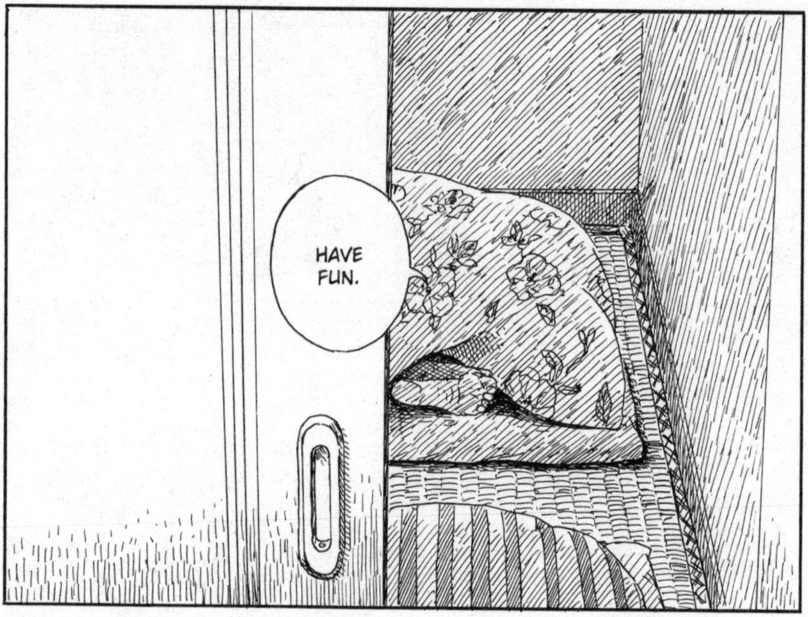
HAVE FUN.
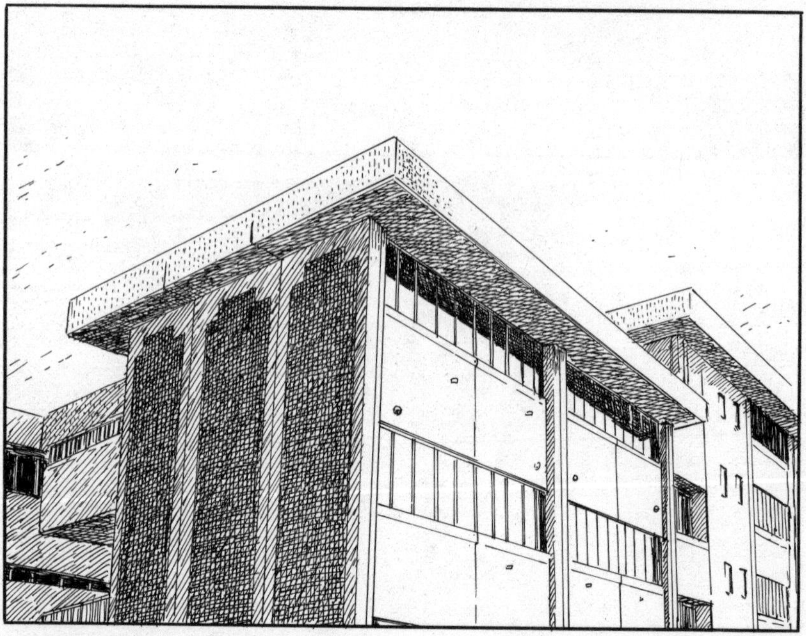

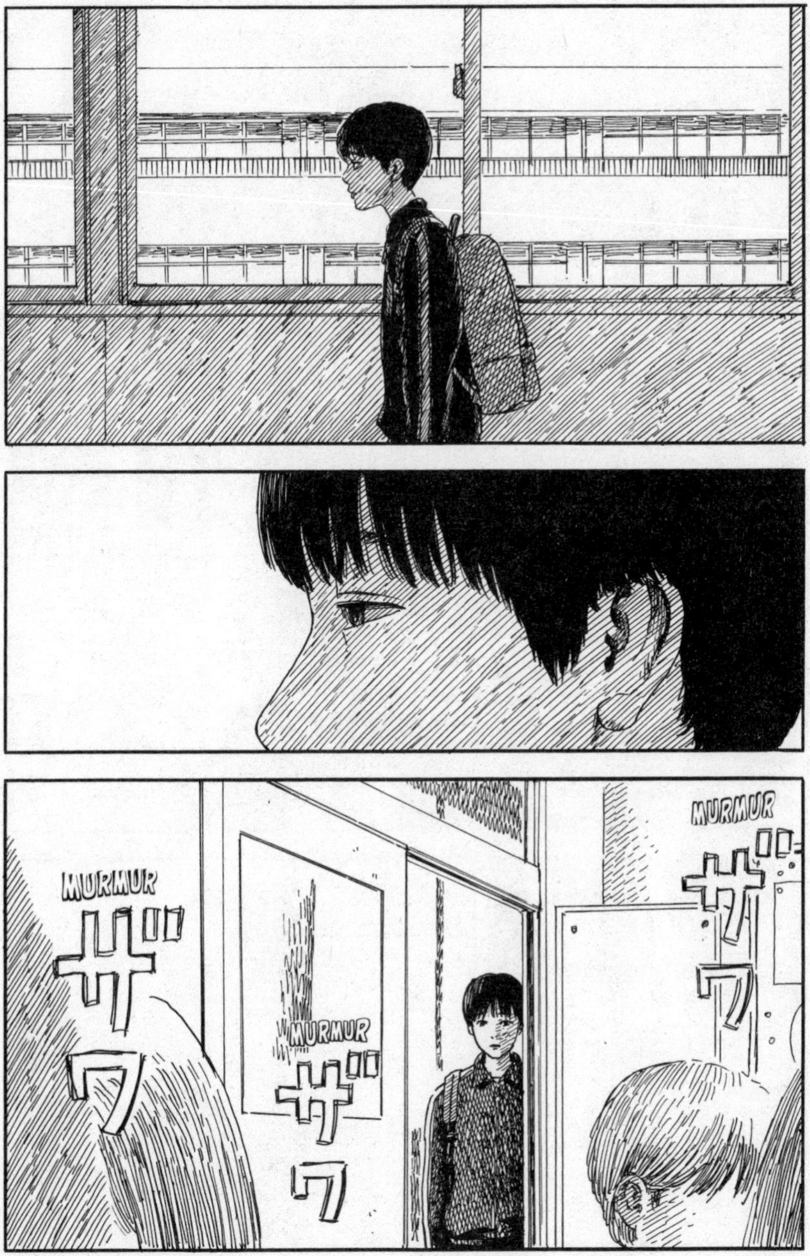
MURMUR
ザワ
MURMUR
ザワ
MURMUR
ザワ

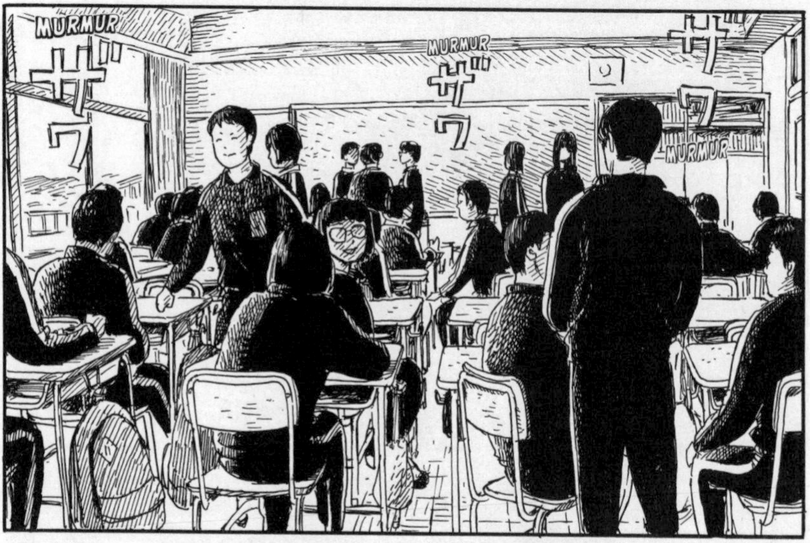
ザワ
MURMUR
MURMUR
ザワ
MURMUR
ザワ

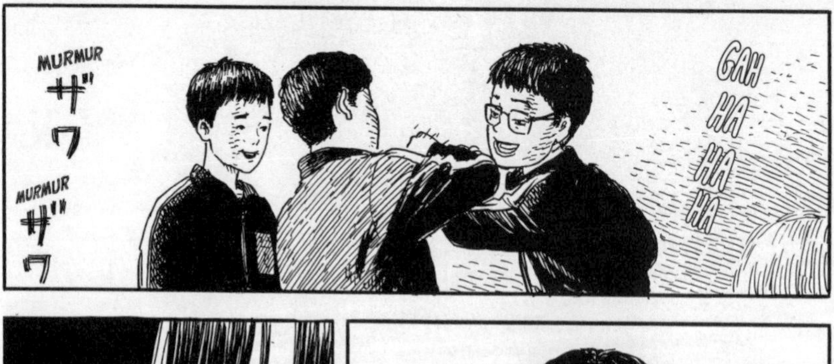
GAH HA HA HA
MURMUR
ザワ
MURMUR
ザワ

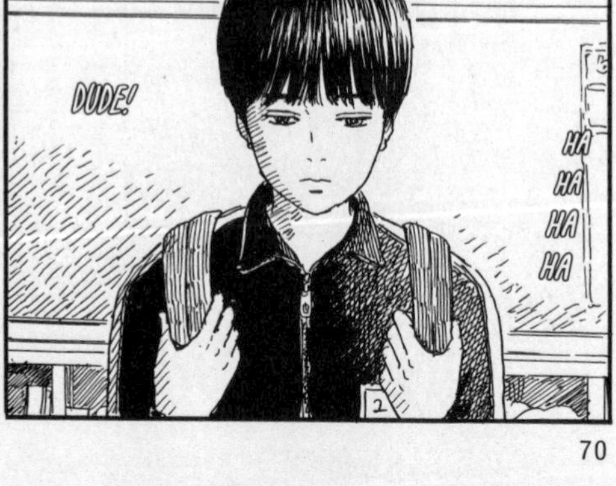
HA HA HA HA HA
DUDE!

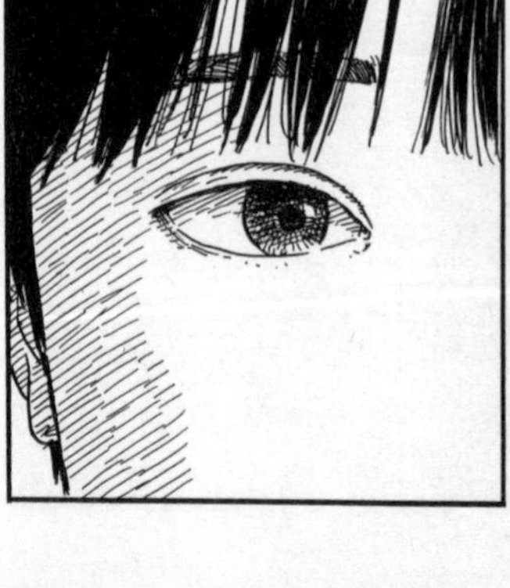

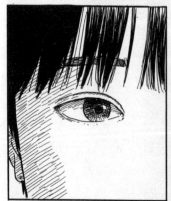

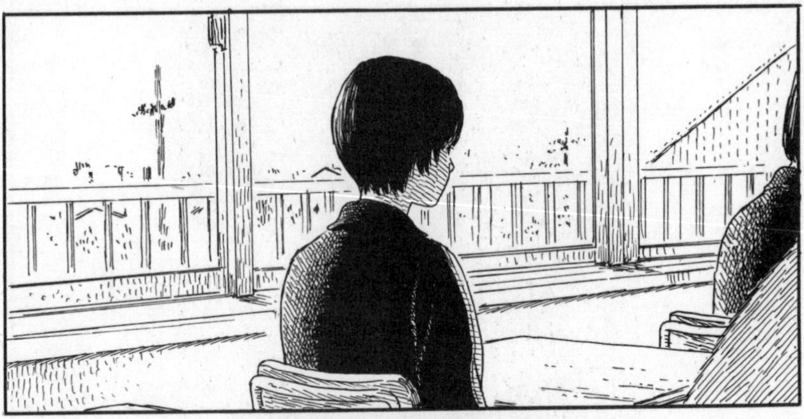
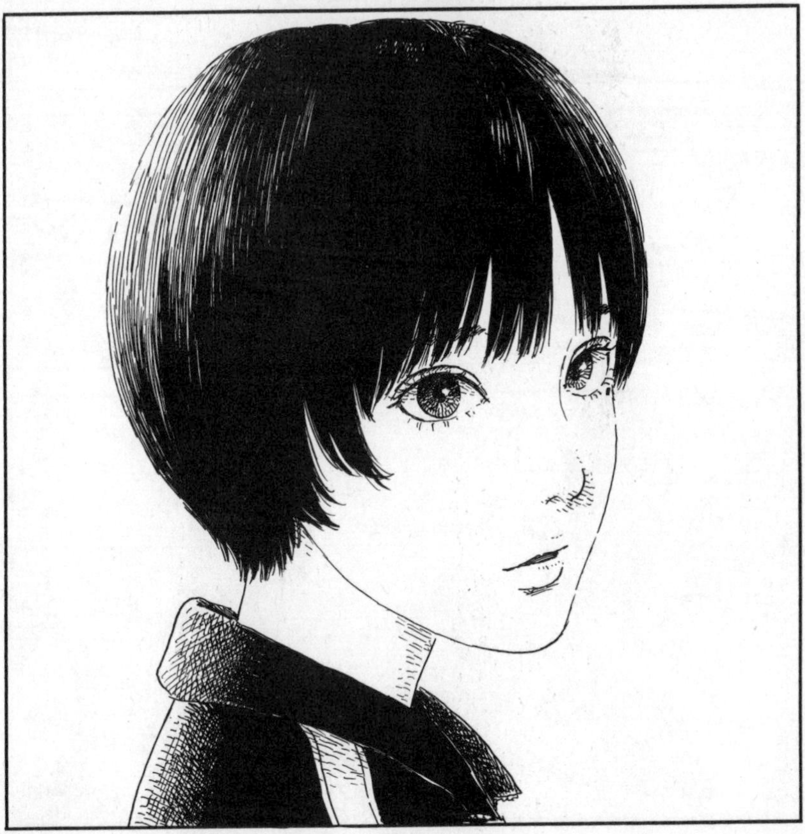

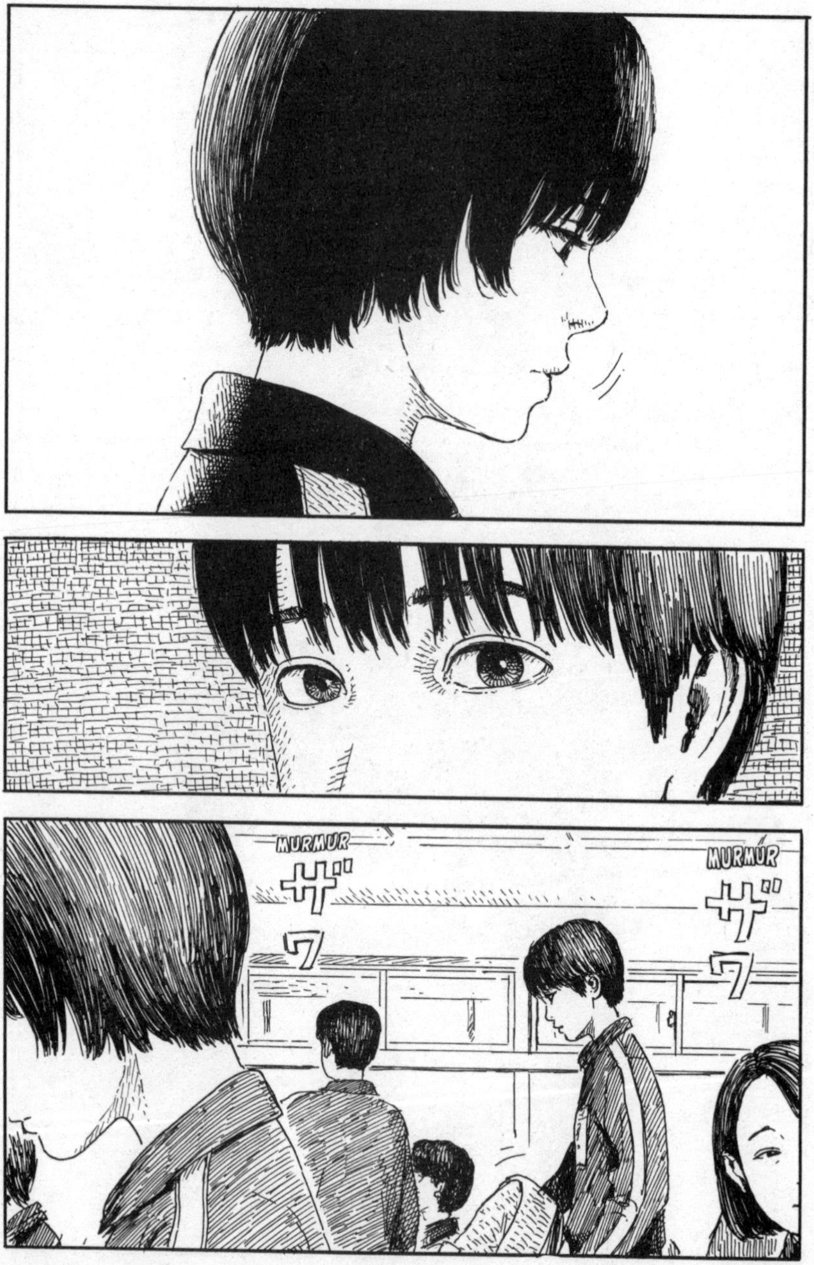
MURMUR
ザワ
MURMUR
ザワ

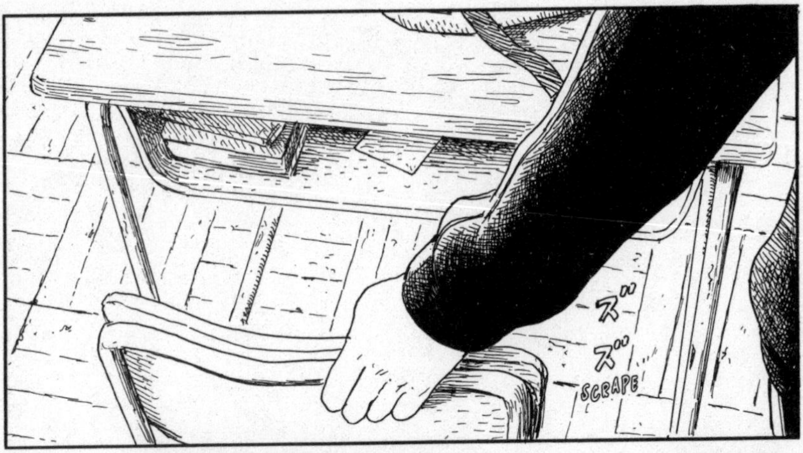
ズズ
SCRAPE

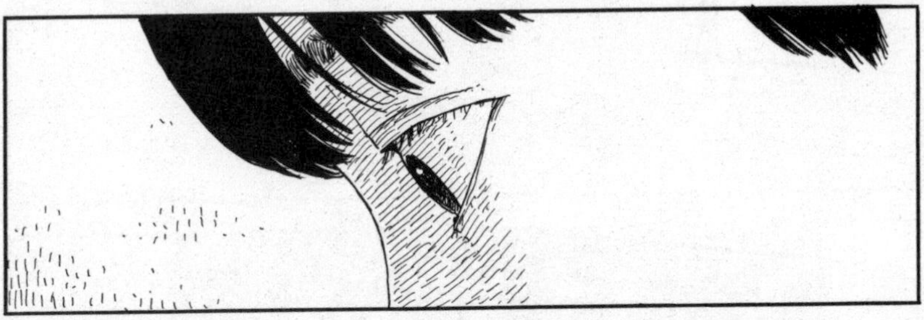

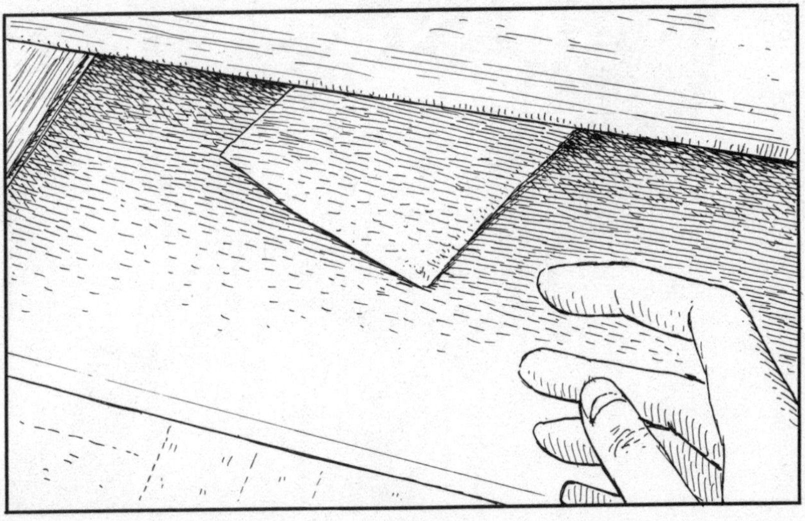

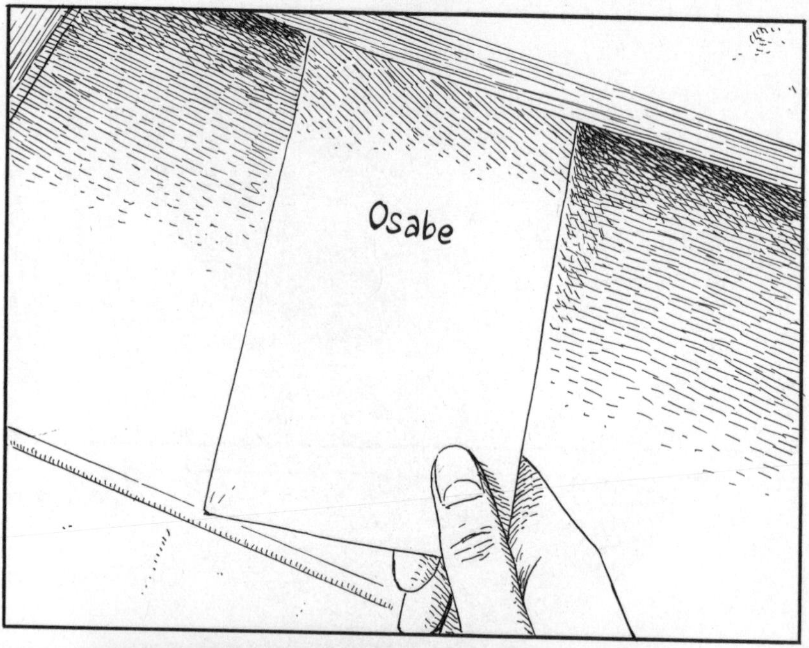
Osabe

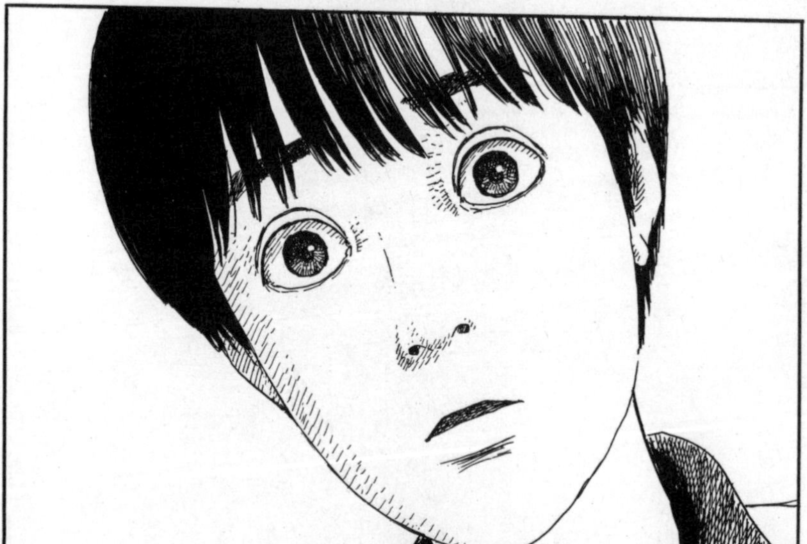

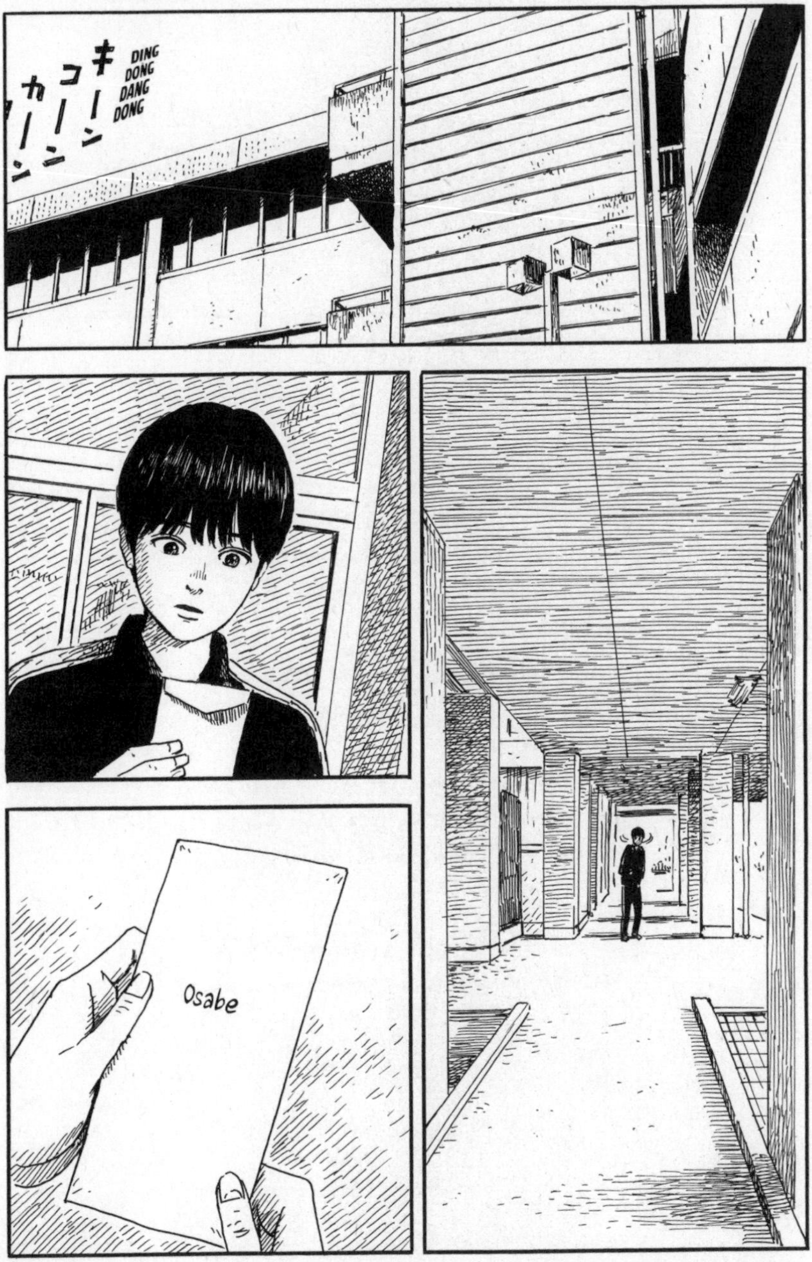
キーンコーンカーンコーン
DING DONG DANG DONG
Osabe

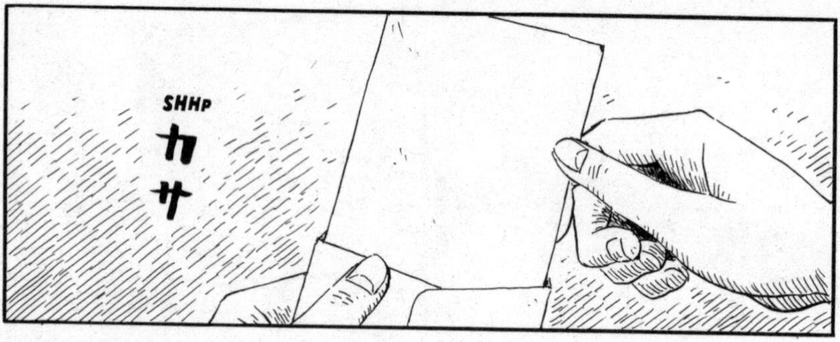
SHHP
カサ

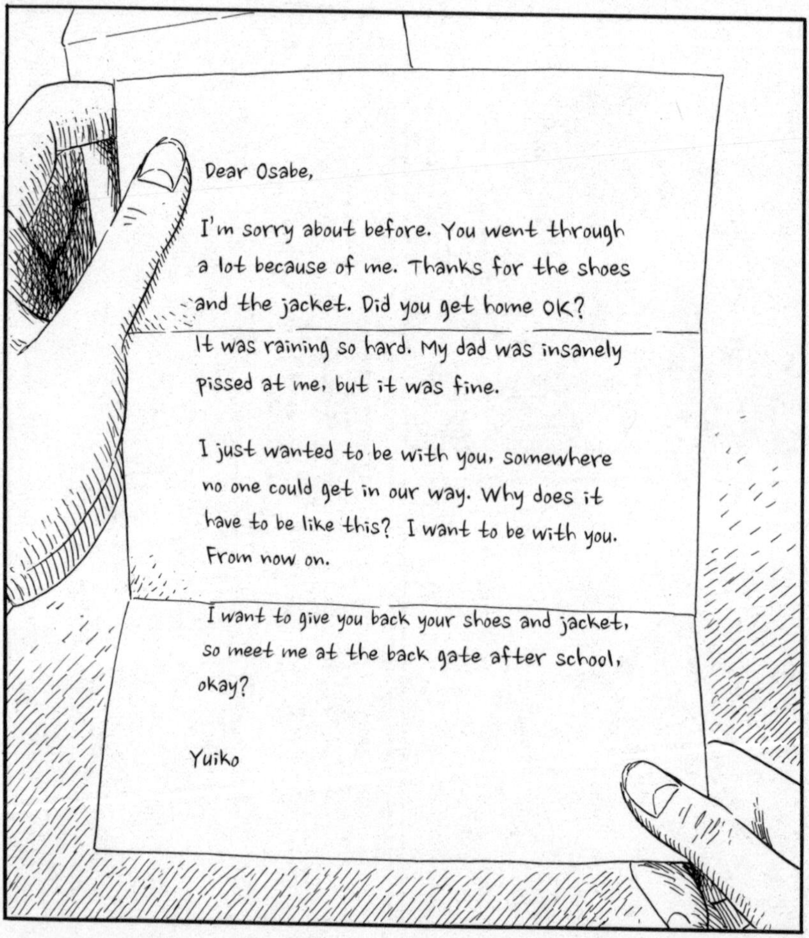
Dear Osabe,
I'm sorry about before. You went through a lot because of me. Thanks for the shoes and the jacket. Did you get home OK? It was raining so hard. My dad was insanely pissed at me, but it was fine.
I just wanted to be with you, somewhere no one could get in our way. Why does it have to be like this? I want to be with you. From now on.
I want to give you back your shoes and jacket, so meet me at the back gate after school, okay?
Yuiko

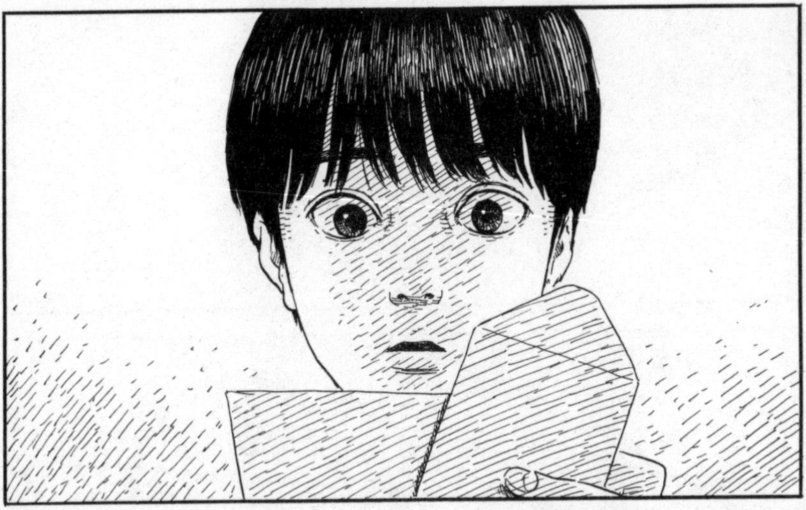

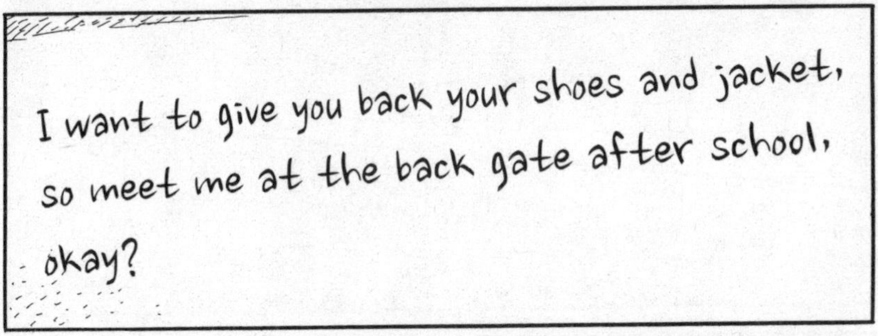
I want to give you back your shoes and jacket,
so meet me at the back gate after school,
okay?

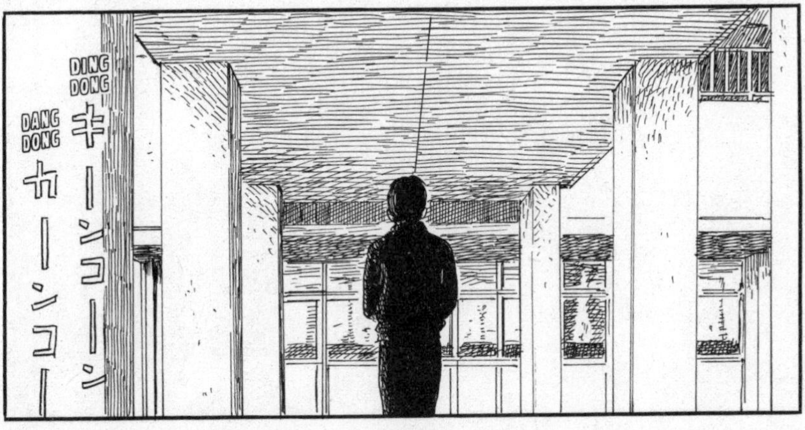
DING DONG
キーンコーン
DANG DONG
カーンコーン

トプ
BLUP
I'M SO HUNGRY
ザワ
MURMUR
AH HA HA HA
ザワ
MURMUR
ザワ
MURMUR
WHAAAT, GIMME MORE THAN THAAAT
HA HA HA HA HA
2-1 OSABE

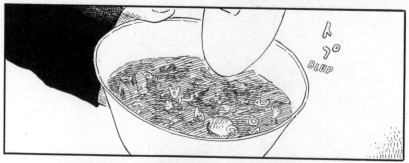

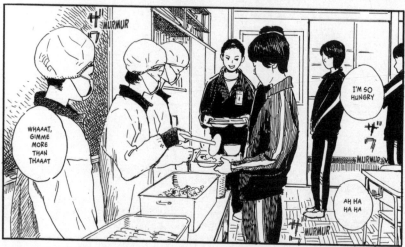

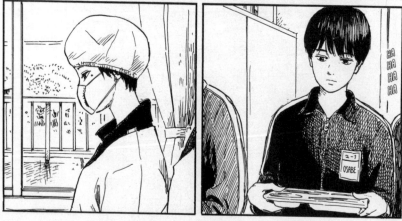

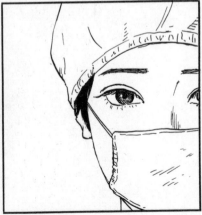

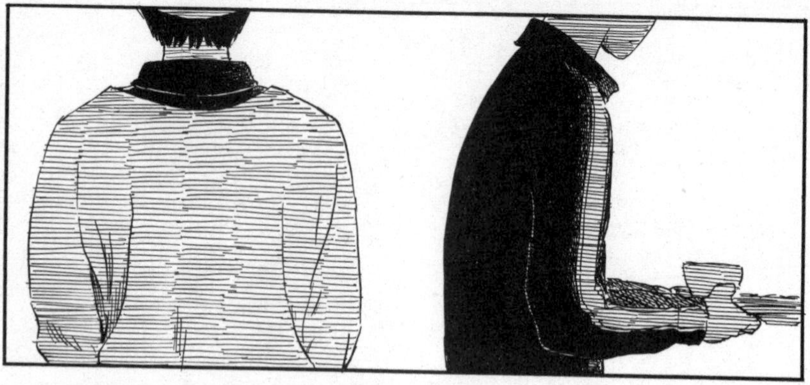

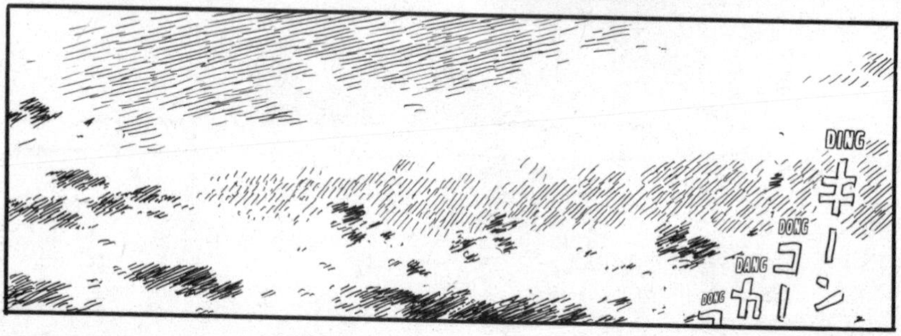
DING
DONG
DANG
DONG

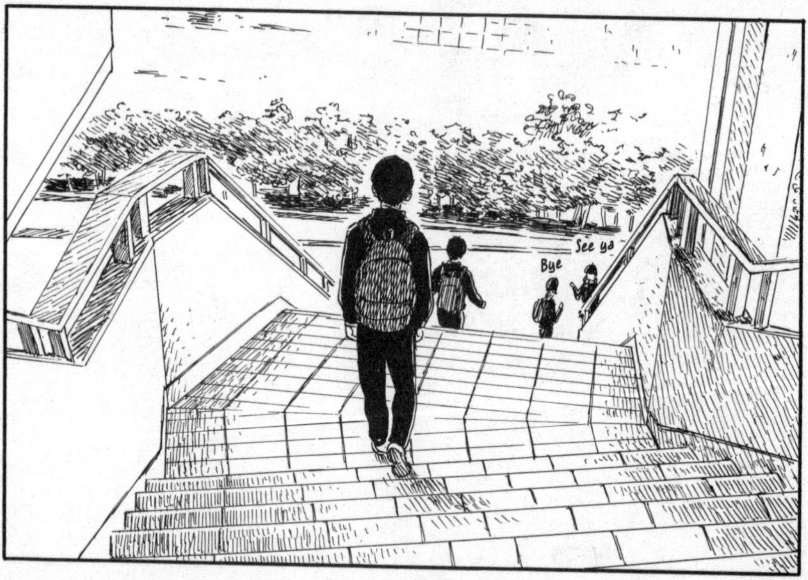
See ya
Bye

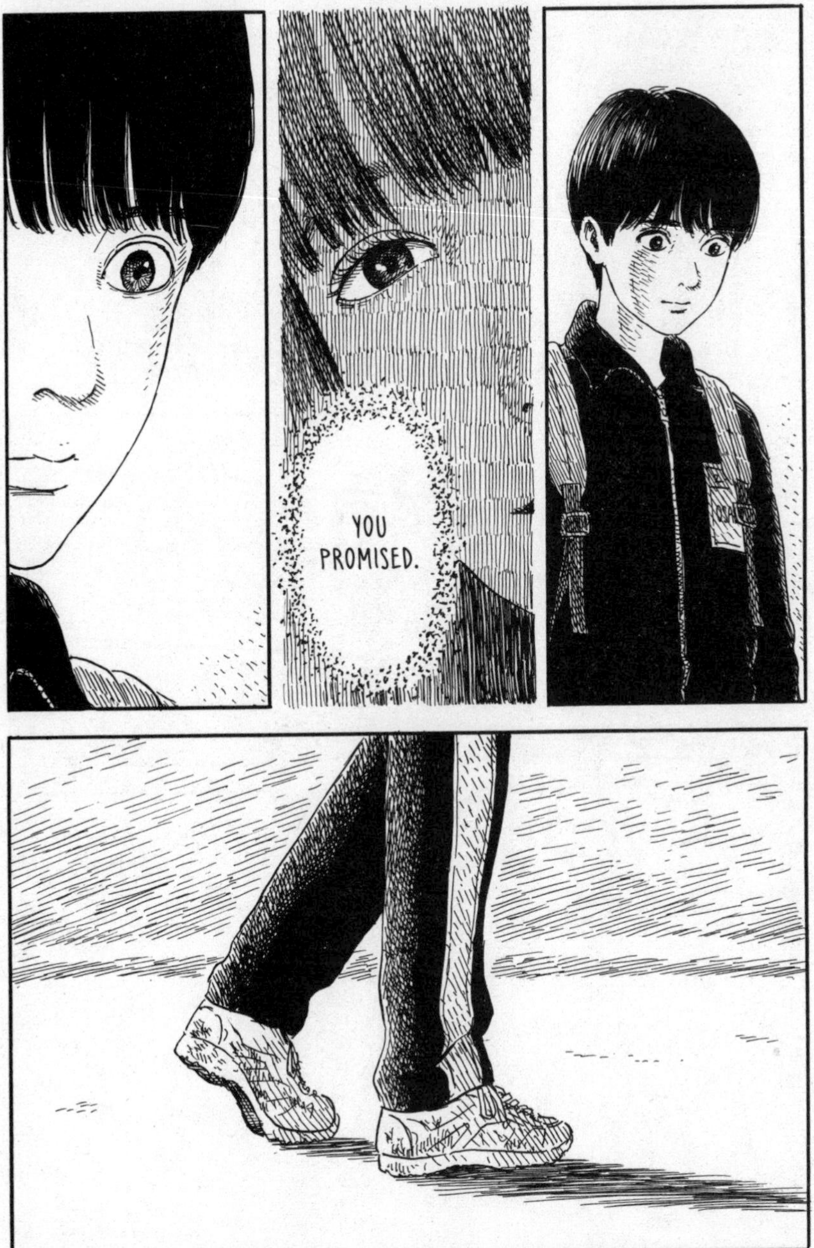
YOU PROMISED.

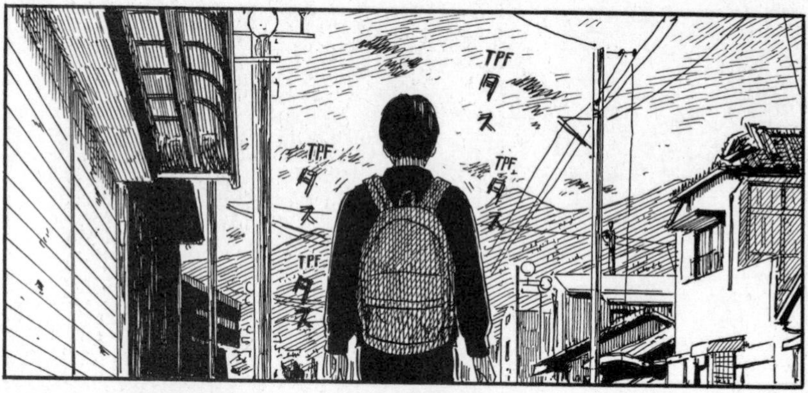
TPF
タス
TPF
タス
TPF
タス
TPF
タス

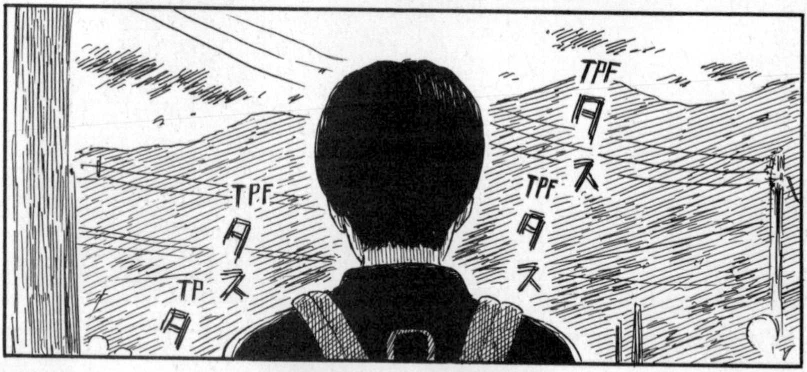
TPF
タス
TPF
タス
TPF
タス
TP
タ

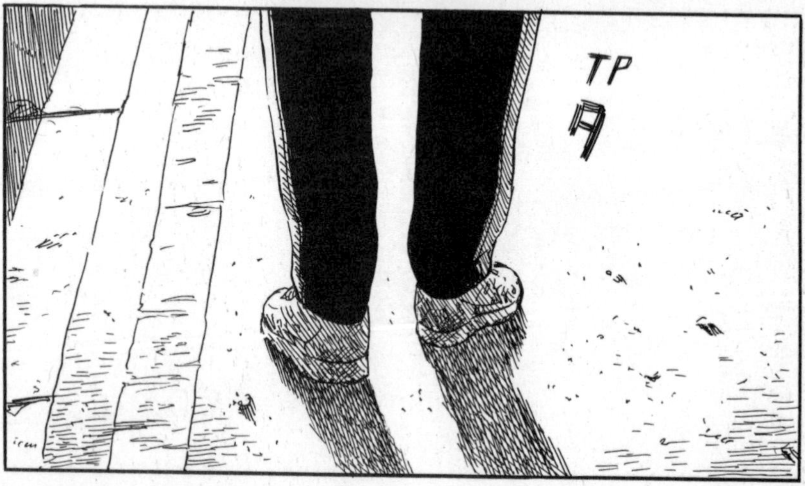
TP
タ

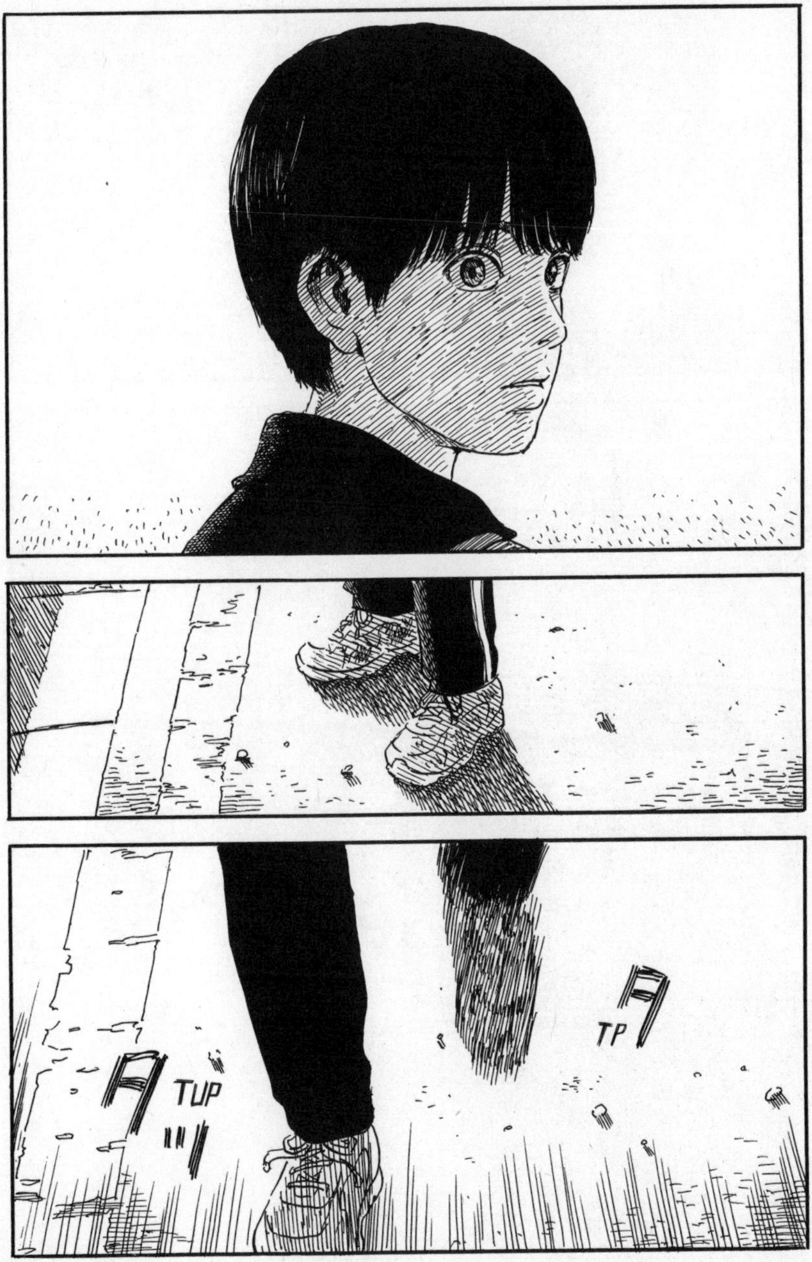
TP
TUP

TPF
タス
TPF
タス
TPF
タス
TP
タッ

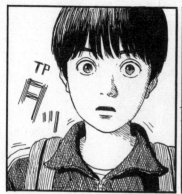

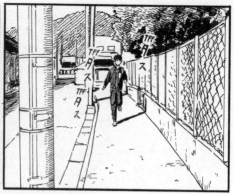

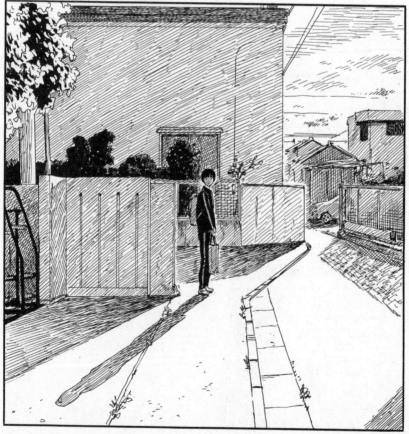

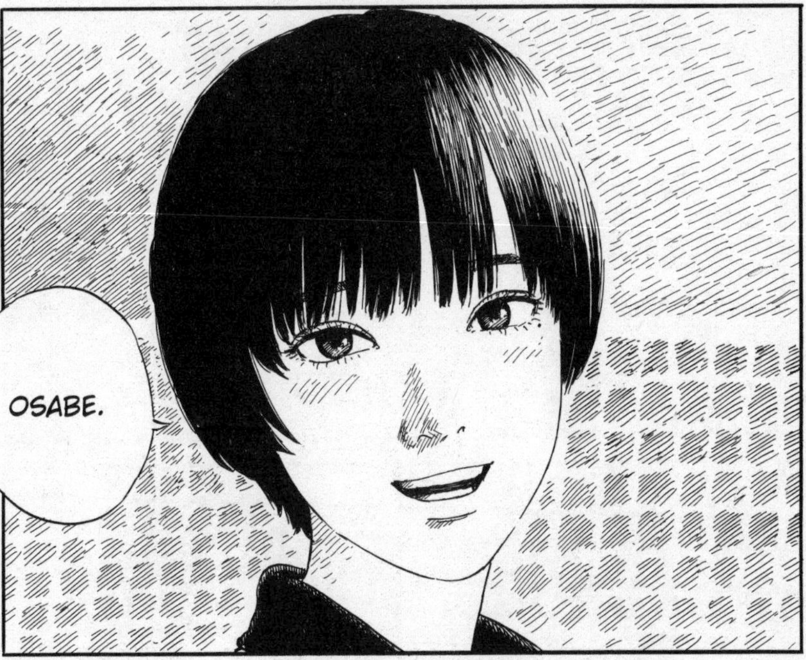
OSABE.
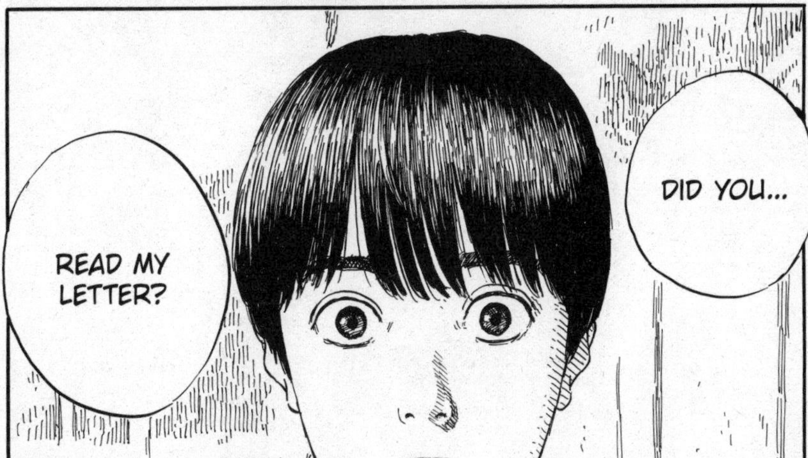
DID YOU...
READ MY LETTER?

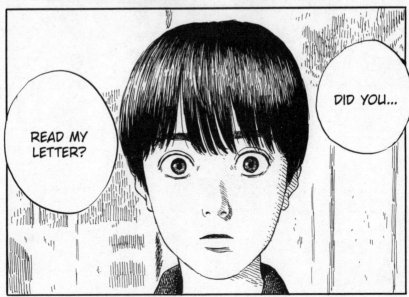

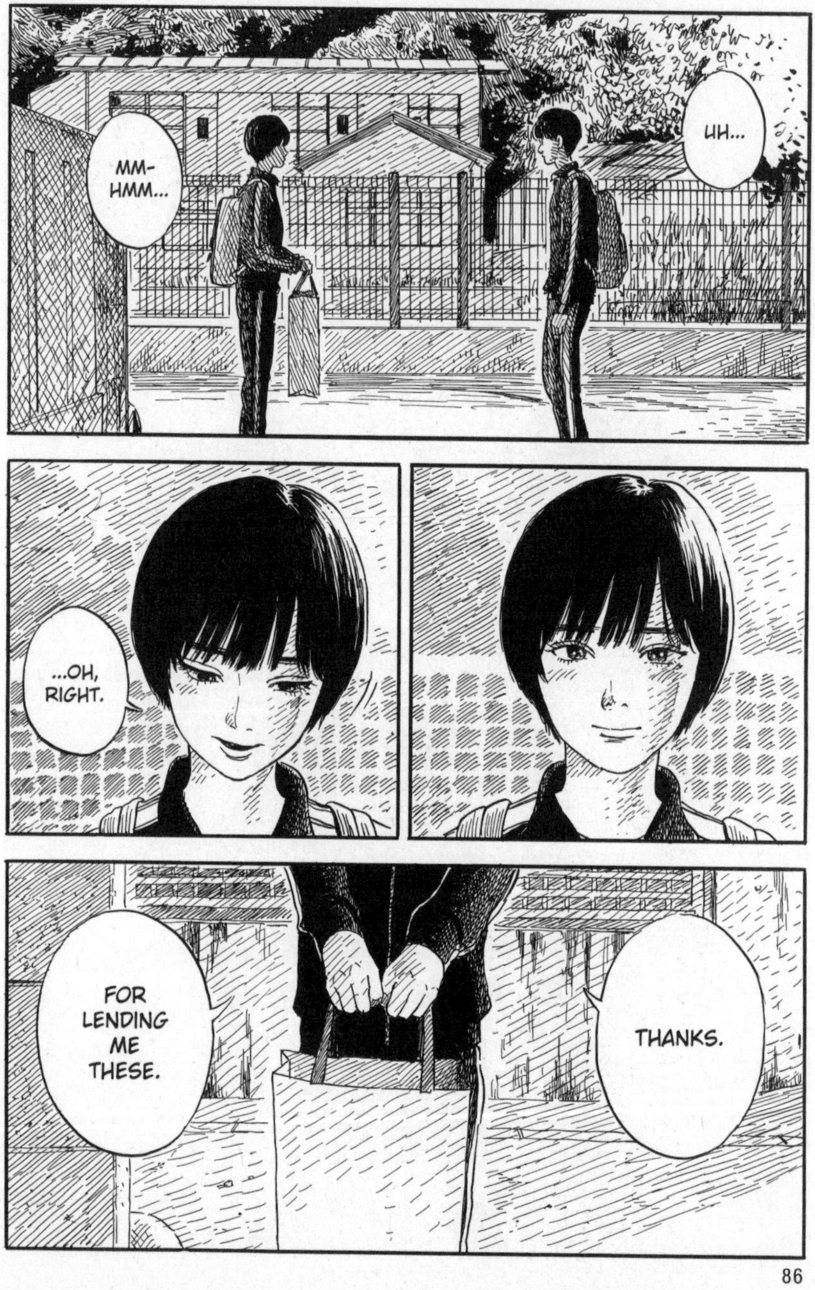
UH...
MM-HMM...
...OH, RIGHT.
THANKS.
FOR LENDING ME THESE.

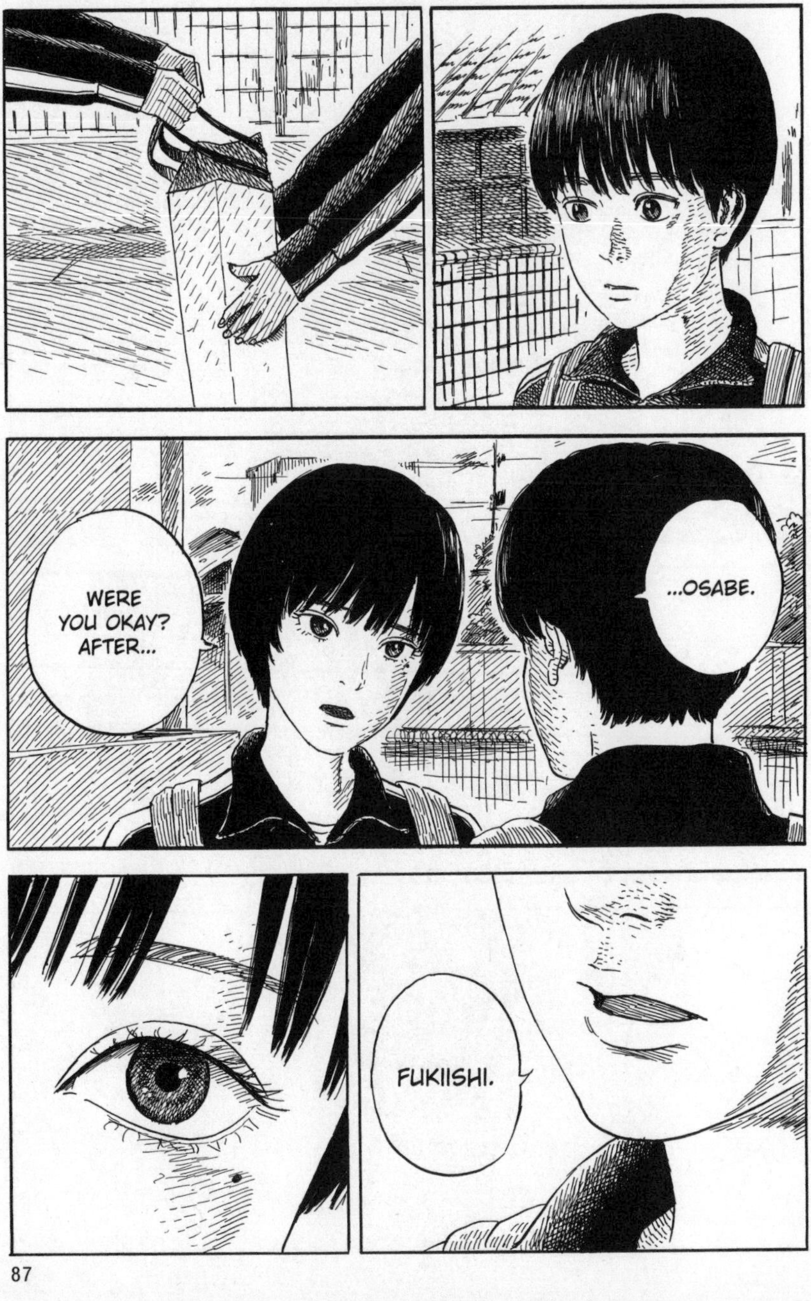
...OSABE.
WERE YOU OKAY? AFTER...
FUKIISHI.

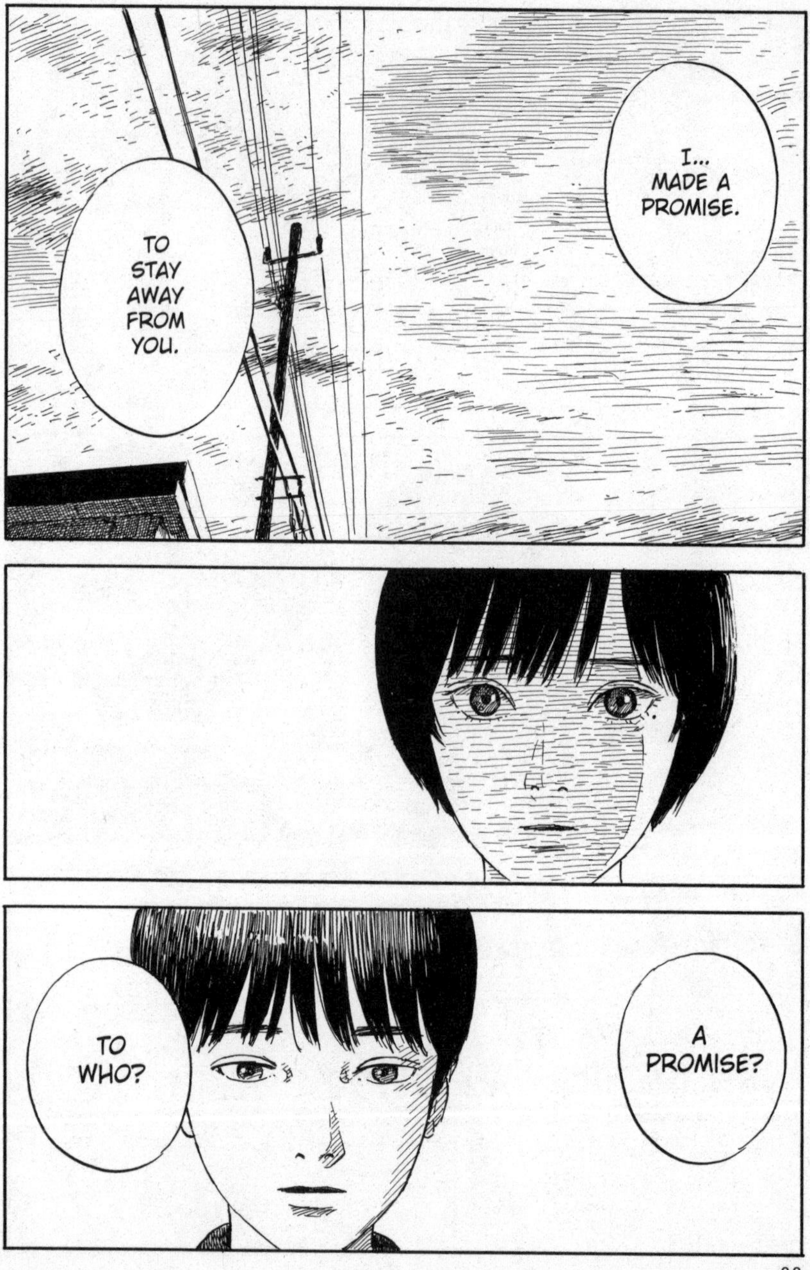
I... MADE A PROMISE.
TO STAY AWAY FROM YOU.
A PROMISE?
TO WHO?

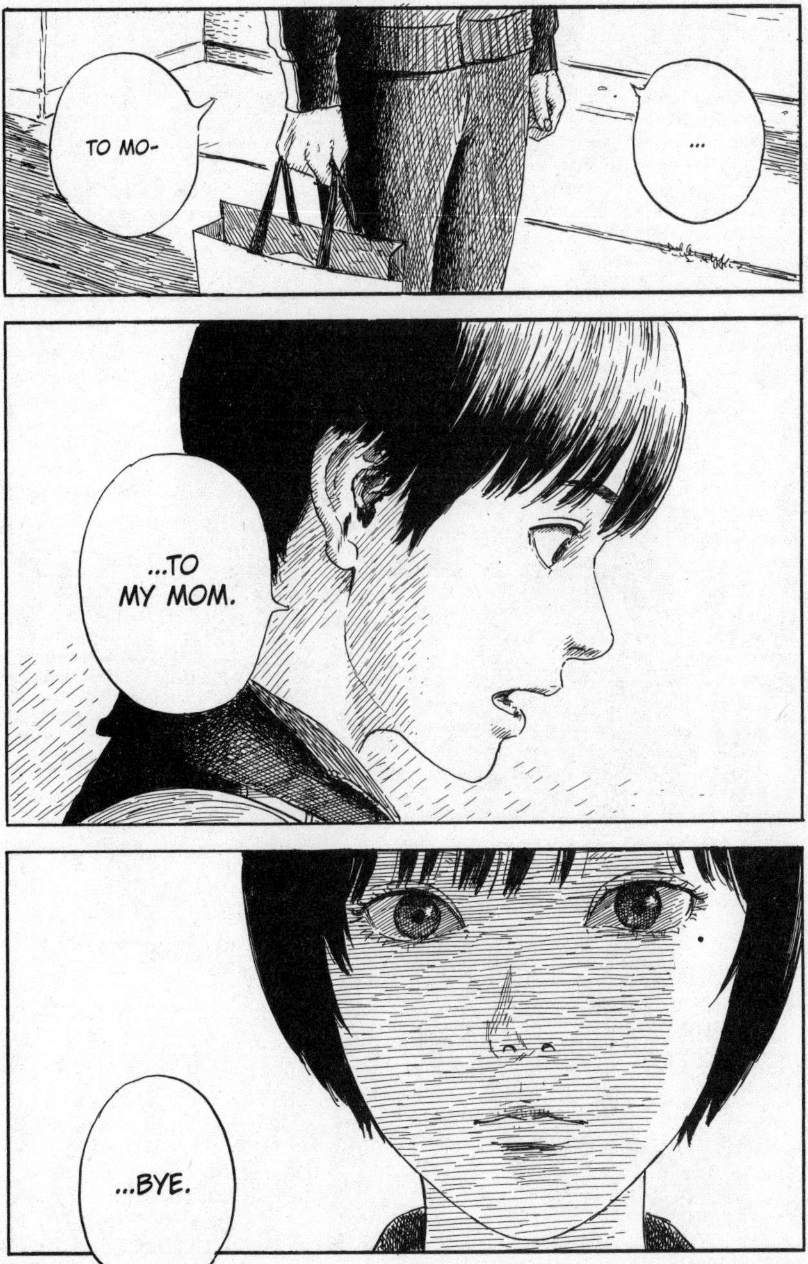
...
TO MO-
...TO MY MOM.
...BYE.

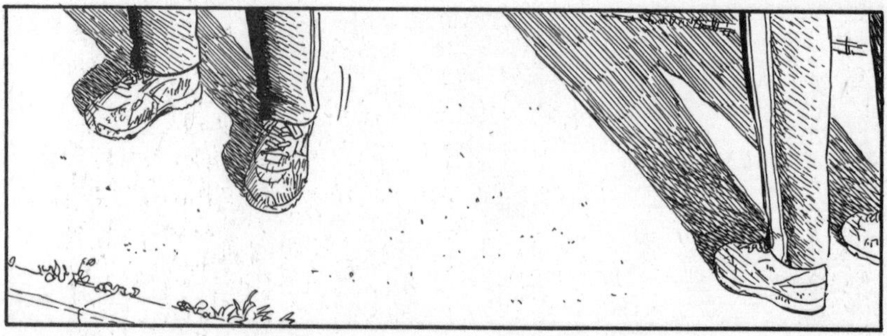

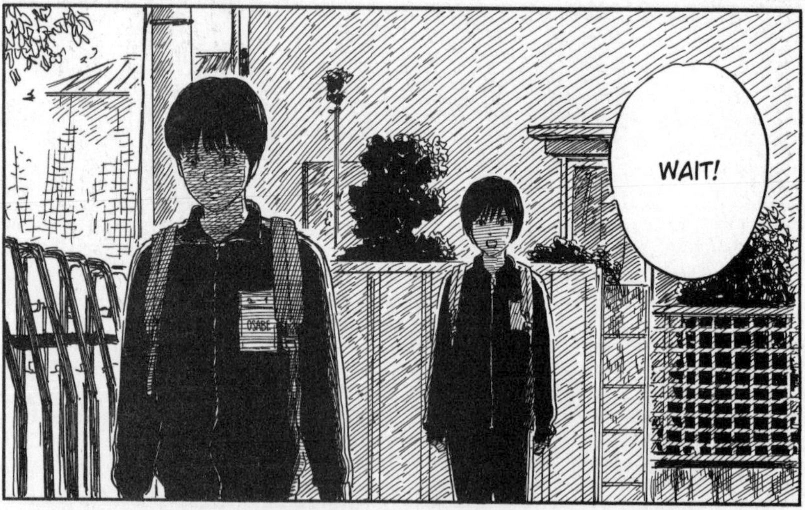
WAIT!
OSABE

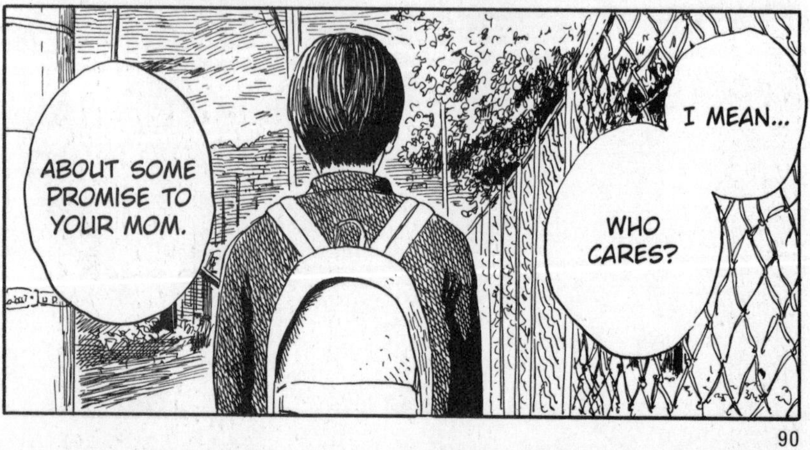
I MEAN...
WHO CARES?
ABOUT SOME PROMISE TO YOUR MOM.

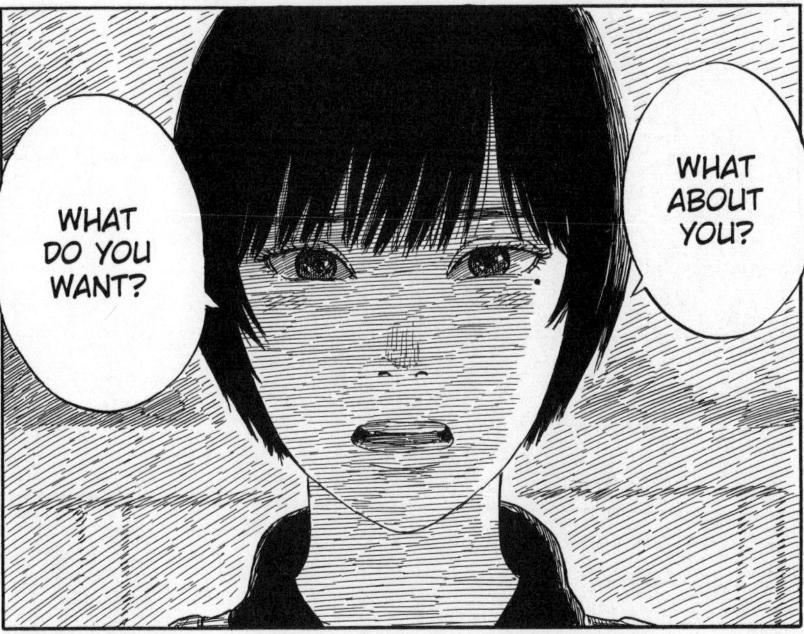
WHAT ABOUT YOU?
WHAT DO YOU WANT?

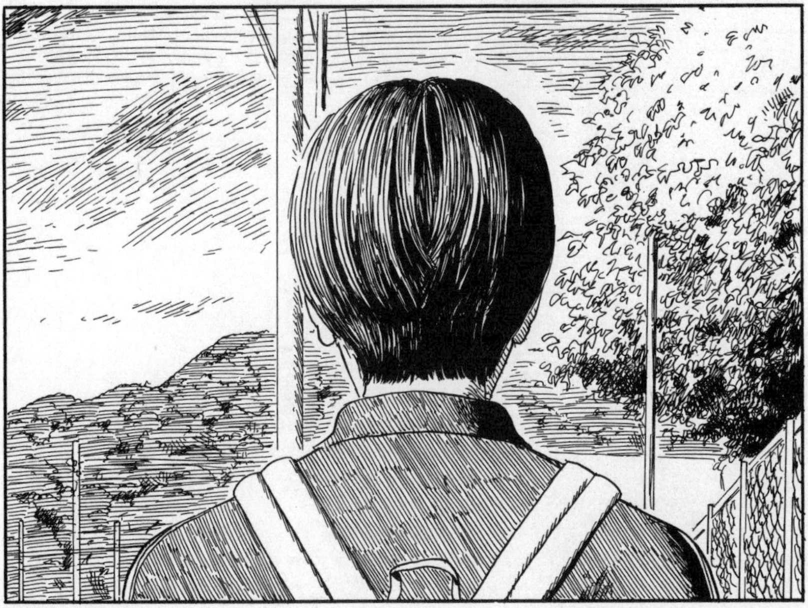

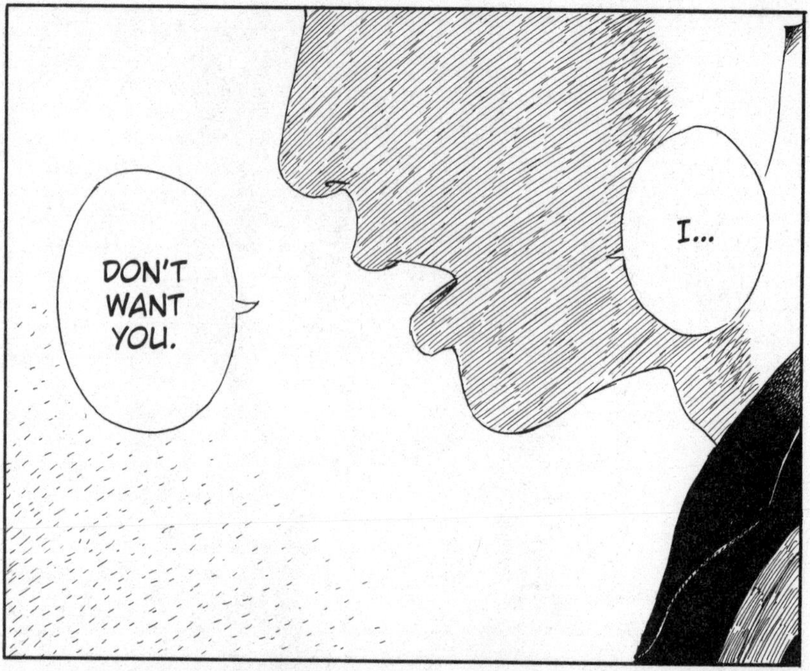
I...
DON'T WANT YOU.

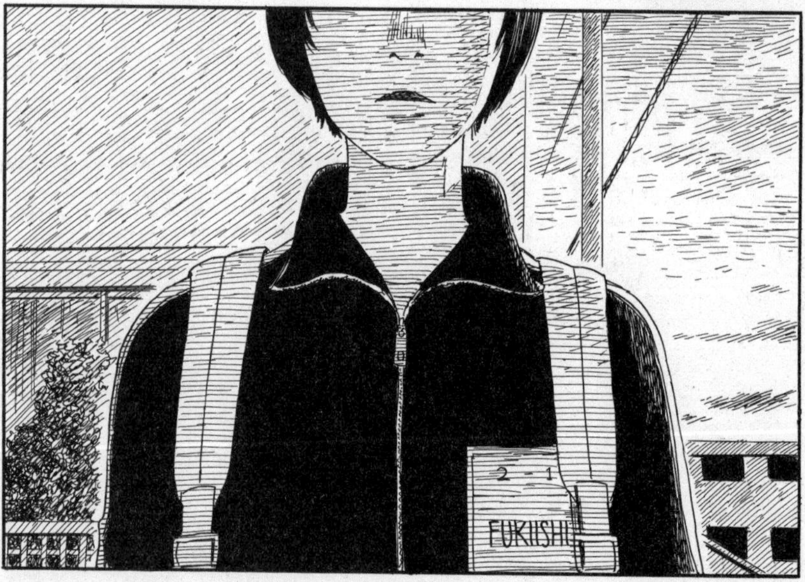
2-1
FUKIISHI

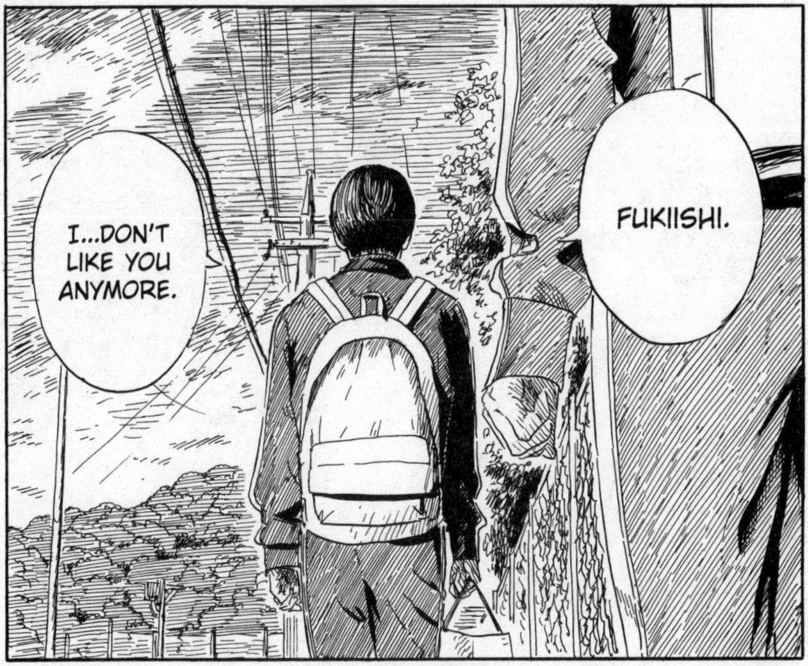
FUKIISHI.
I...DON'T LIKE YOU ANYMORE.

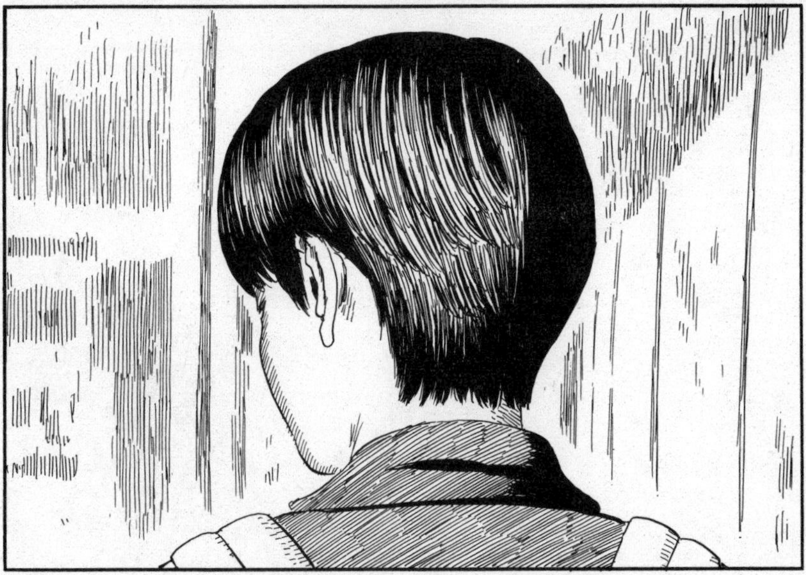

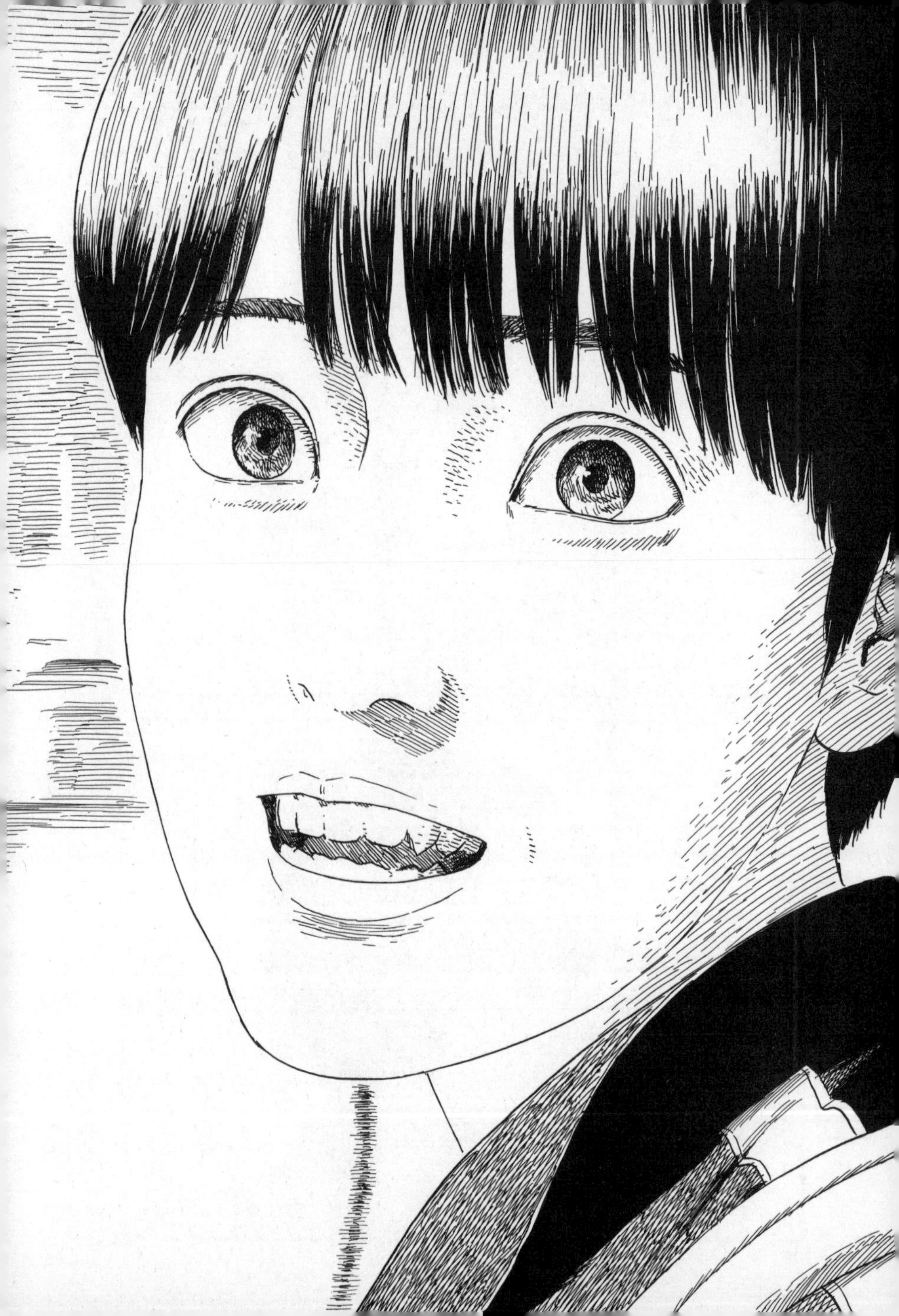

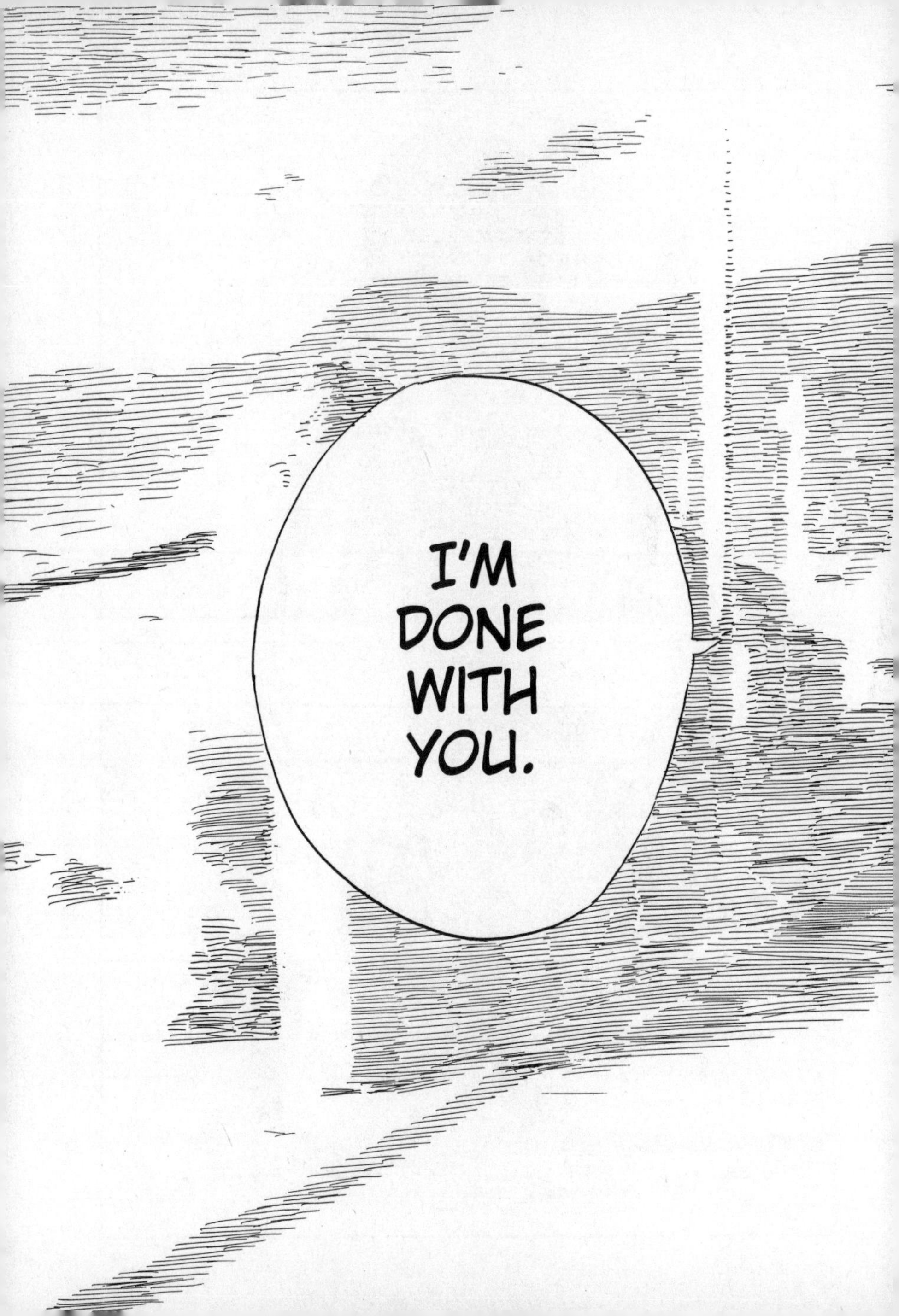
I'M DONE WITH YOU.

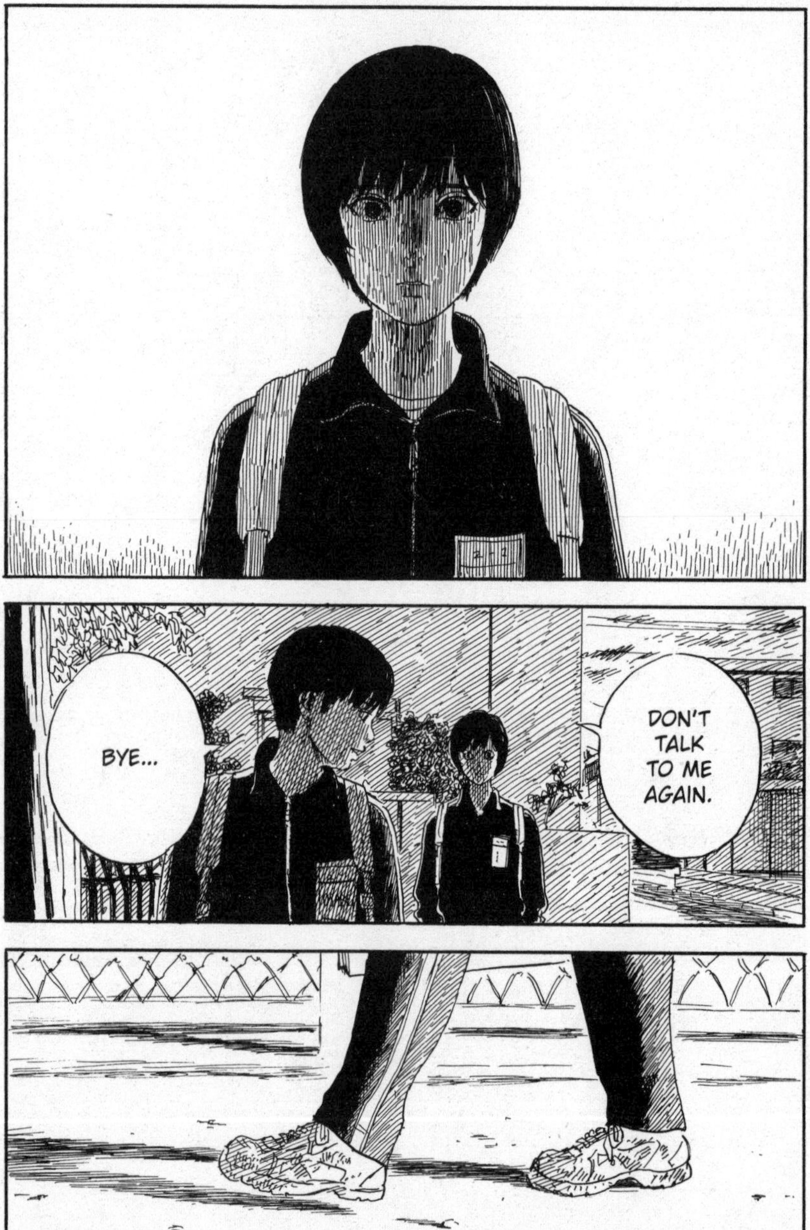
DON'T TALK TO ME AGAIN.
BYE...

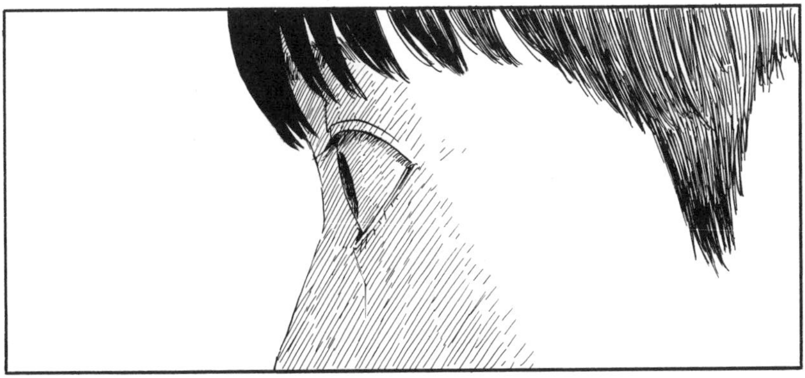
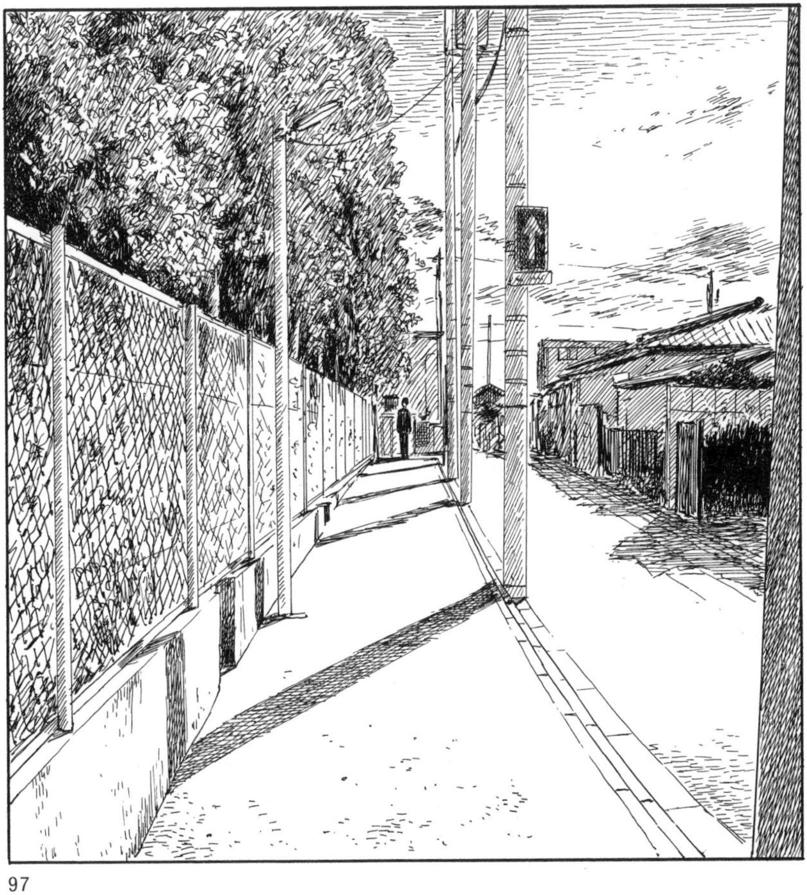

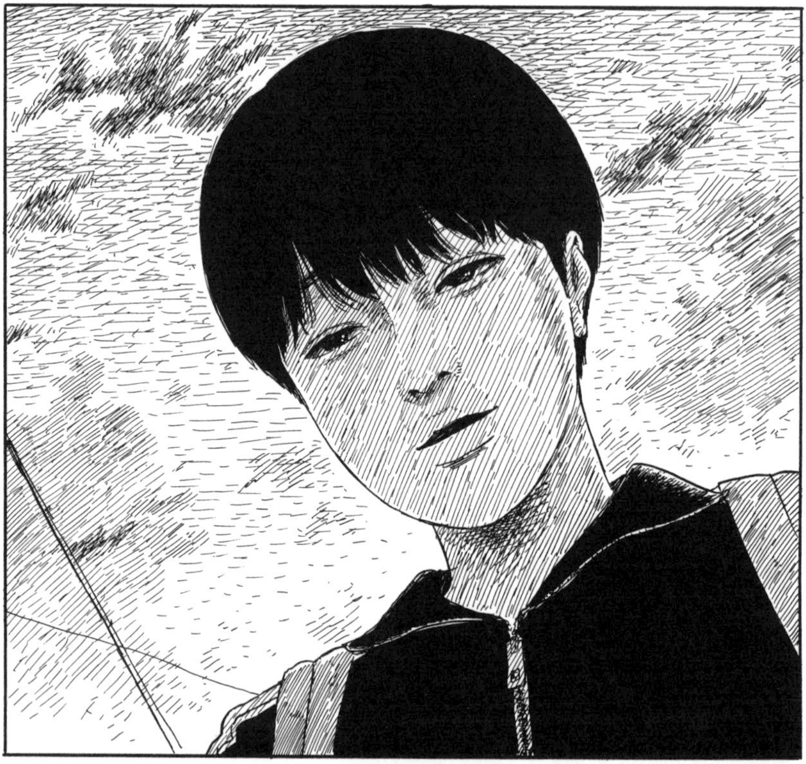

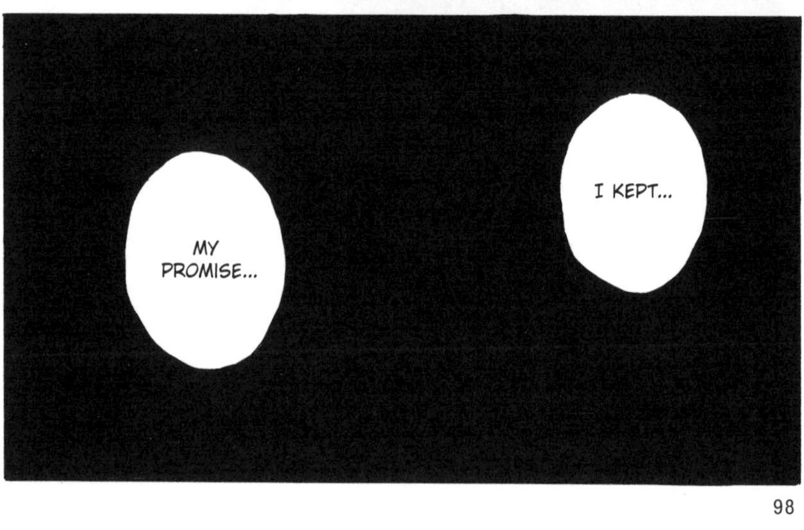
I KEPT...
MY PROMISE...

Blood
on
the
Tracks

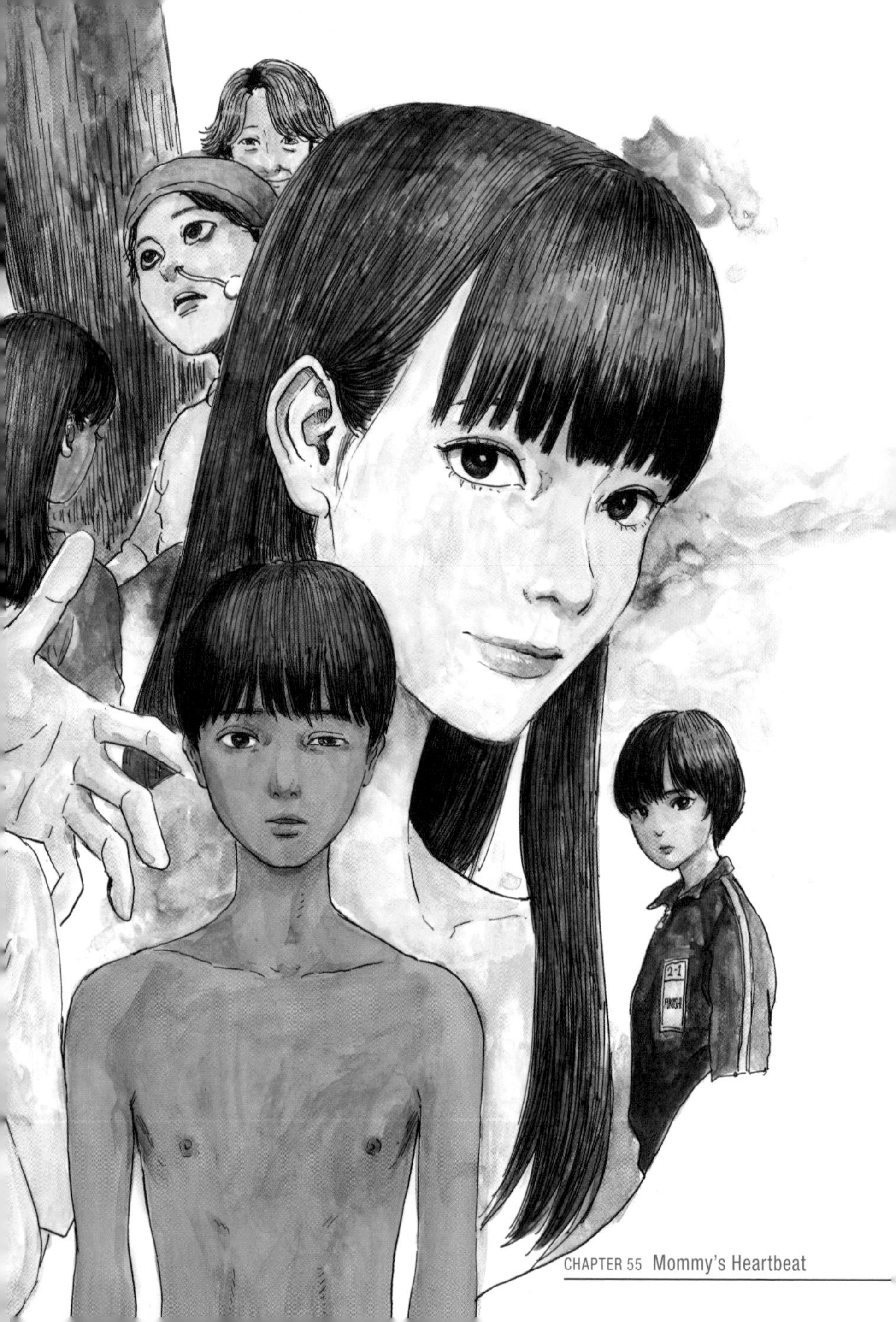

## CHAPTER 55 Mommy's Heartbeat

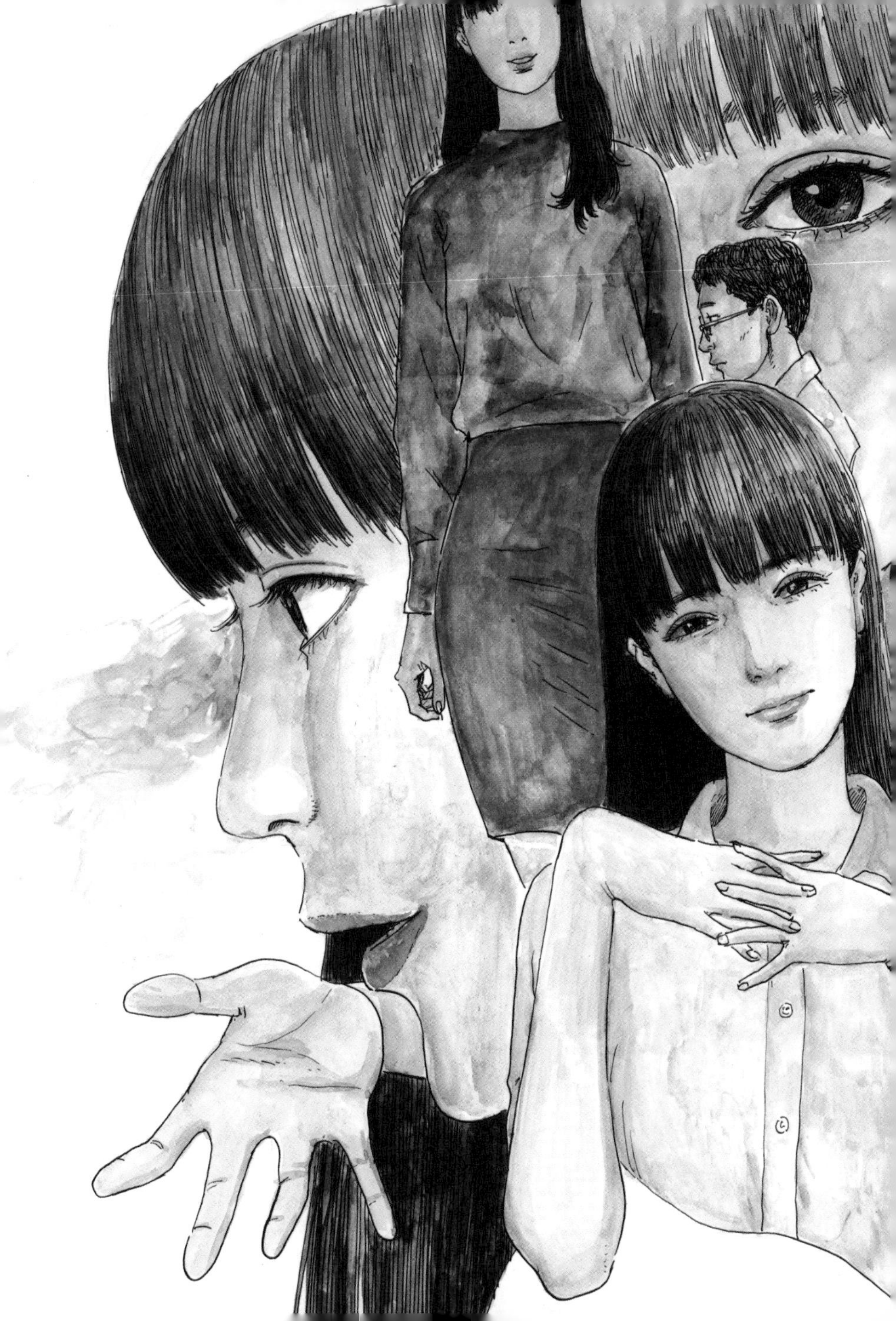

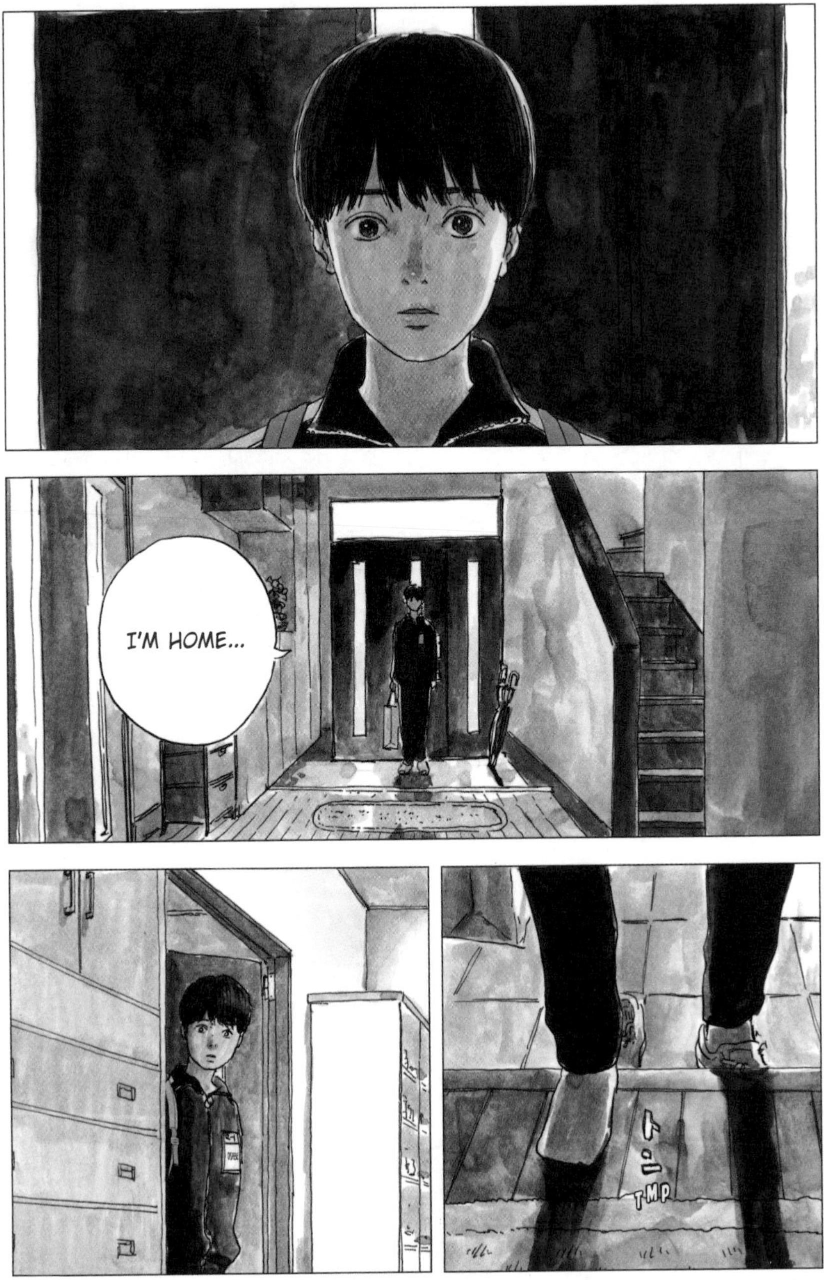
I'M HOME...
TMP

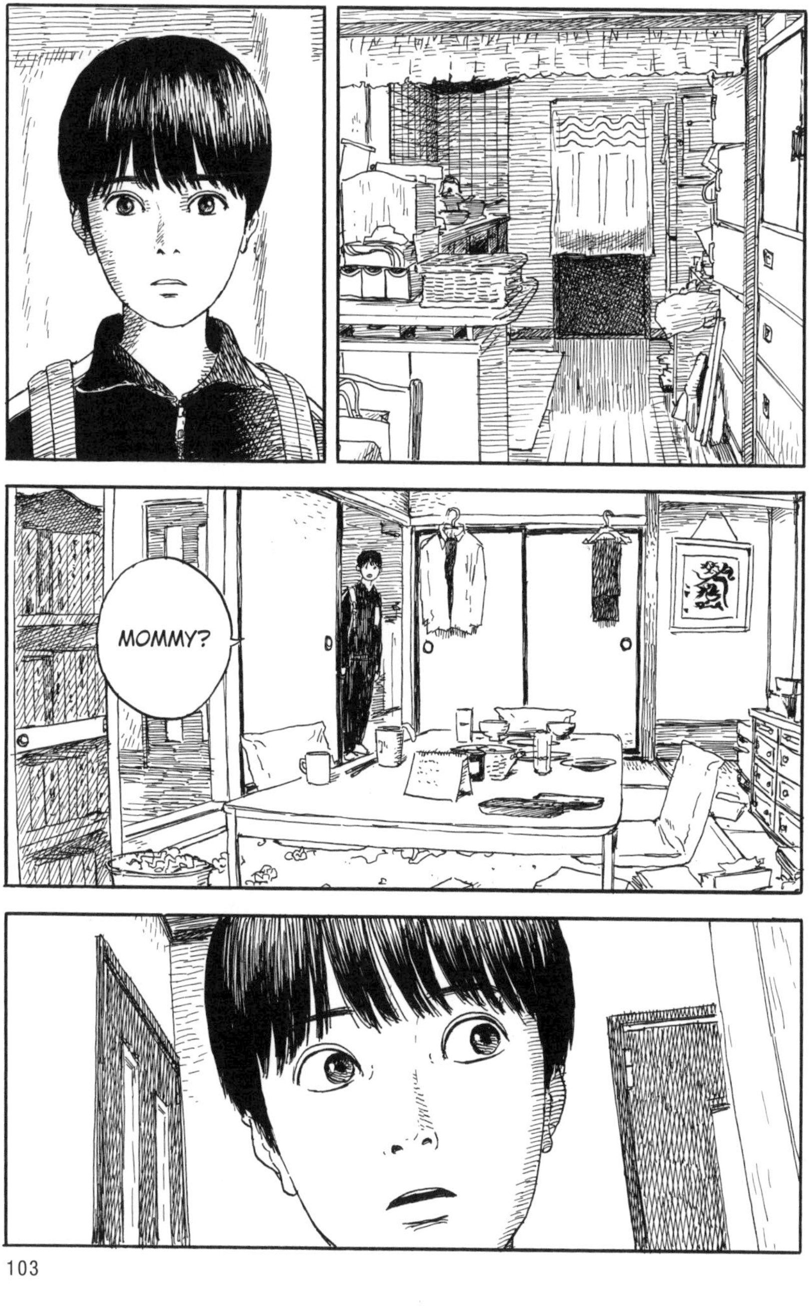
MOMMY?

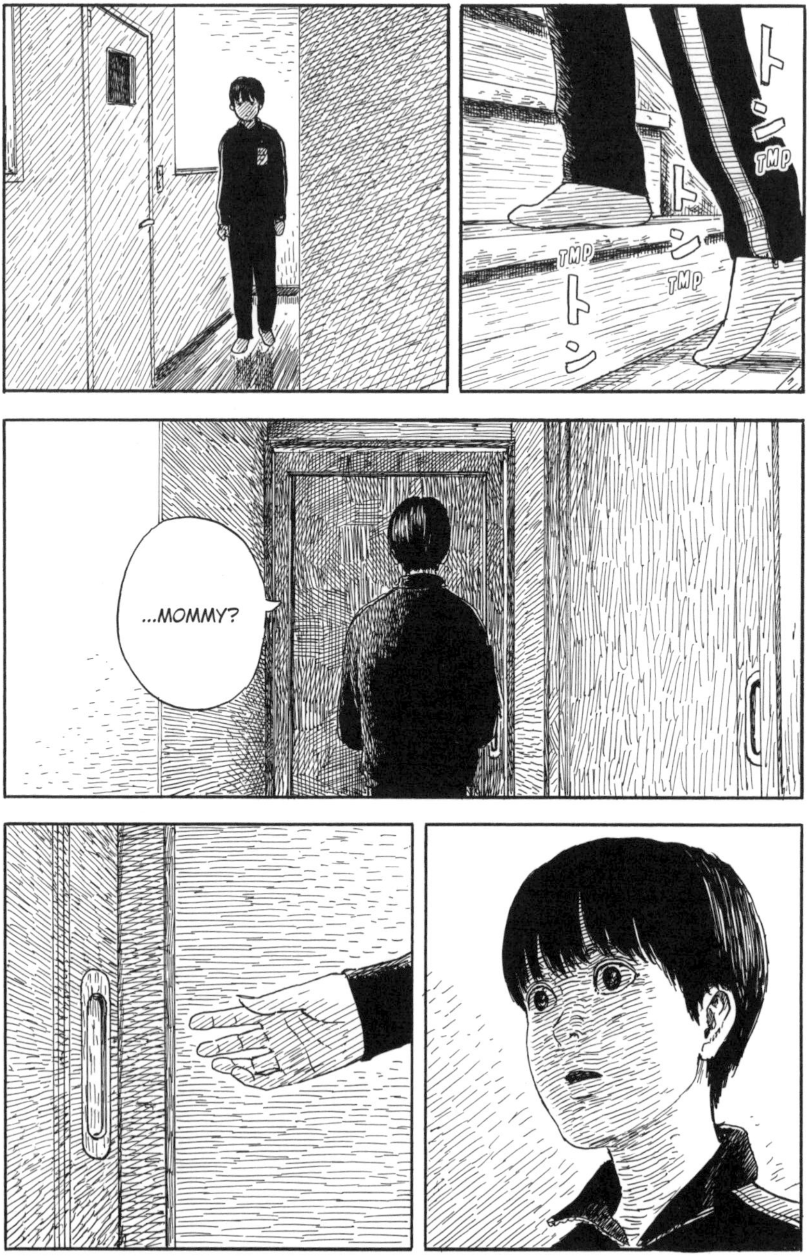
トン
TMP
トン
TMP
TMP
トン
...MOMMY?

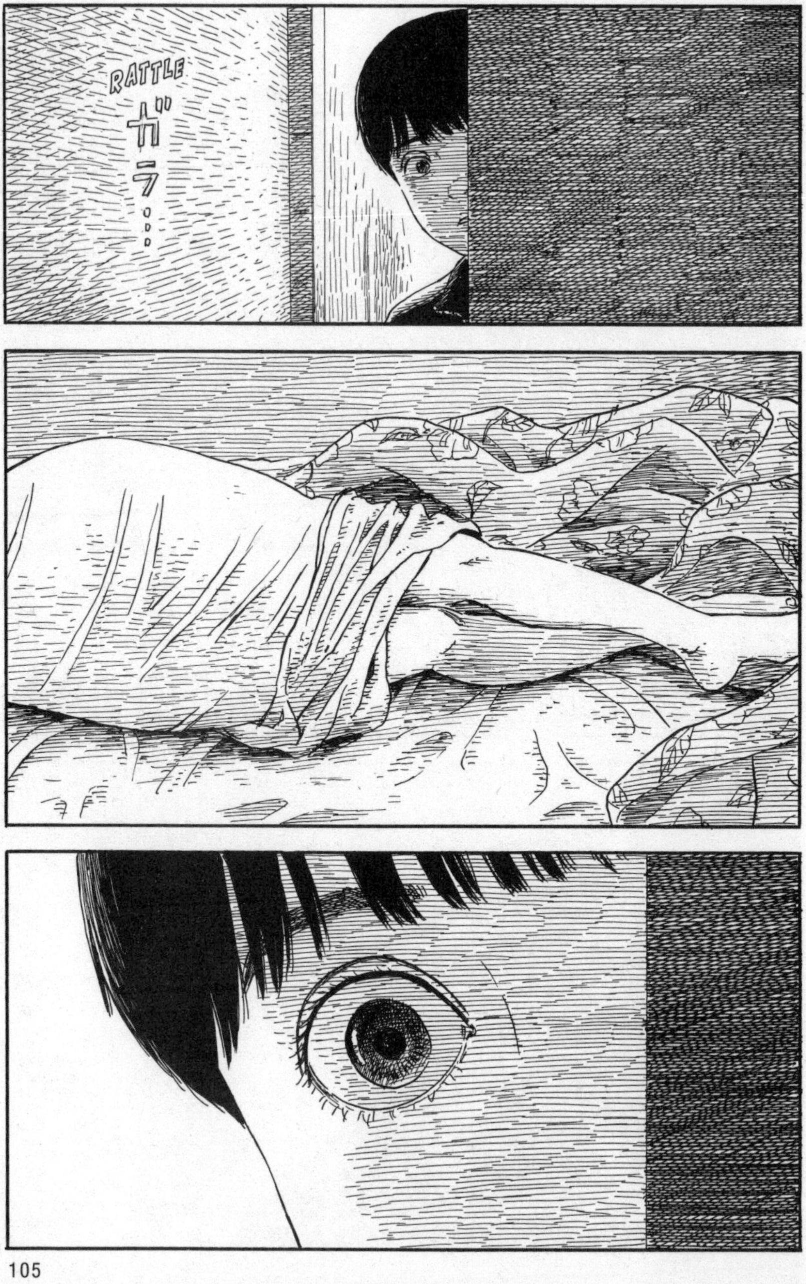
RATTLE
ガラ…

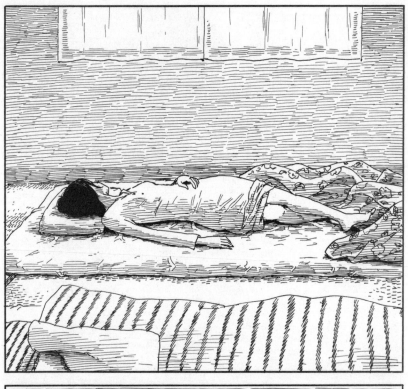

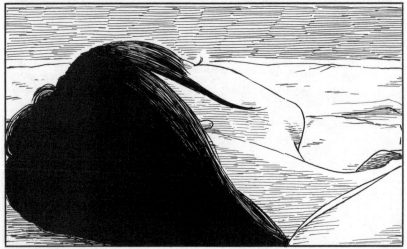

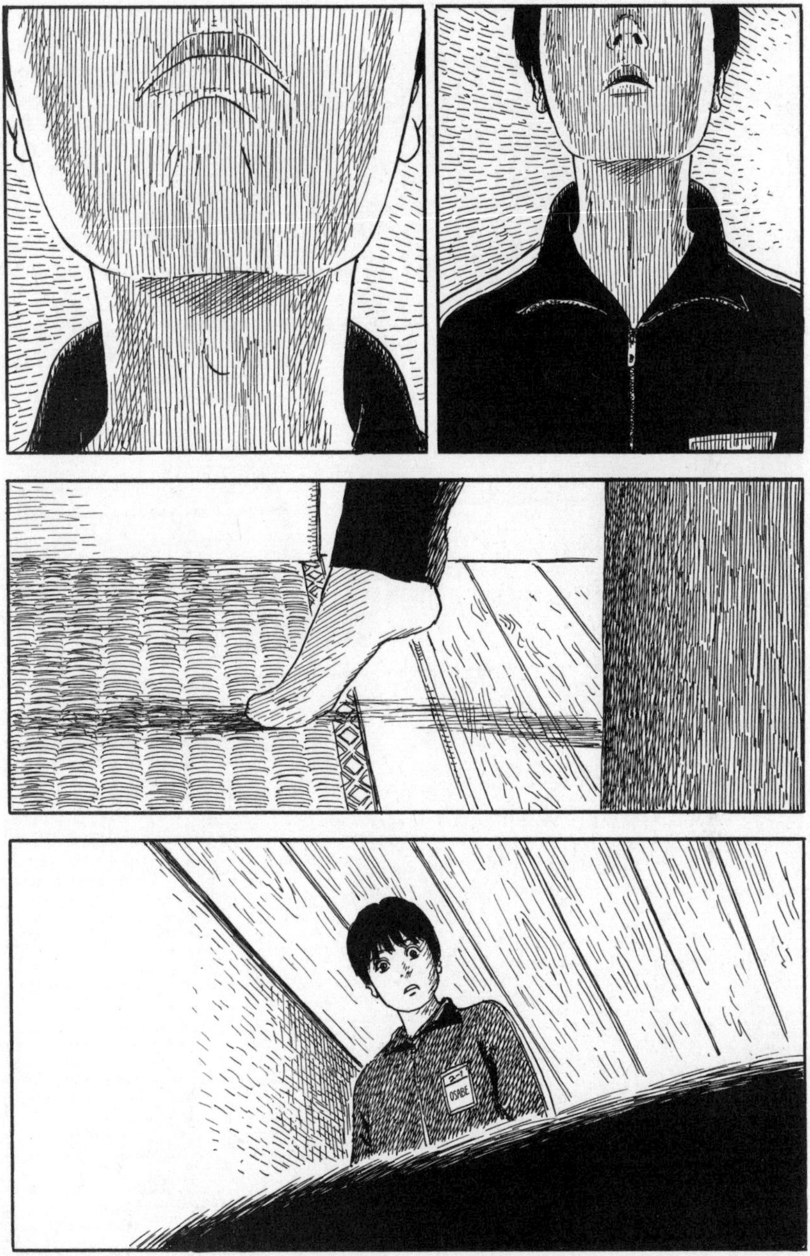
2-1
OSABE

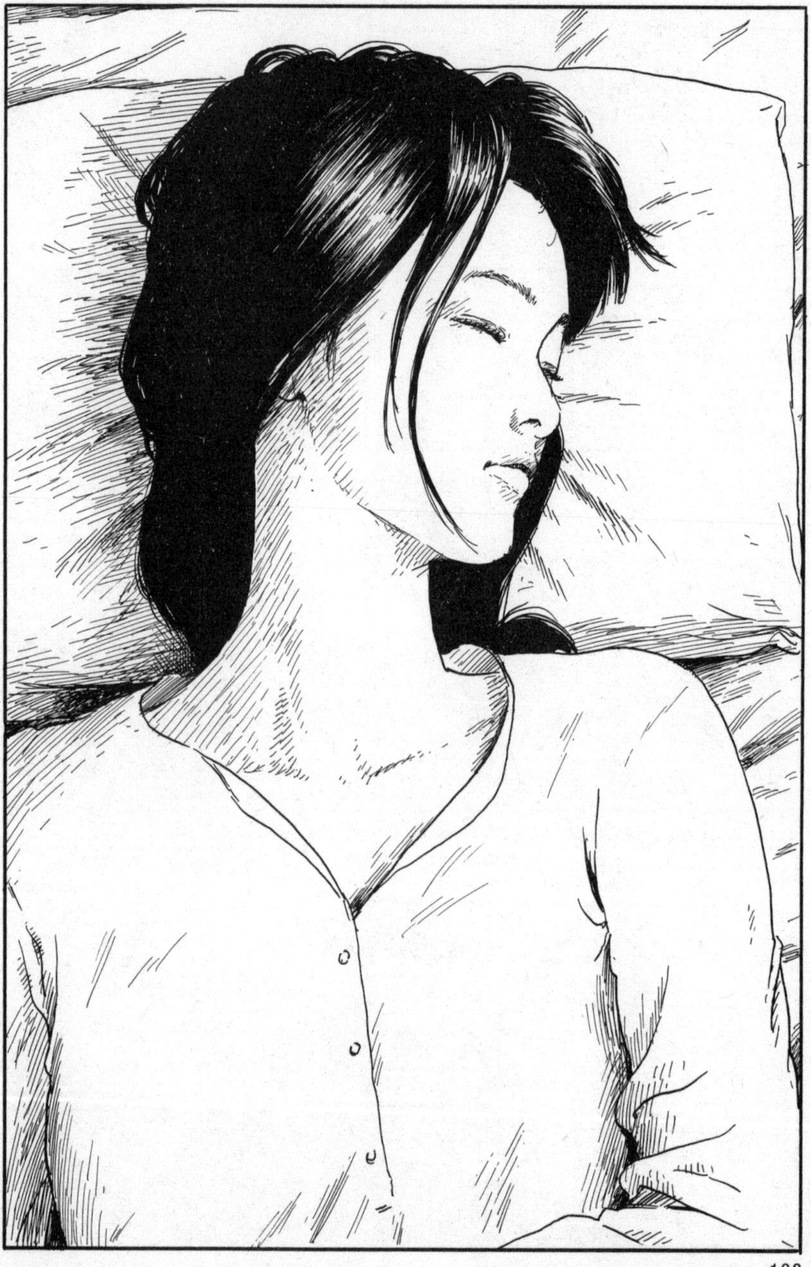

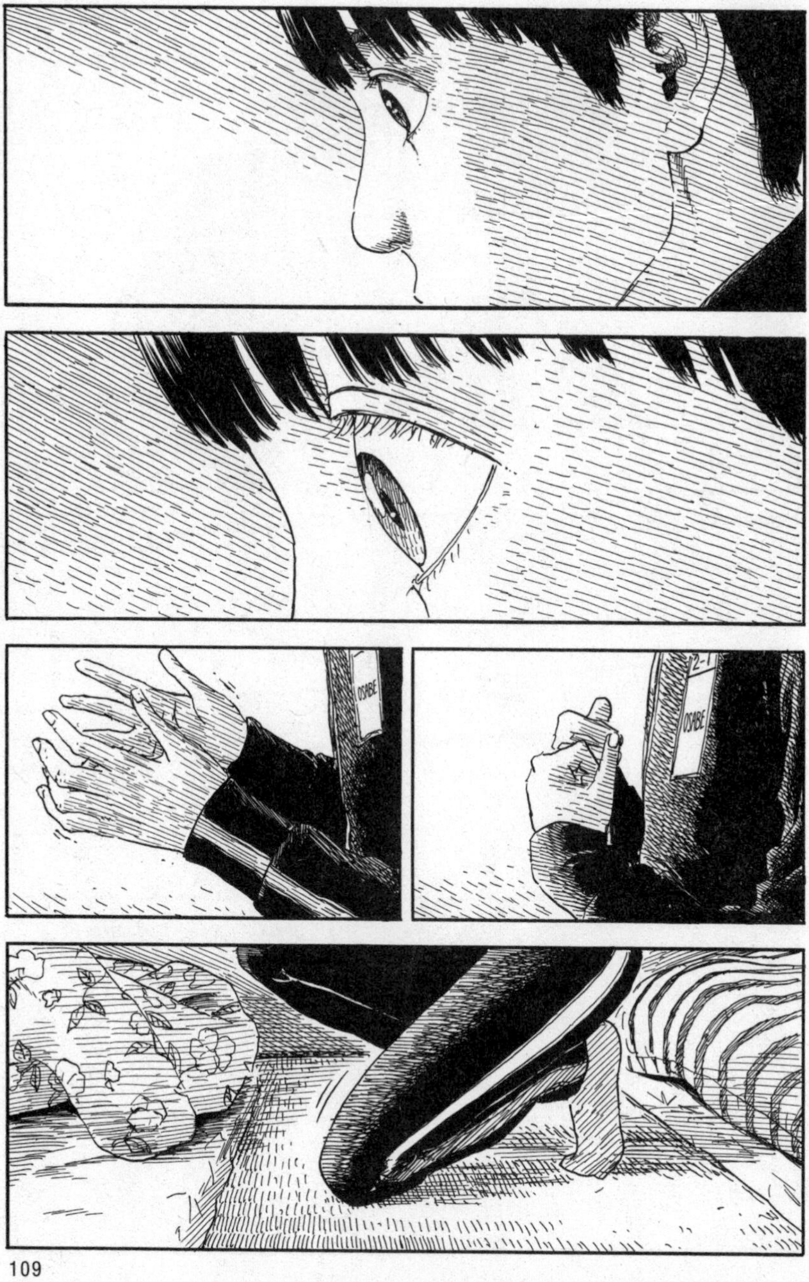
2-1
OSABE
OSABE

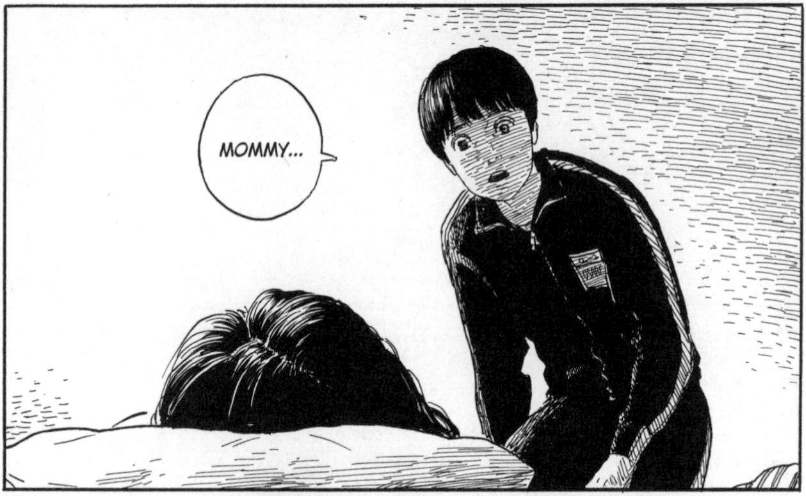
MOMMY...
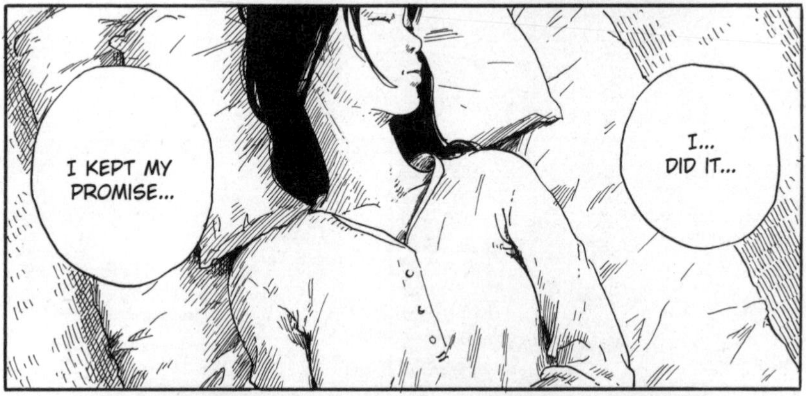
I... DID IT...
I KEPT MY PROMISE...
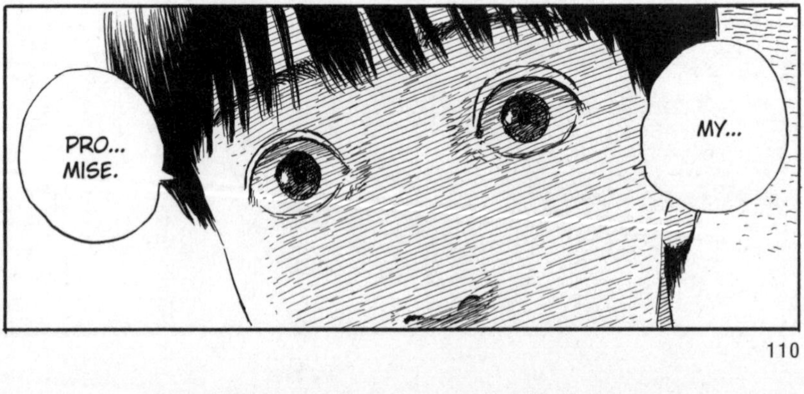
MY...
PRO... MISE.

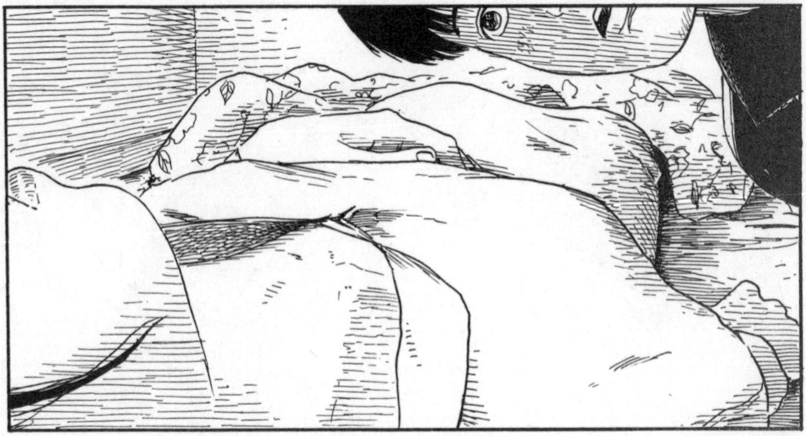
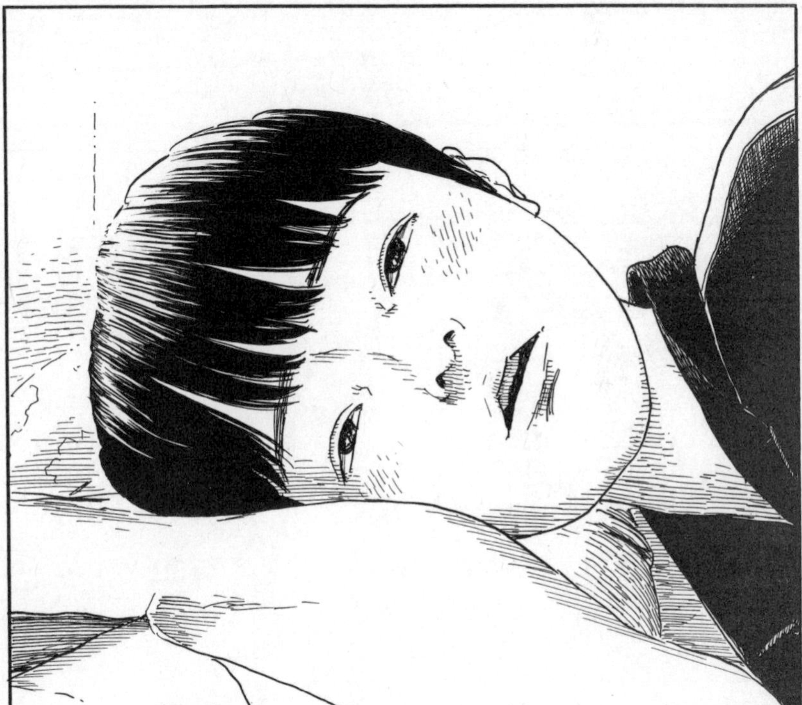

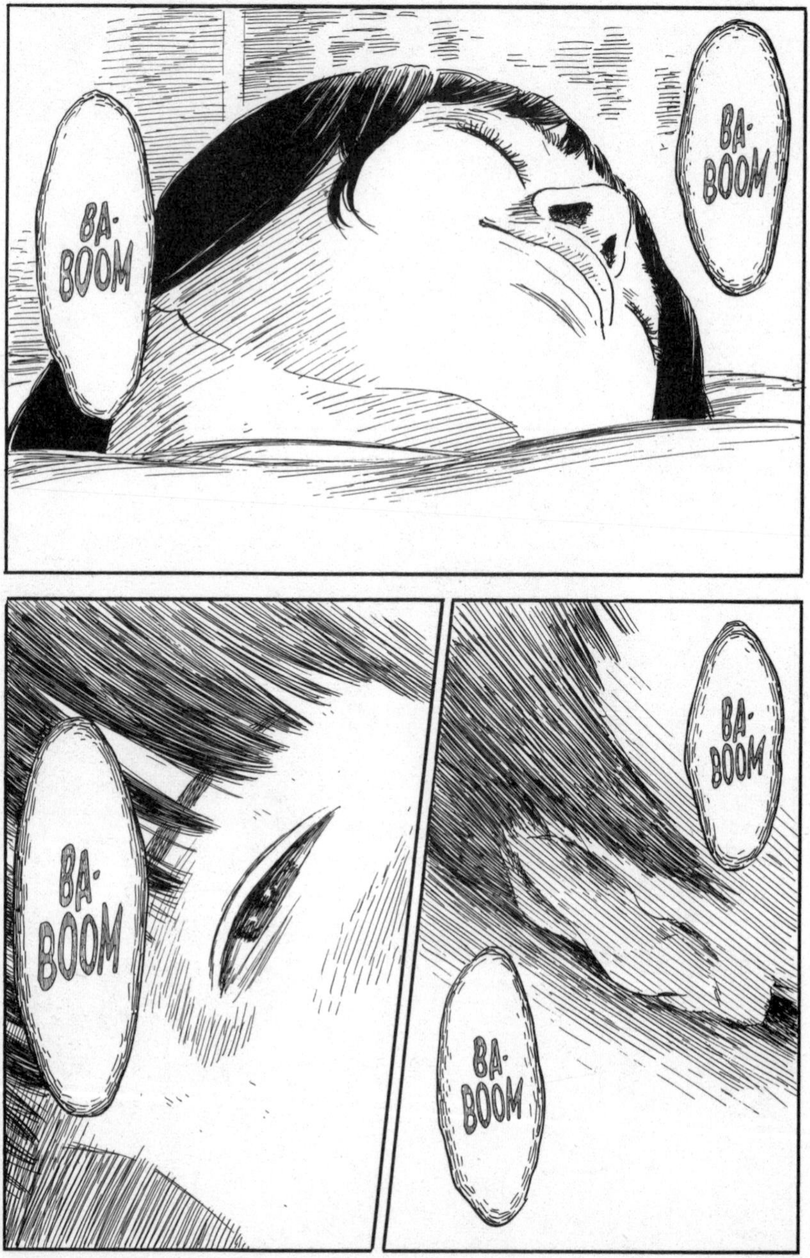
BA-BOOM
BA-BOOM
BA-BOOM
BA-BOOM
BA-BOOM
BA-BOOM

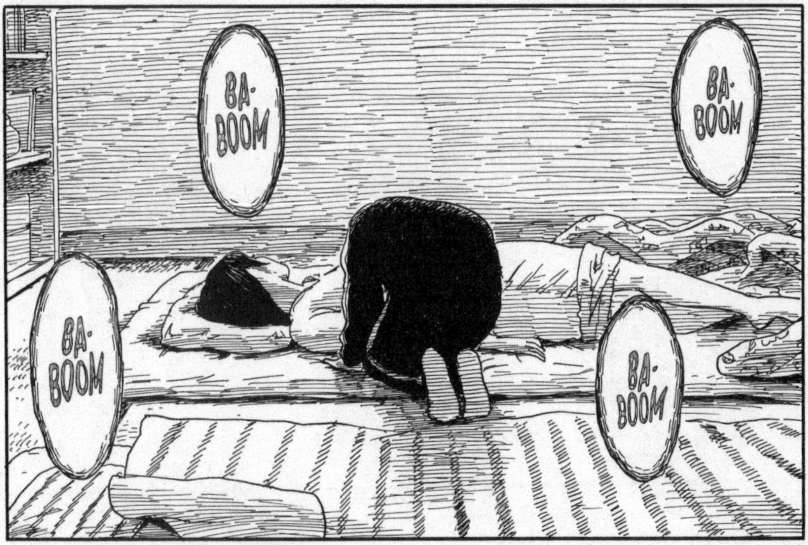
BA-BOOM
BA-BOOM
BA-BOOM
BA-BOOM
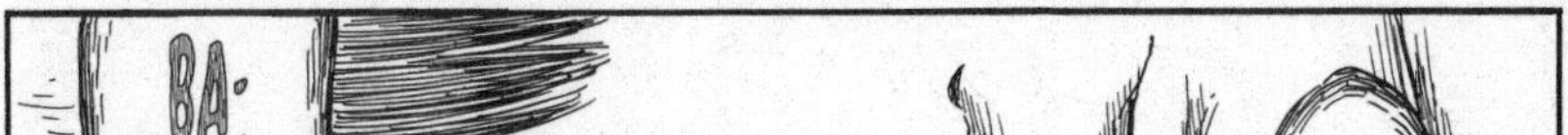
BA-BOOM
BA-BOOM
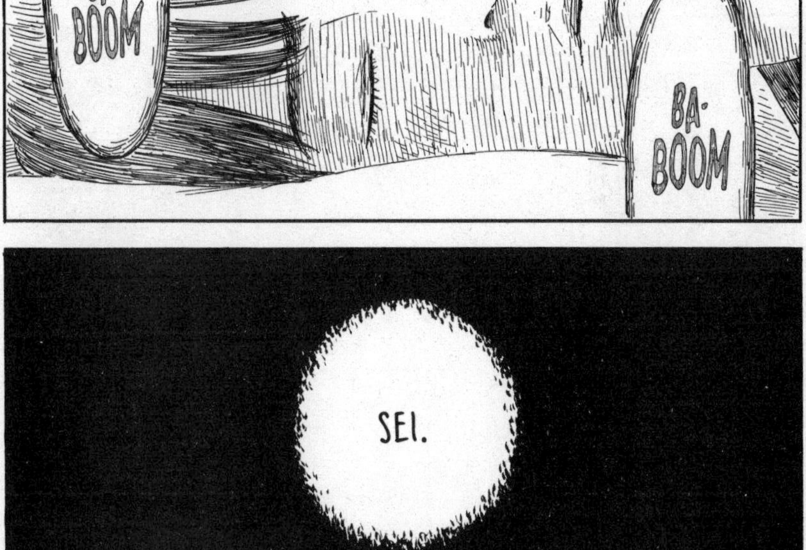
SEI.

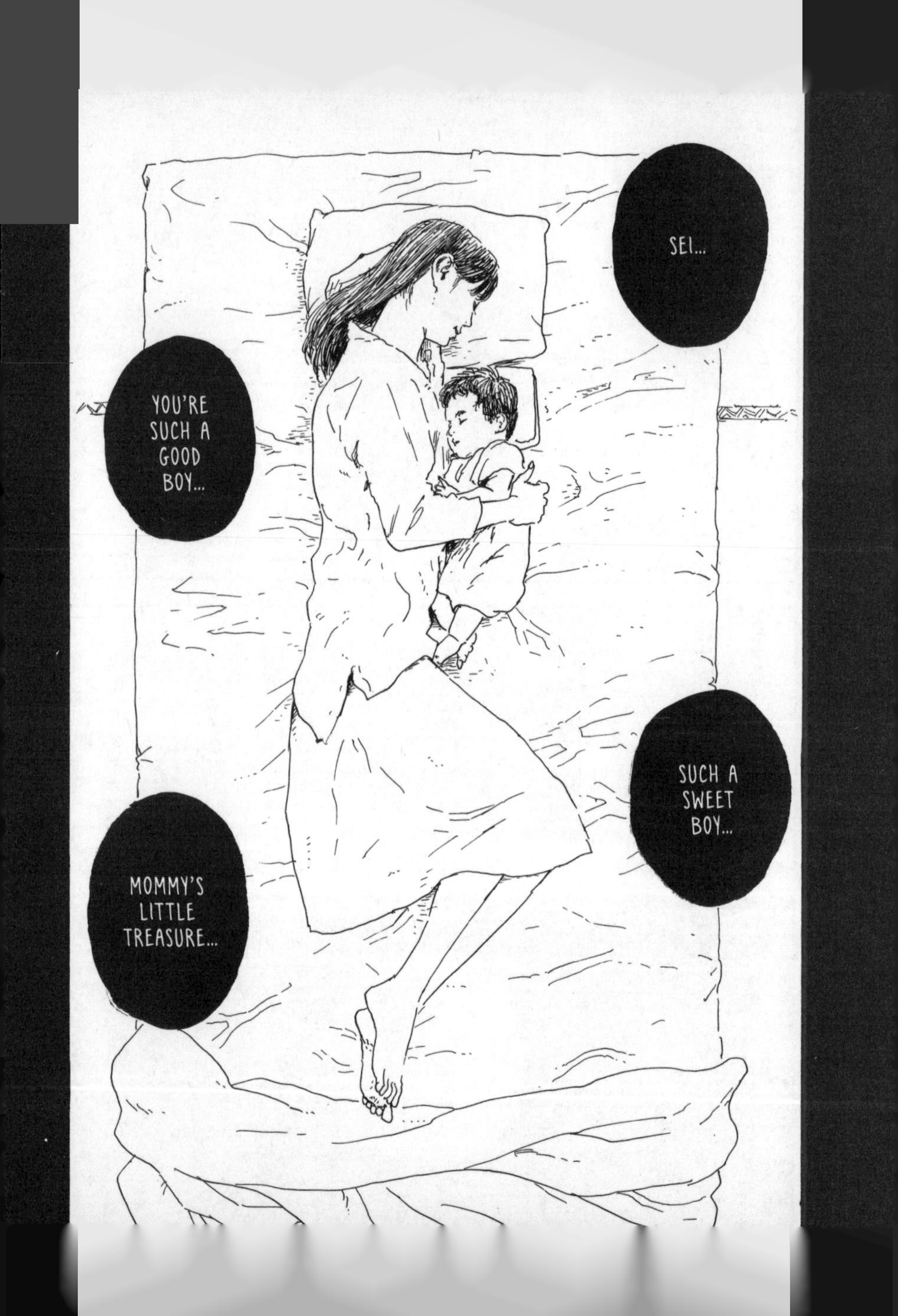
SEI...
YOU'RE SUCH A GOOD BOY...
SUCH A SWEET BOY...
MOMMY'S LITTLE TREASURE...

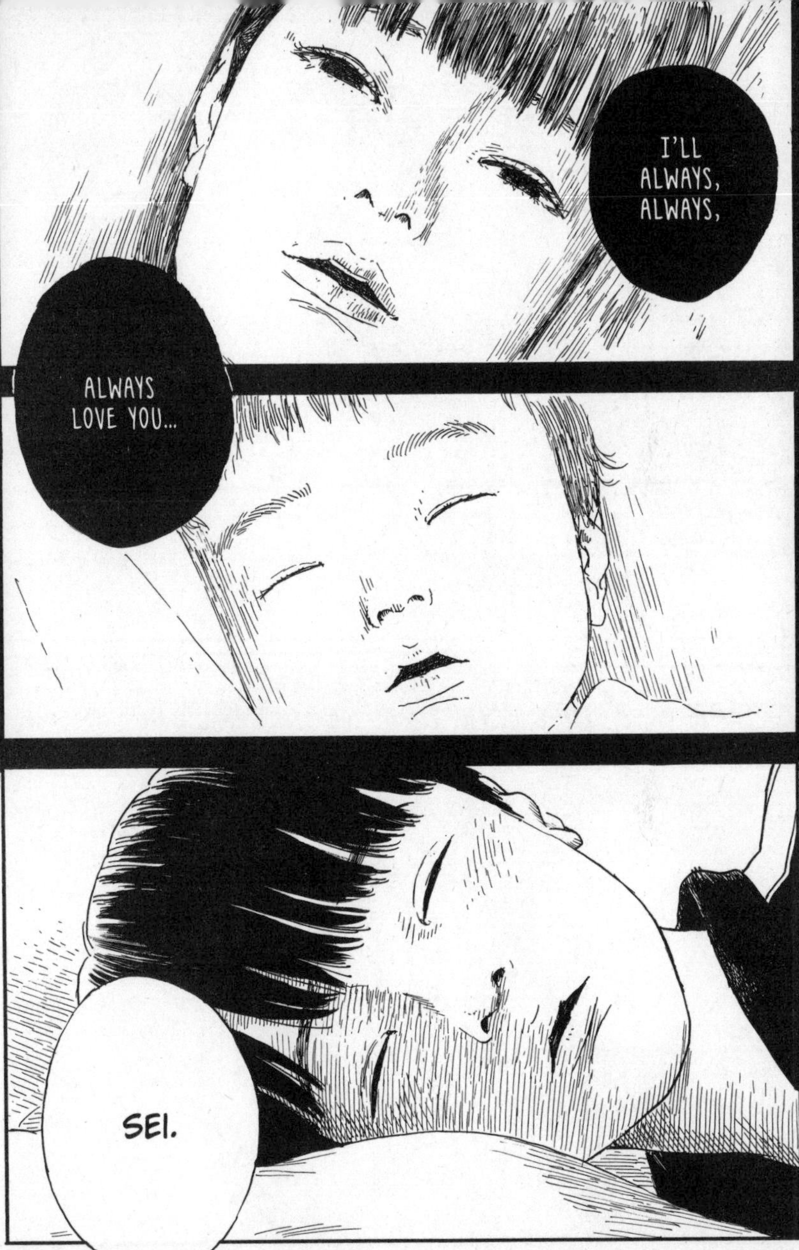
I'LL ALWAYS, ALWAYS,
ALWAYS LOVE YOU...
SEI.

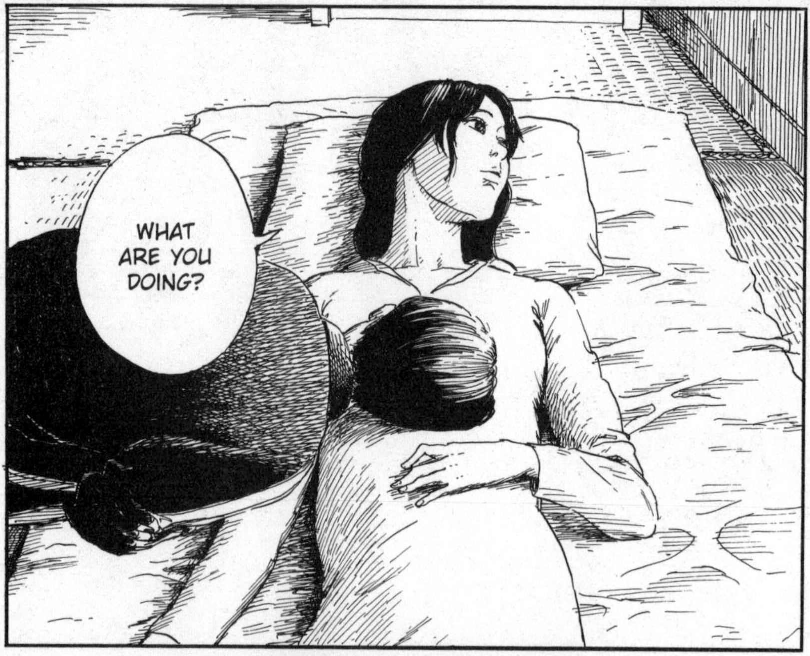
WHAT ARE YOU DOING?
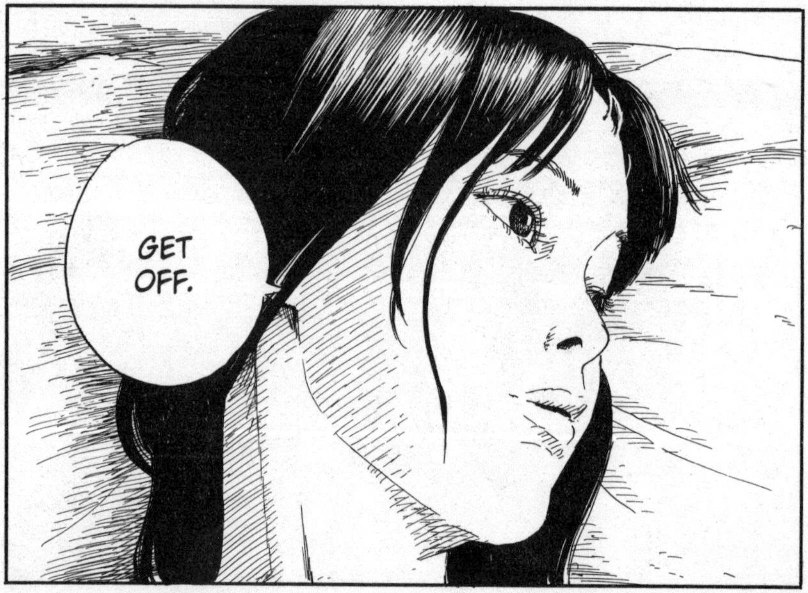
GET OFF.

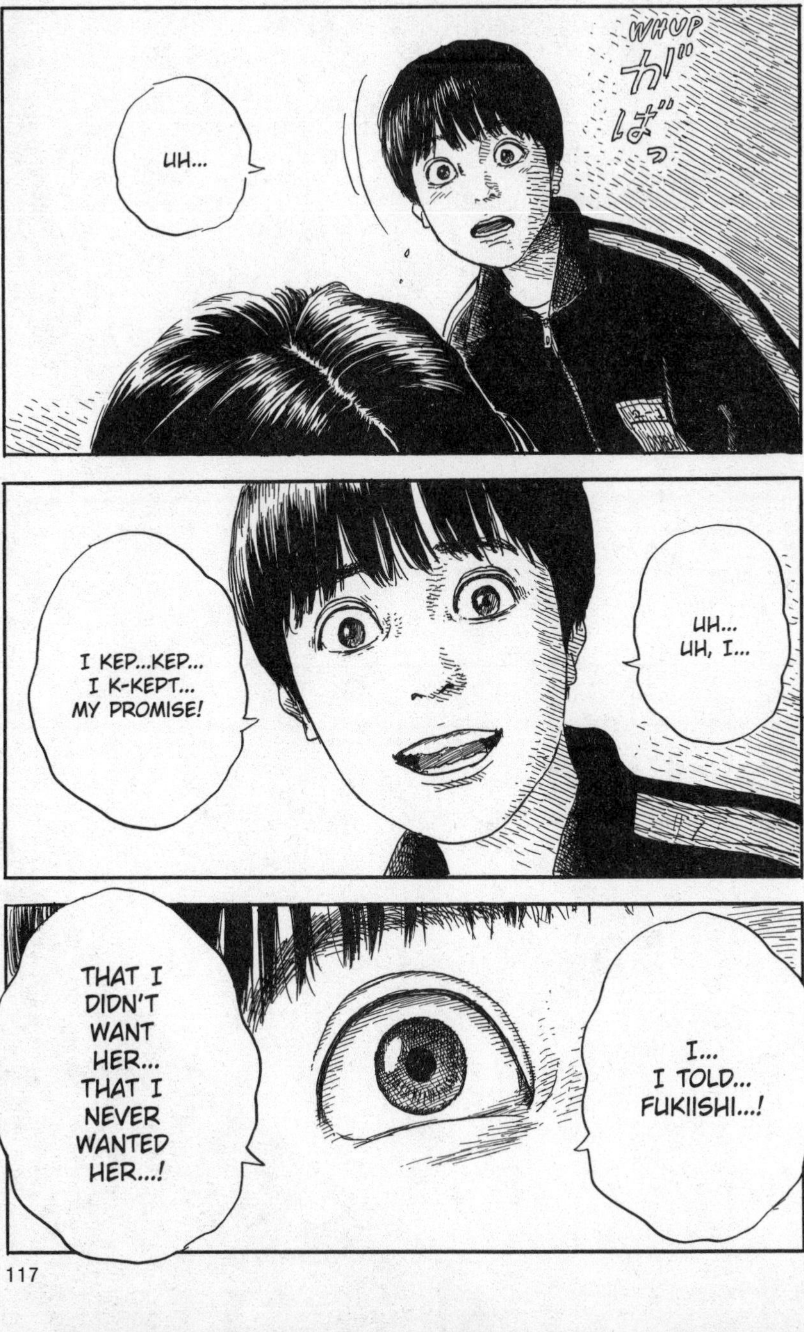
WHUP
がばっ
UH...
UH... UH, I...
I KEP...KEP... I K-KEPT... MY PROMISE!
I... I TOLD... FUKIISHI...!
THAT I DIDN'T WANT HER... THAT I NEVER WANTED HER...!

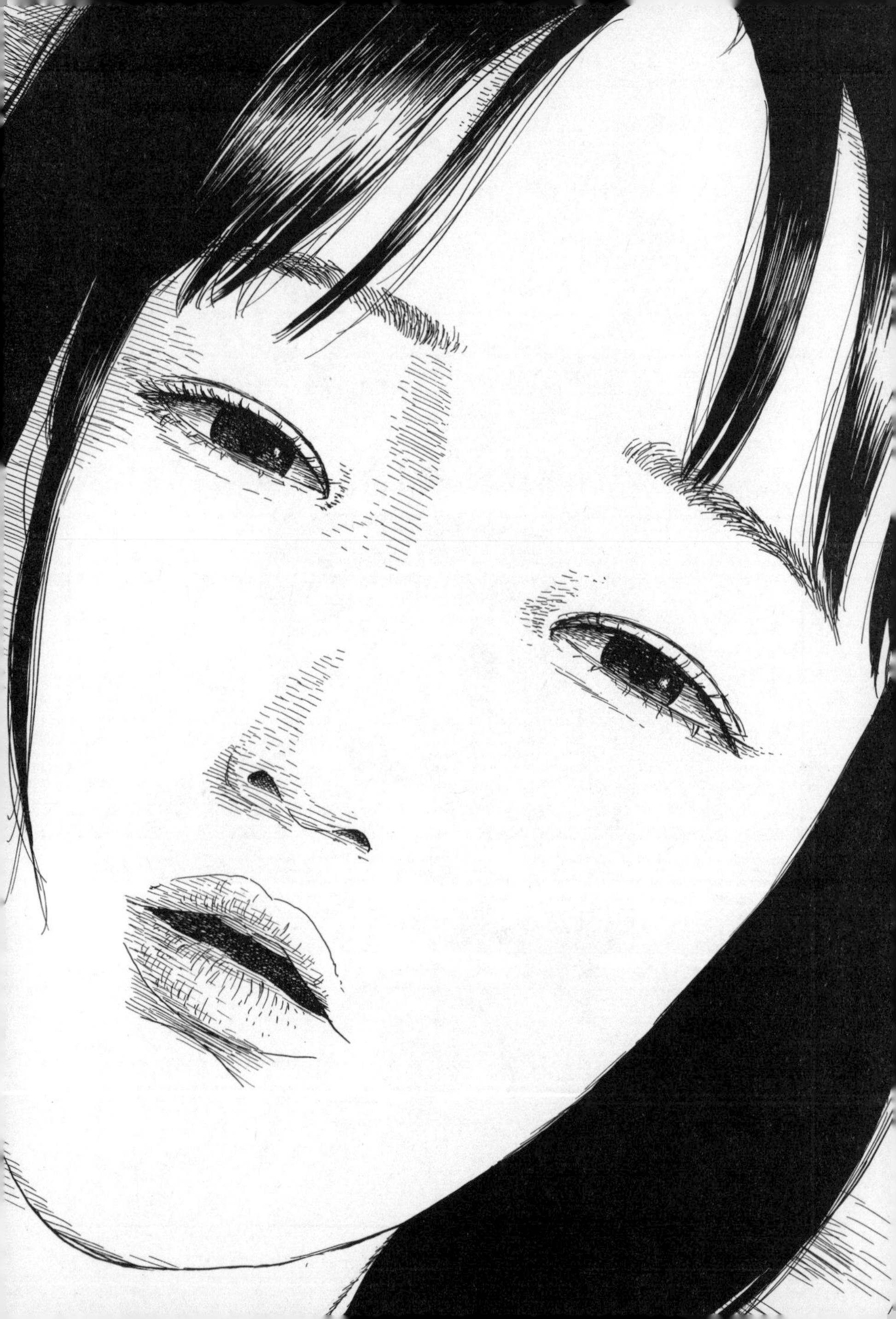

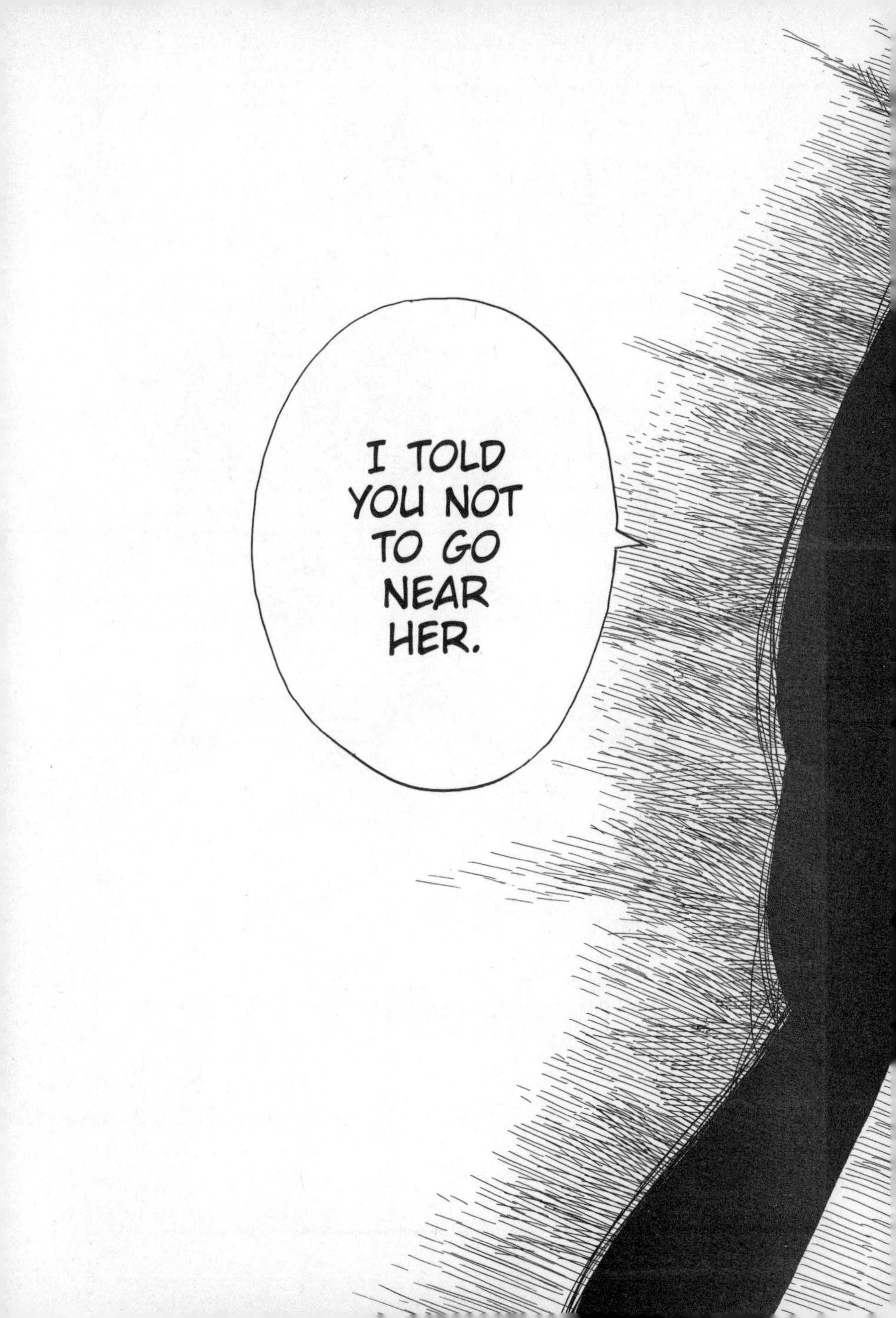
I TOLD YOU NOT TO GO NEAR HER.

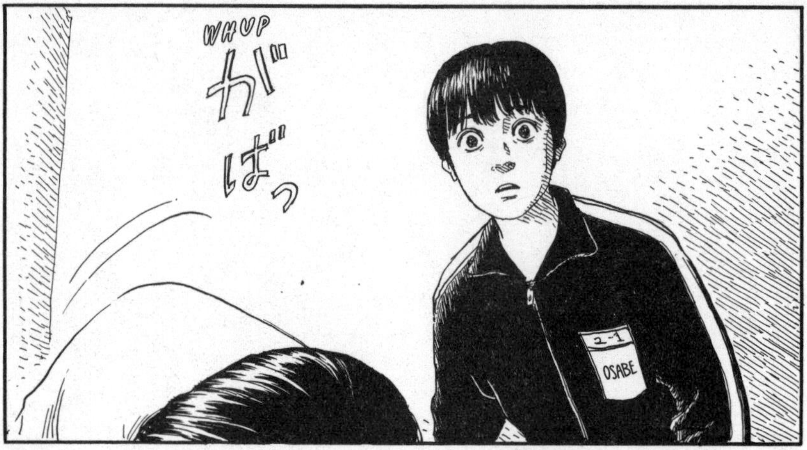
WHUP
がばっ
2-1
OSABE
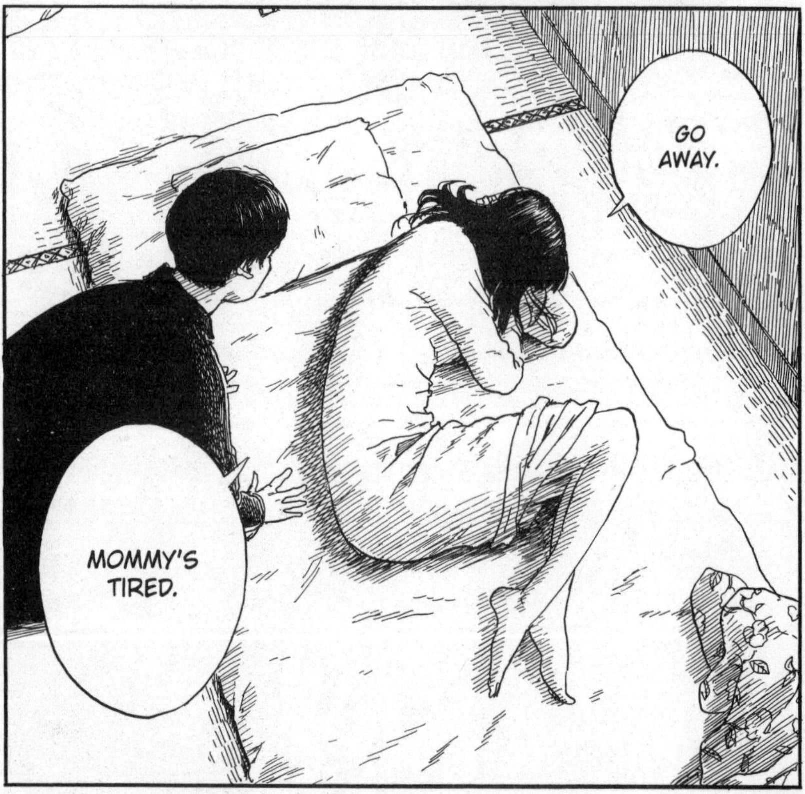
GO AWAY.
MOMMY'S TIRED.

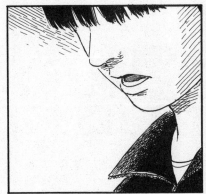
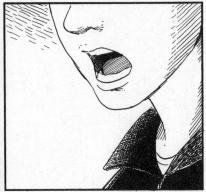

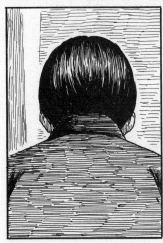

RATTLE
ガラ！

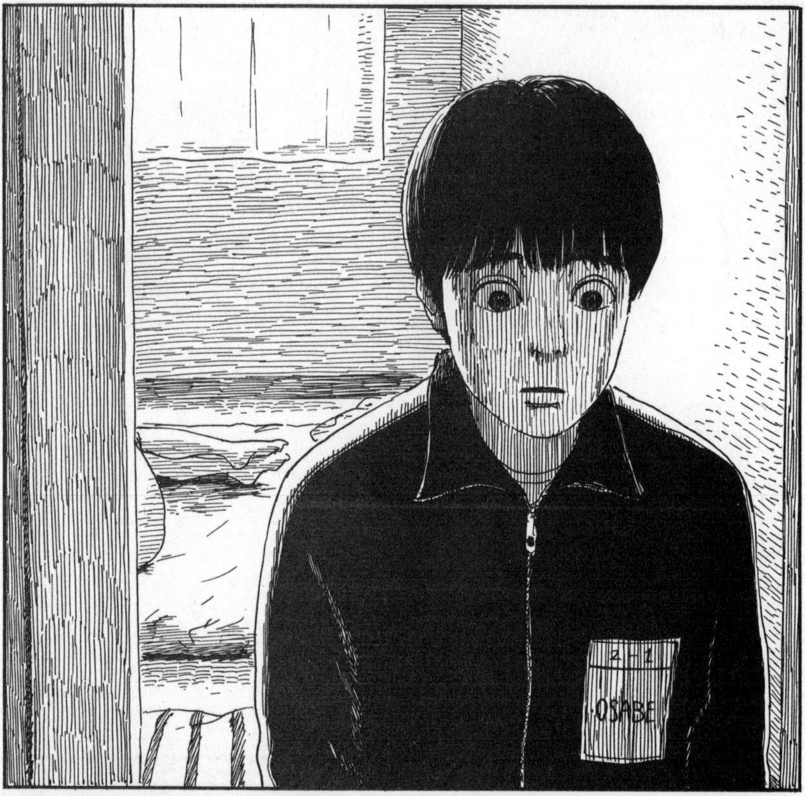
2-1
OSABE
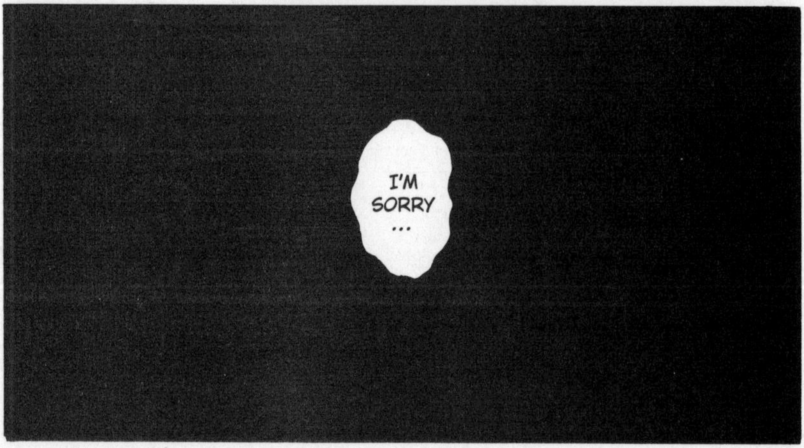
I'M SORRY ...

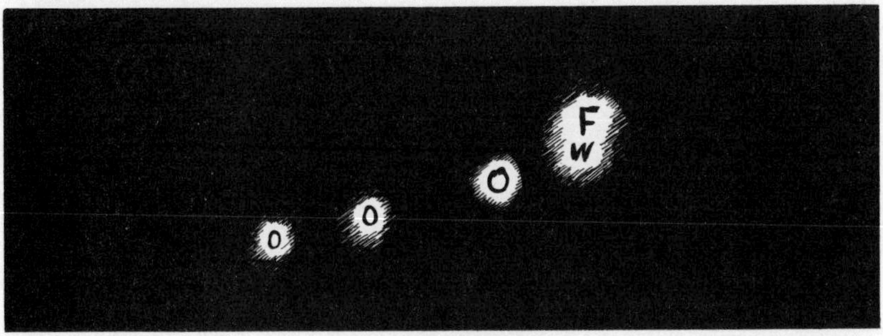
o O O O F W

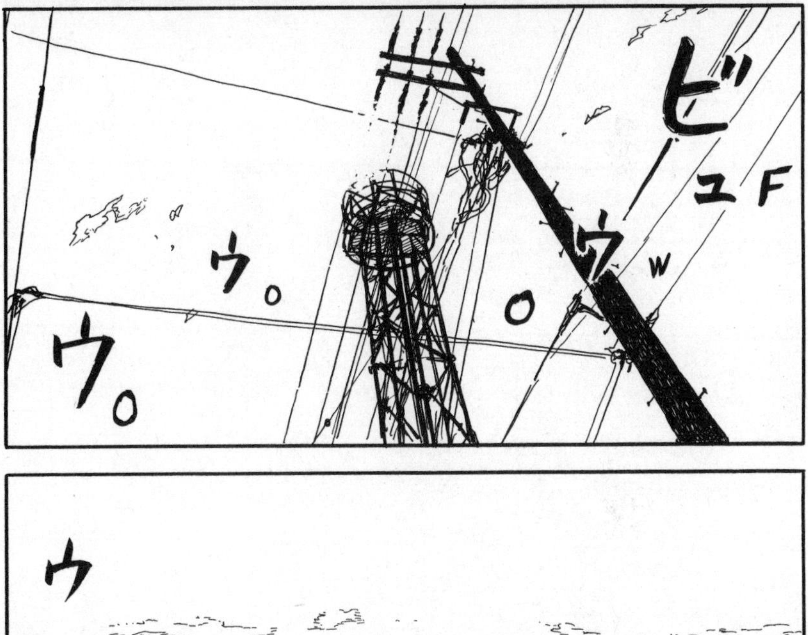
ビュウ
F W O
ウo
ウO

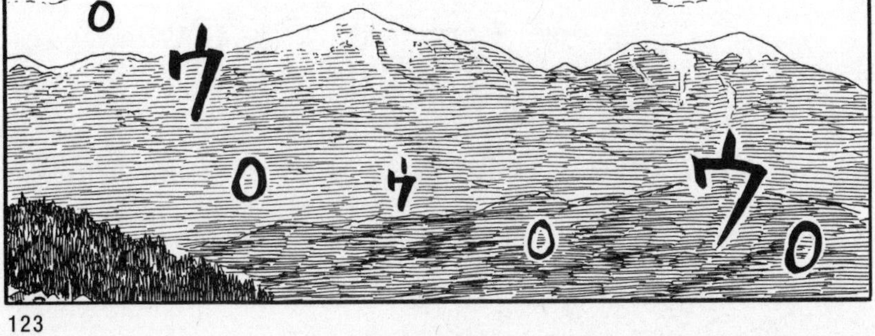
ウO
ウO
ゥO
ウO

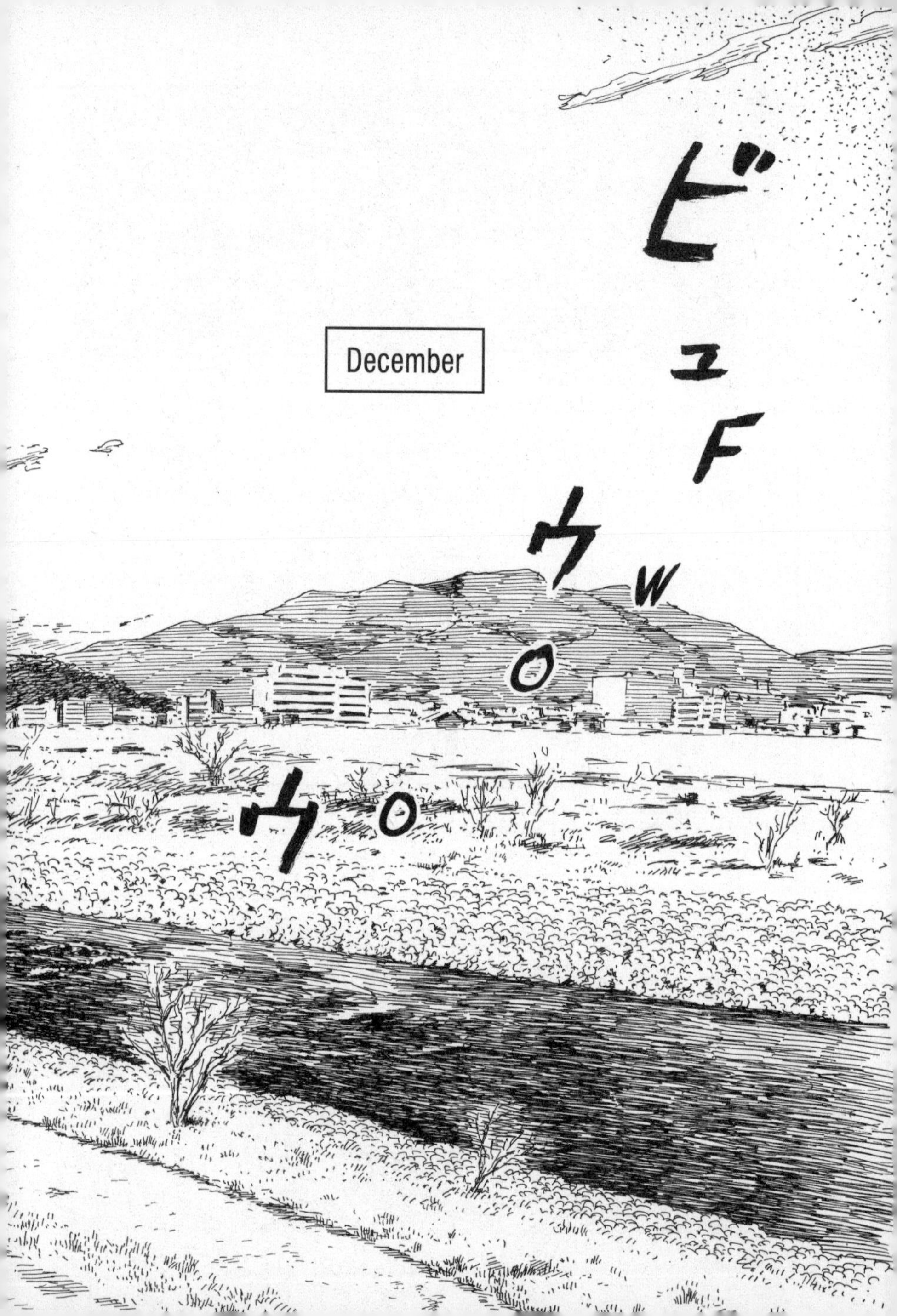
December
ビュFウwo
ウo

# CHAPTER 56 Afterwards

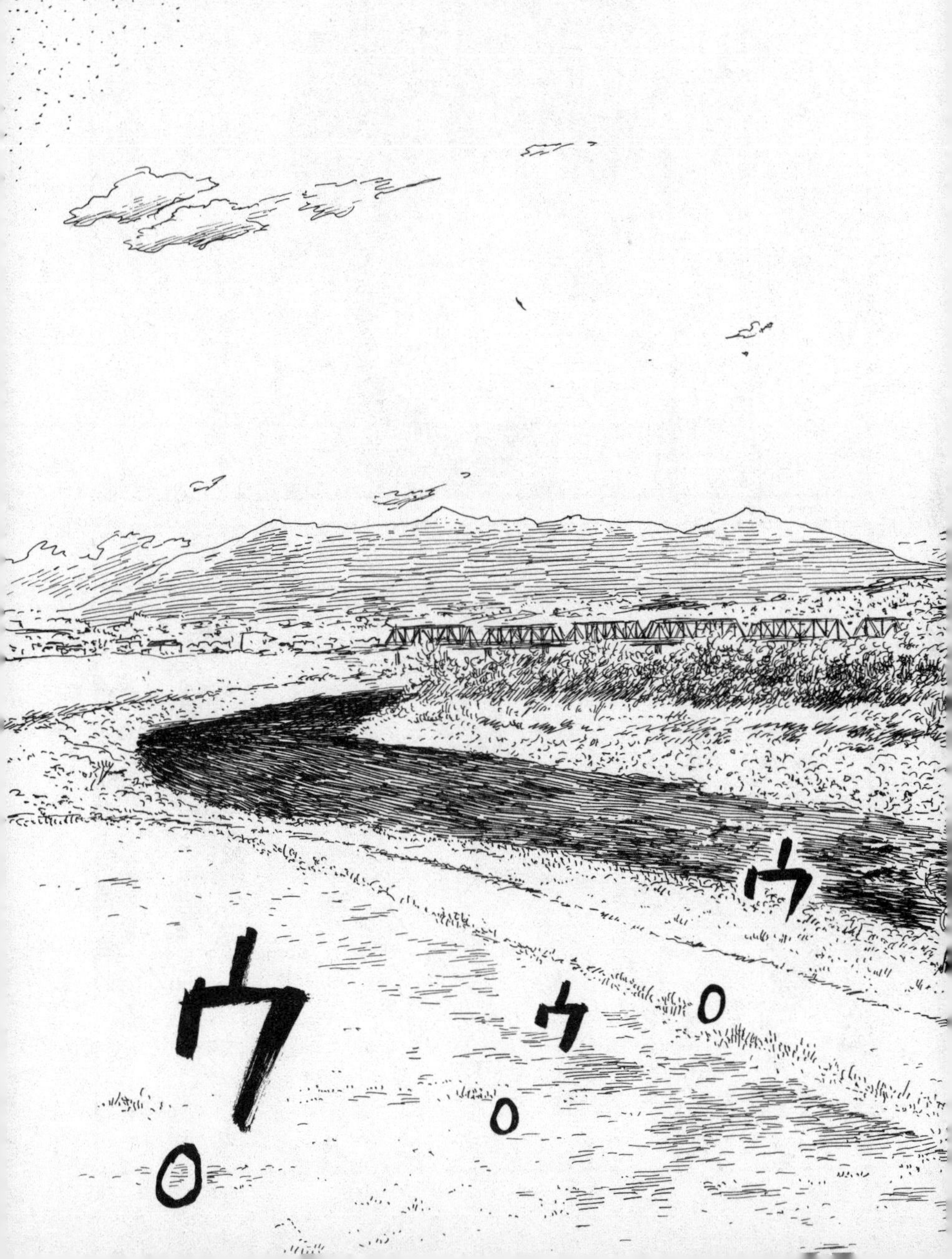
ウ
。
ウ
。
ウ
。

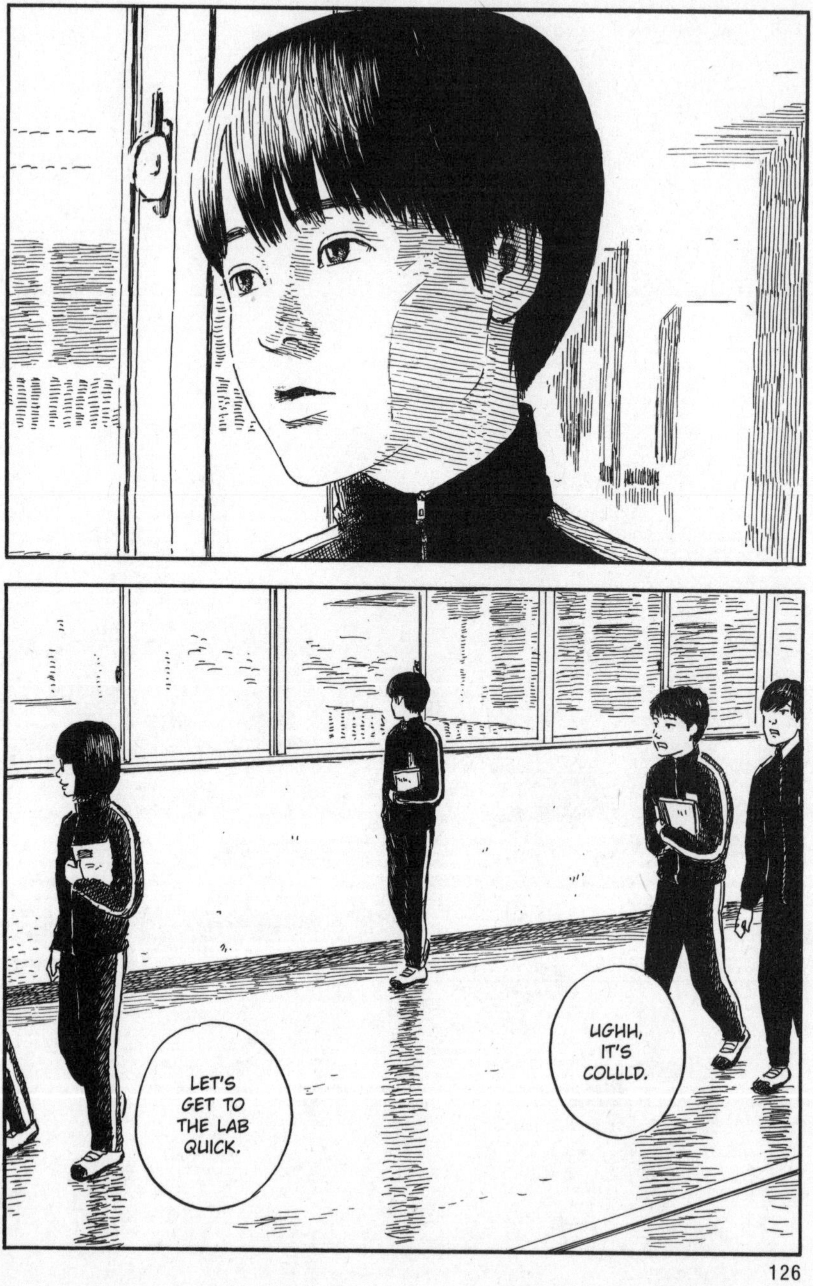
UGHH, IT'S COLLLD.
LET'S GET TO THE LAB QUICK.

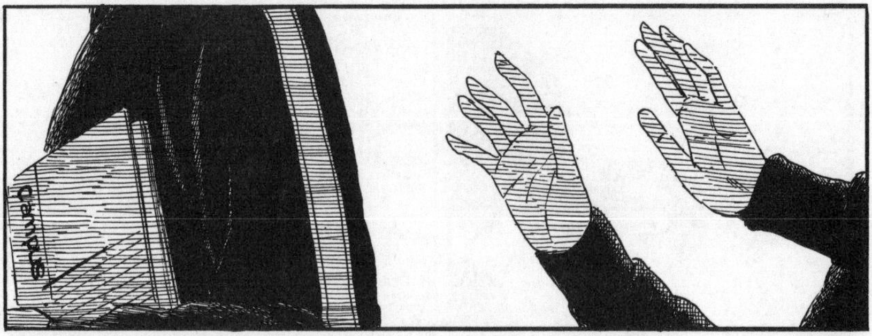
Campus
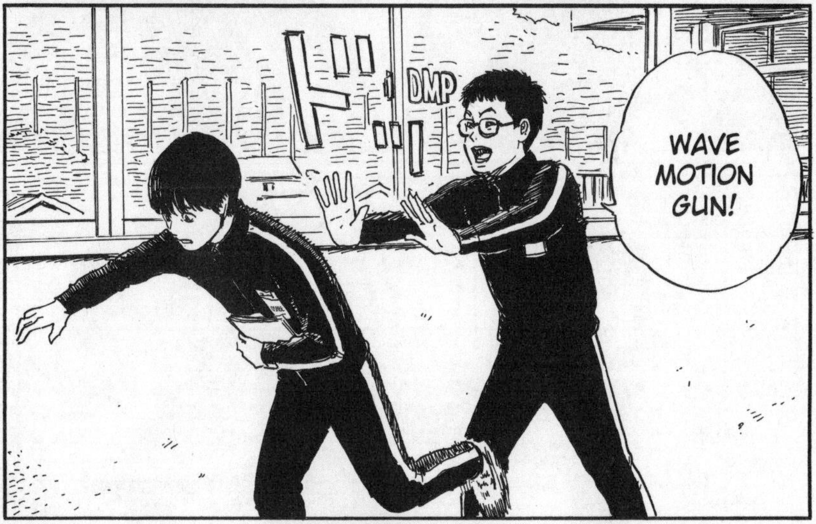
DMP
WAVE MOTION GUN!
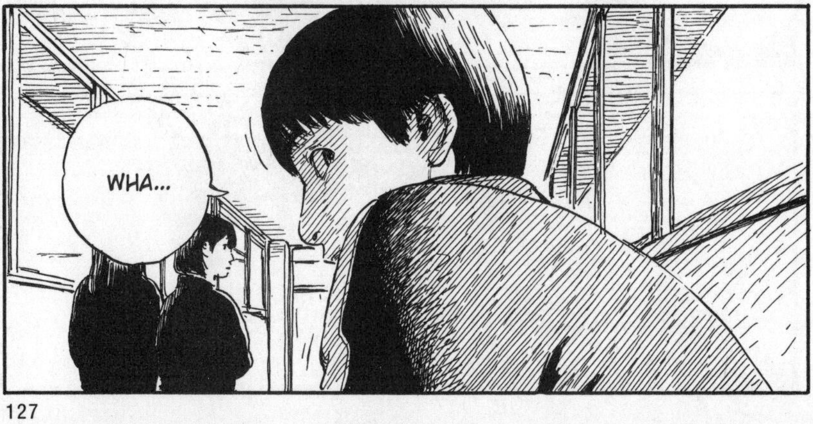
WHA...

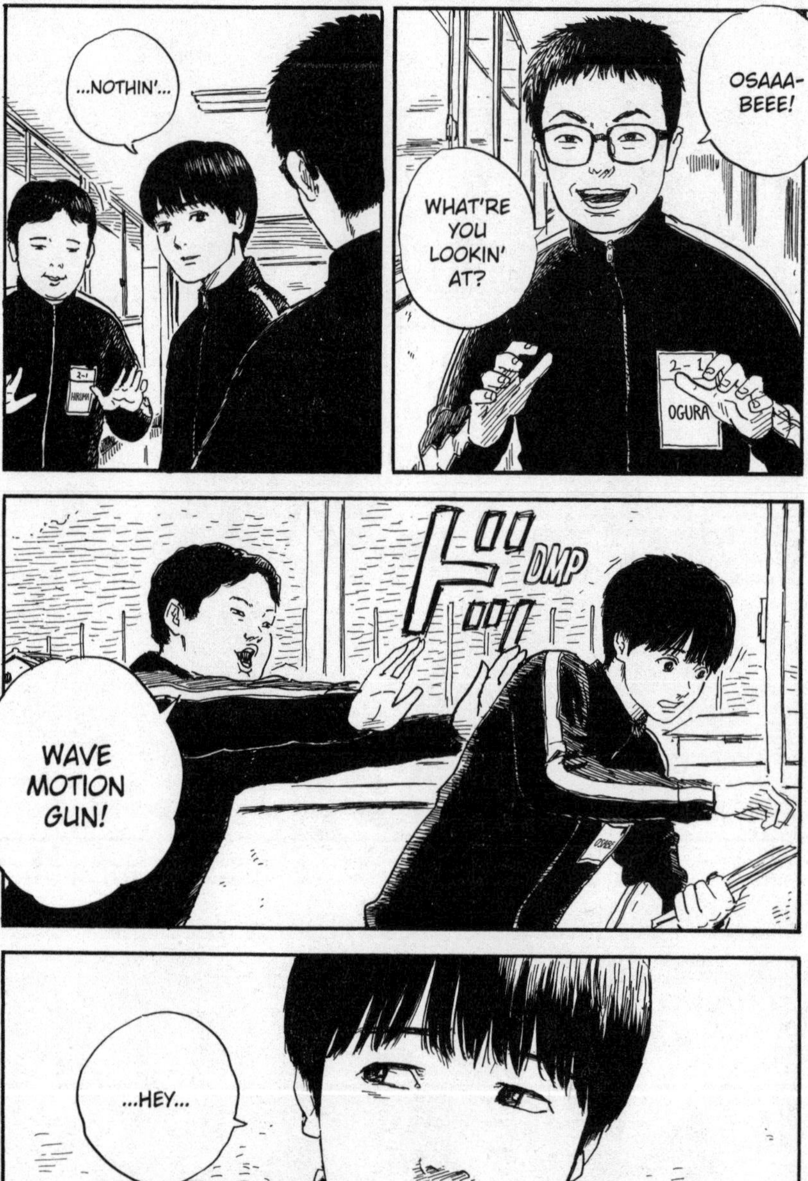
OSAAA-BEEE!
WHAT'RE YOU LOOKIN' AT?
2-1
OGURA
...NOTHIN'...
DMP
WAVE MOTION GUN!
...HEY...

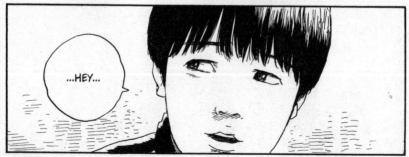

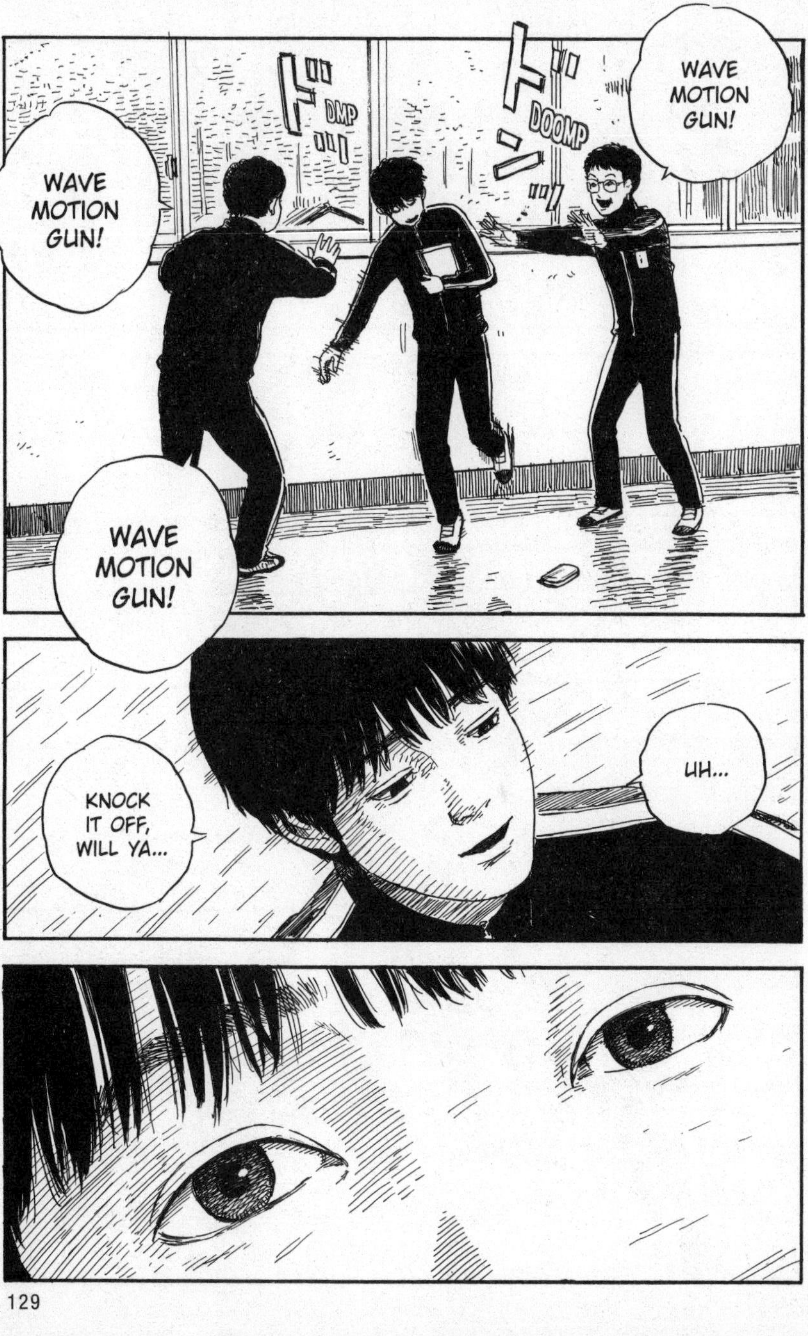
WAVE MOTION GUN!
DOOMP
DMP
WAVE MOTION GUN!
WAVE MOTION GUN!
UH...
KNOCK IT OFF, WILL YA...

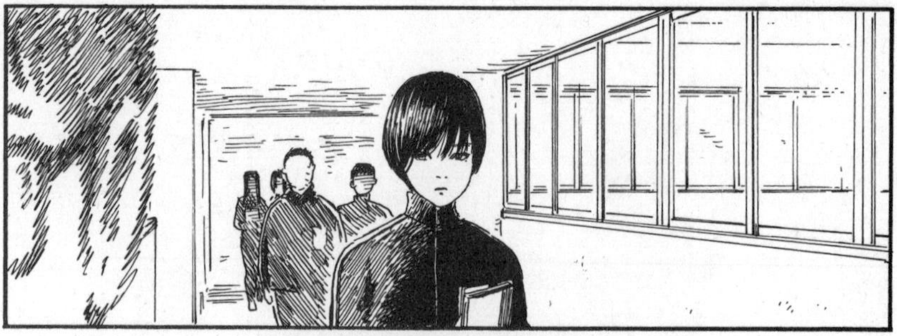
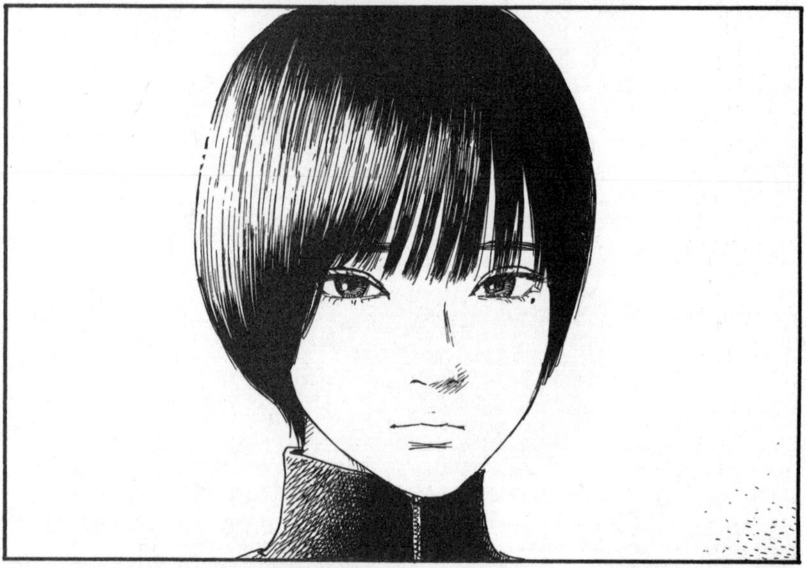
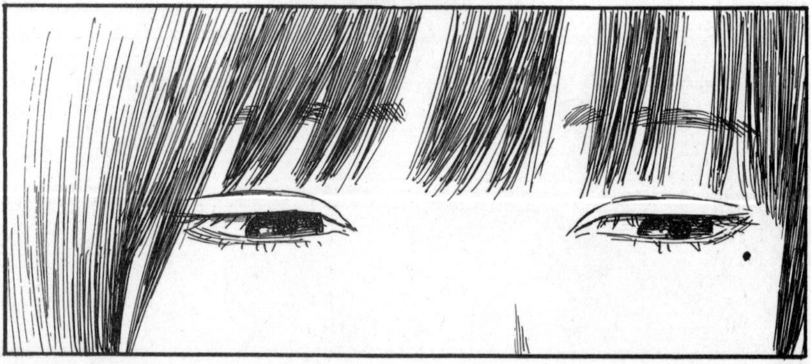

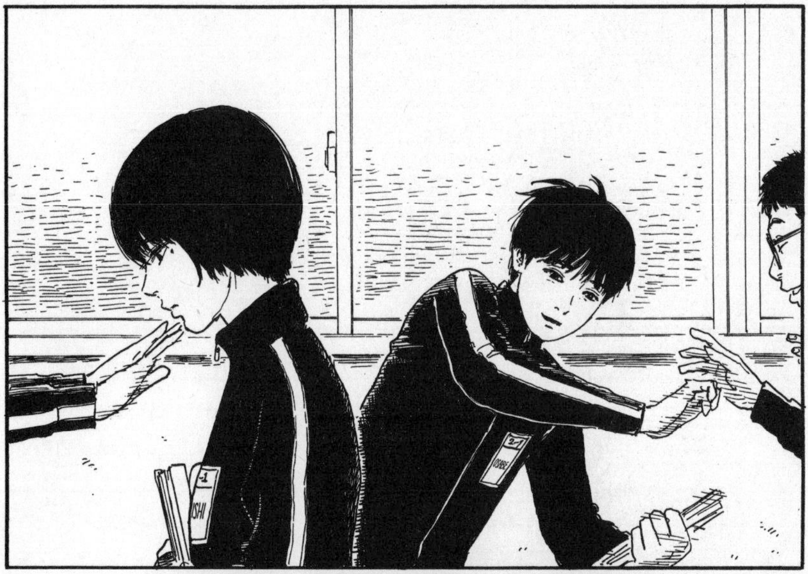
2-1
-1
ISHI
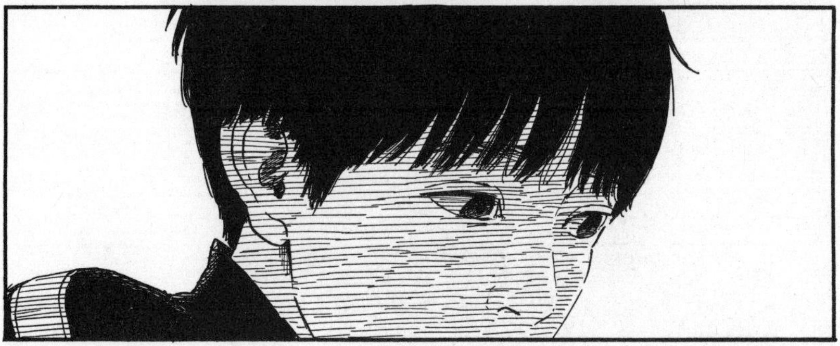
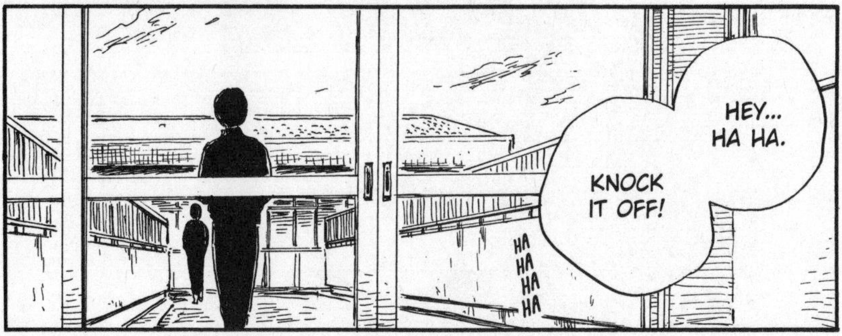
HEY... HA HA.
KNOCK IT OFF!
HA HA HA HA HA

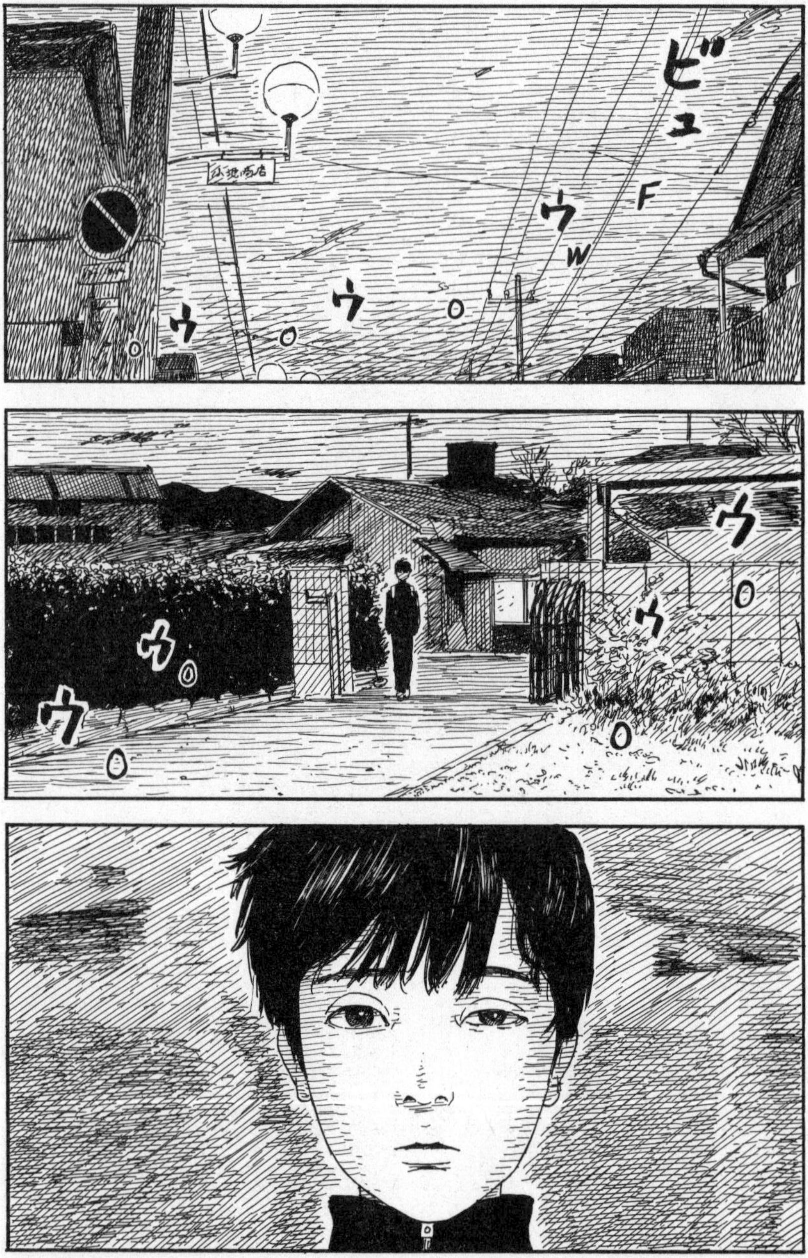
ビュ
ウ
ウ
ウ
ウ
ウ
ウ
ウ

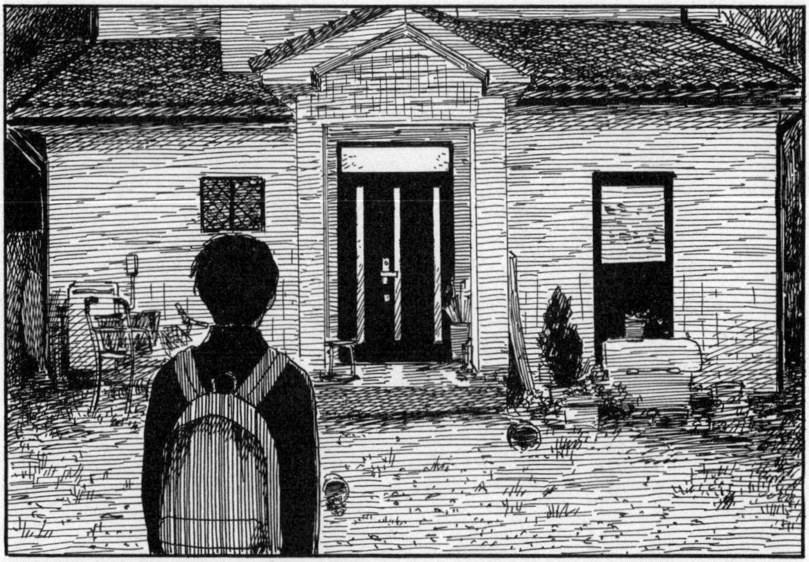

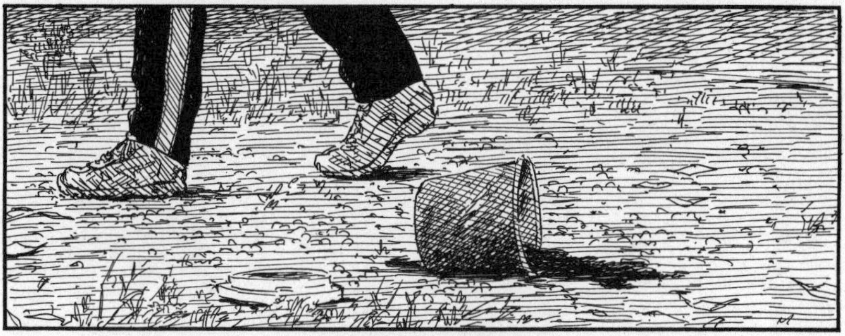

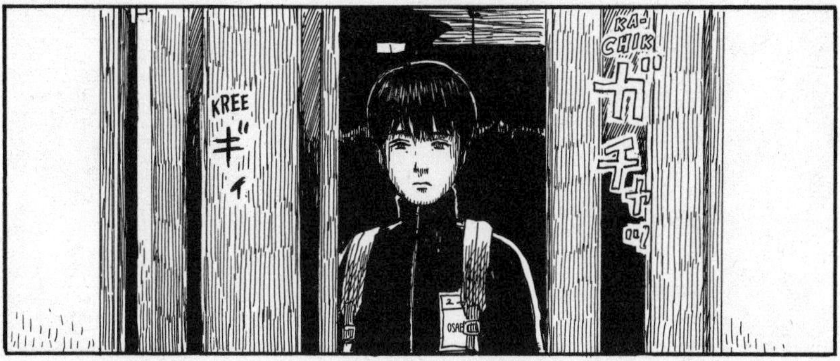
KA-CHIK
ガチャッ
KREE
ギィ

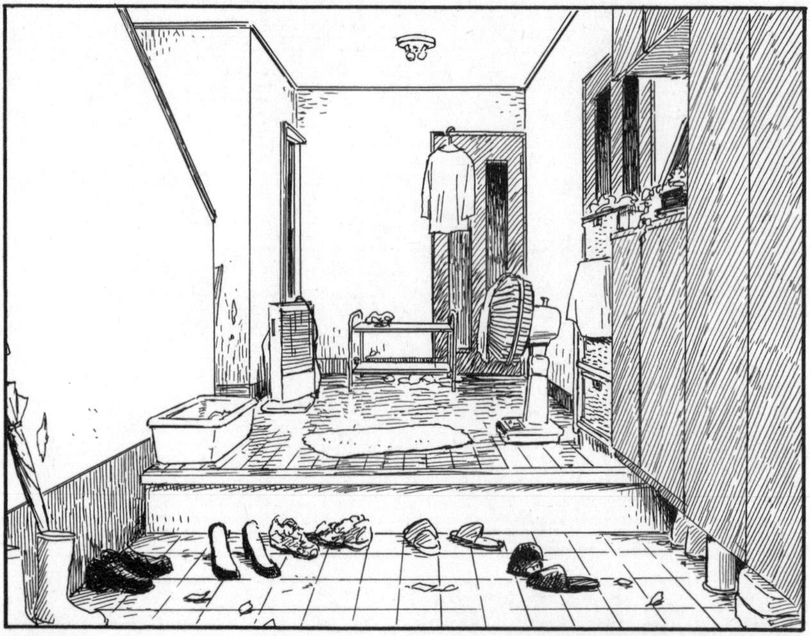

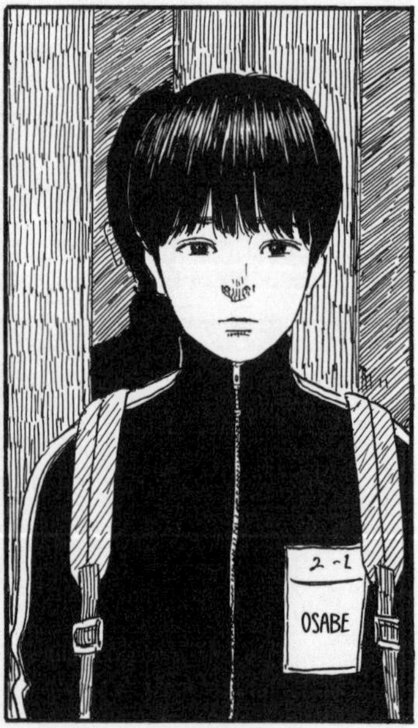
2-1
OSABE

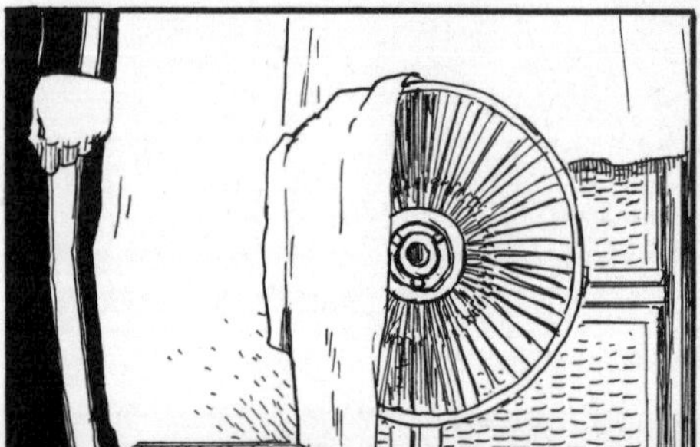

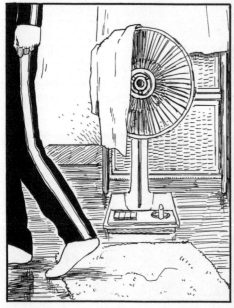

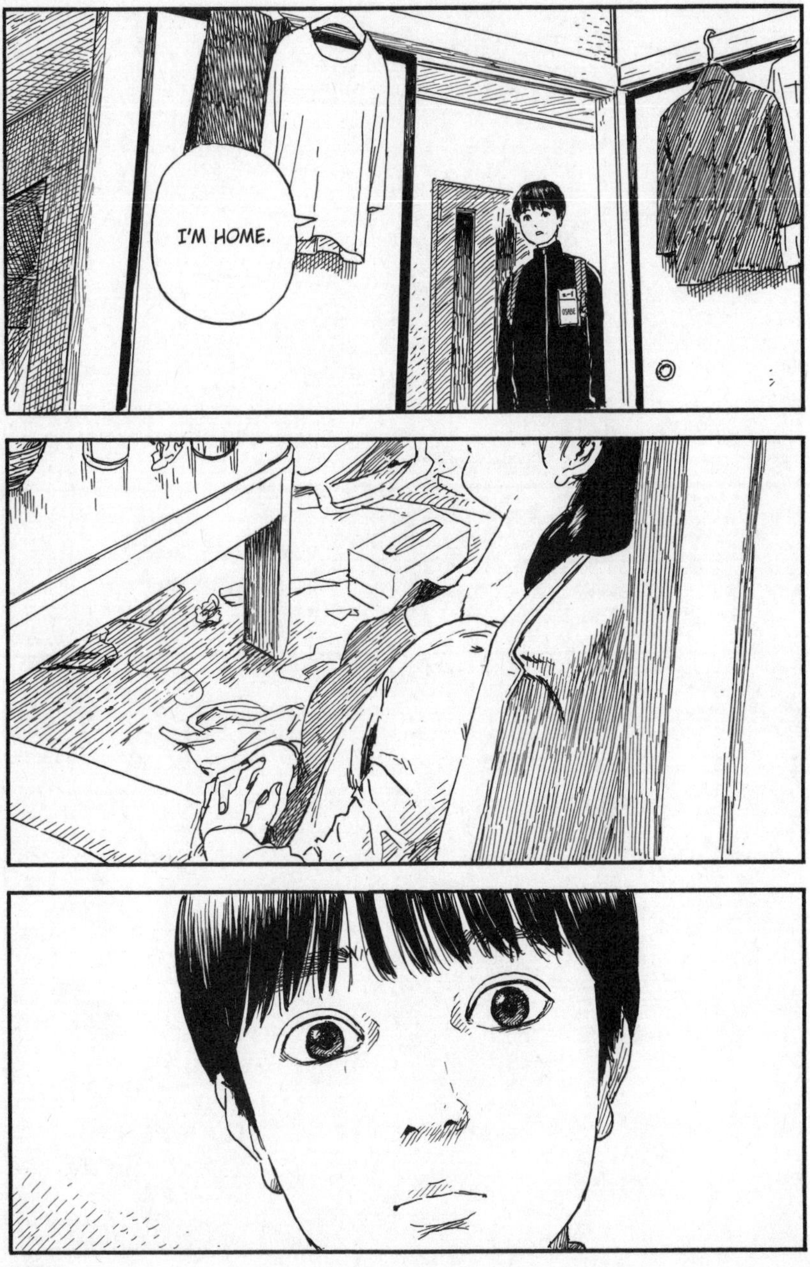
I'M HOME.

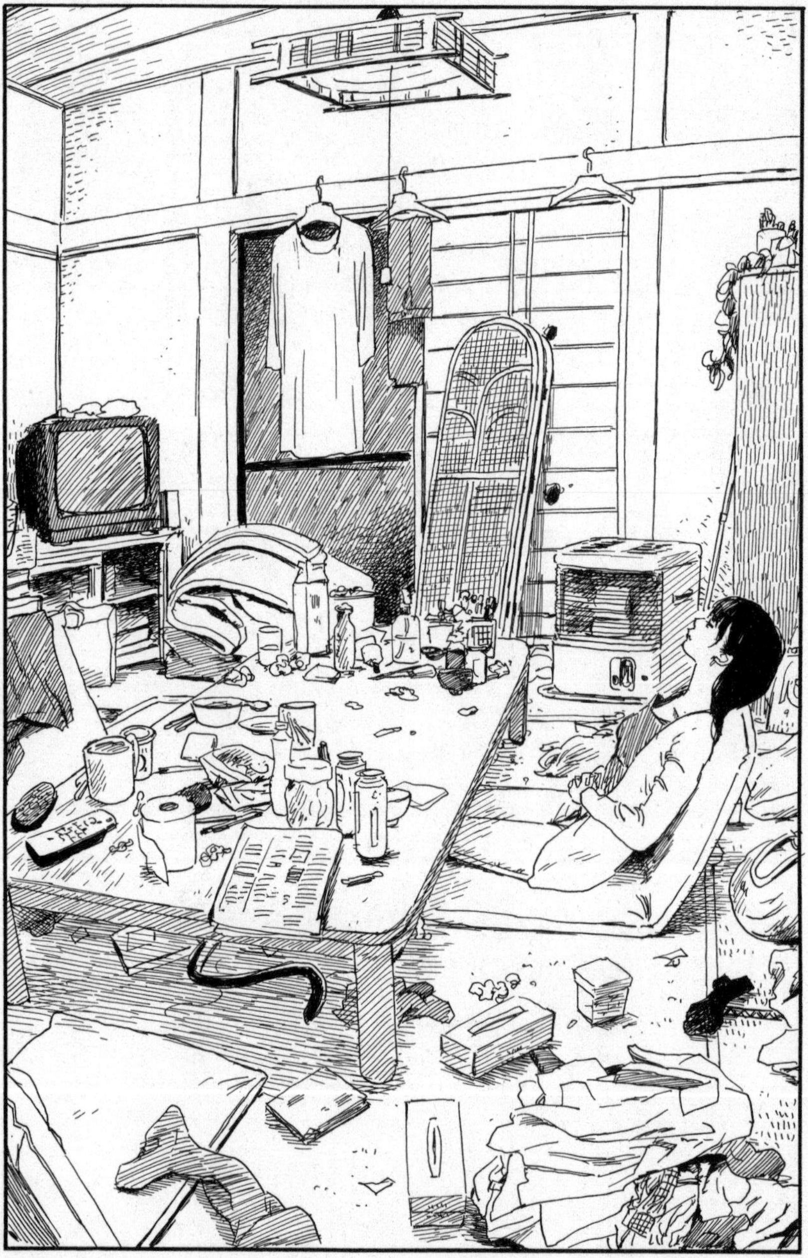

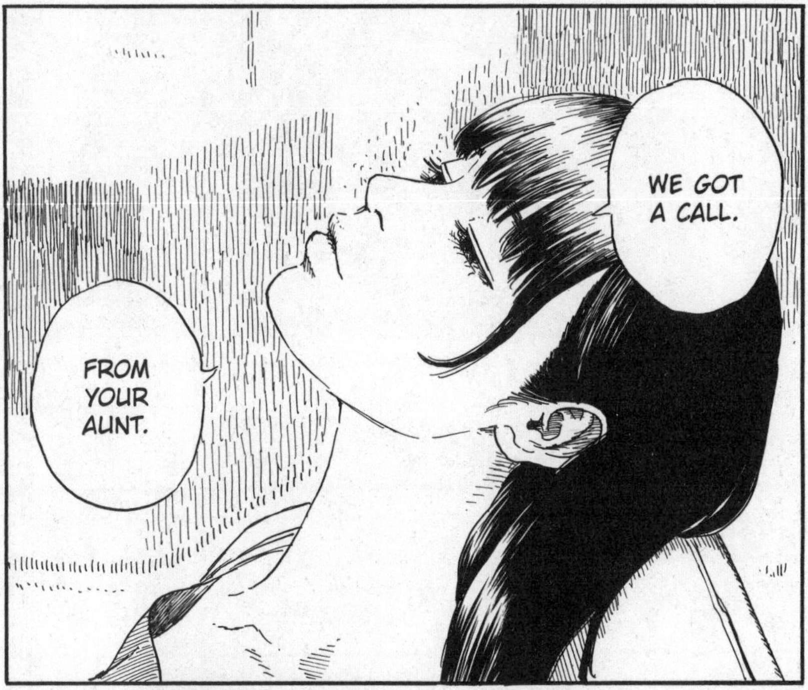
WE GOT A CALL.
FROM YOUR AUNT.
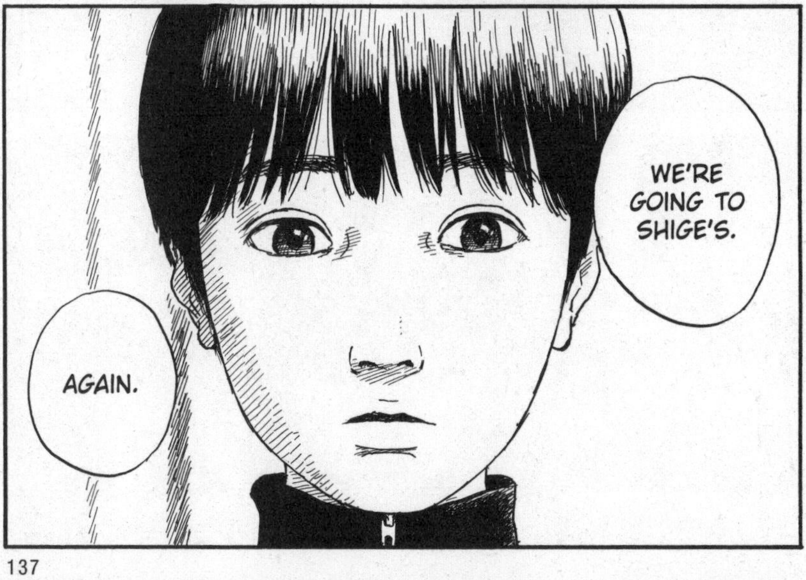
WE'RE GOING TO SHIGE'S.
AGAIN.

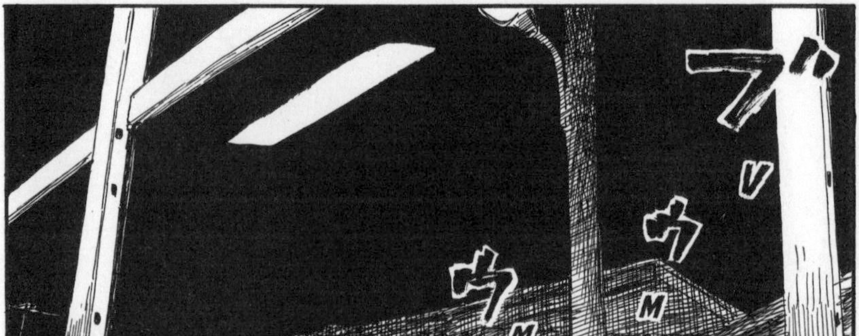
ブVウMウM
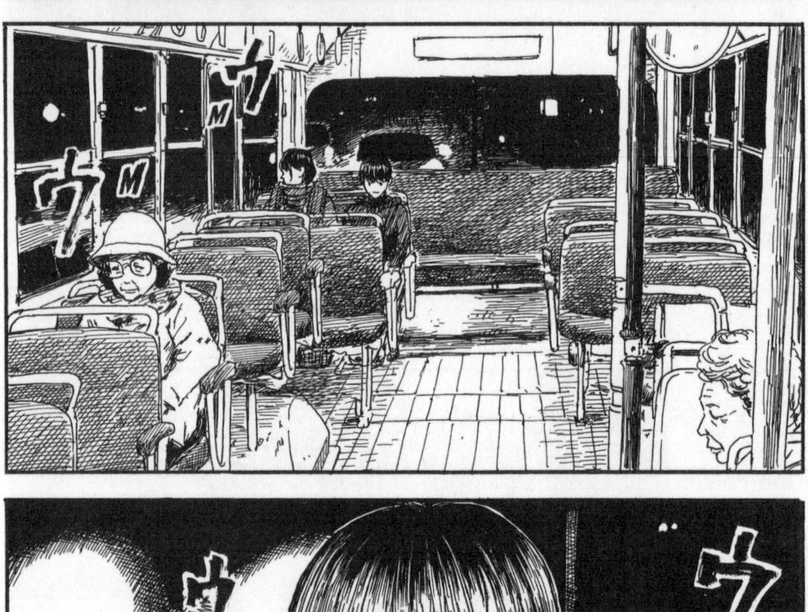
ウMウM
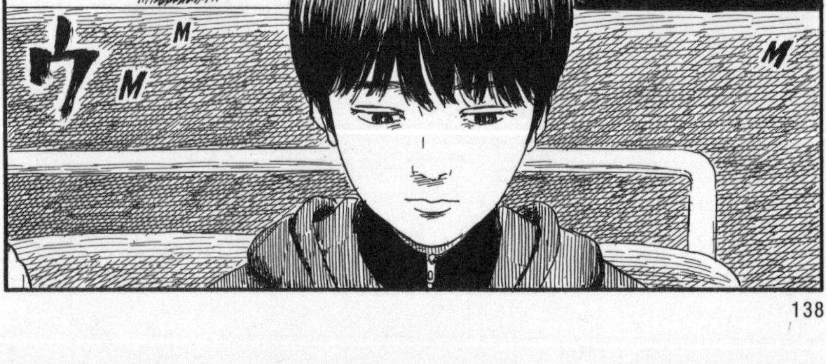
ウMウMウM

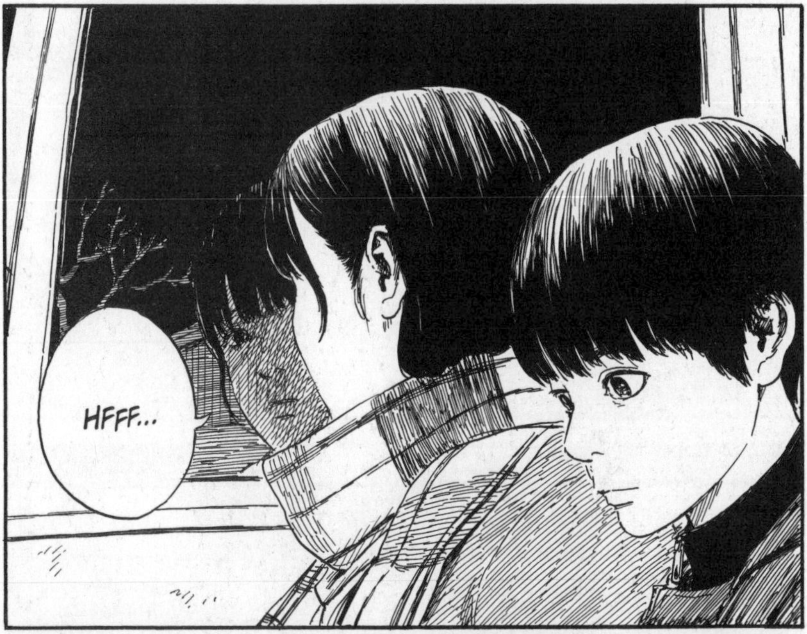
HFFF...

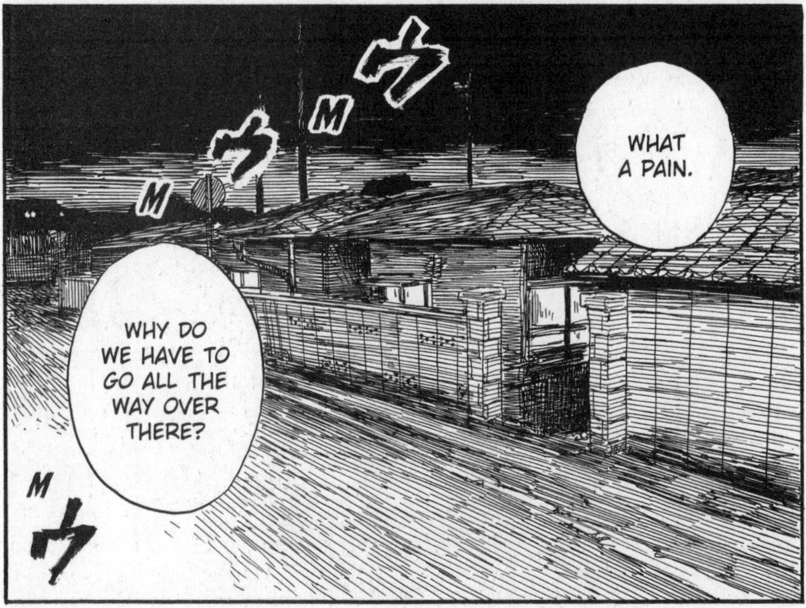
WHAT A PAIN.
ウ
M
ウ
M
WHY DO WE HAVE TO GO ALL THE WAY OVER THERE?
M
ウ

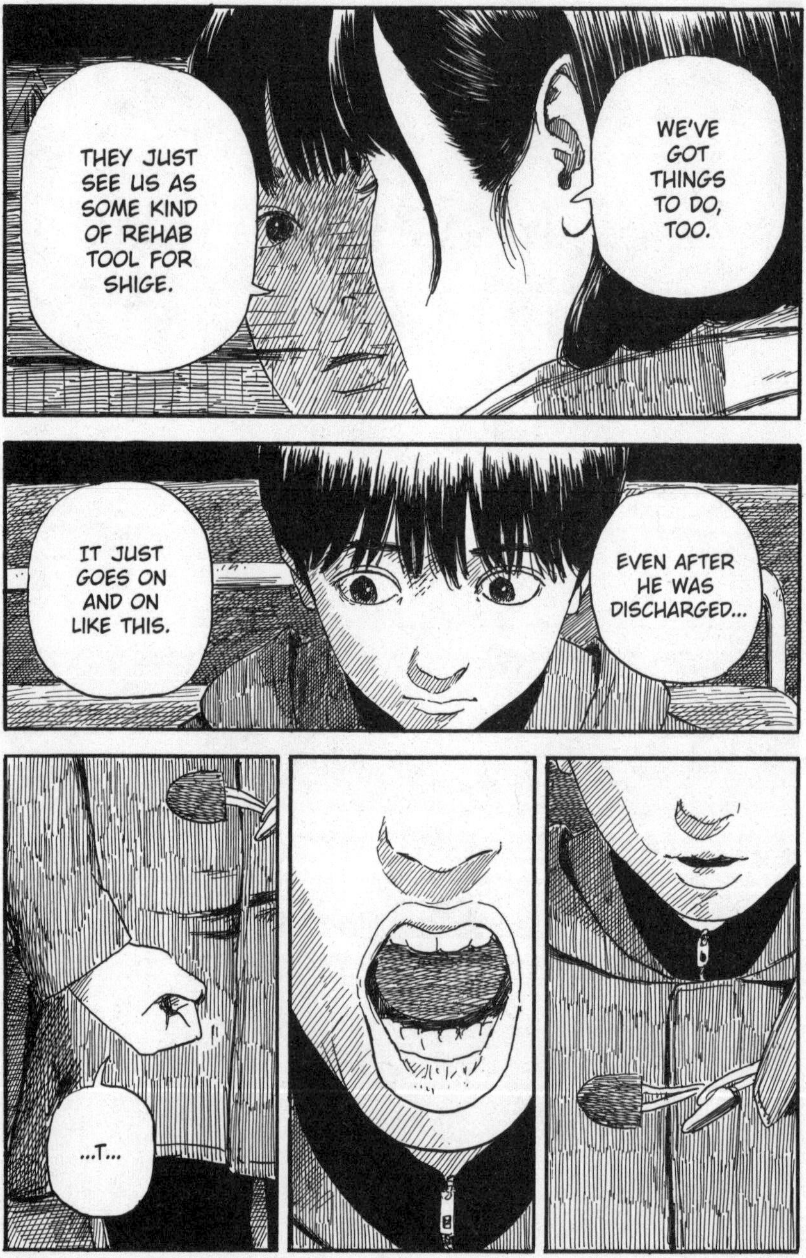
WE'VE GOT THINGS TO DO, TOO.
THEY JUST SEE US AS SOME KIND OF REHAB TOOL FOR SHIGE.
EVEN AFTER HE WAS DISCHARGED...
IT JUST GOES ON AND ON LIKE THIS.
...T...

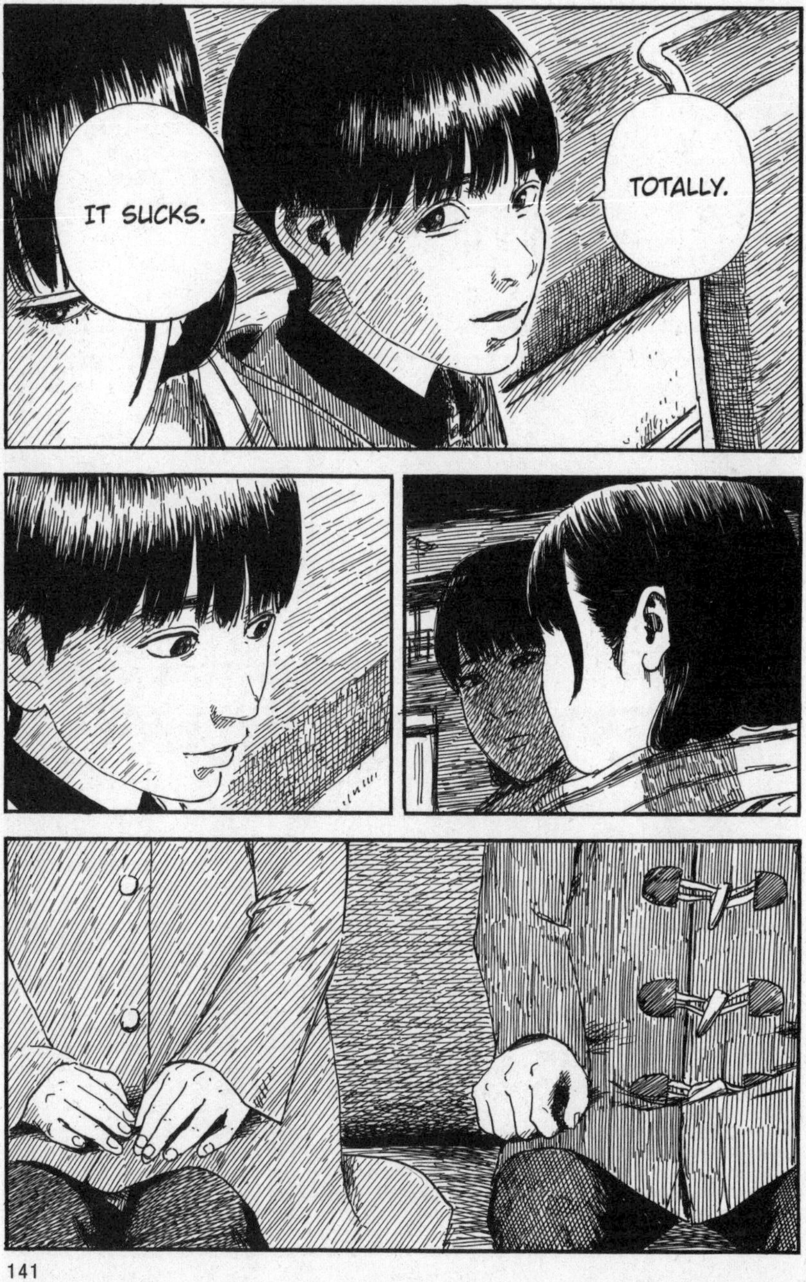
TOTALLY.
IT SUCKS.

YO

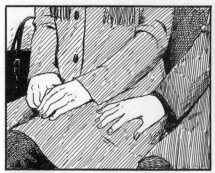

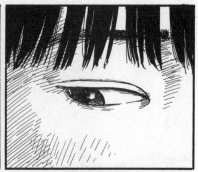

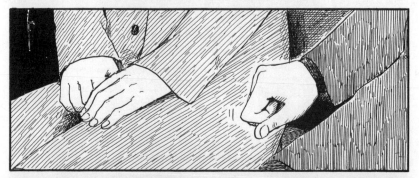

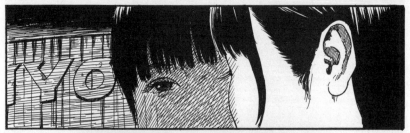

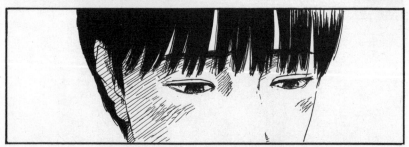

...MOMMY...

CAN I...
DO ANYTHING?

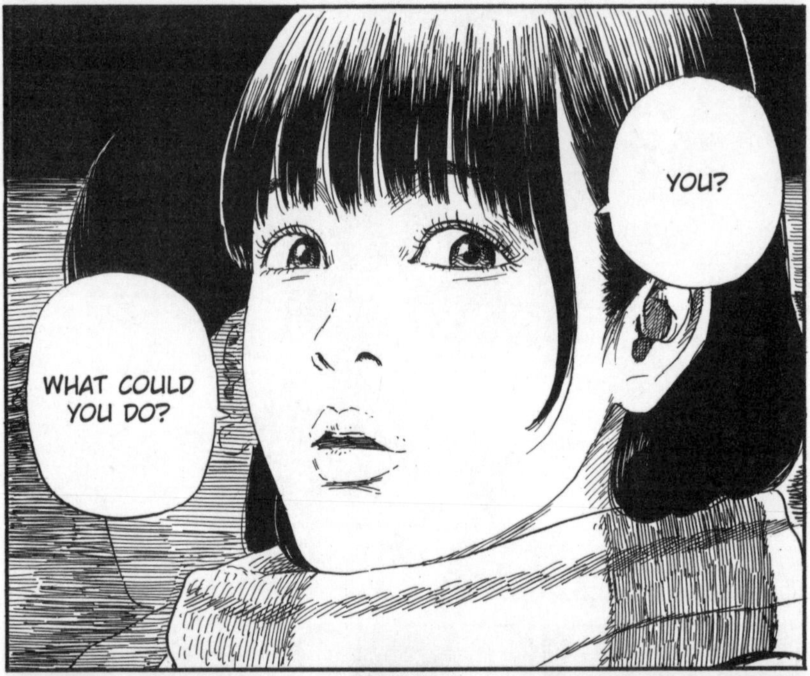
YOU?
WHAT COULD YOU DO?
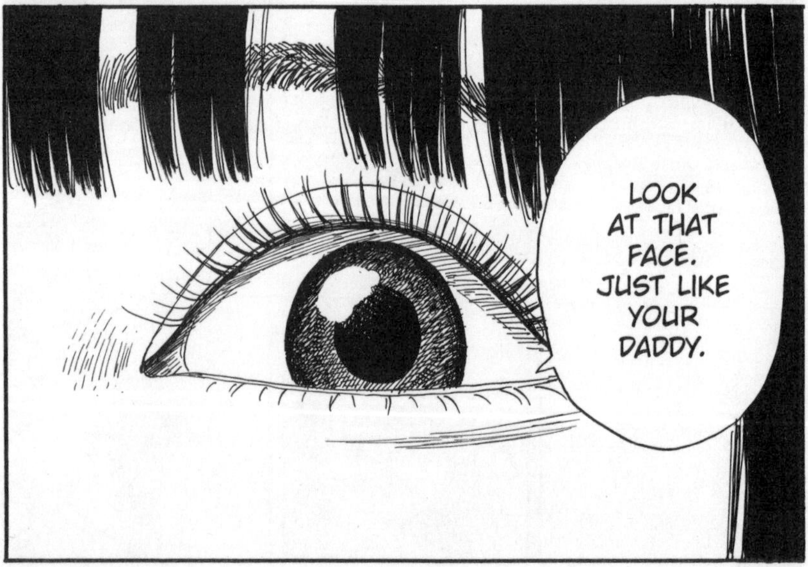
LOOK AT THAT FACE. JUST LIKE YOUR DADDY.

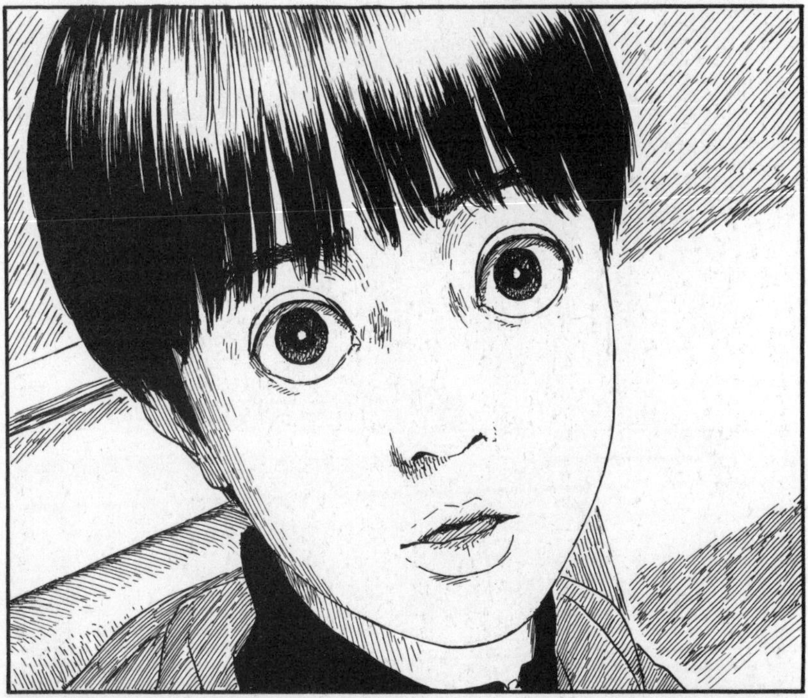
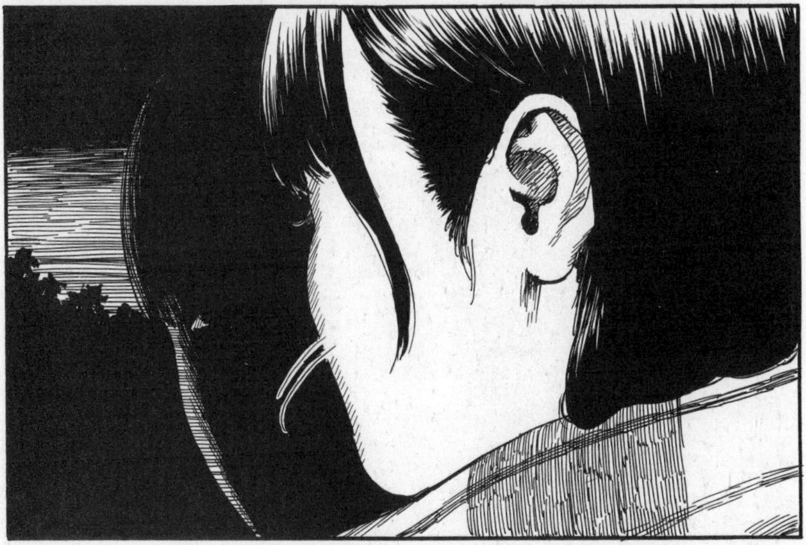

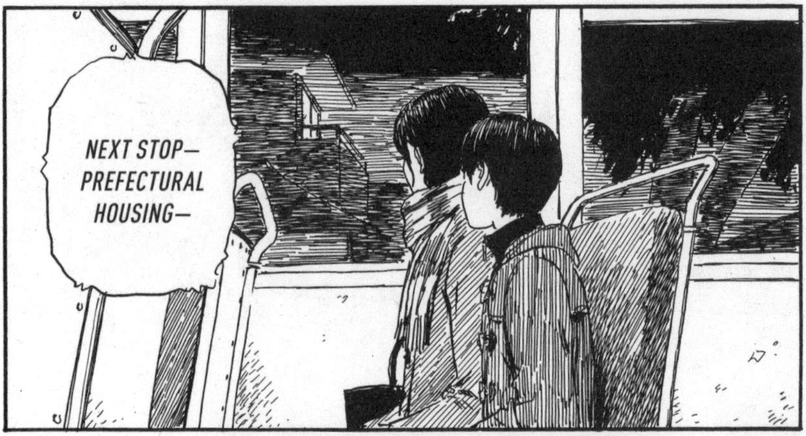
NEXT STOP—
PREFECTURAL
HOUSING—
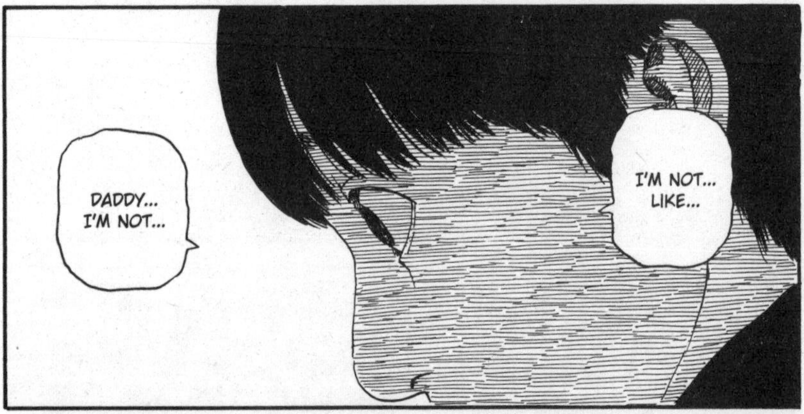
DADDY... I'M NOT...
I'M NOT... LIKE...
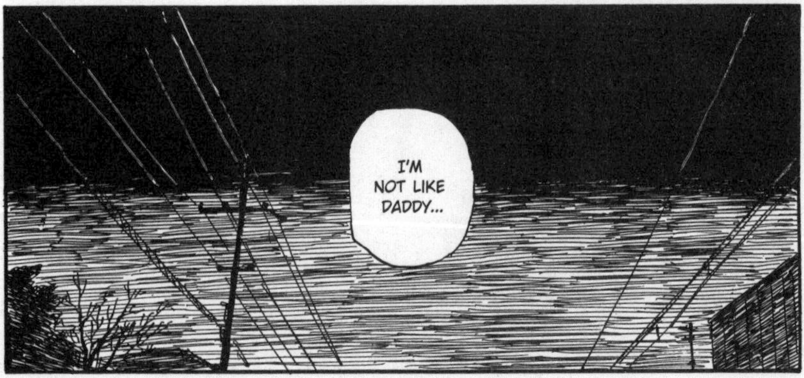
I'M NOT LIKE DADDY...

## CHAPTER 57 Paying a Call

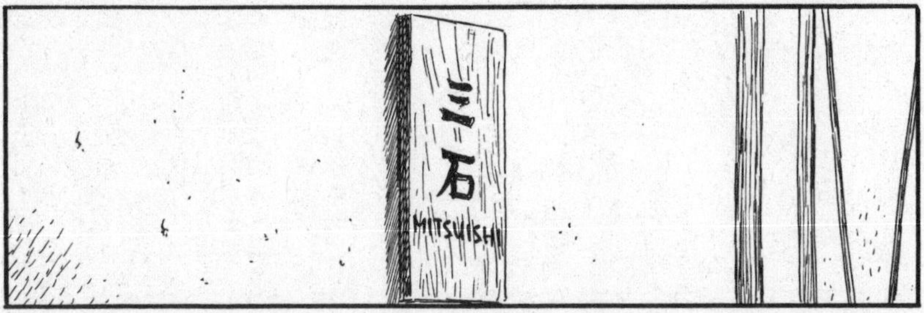
三石
MITSUISHI

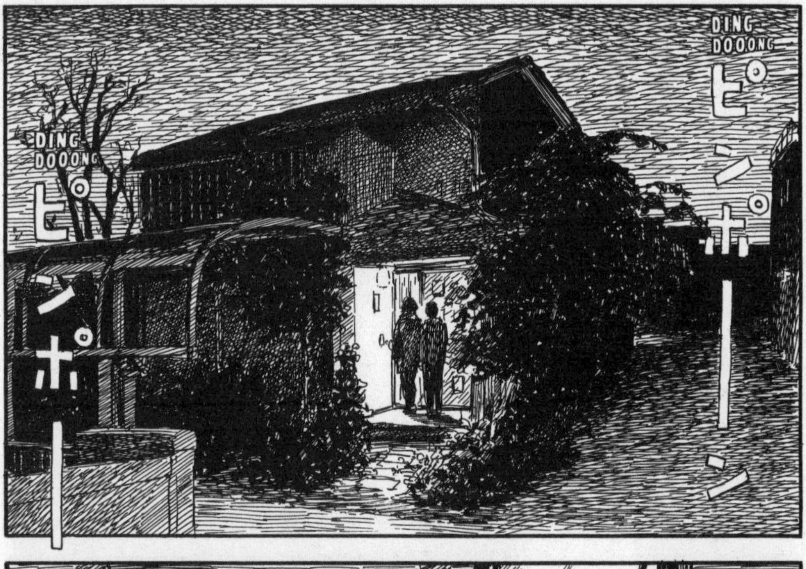
DING DOOONG
ピンポーン
DING-DOOONG
ピンポーン

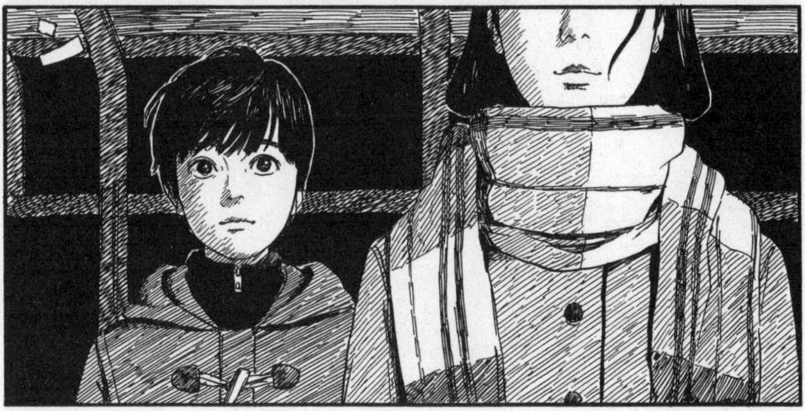

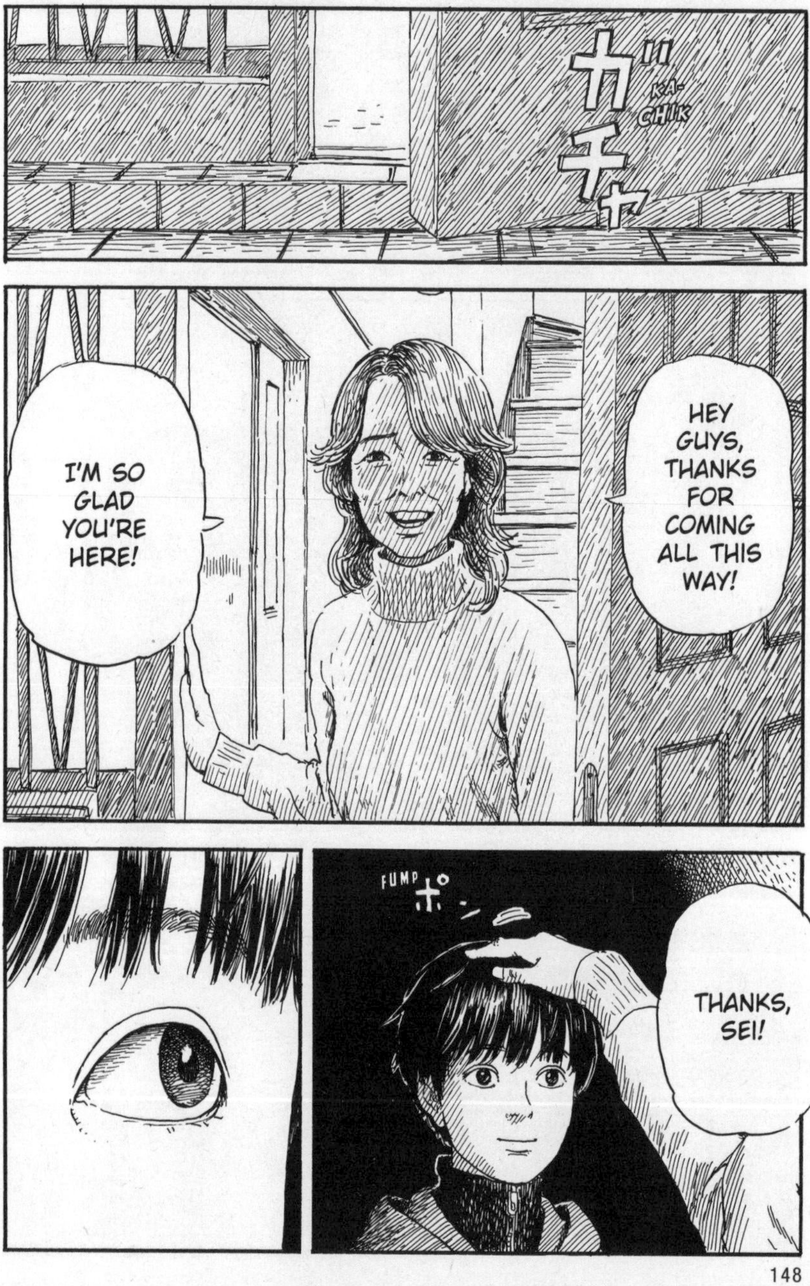
ガチャ
KA-CHIK
HEY GUYS, THANKS FOR COMING ALL THIS WAY!
I'M SO GLAD YOU'RE HERE!
FUMP
ポ
THANKS, SEI!

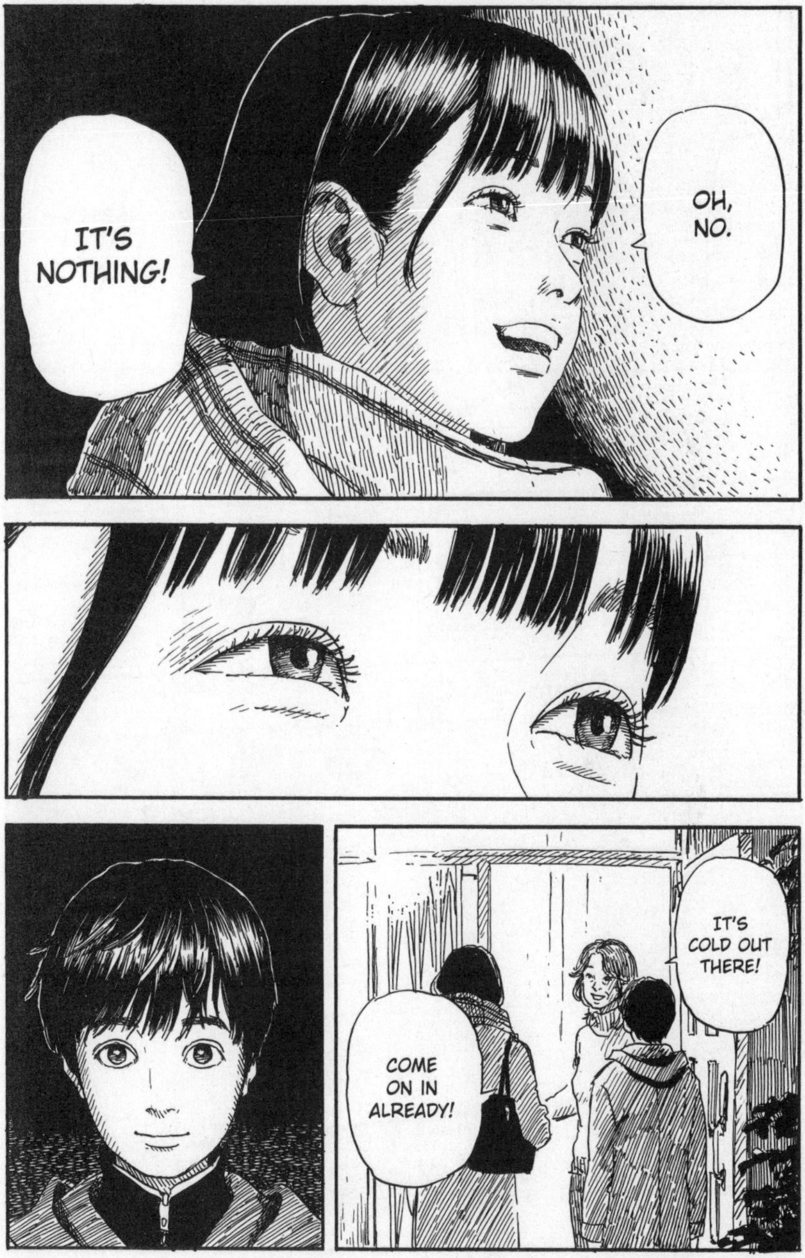
OH, NO.
IT'S NOTHING!
IT'S COLD OUT THERE!
COME ON IN ALREADY!

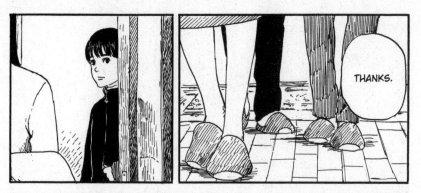

THANKS.

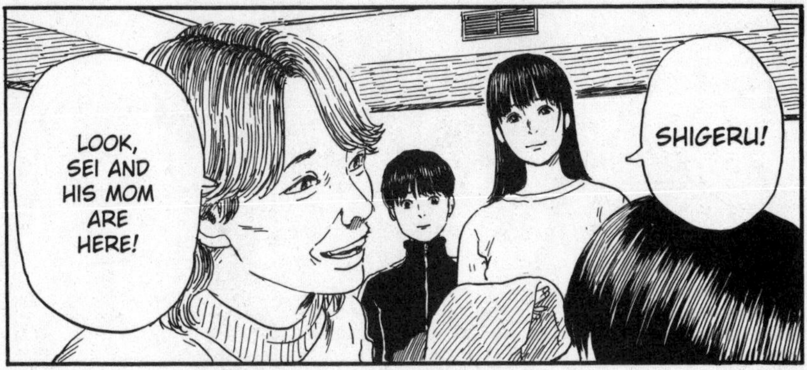
SHIGERU!
LOOK, SEI AND HIS MOM ARE HERE!

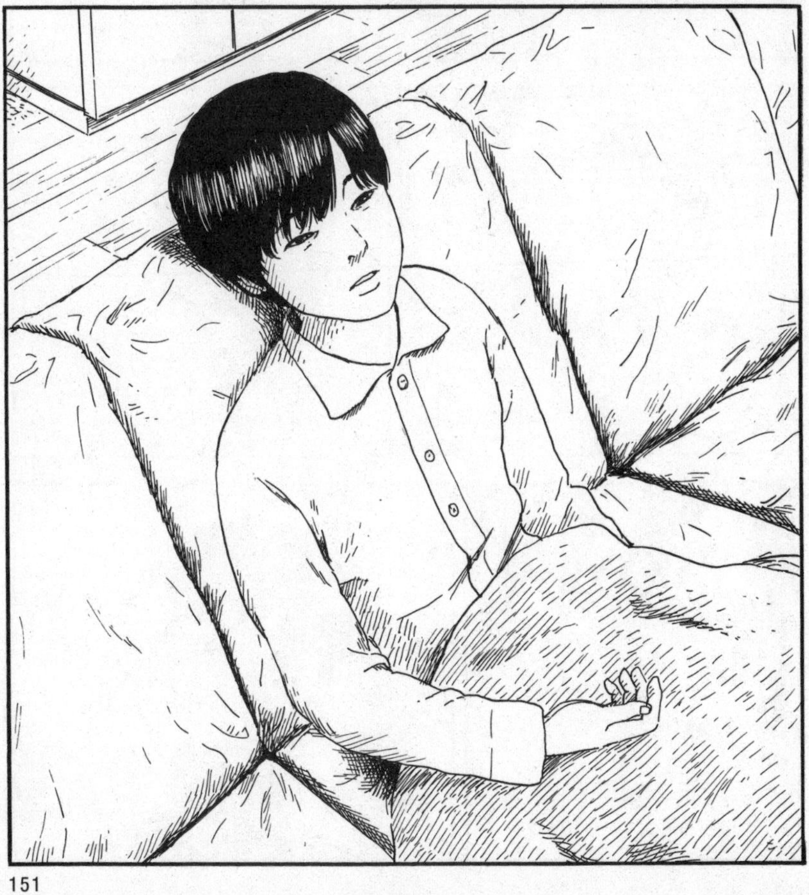

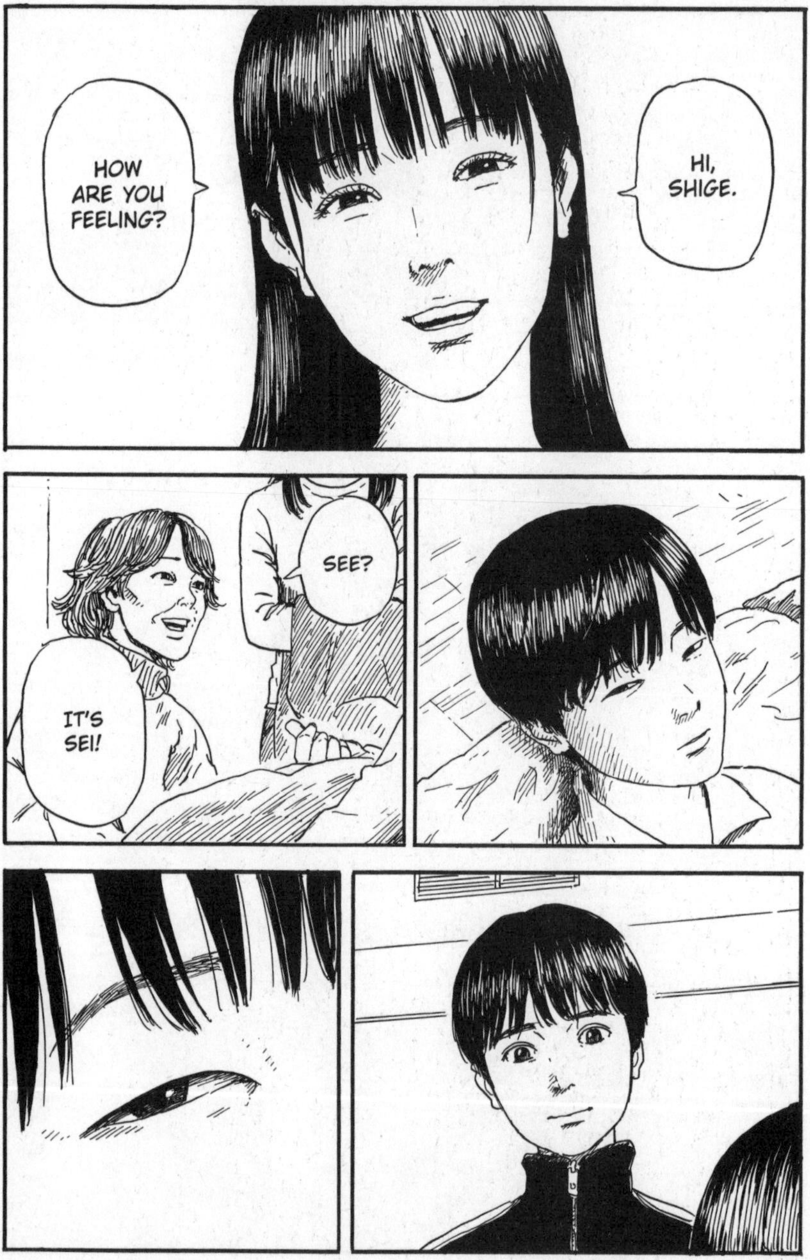
HI, SHIGE.
HOW ARE YOU FEELING?
SEE?
IT'S SEI!

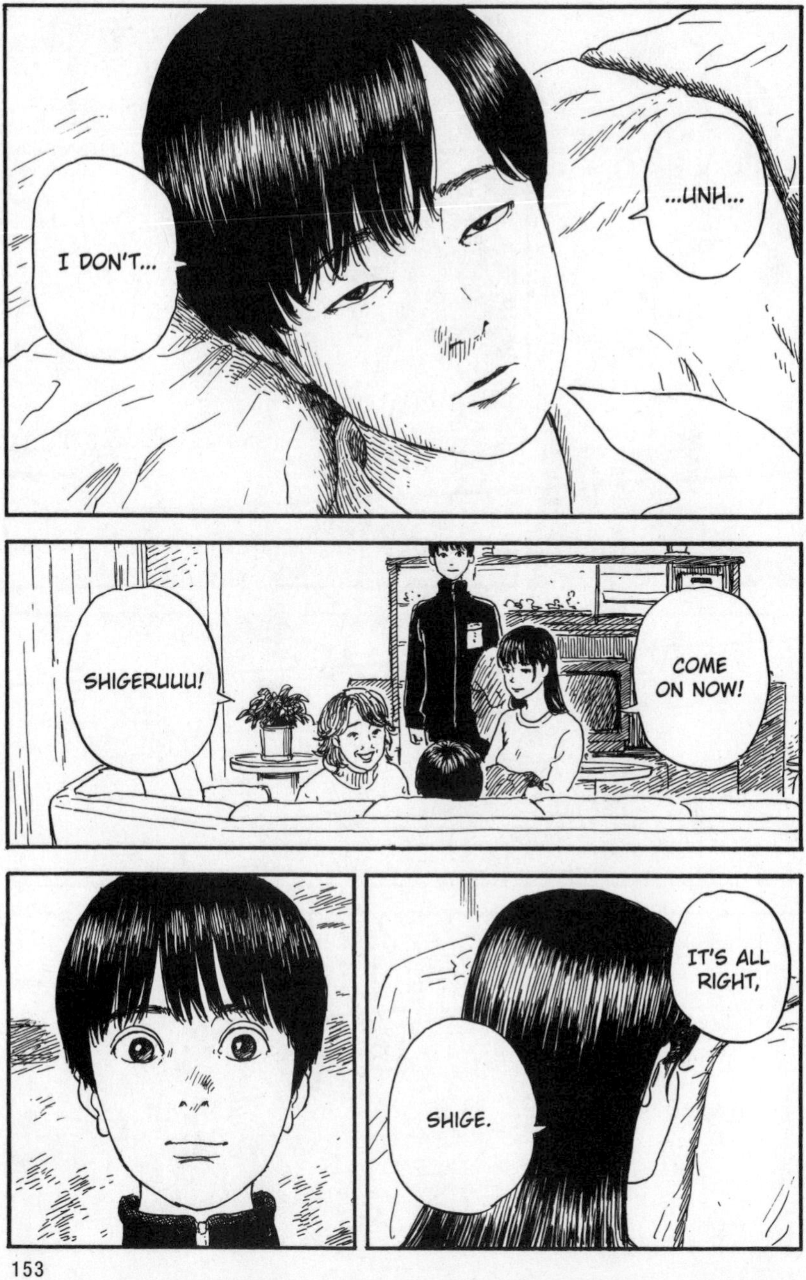
...UNH...
I DON'T...
COME ON NOW!
SHIGERUUU!
IT'S ALL RIGHT,
SHIGE.

I HOPE YOU REMEMBER US SOON.

SEI AND ME.

WENT TO THE HOSPITAL TODAY.

FOR P.T.

...WE

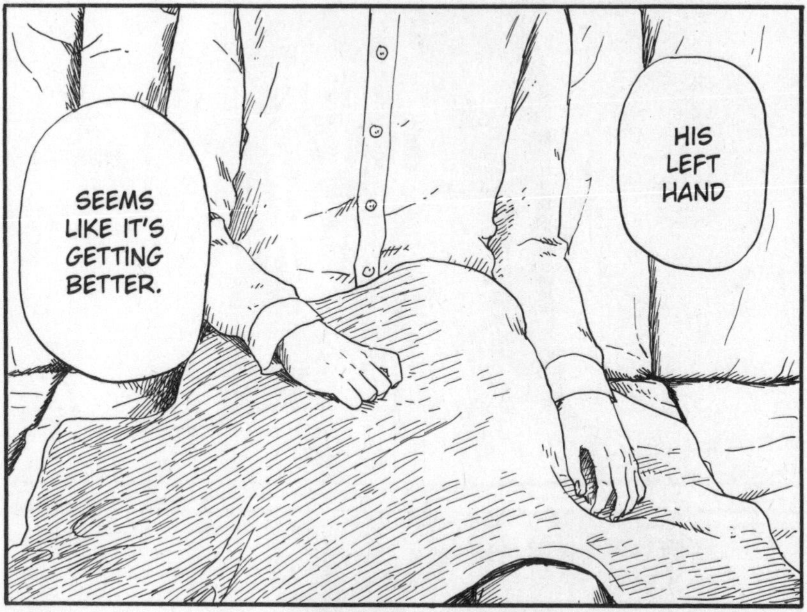
HIS LEFT HAND
SEEMS LIKE IT'S GETTING BETTER.

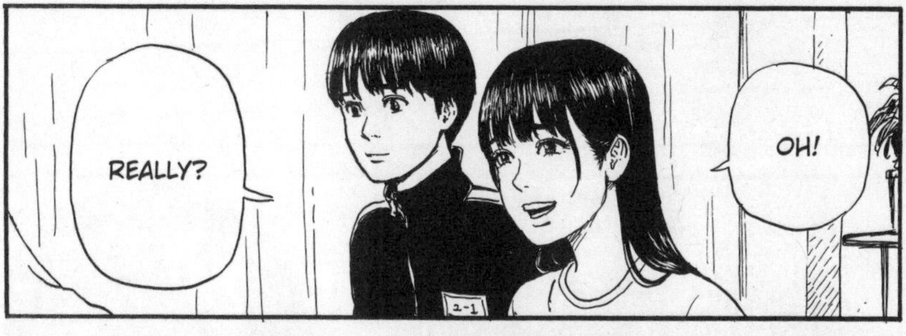
OH!
REALLY?

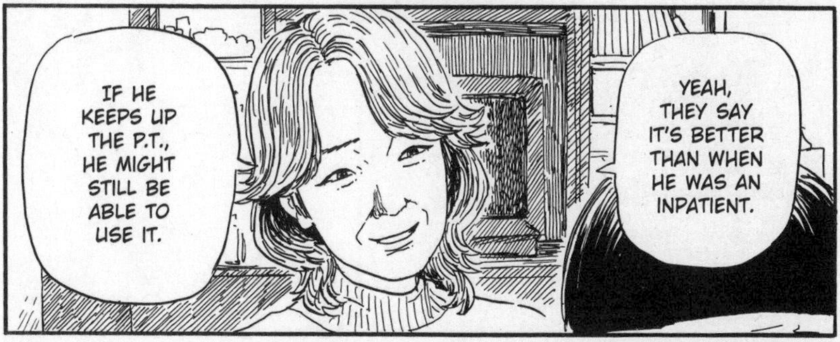
YEAH, THEY SAY IT'S BETTER THAN WHEN HE WAS AN INPATIENT.
IF HE KEEPS UP THE P.T., HE MIGHT STILL BE ABLE TO USE IT.

WOW...
THAT'S SO GREAT, SHIGE...
I'M SO GLAD YOU COULD COME OUT.
CREAK
ぎし
SHIGERU LOOKS SO HAPPY, TOO.

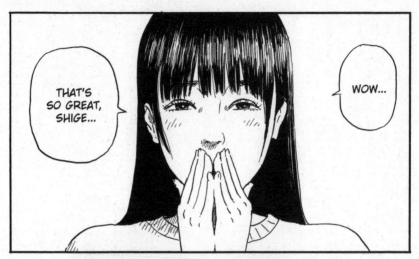

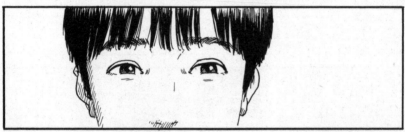

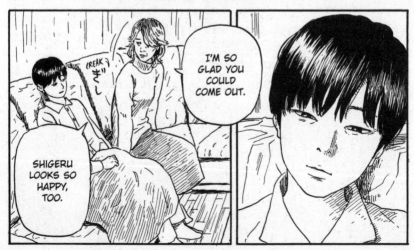

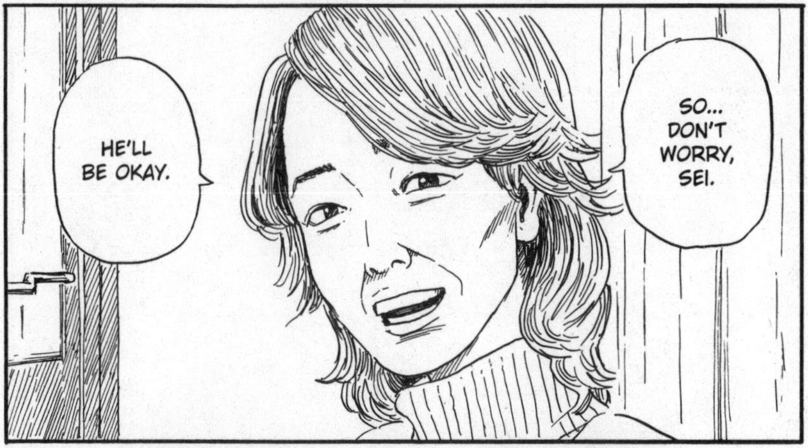
SO... DON'T WORRY, SEI.
HE'LL BE OKAY.

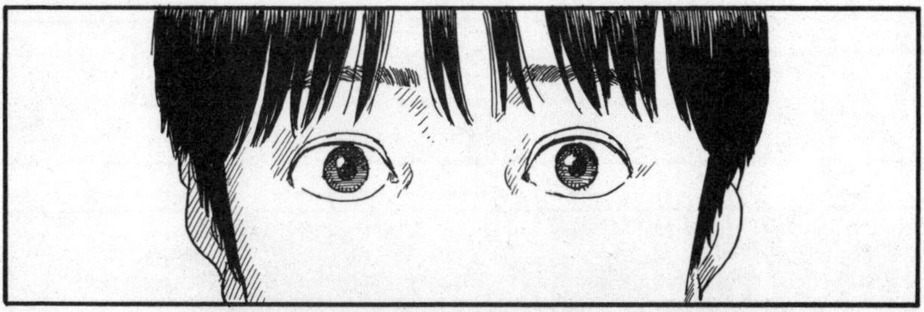

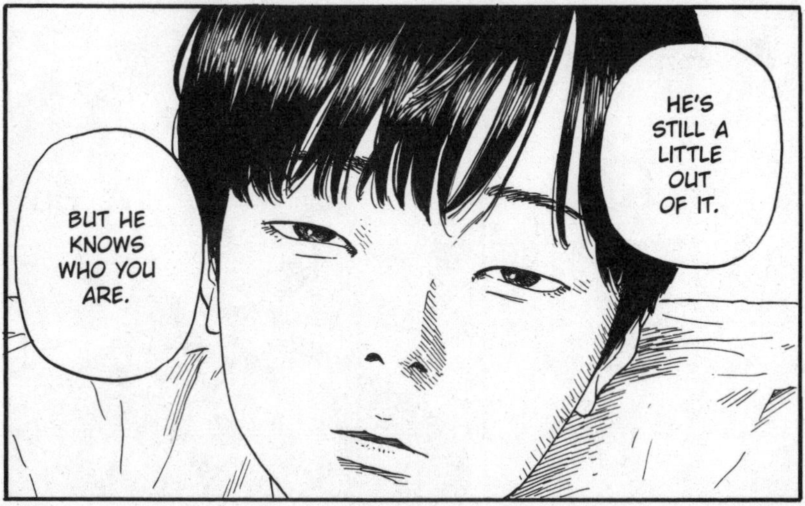
HE'S STILL A LITTLE OUT OF IT.
BUT HE KNOWS WHO YOU ARE.

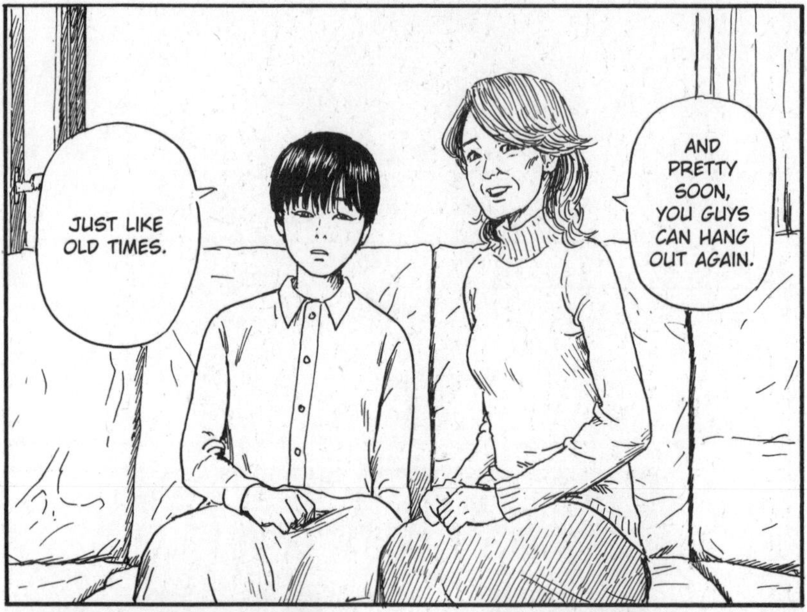
AND PRETTY SOON, YOU GUYS CAN HANG OUT AGAIN.
JUST LIKE OLD TIMES.
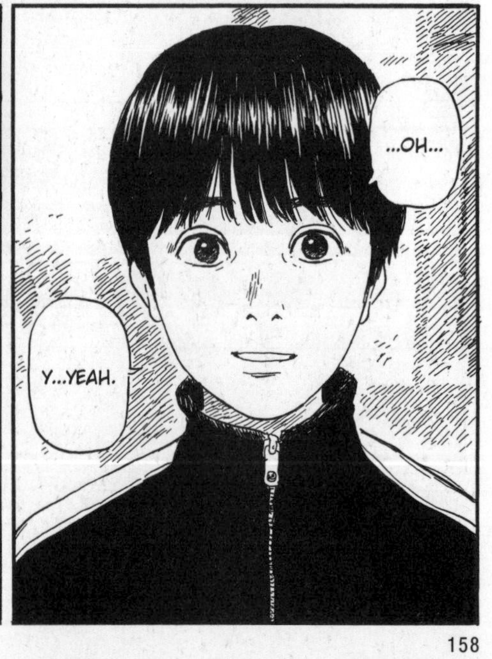
...OH...
Y...YEAH.
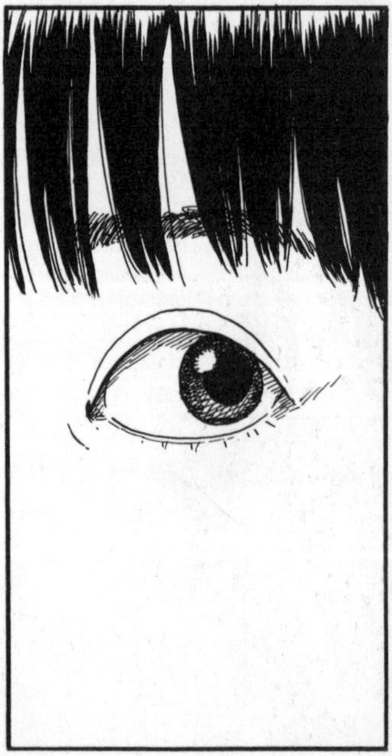

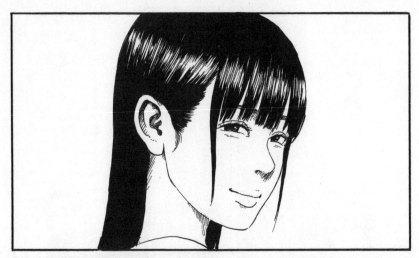

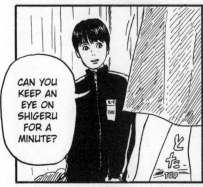

OH, LOOK AT THE TIME.
I'D BETTER GET DINNER STARTED.
CAN YOU KEEP AN EYE ON SHIGERU FOR A MINUTE?
とた
TUP
HERE.

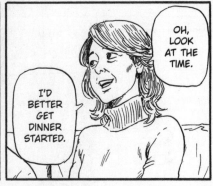

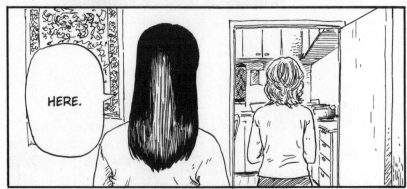

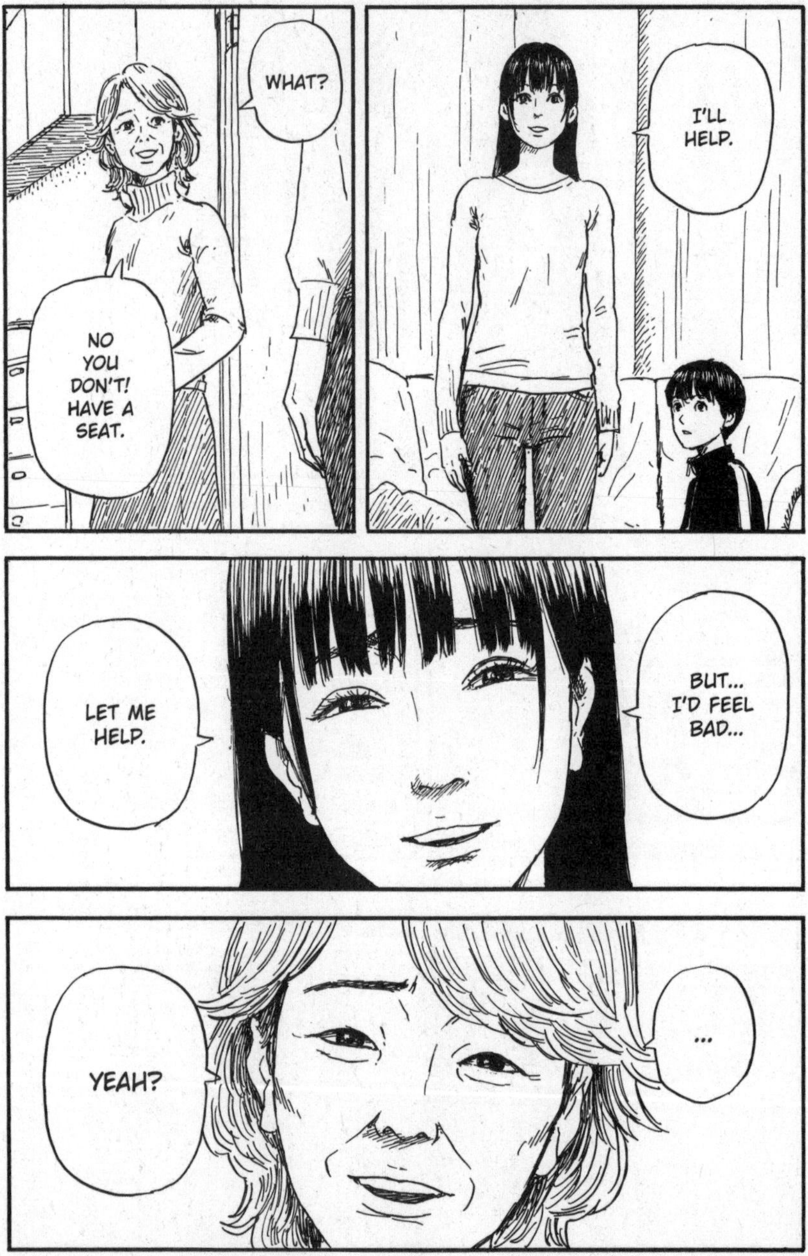
I'LL HELP.
WHAT?
NO YOU DON'T! HAVE A SEAT.
BUT... I'D FEEL BAD...
LET ME HELP.
...
YEAH?

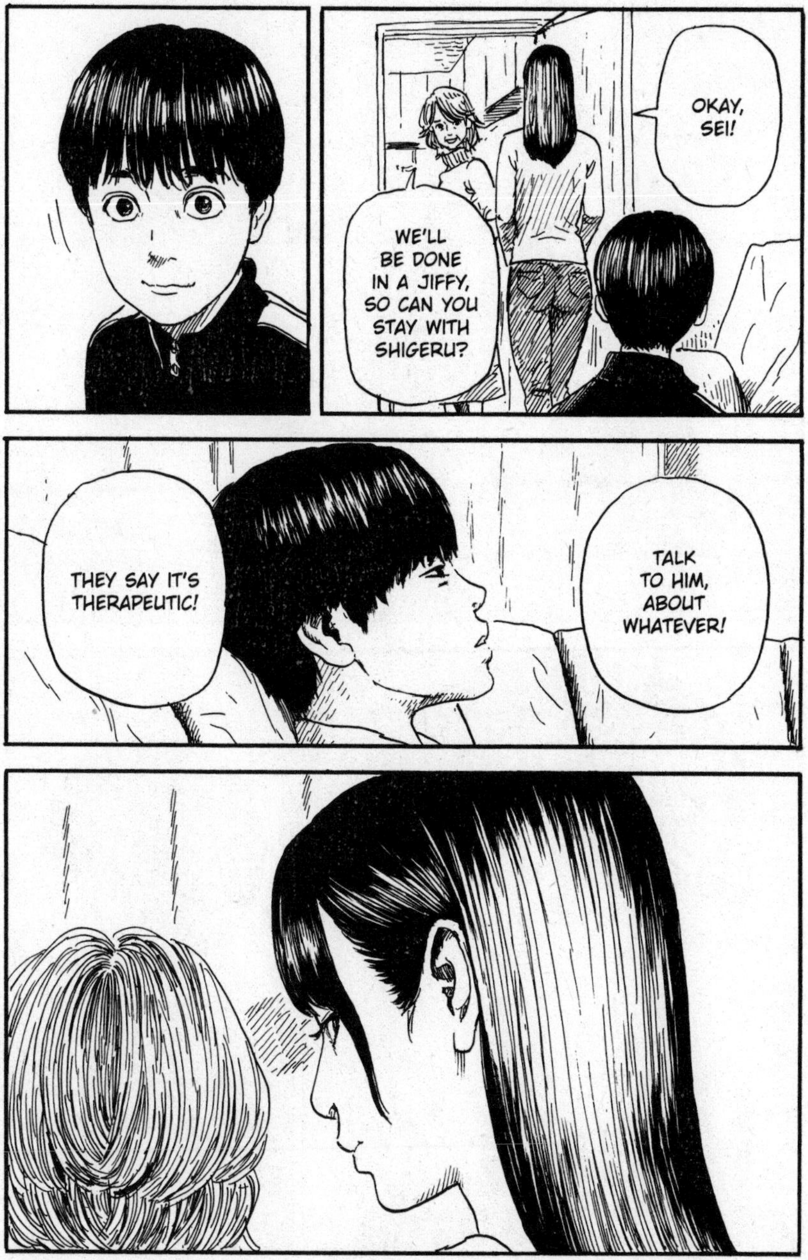
OKAY, SEI!
WE'LL BE DONE IN A JIFFY, SO CAN YOU STAY WITH SHIGERU?
TALK TO HIM, ABOUT WHATEVER!
THEY SAY IT'S THERAPEUTIC!

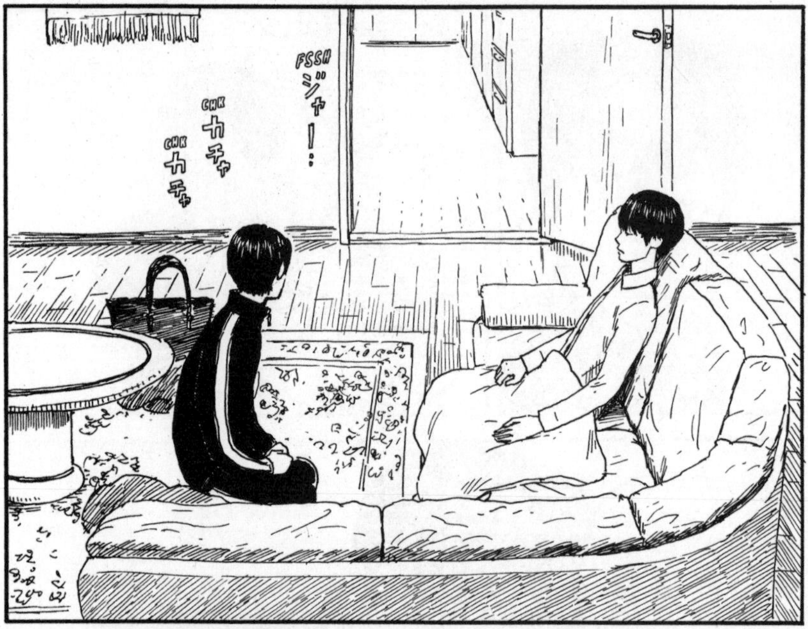
FSSH
ジャー!!
CHK
カチャ
CHK
カチャ

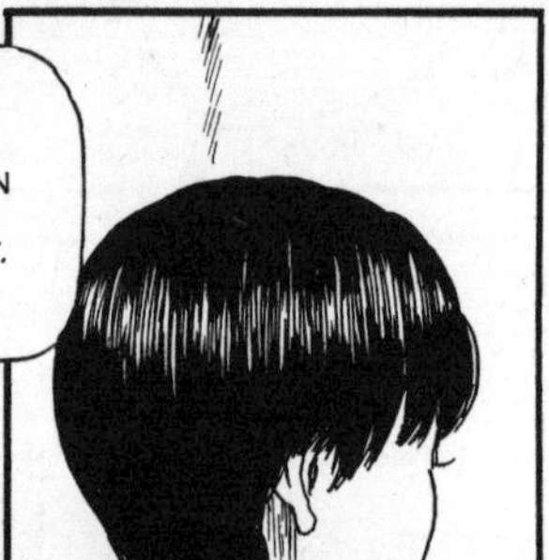
OH, I CAN DO THAT.
2-1
OSABE

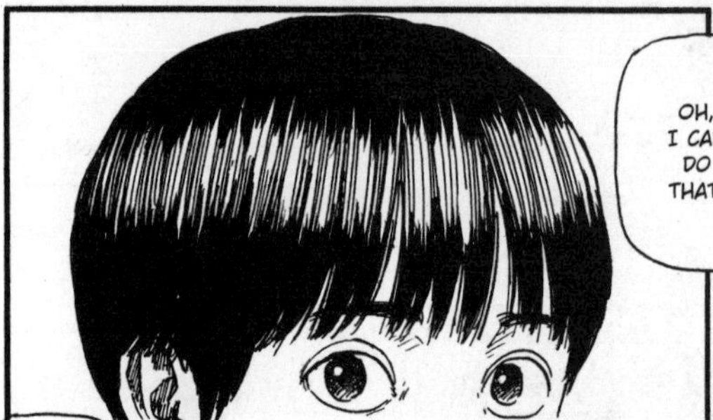
DON'T BOTHER! JUST TAKE THIS.

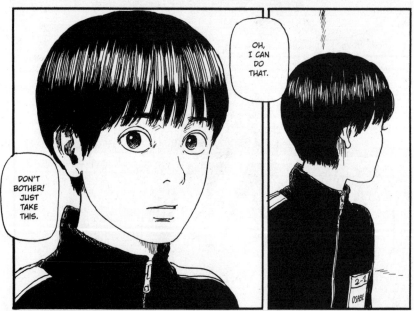

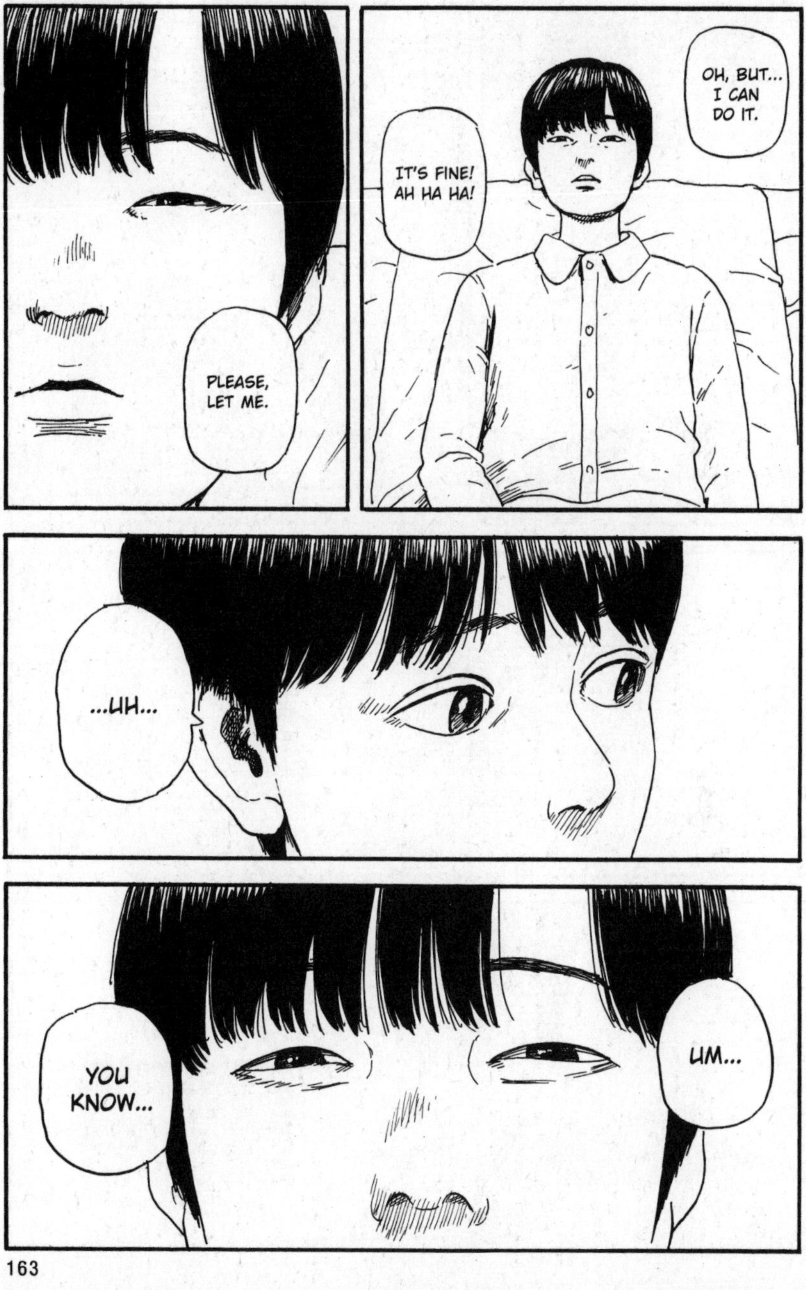
OH, BUT... I CAN DO IT.
IT'S FINE! AH HA HA!
PLEASE, LET ME.
...UH...
UM...
YOU KNOW...

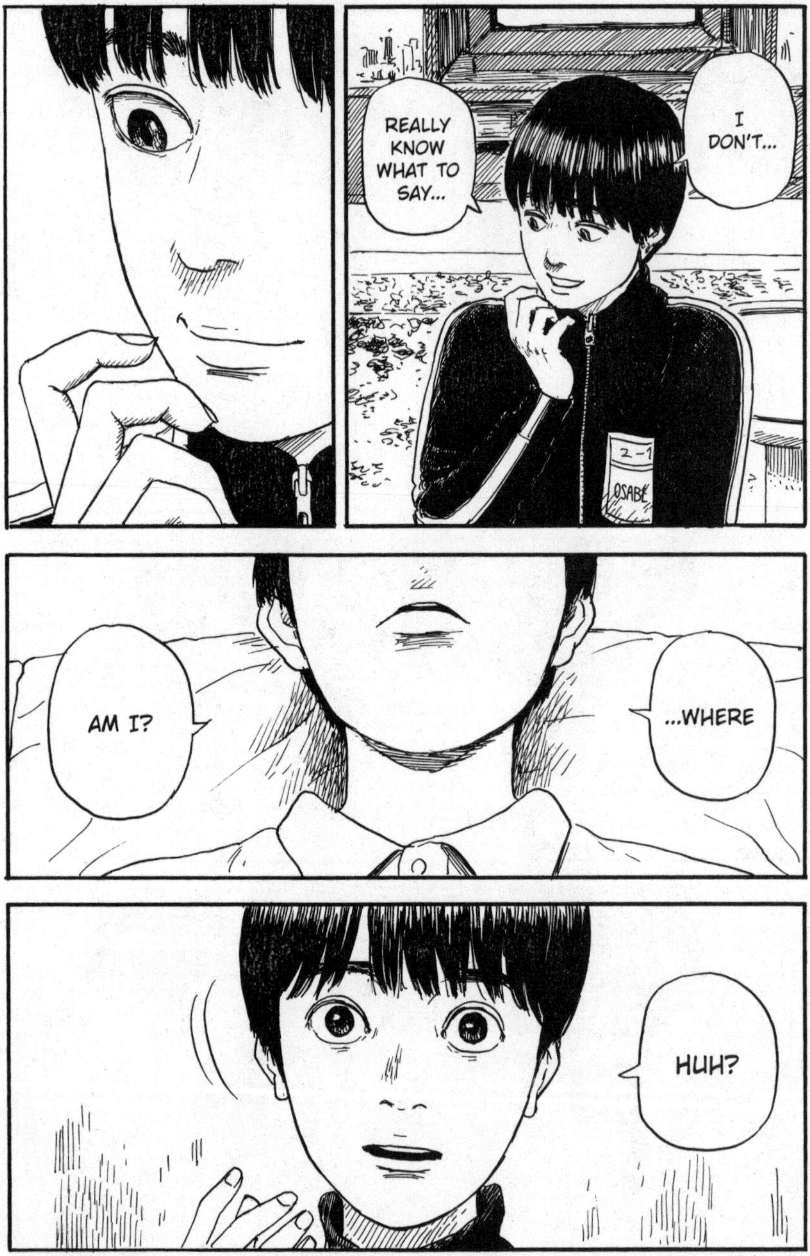
I DON'T...
REALLY KNOW WHAT TO SAY...
2-1
OSABE
...WHERE
AM I?
HUH?

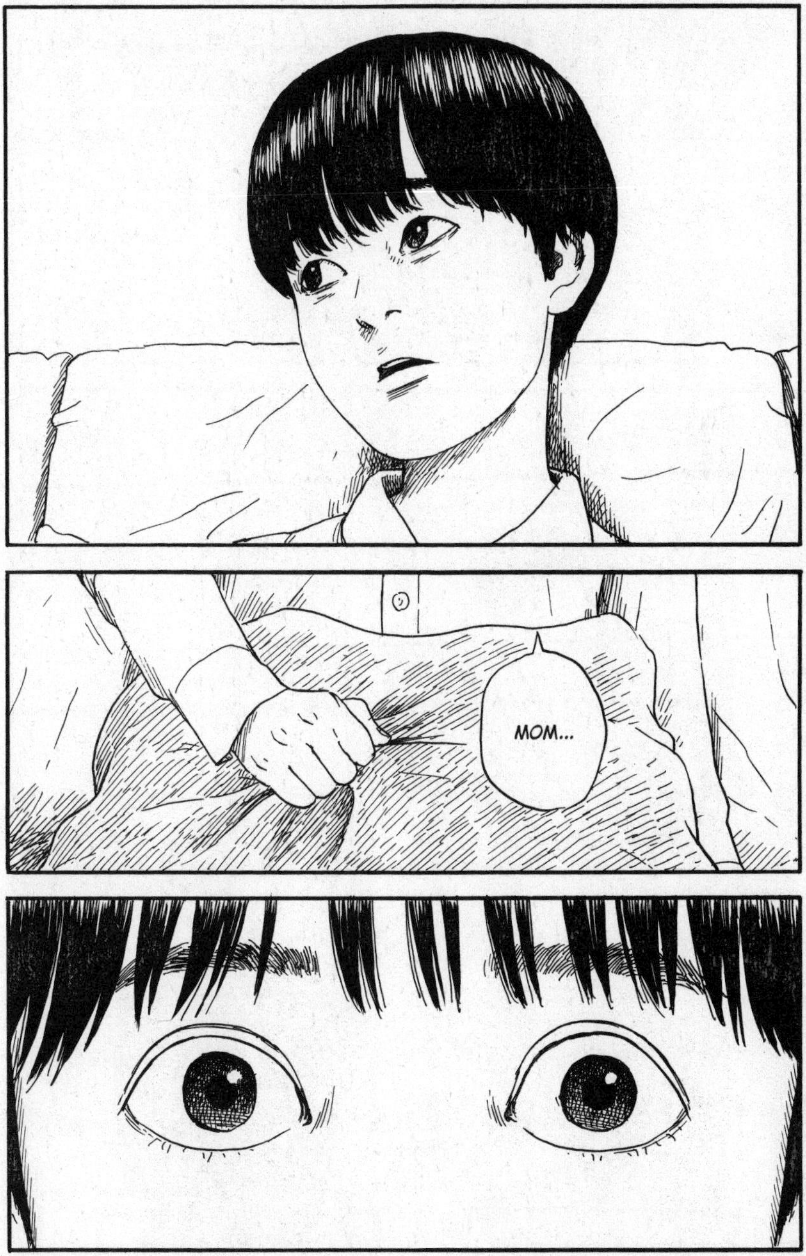
MOM...

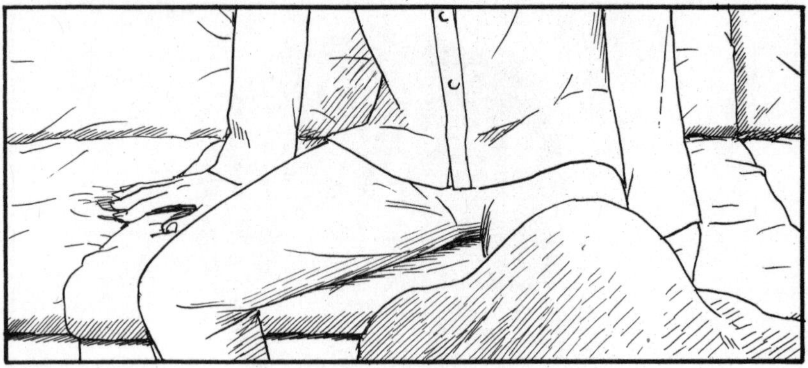

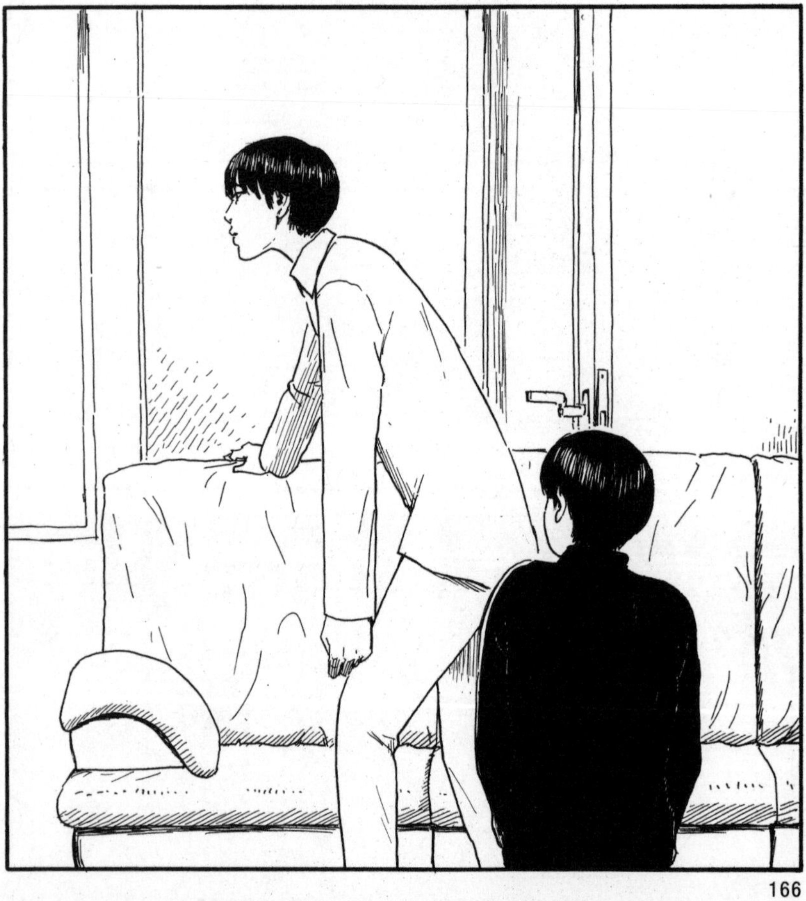

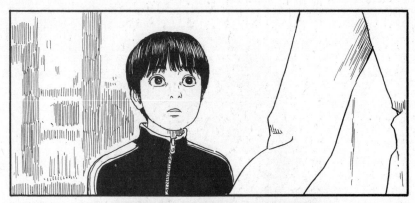

WHAT IS IT?

SHIGE...

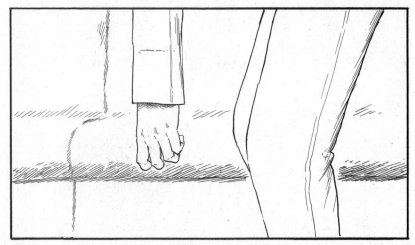

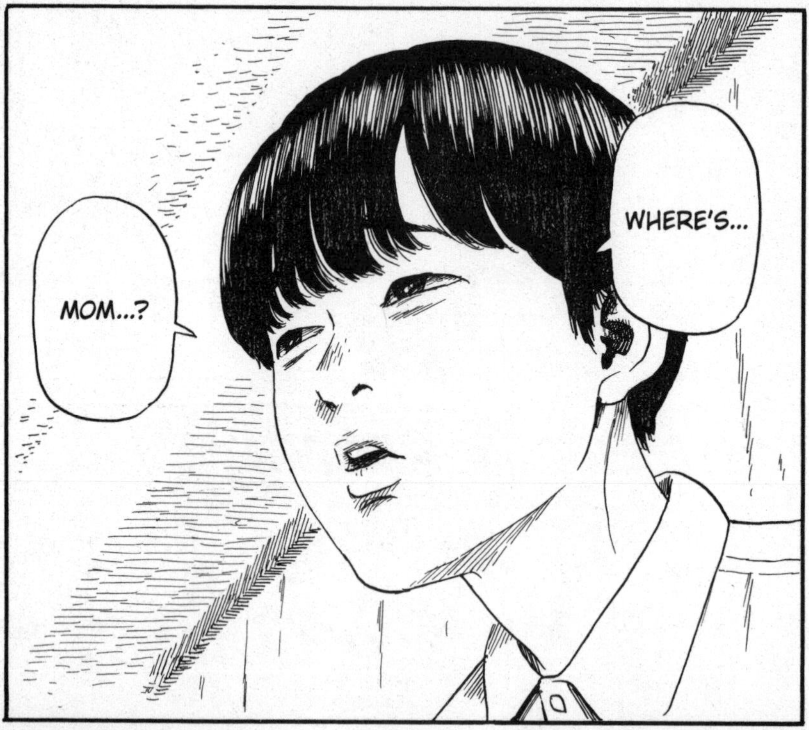
WHERE'S...
MOM...?
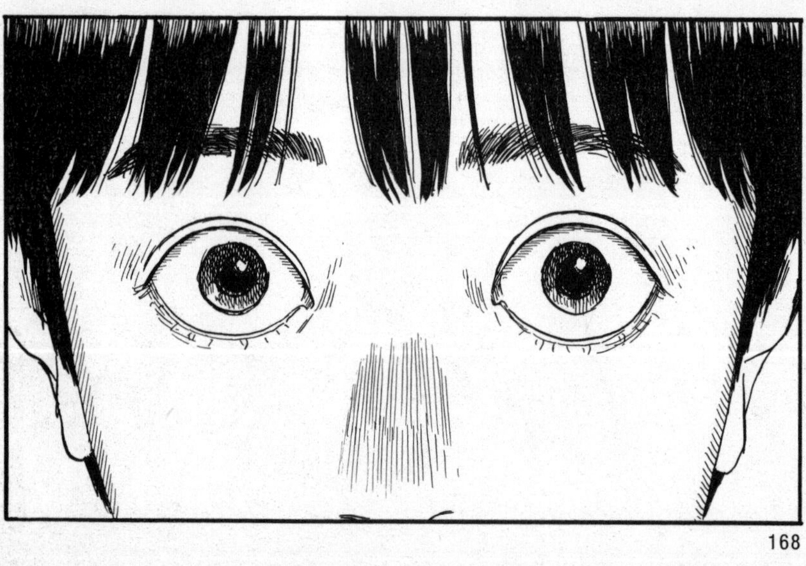

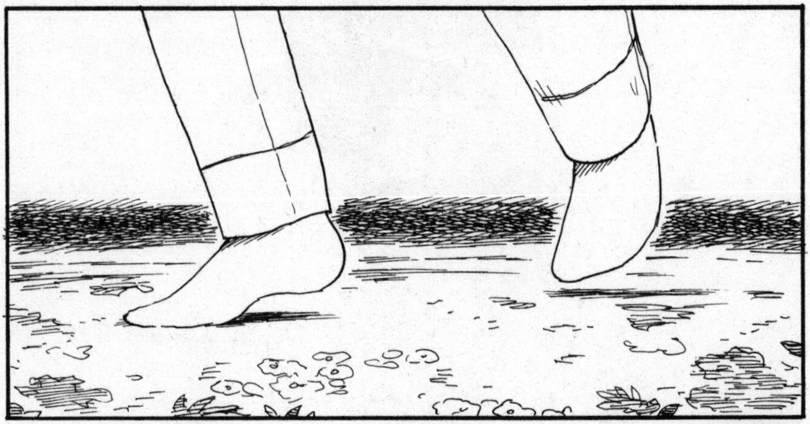
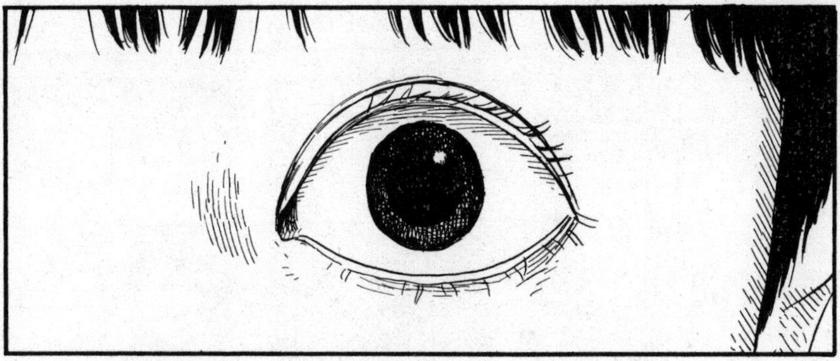
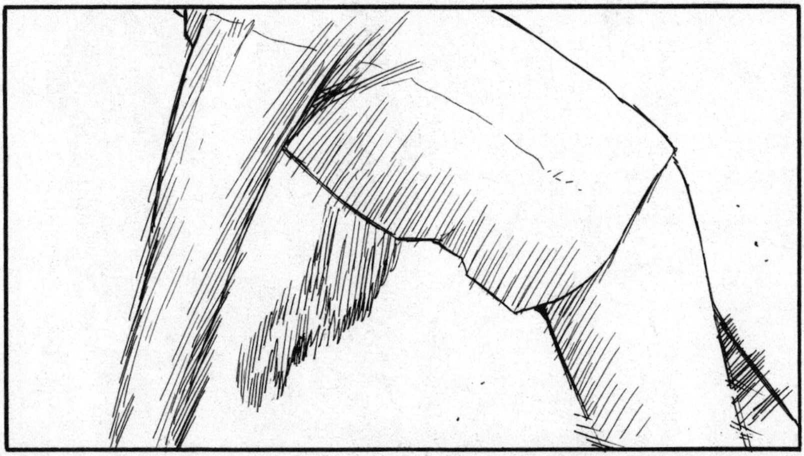

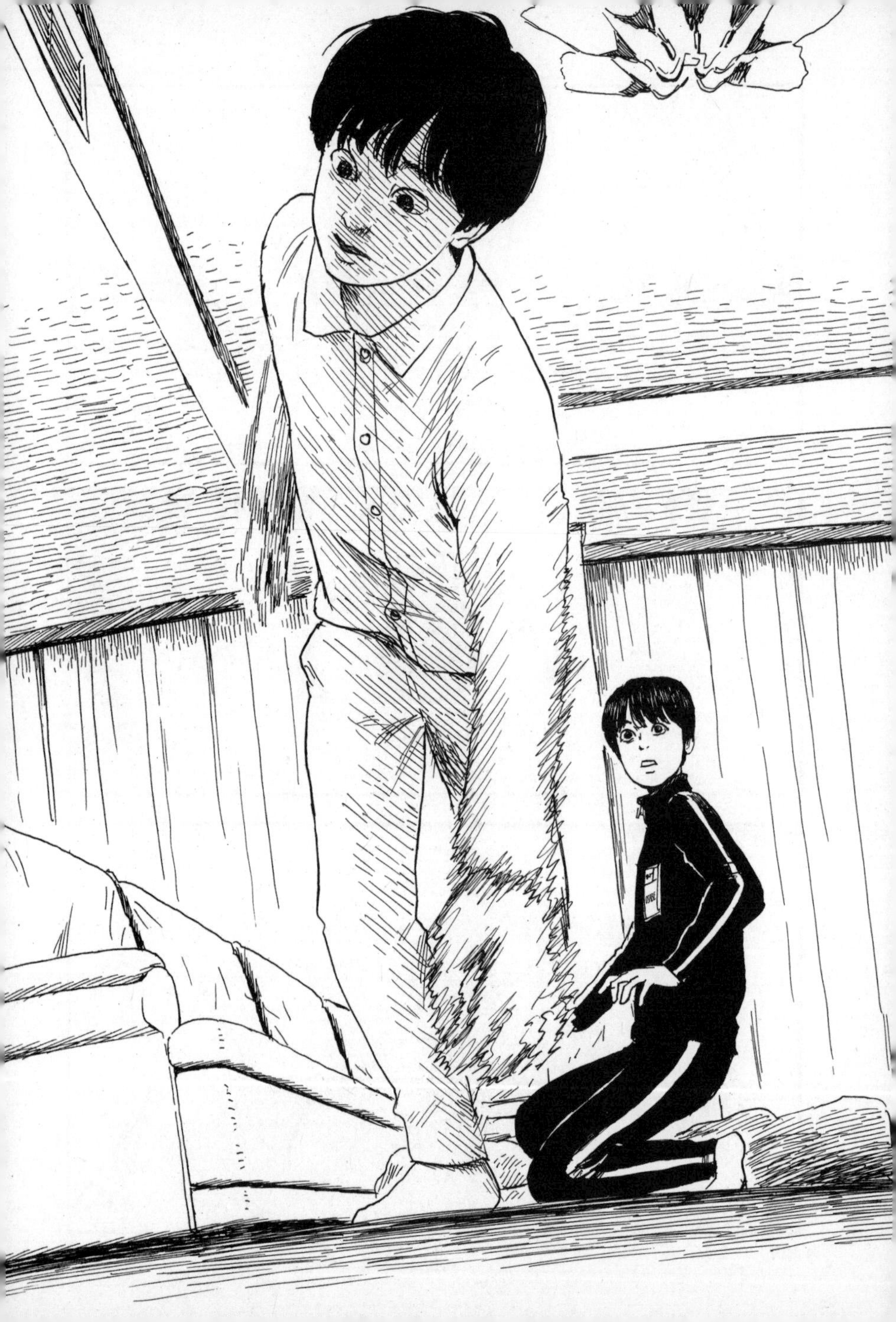

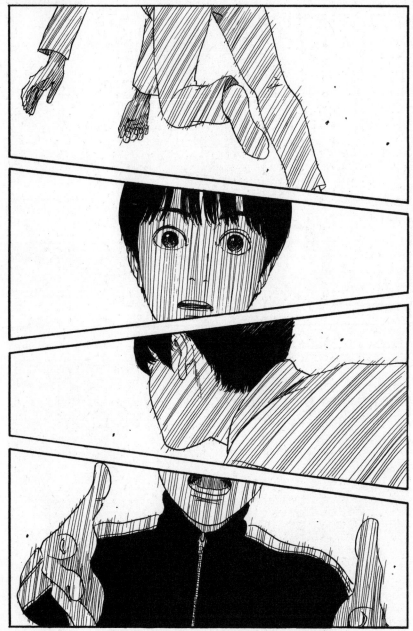

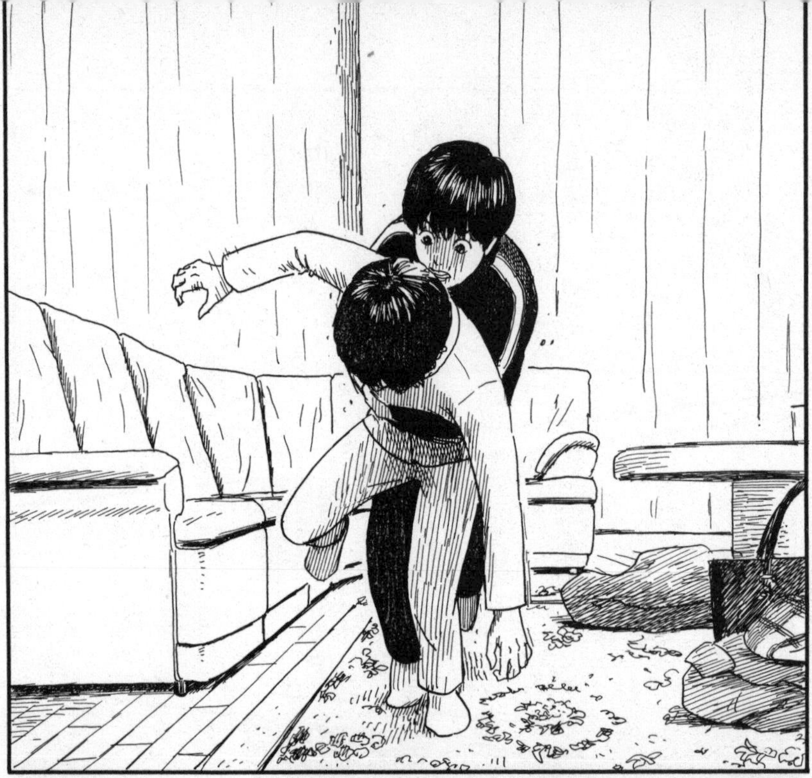
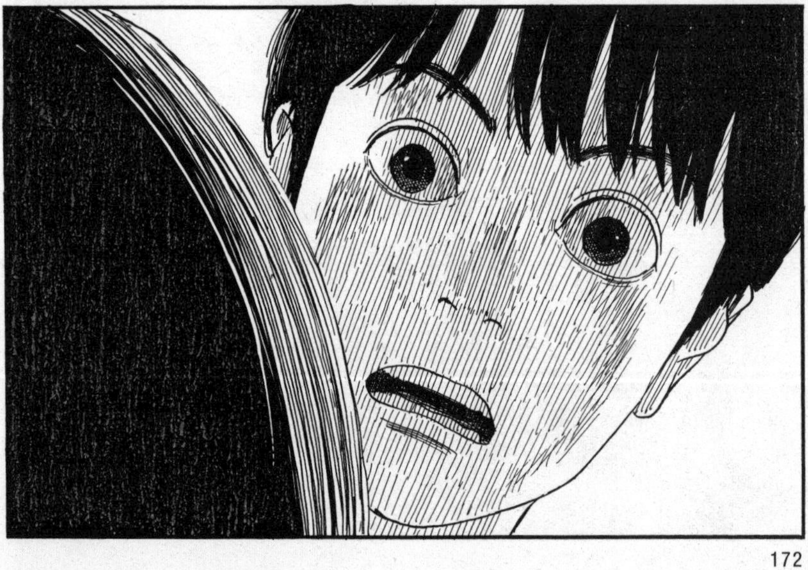

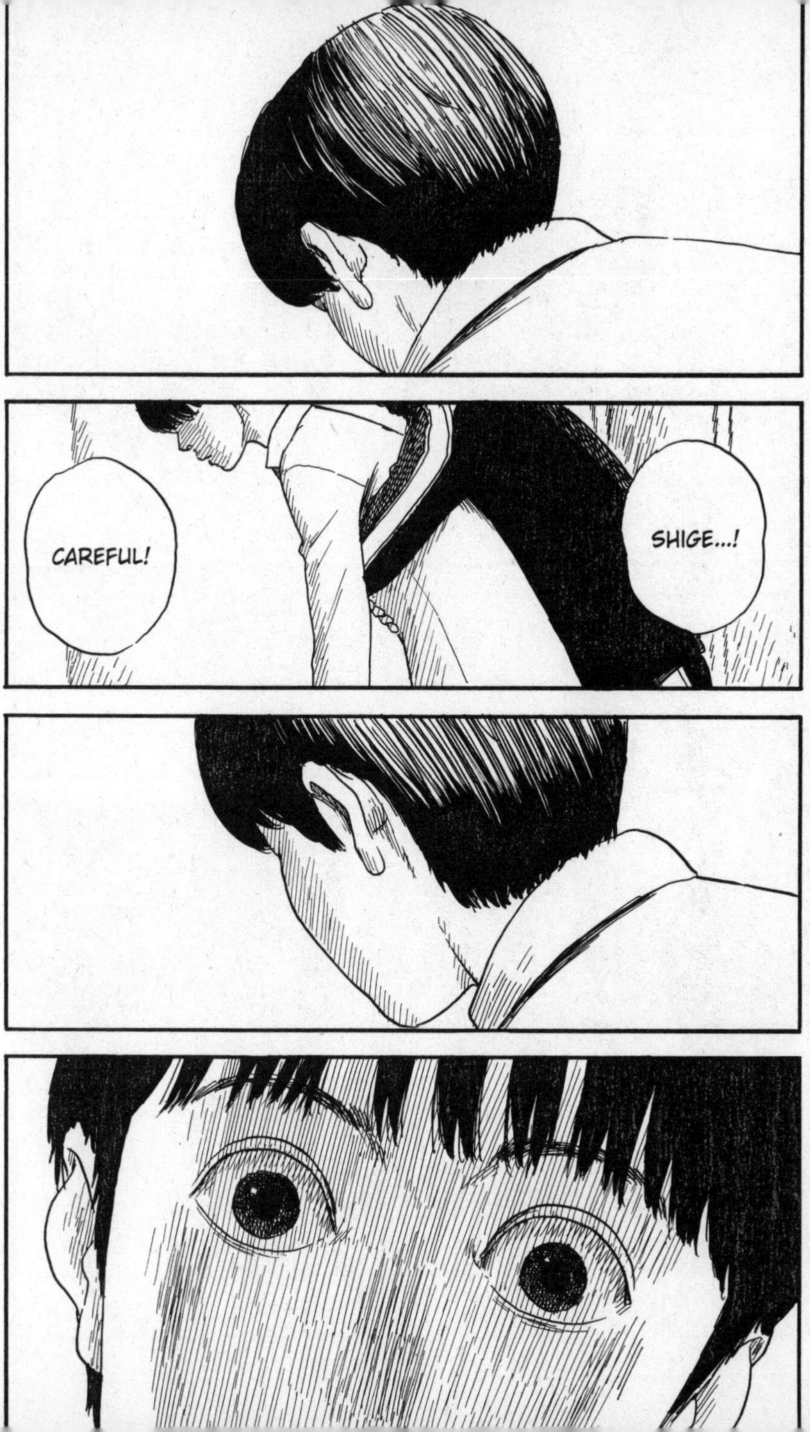
SHIGE...!
CAREFUL!

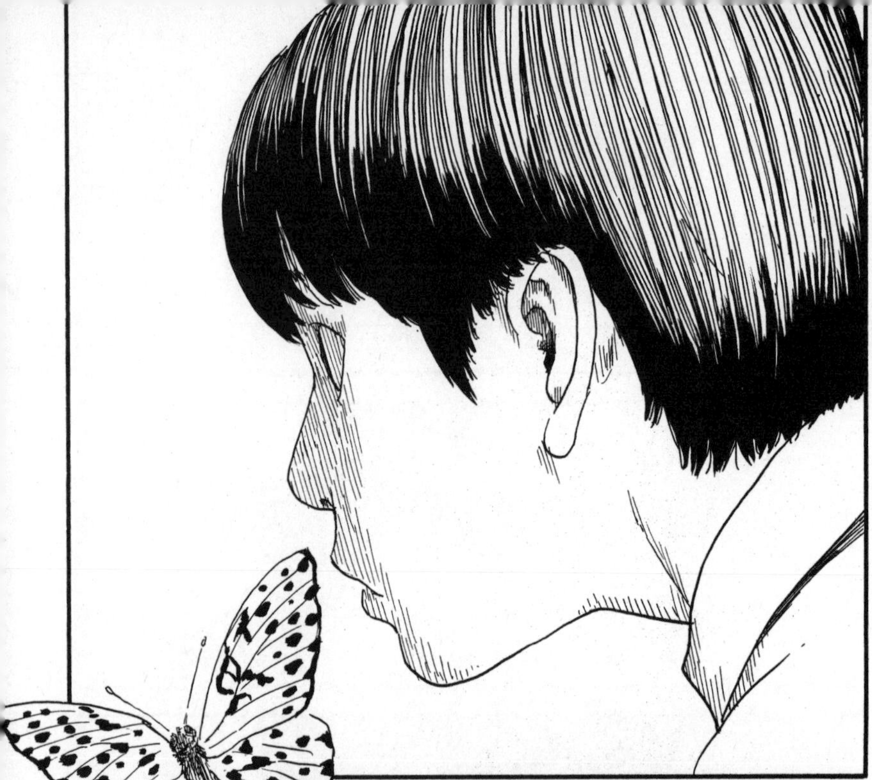
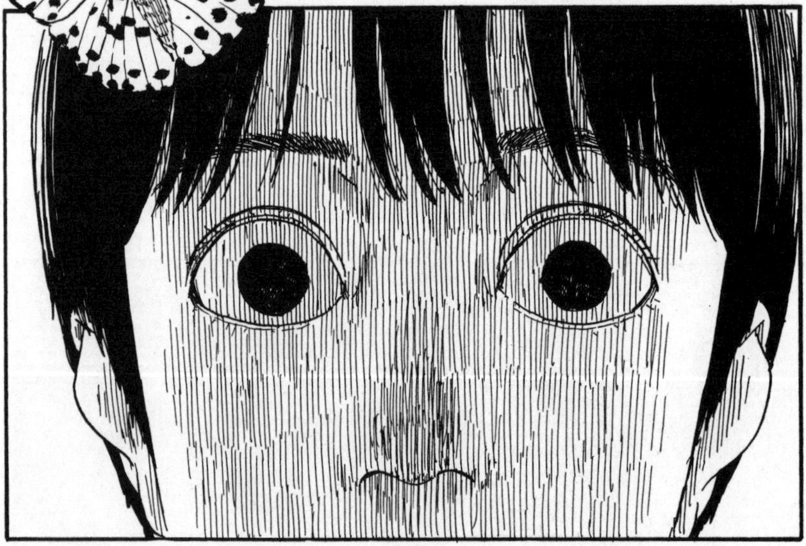

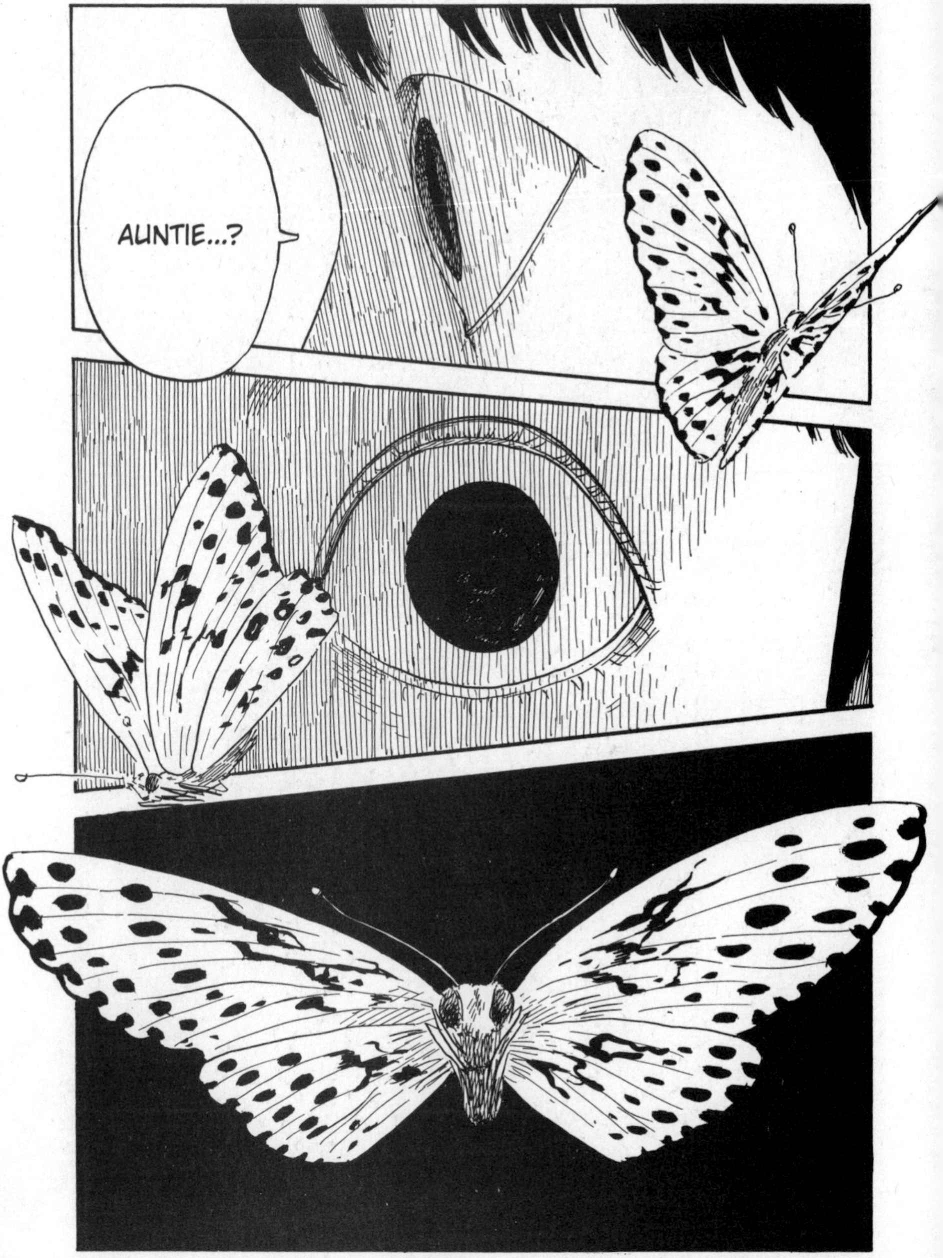
AUNTIE...?

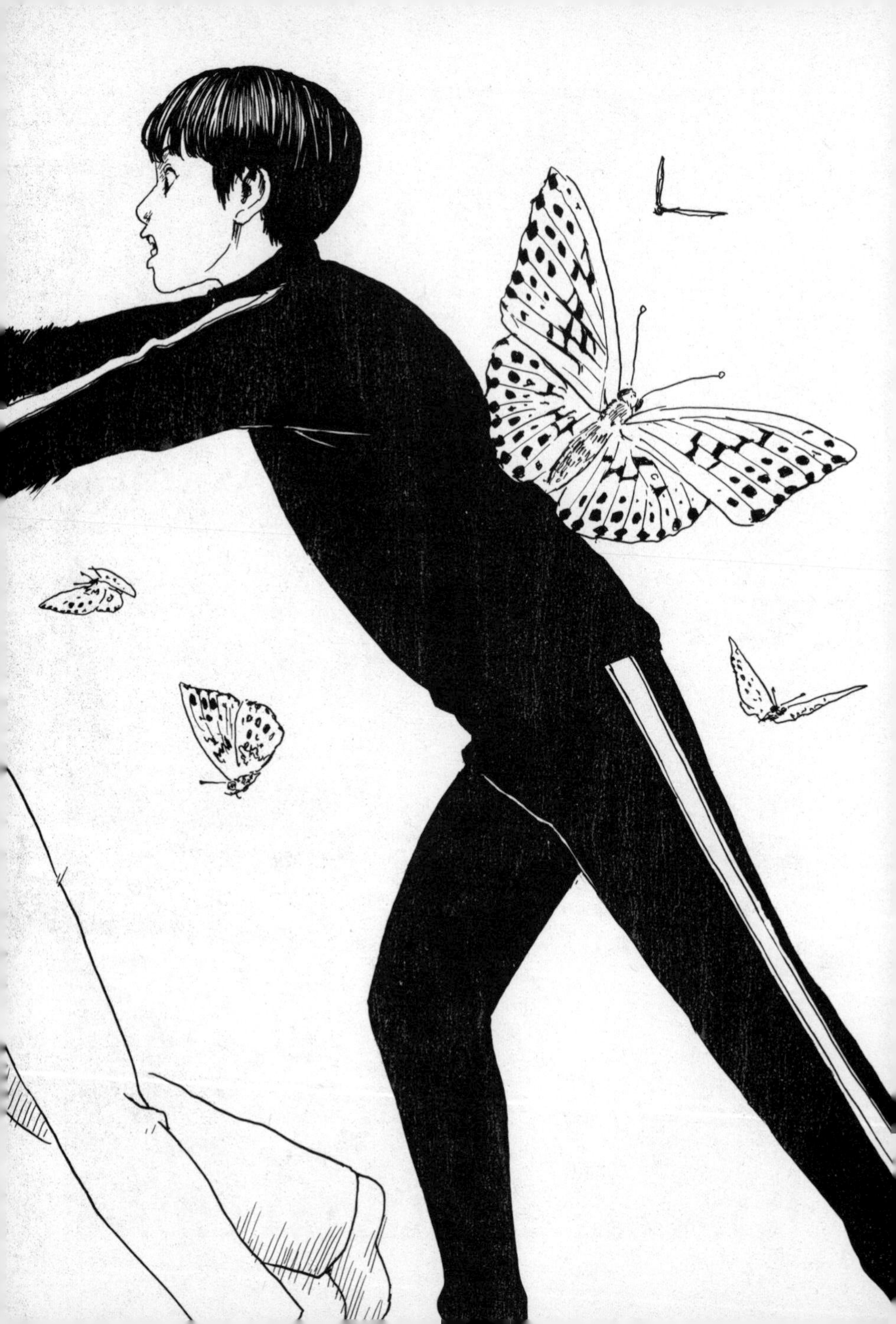

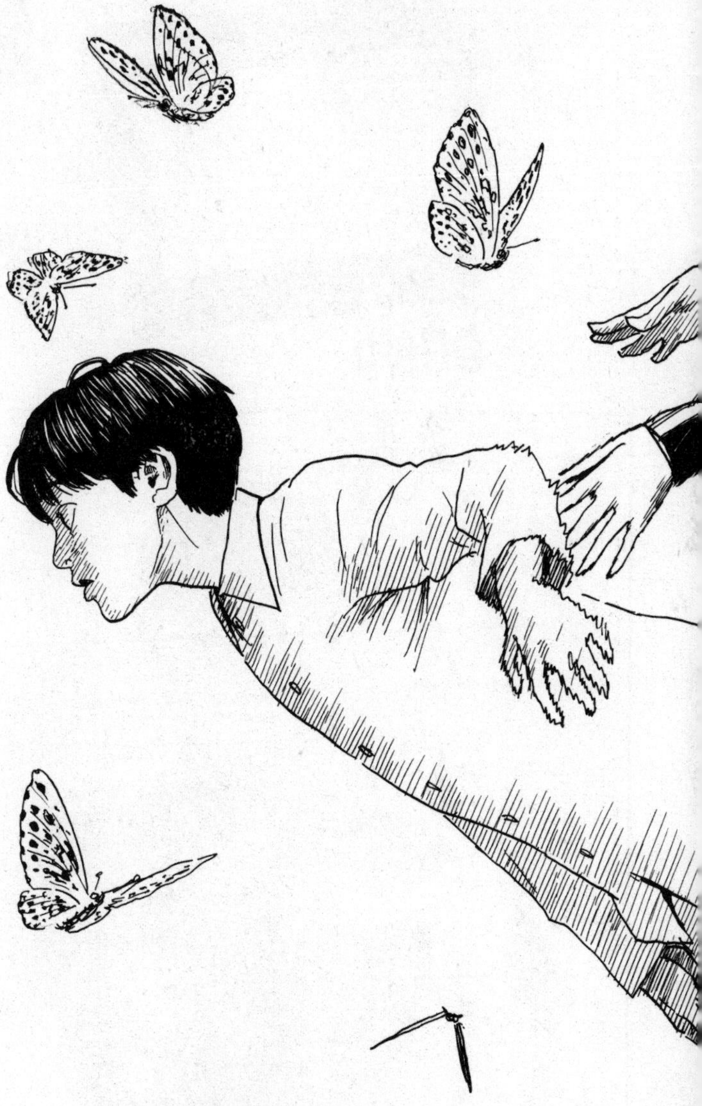

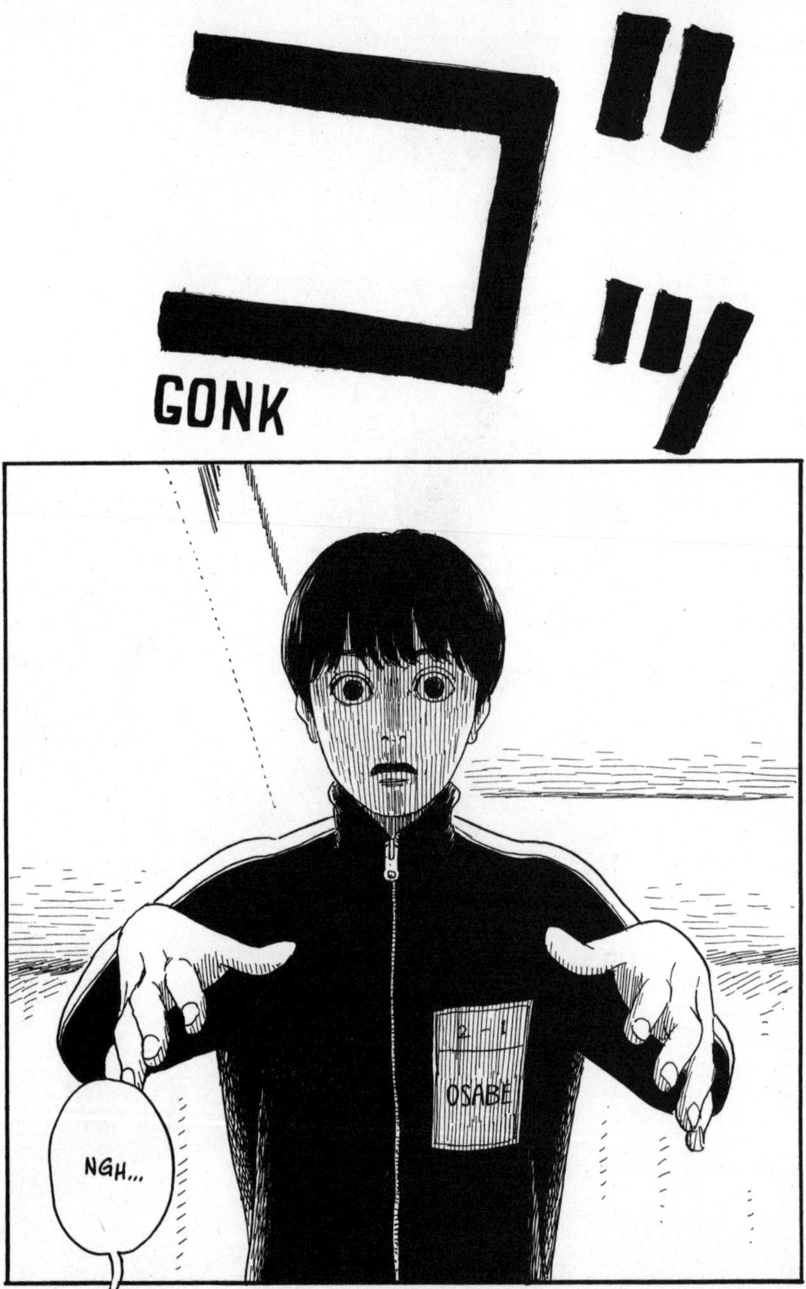
ゴッ
GONK
2-1
OSABE
NGH...

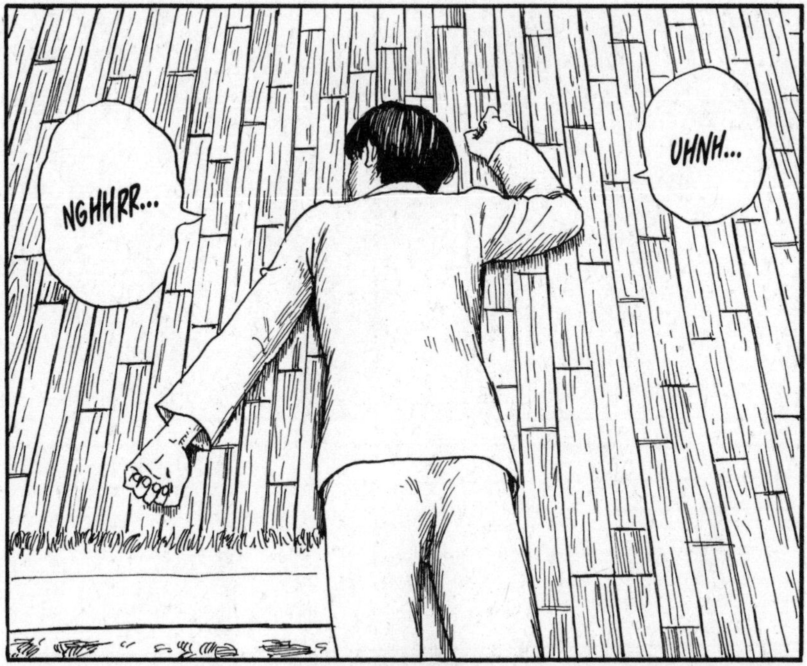
UHNH...
NGHHRR...
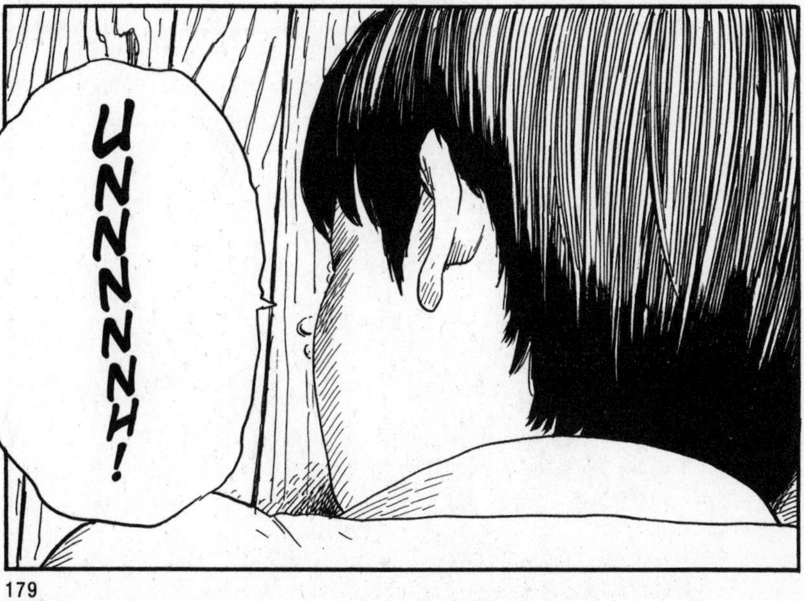
UNNNNH!

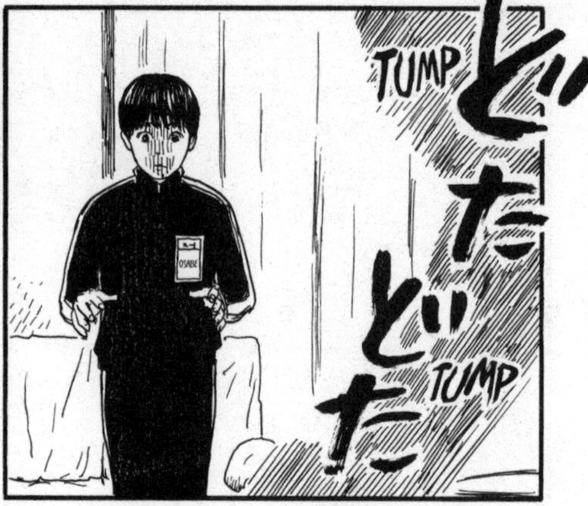
TUMP
どたどた
TUMP
OSABE
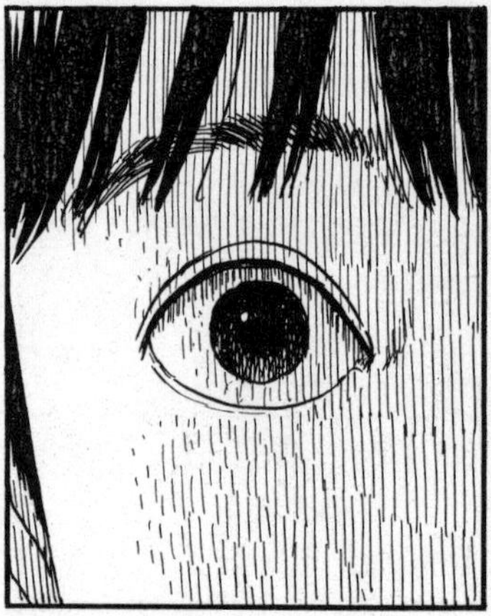
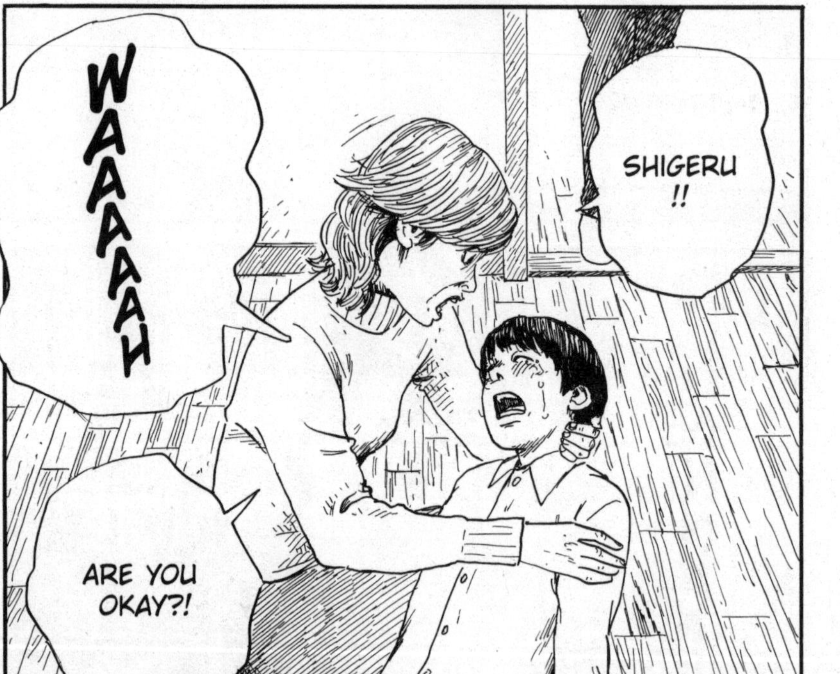
SHIGERU !!
WAAAAAH
ARE YOU OKAY?!

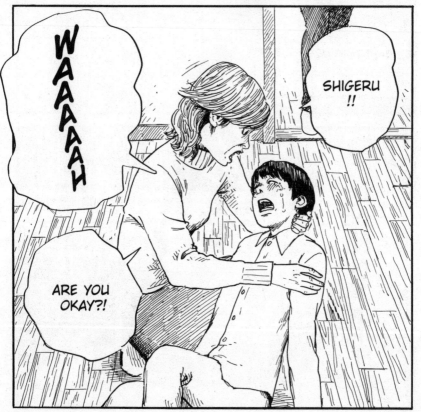

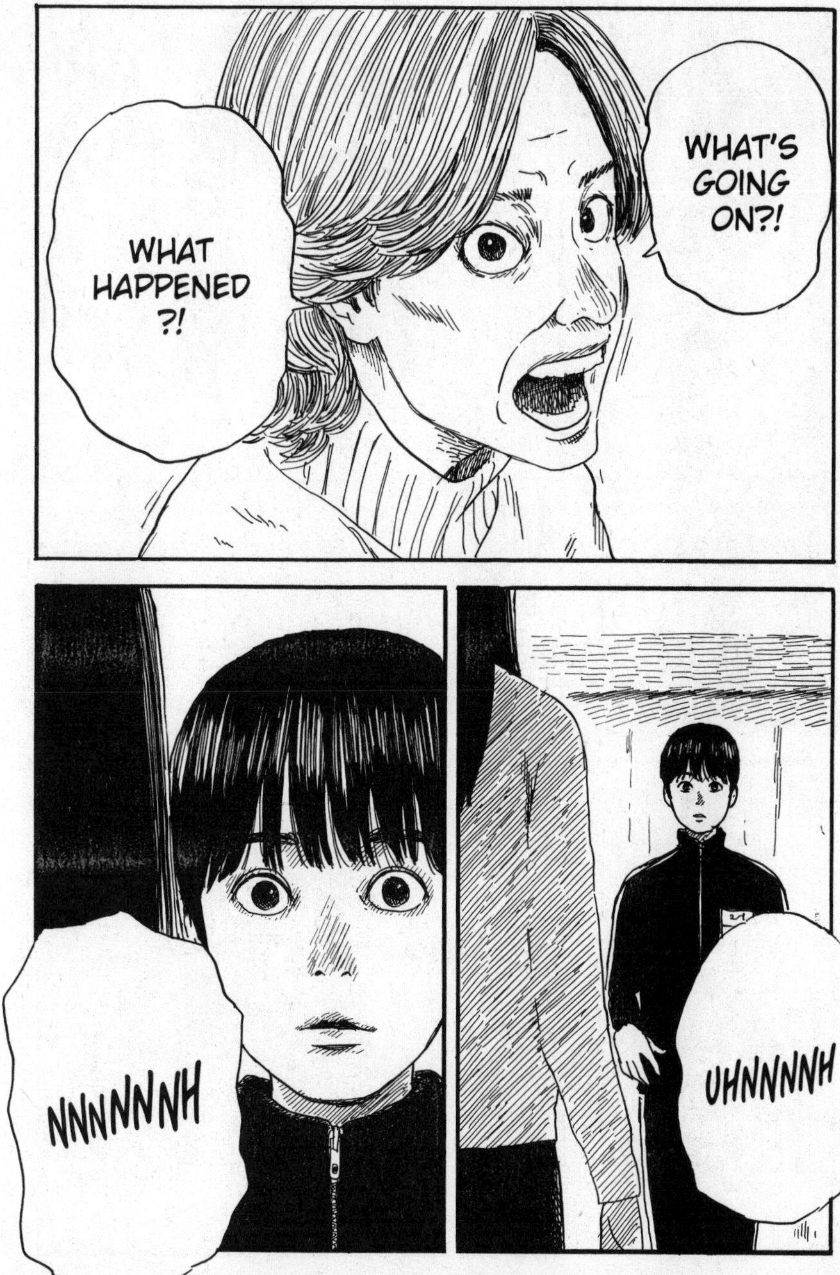
WHAT'S GOING ON?!
WHAT HAPPENED ?!
UHNNNNH
NNNNNNH

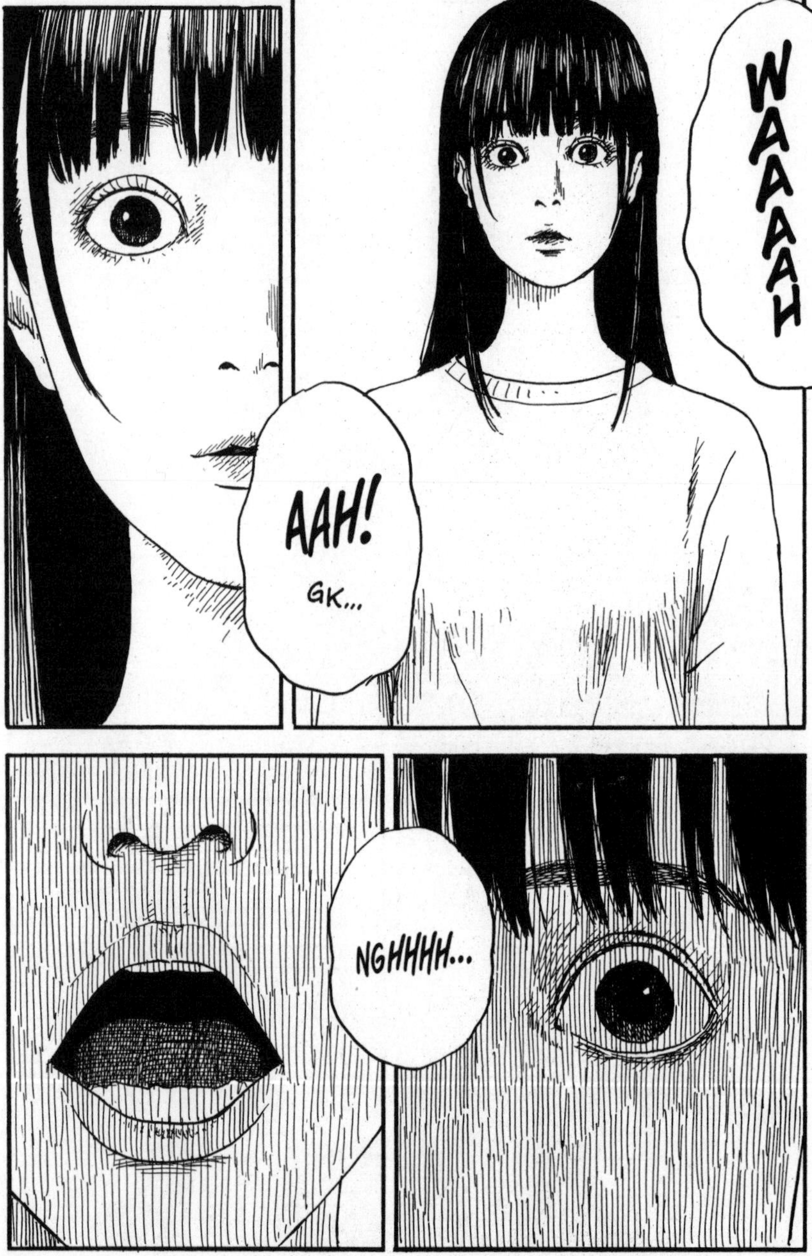
WAAAAH
AAH!
GK...
NGHHHH...

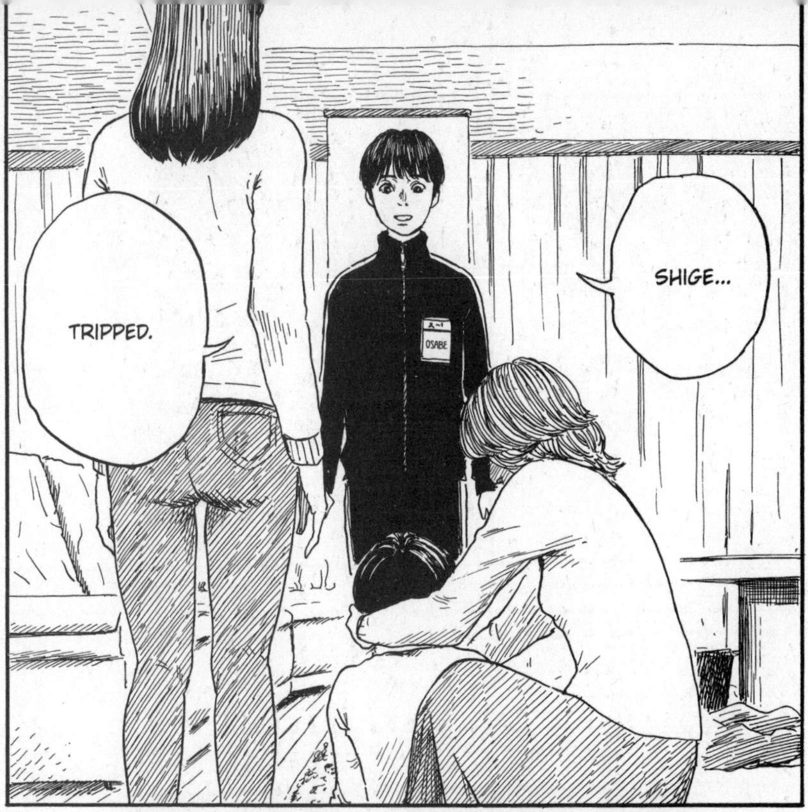
SHIGE...
OSABE
TRIPPED.
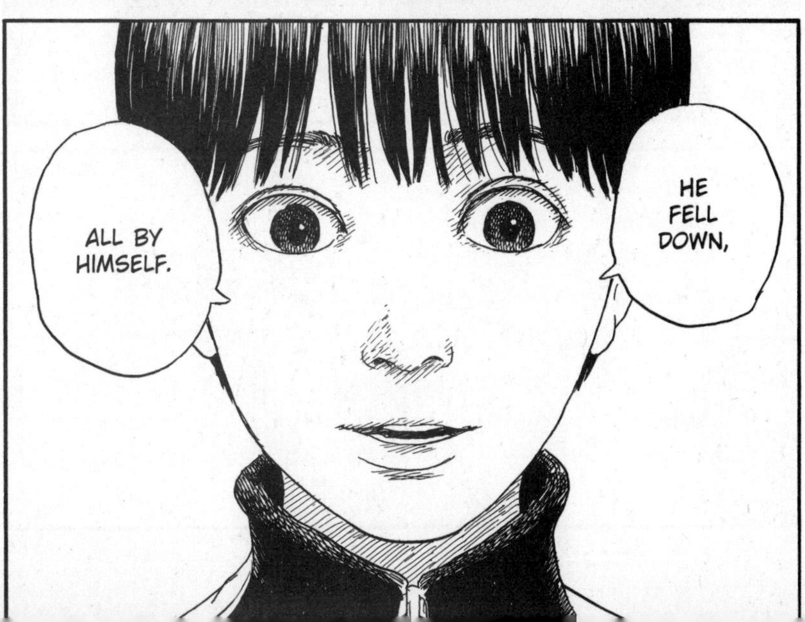
HE FELL DOWN,
ALL BY HIMSELF.

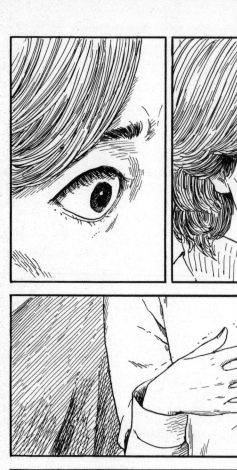

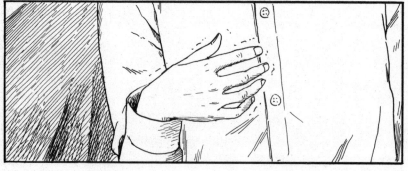
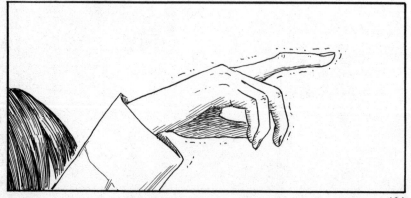

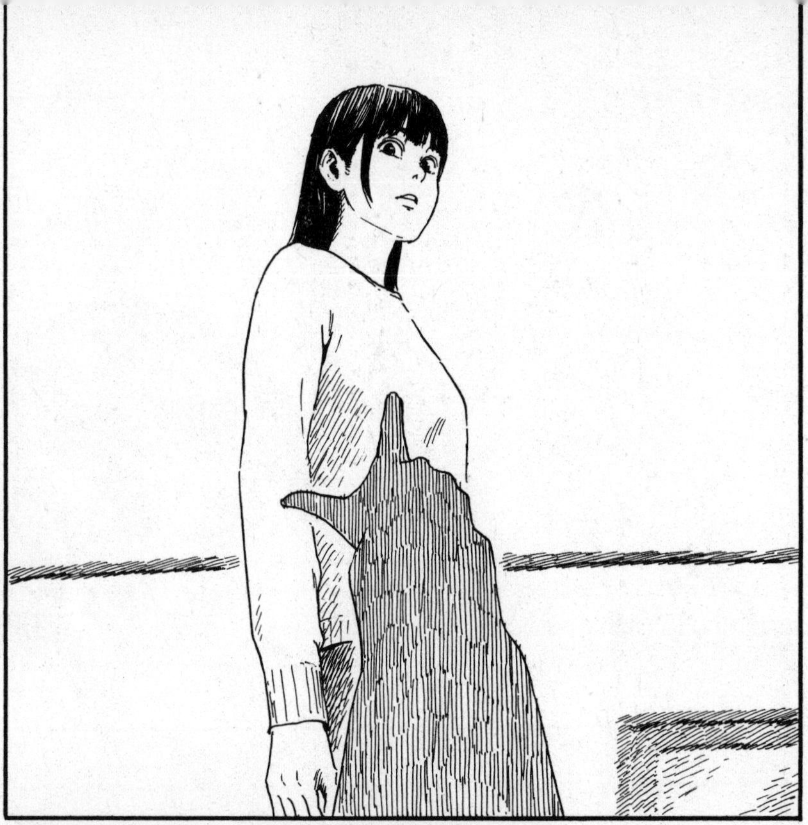
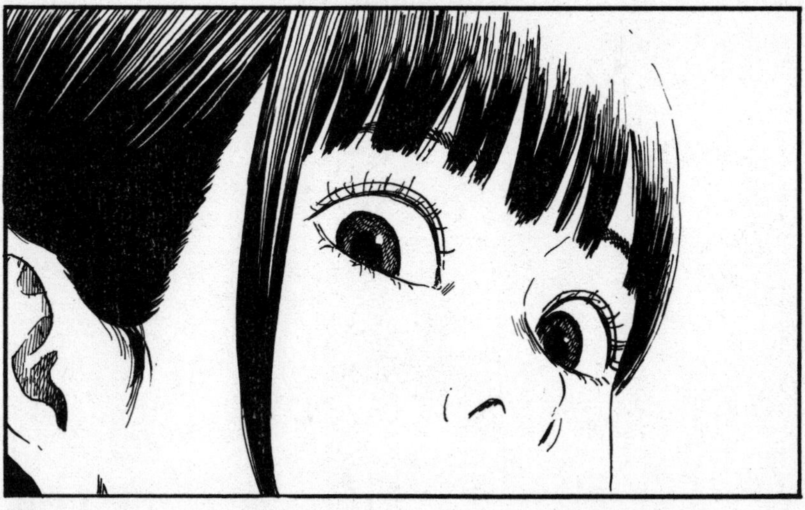

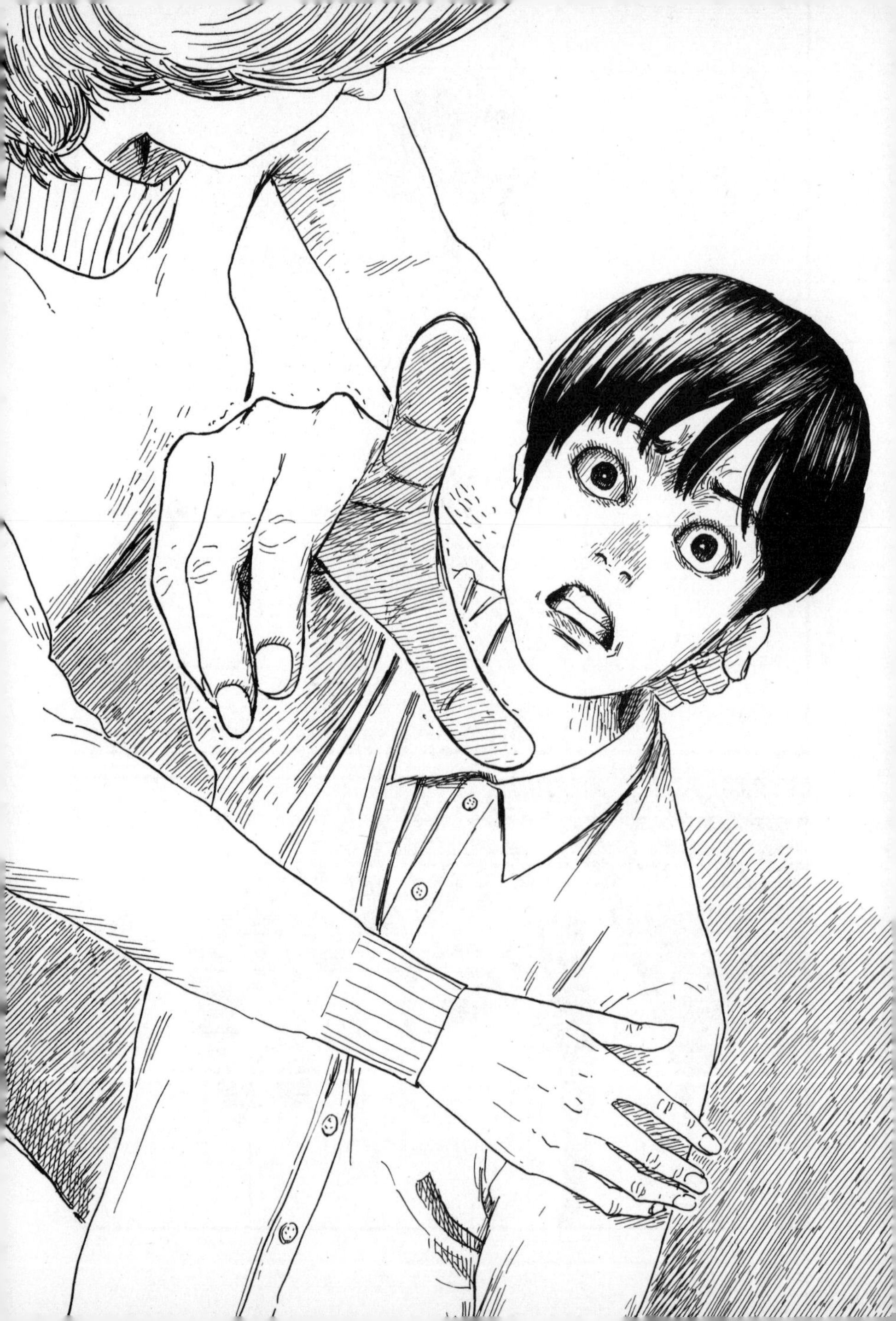

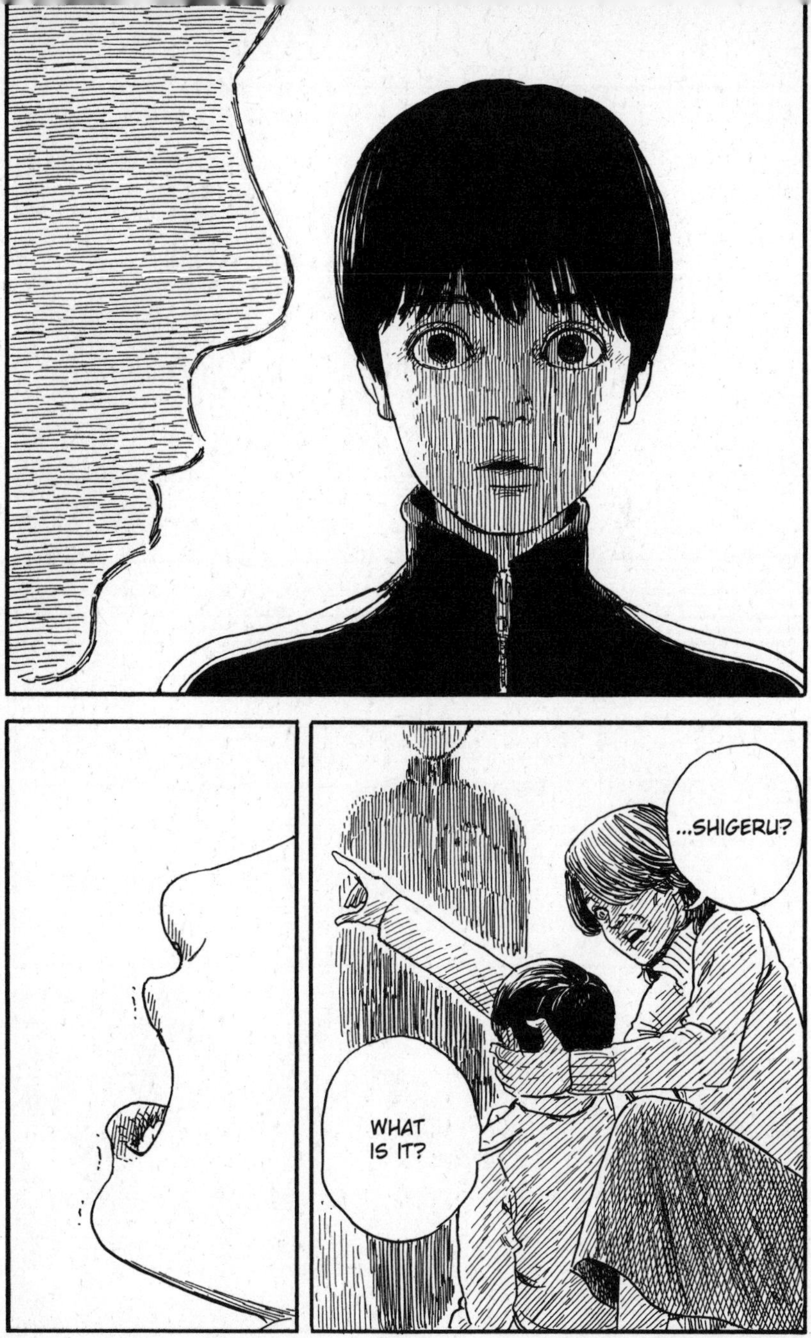
...SHIGERU?
WHAT IS IT?

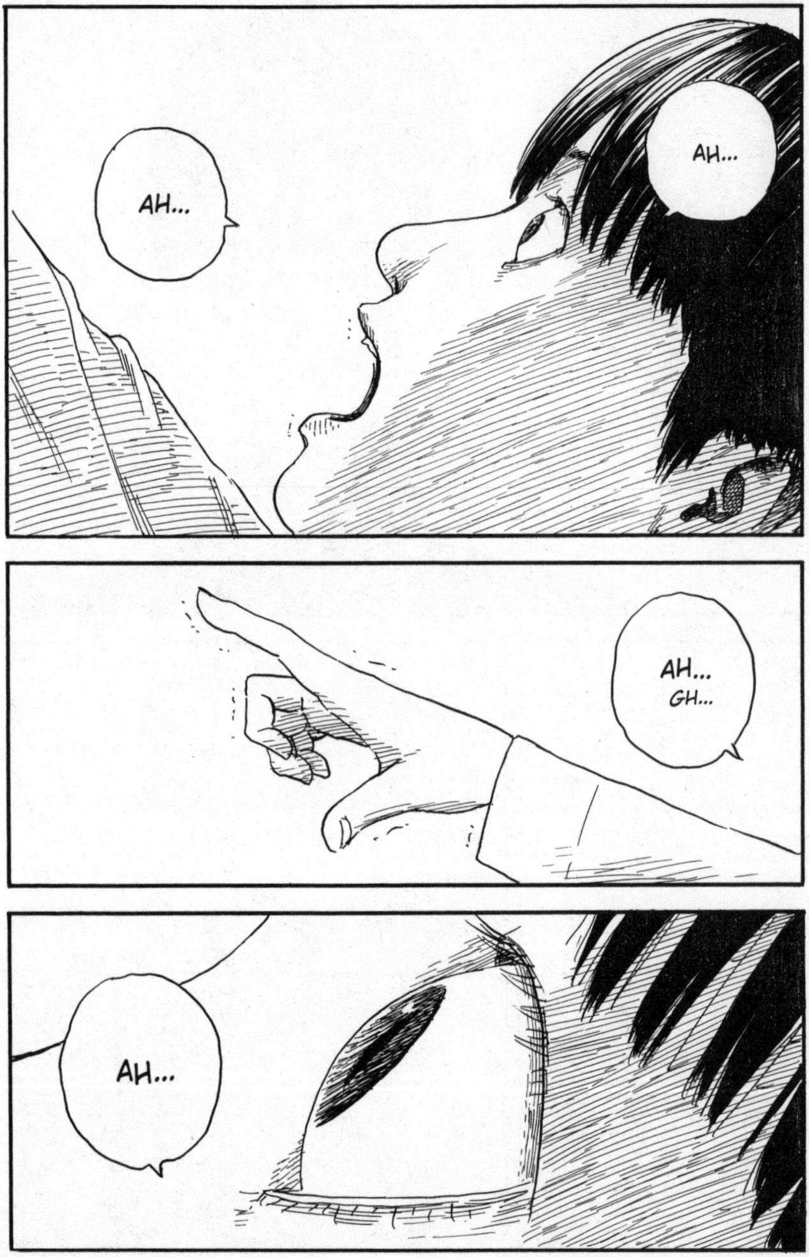
AH...
AH...
AH... GH...
AH...

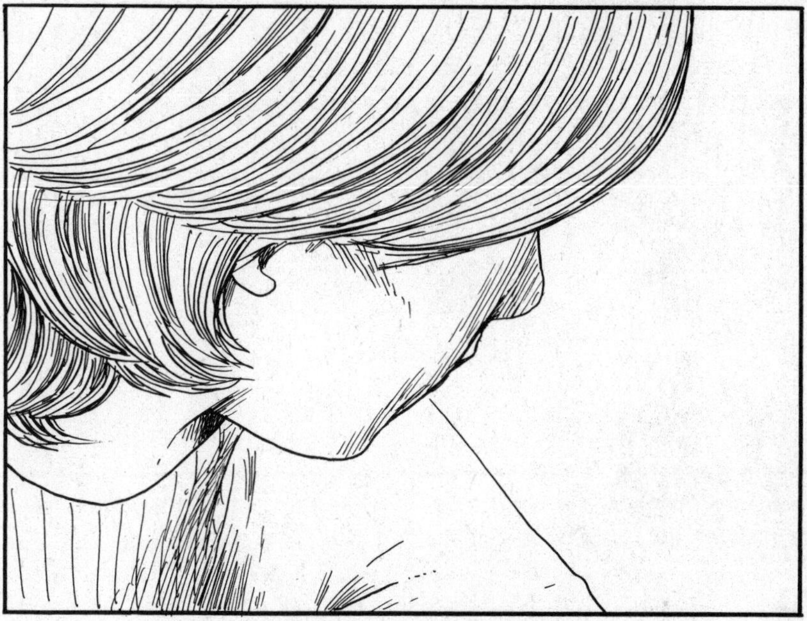

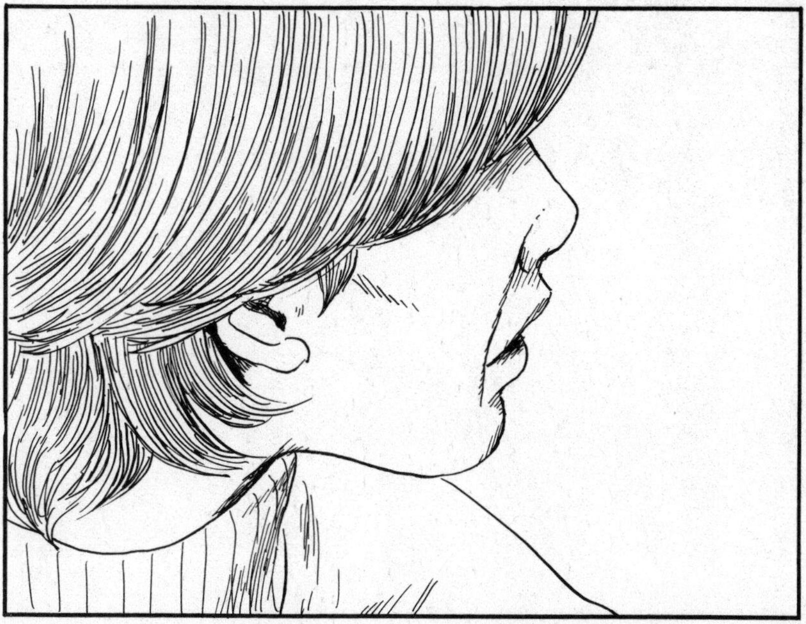

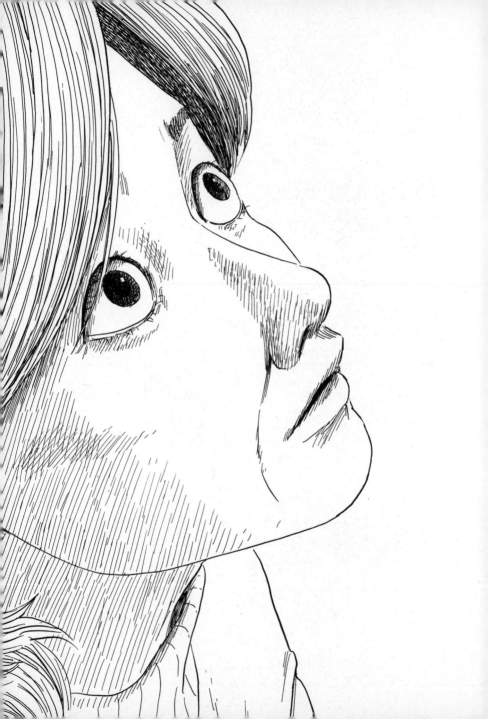

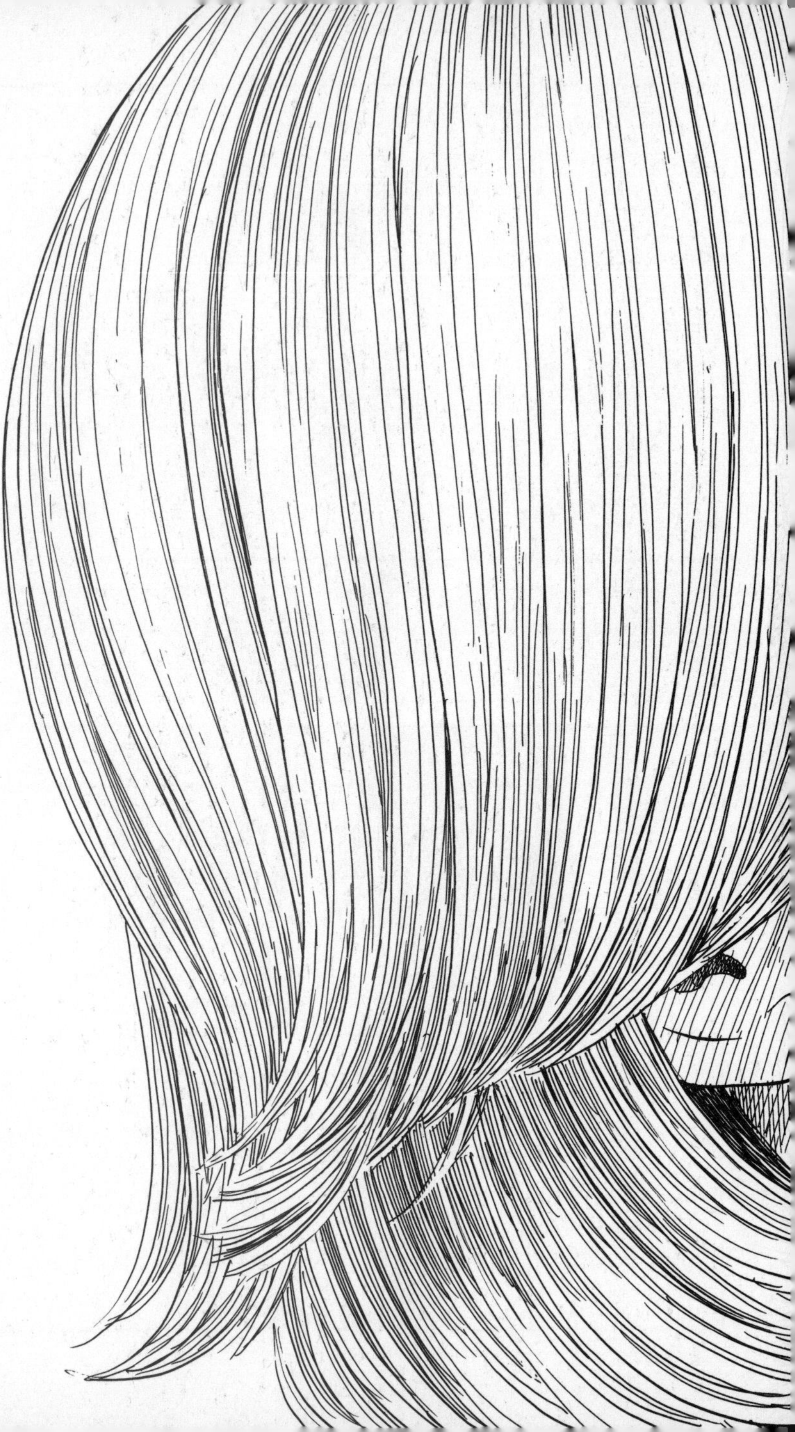

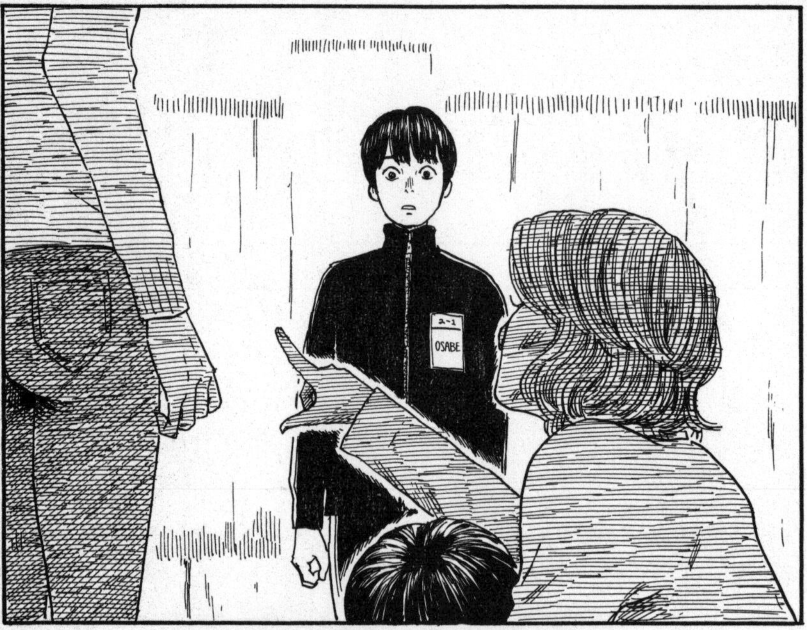
2-1
OSABE
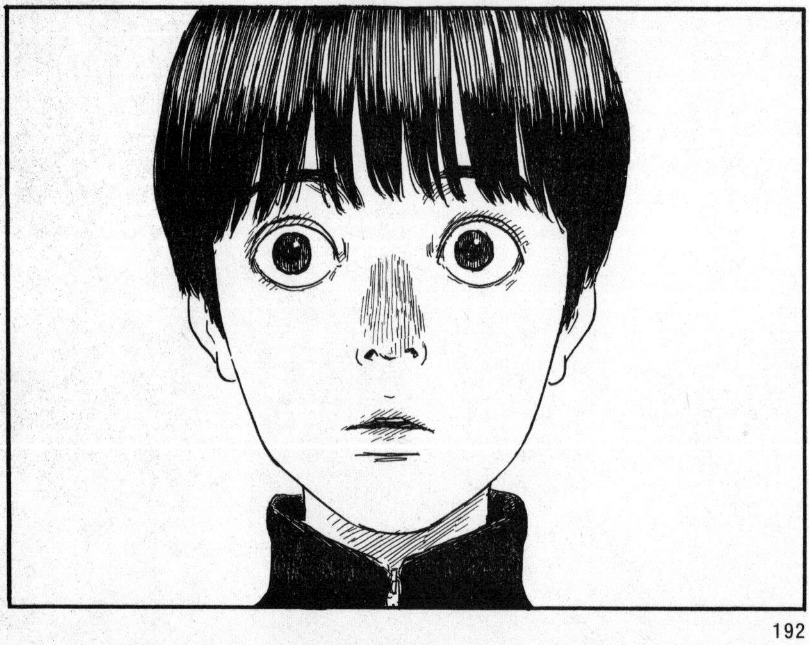

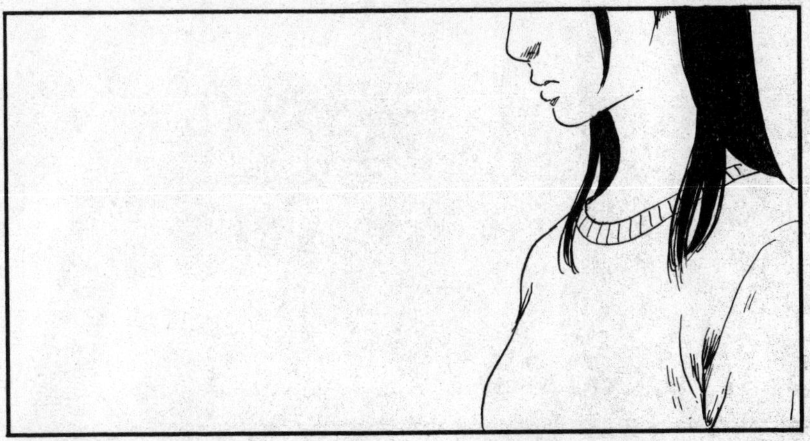
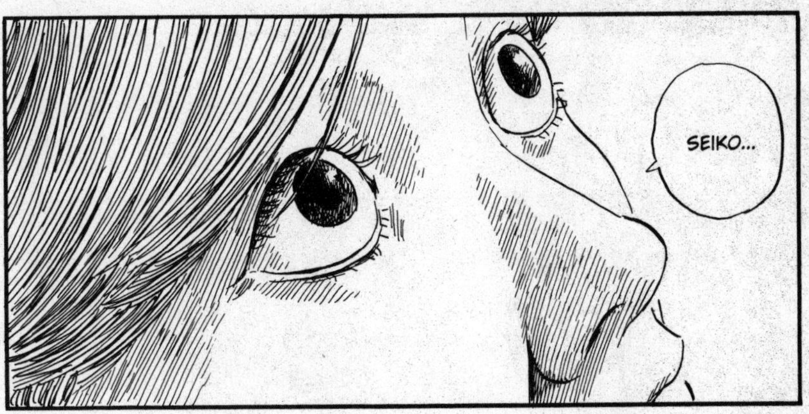
SEIKO...
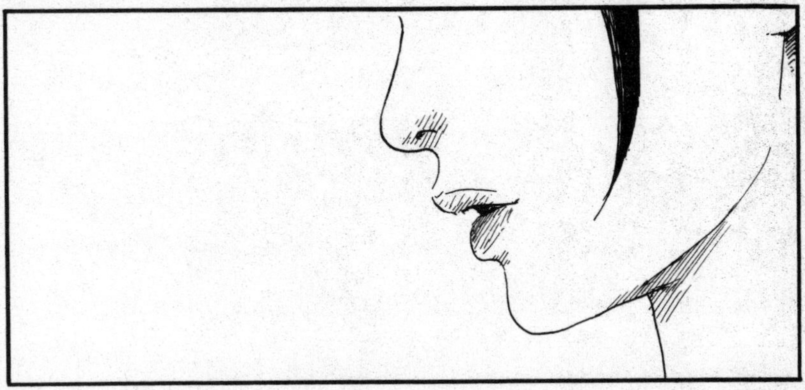

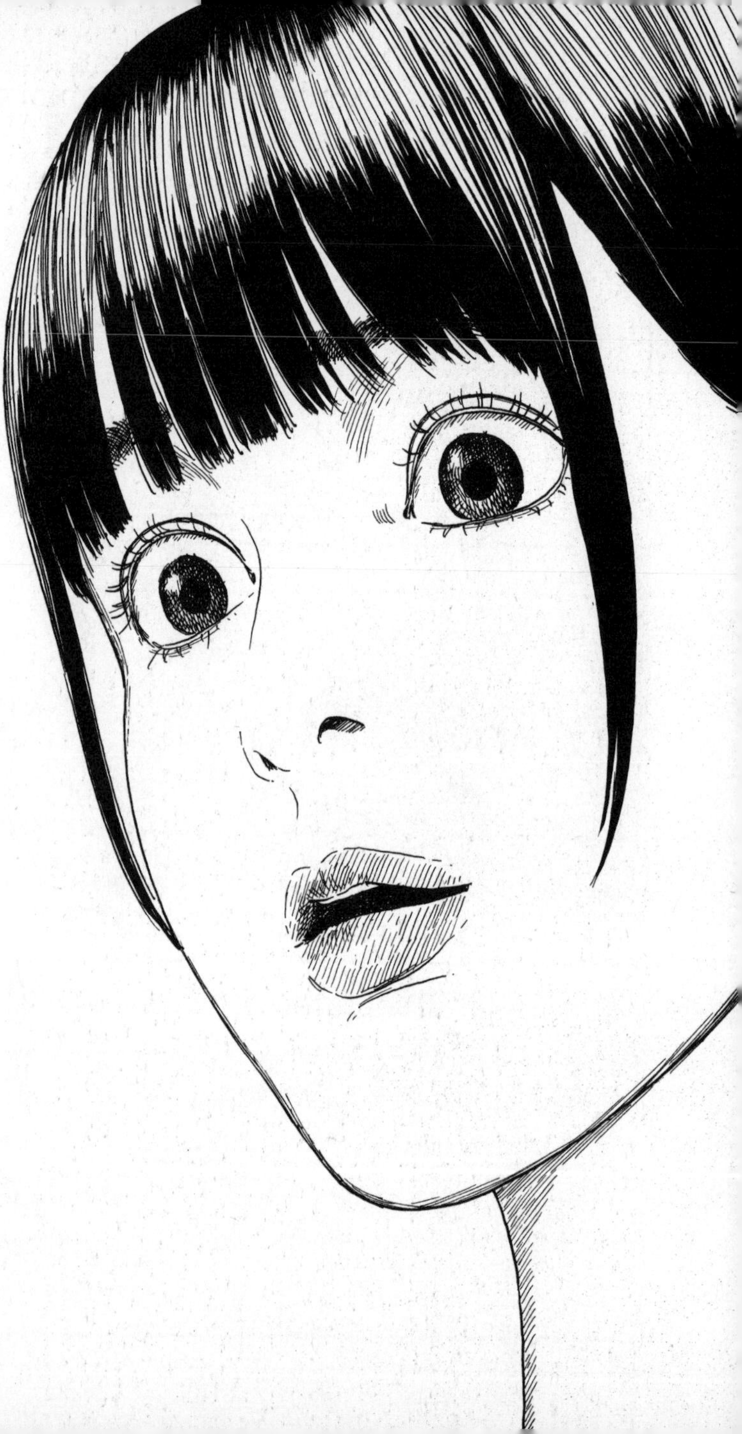

## CHAPTER 59 To the Quick

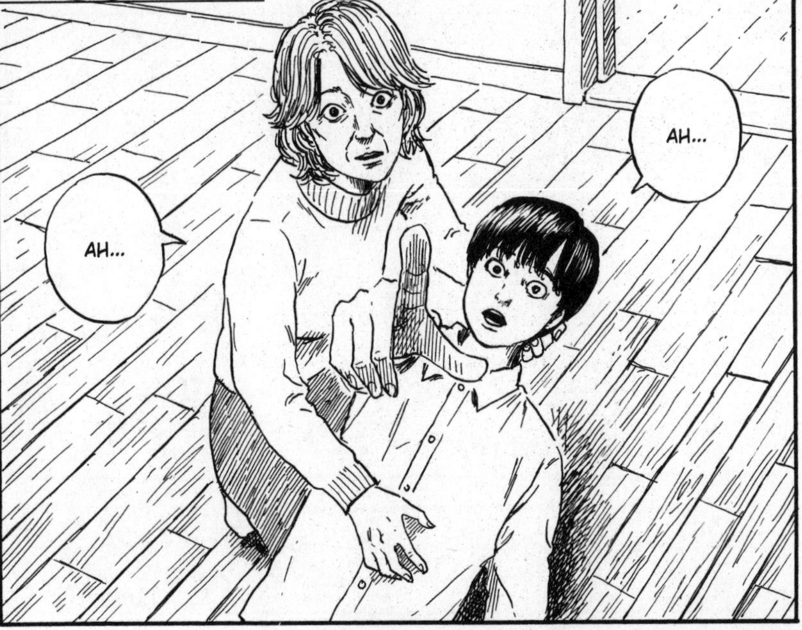
AH...
AH...

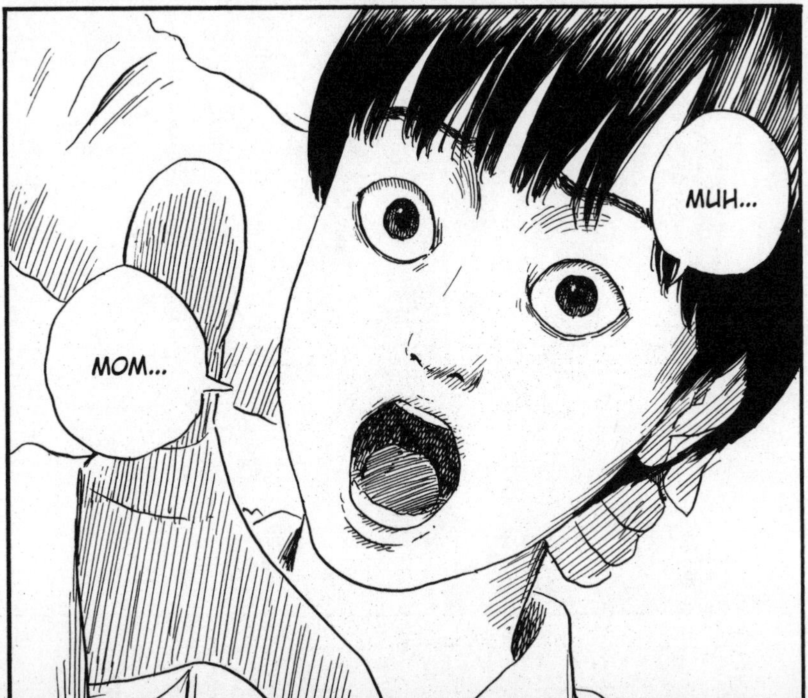
MUH...
MOM...

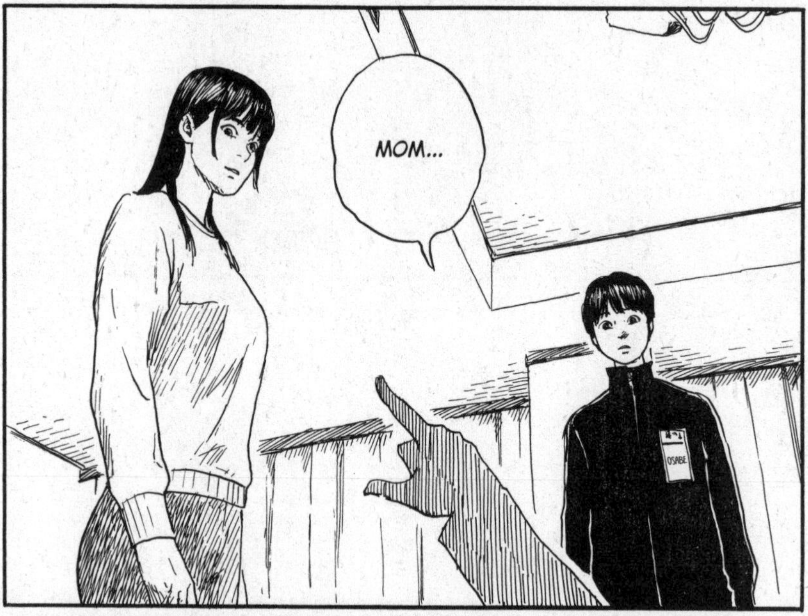
MOM...

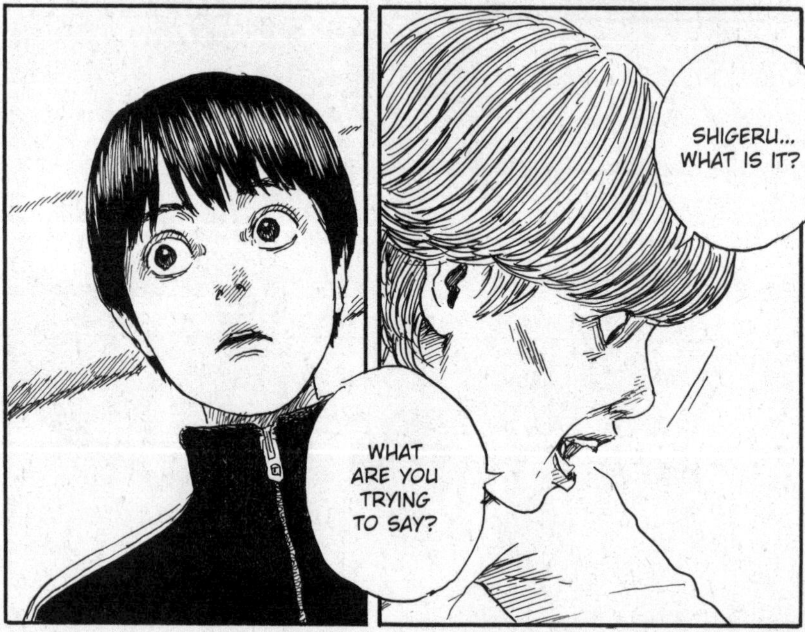
SHIGERU... WHAT IS IT?
WHAT ARE YOU TRYING TO SAY?

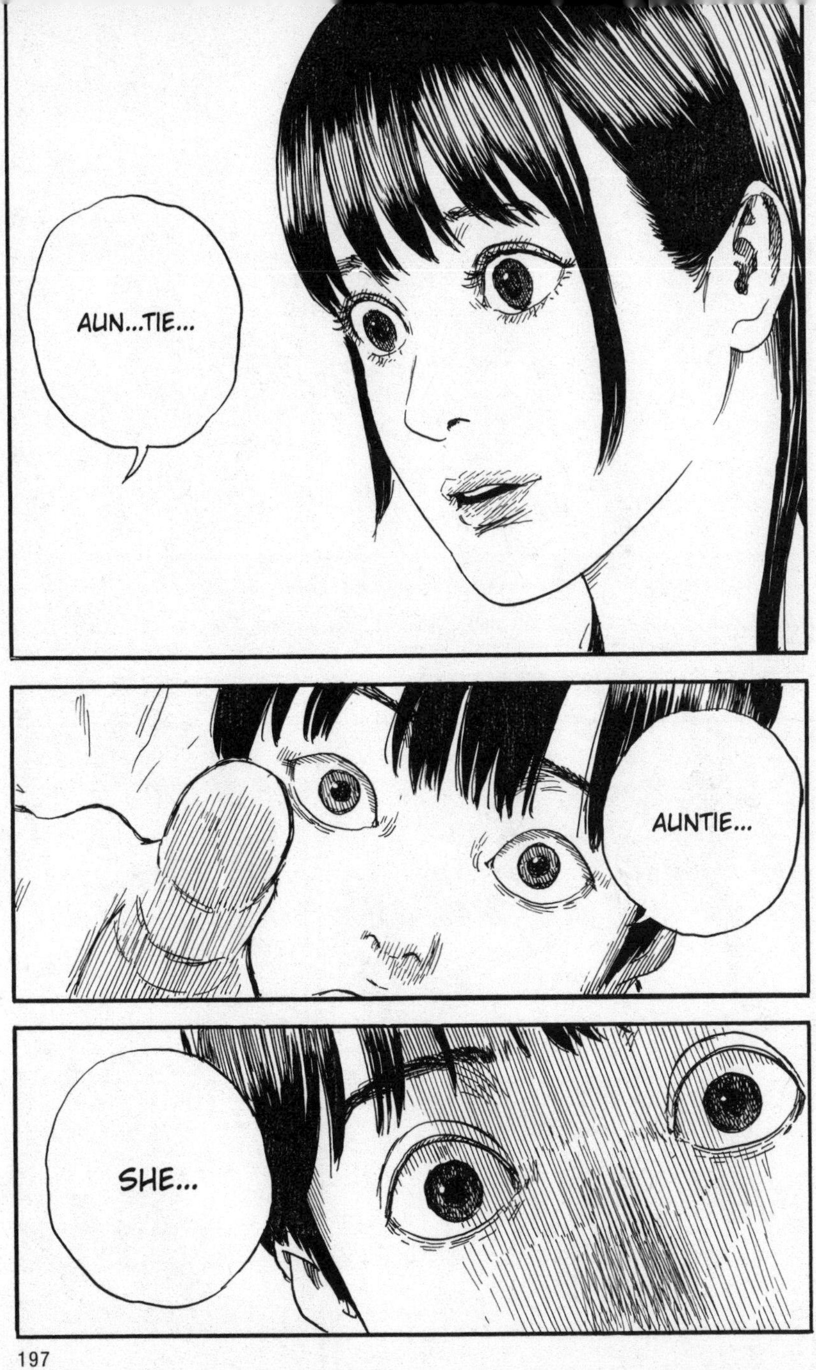
AUN...TIE...
AUNTIE...
SHE...

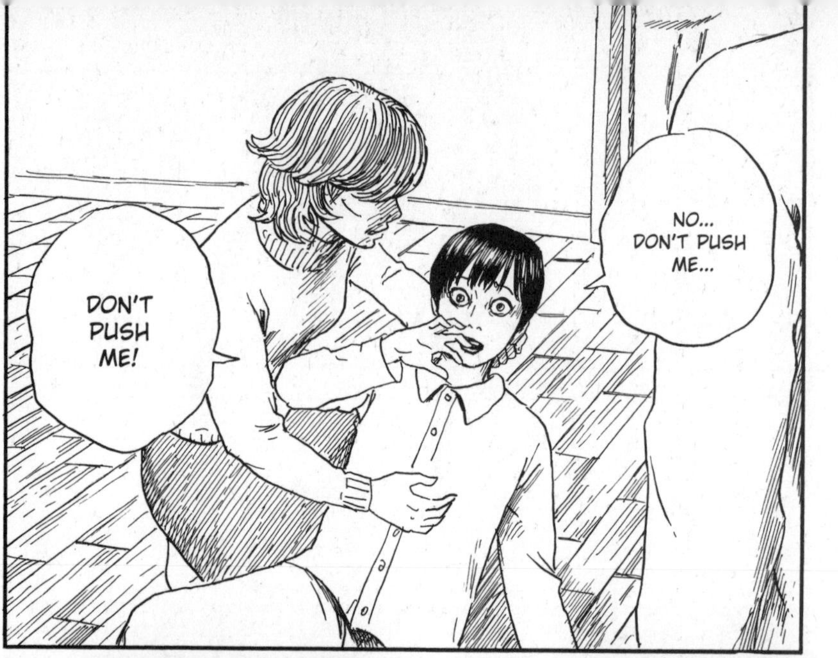
NO... DON'T PUSH ME...
DON'T PUSH ME!
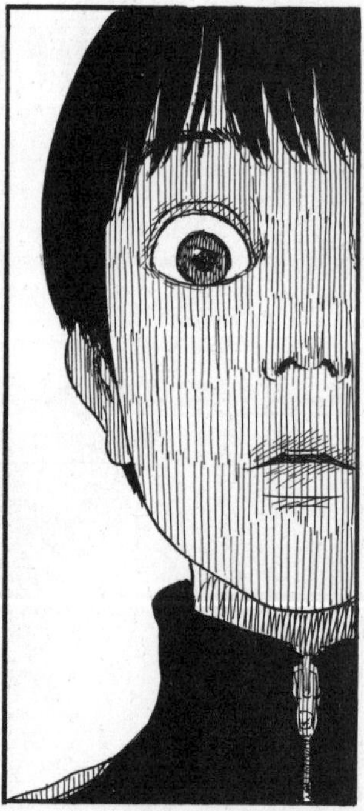
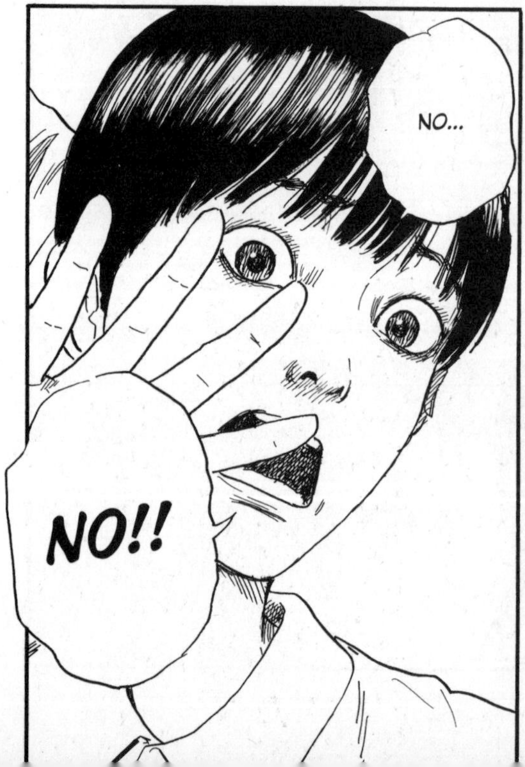
NO...
NO!!

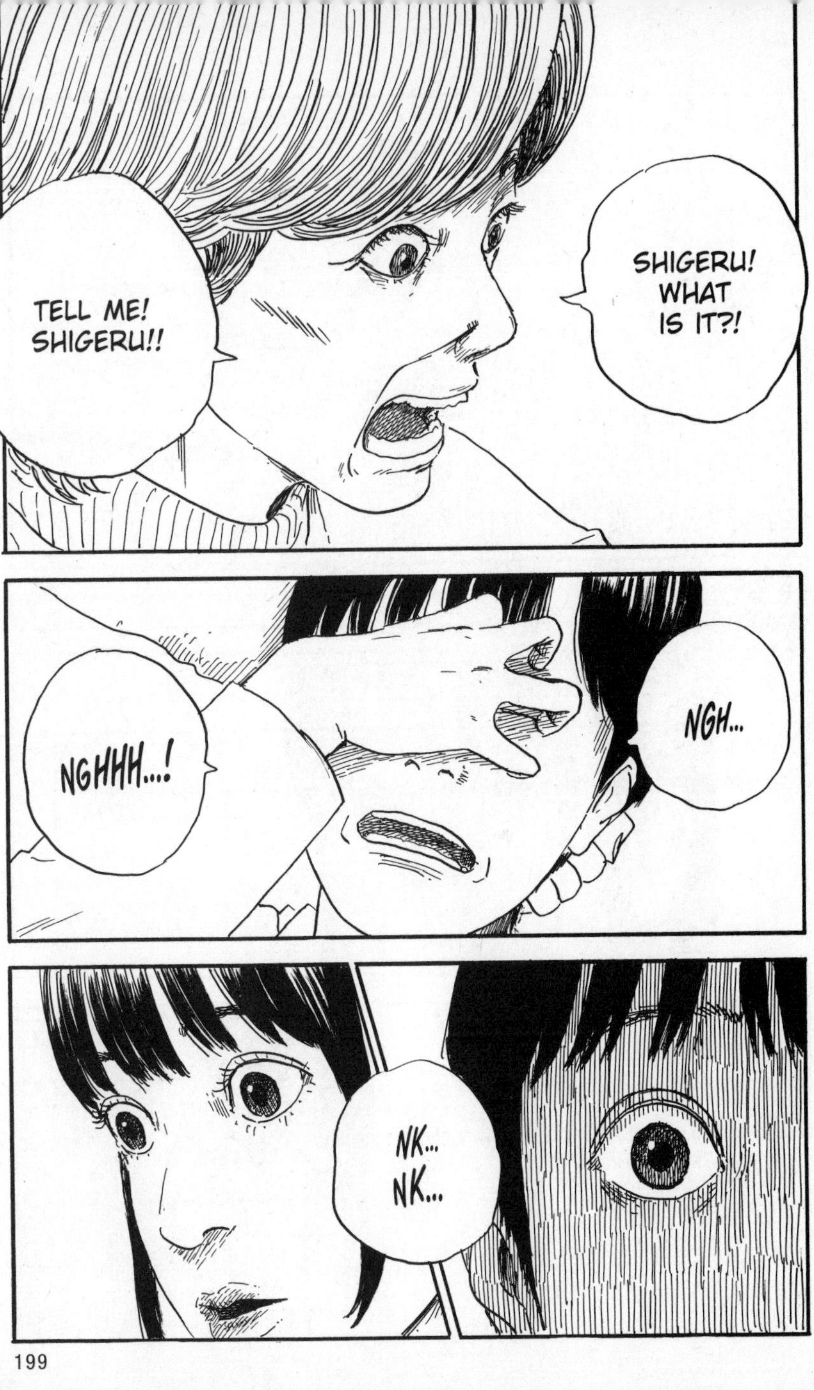
SHIGERU! WHAT IS IT?!
TELL ME! SHIGERU!!
NGH...
NGHHH...!
NK... NK...

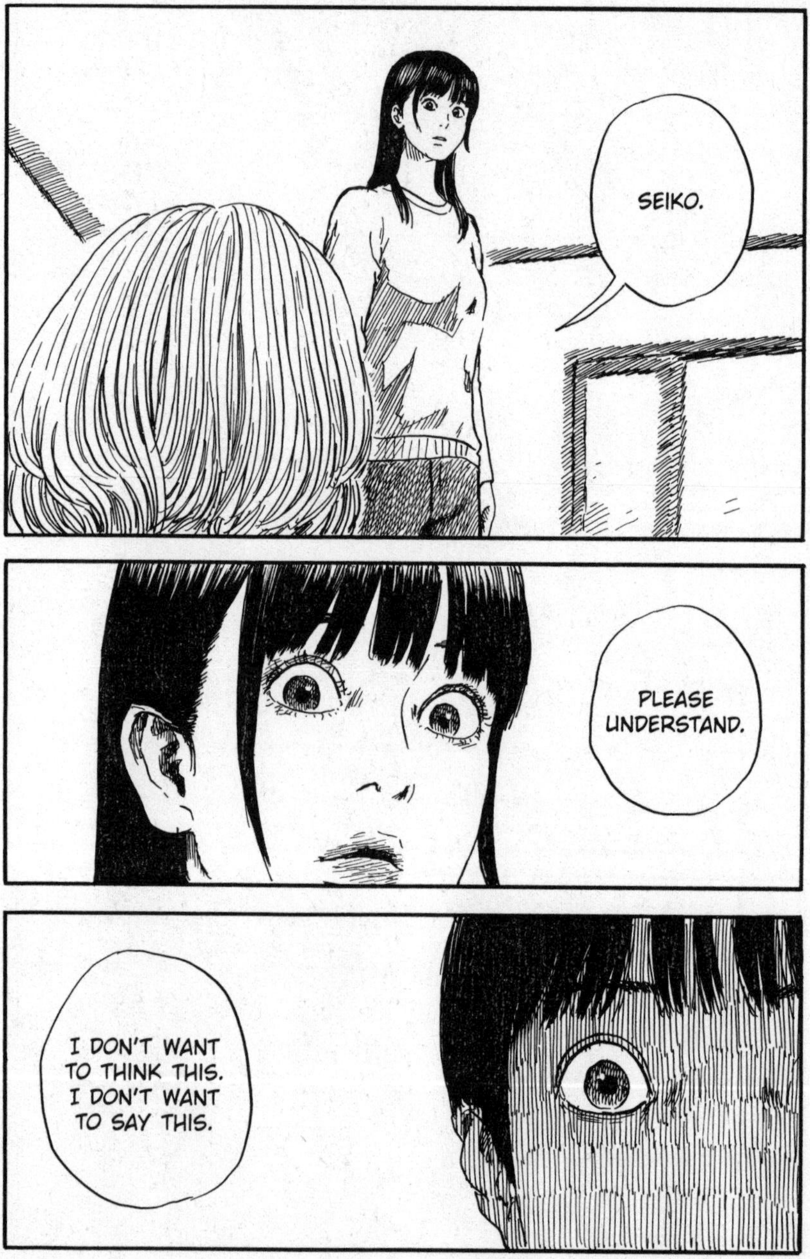
SEIKO.
PLEASE UNDERSTAND.
I DON'T WANT TO THINK THIS. I DON'T WANT TO SAY THIS.

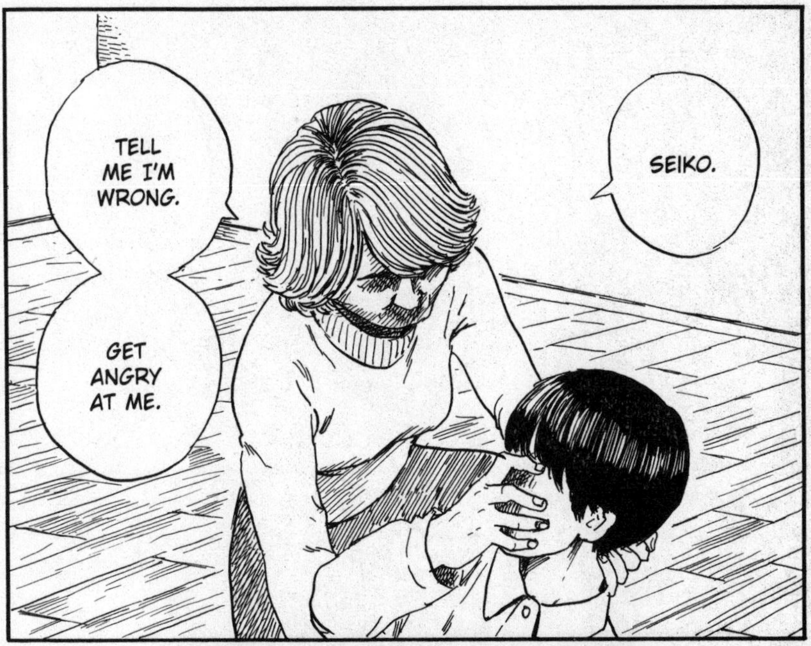
SEIKO.
TELL ME I'M WRONG.
GET ANGRY AT ME.

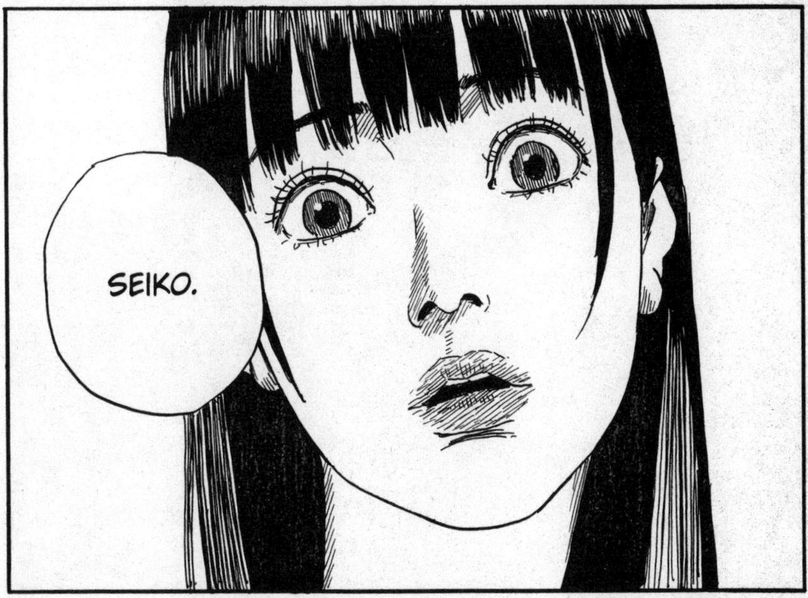
SEIKO.

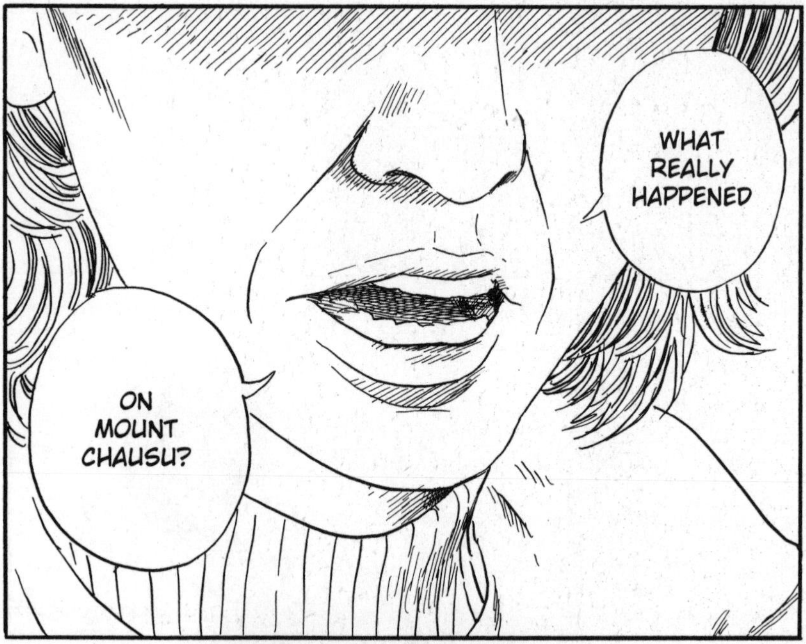
WHAT REALLY HAPPENED
ON MOUNT CHAUSU?
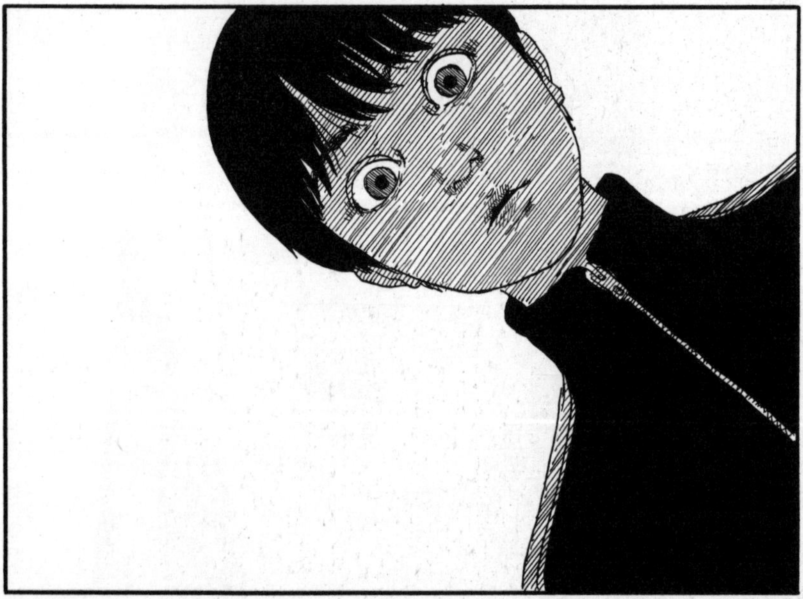

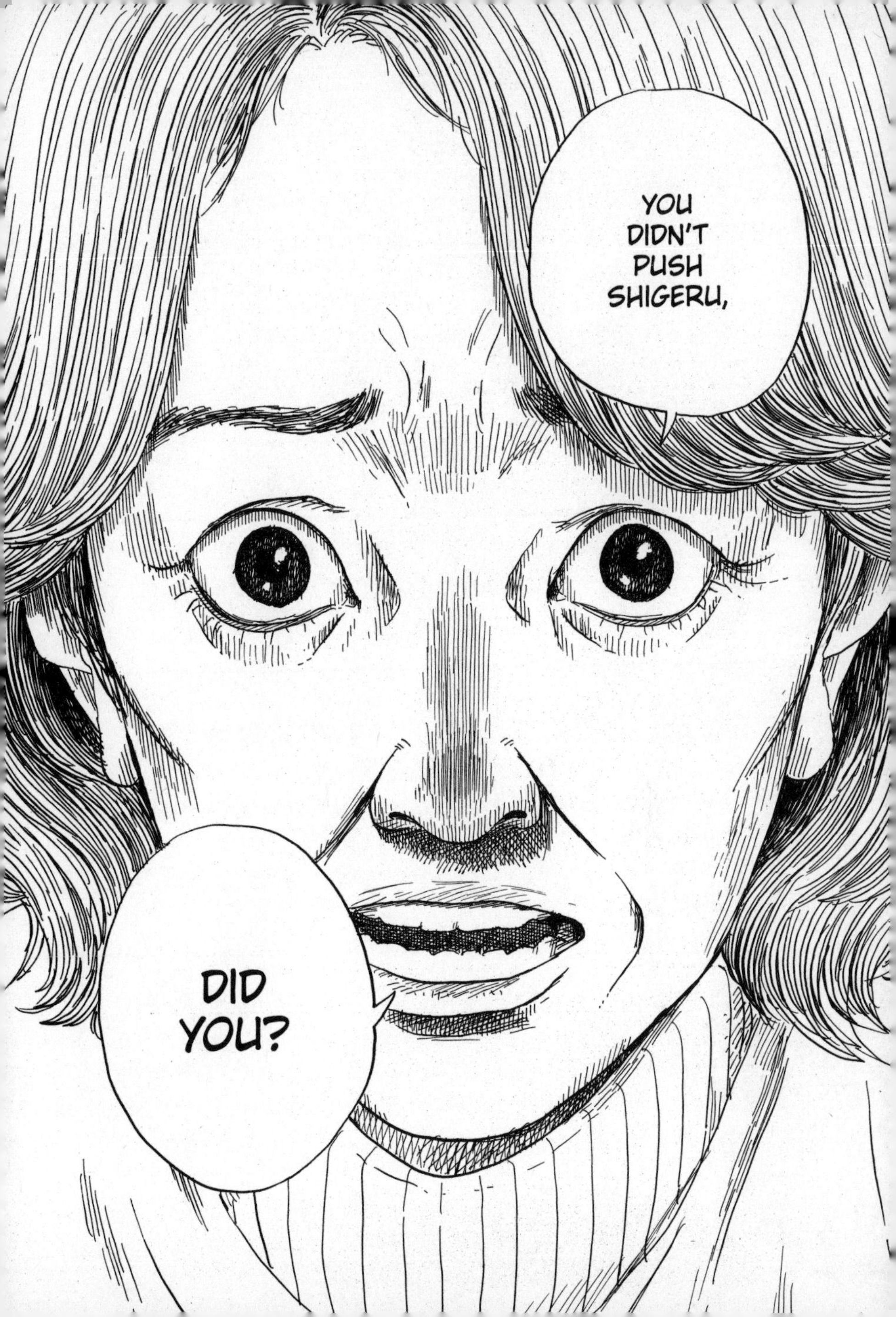
YOU DIDN'T PUSH SHIGERU,
DID YOU?

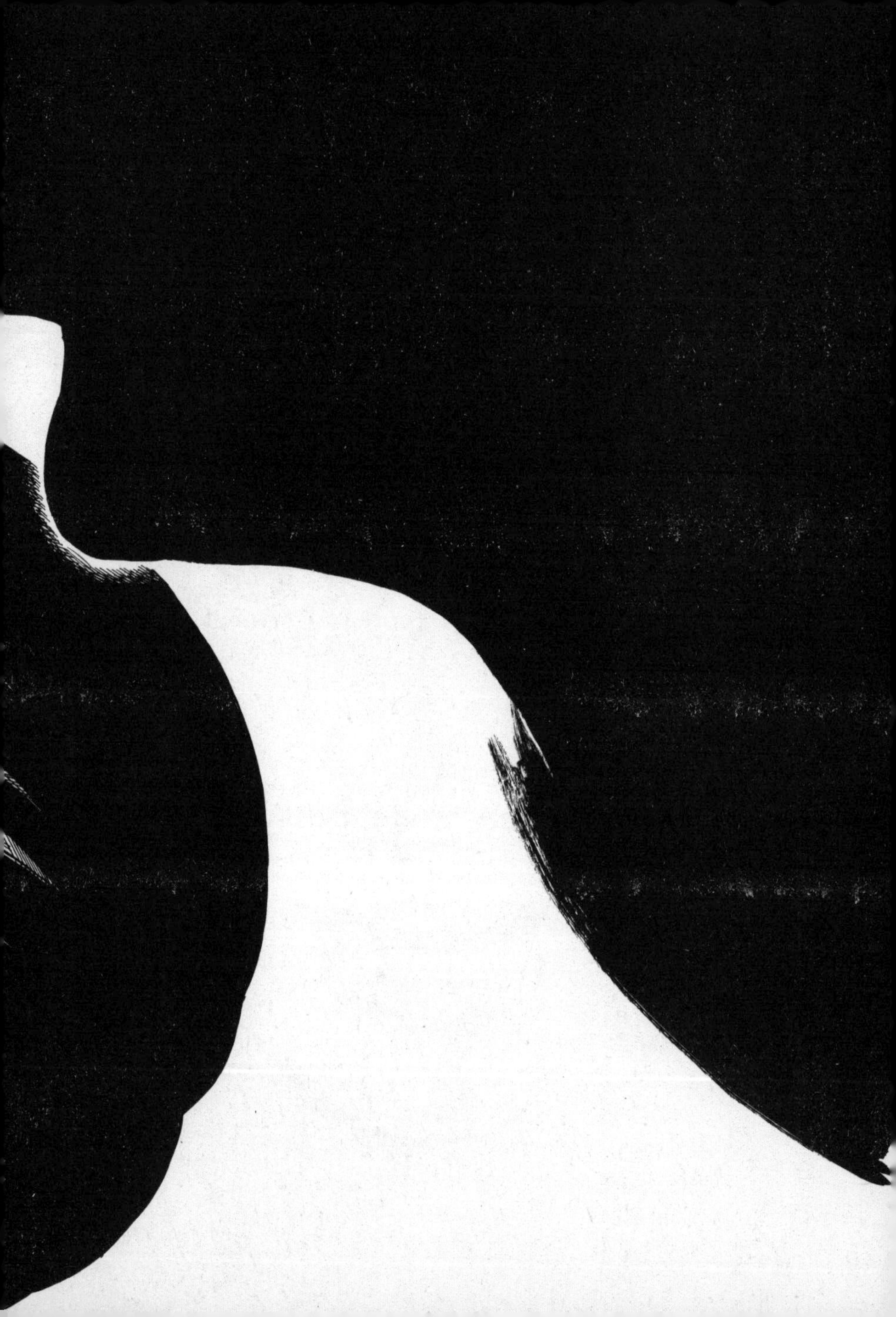

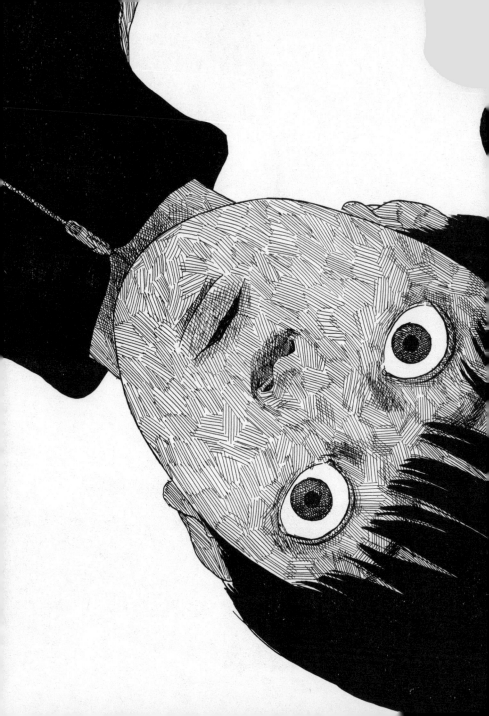

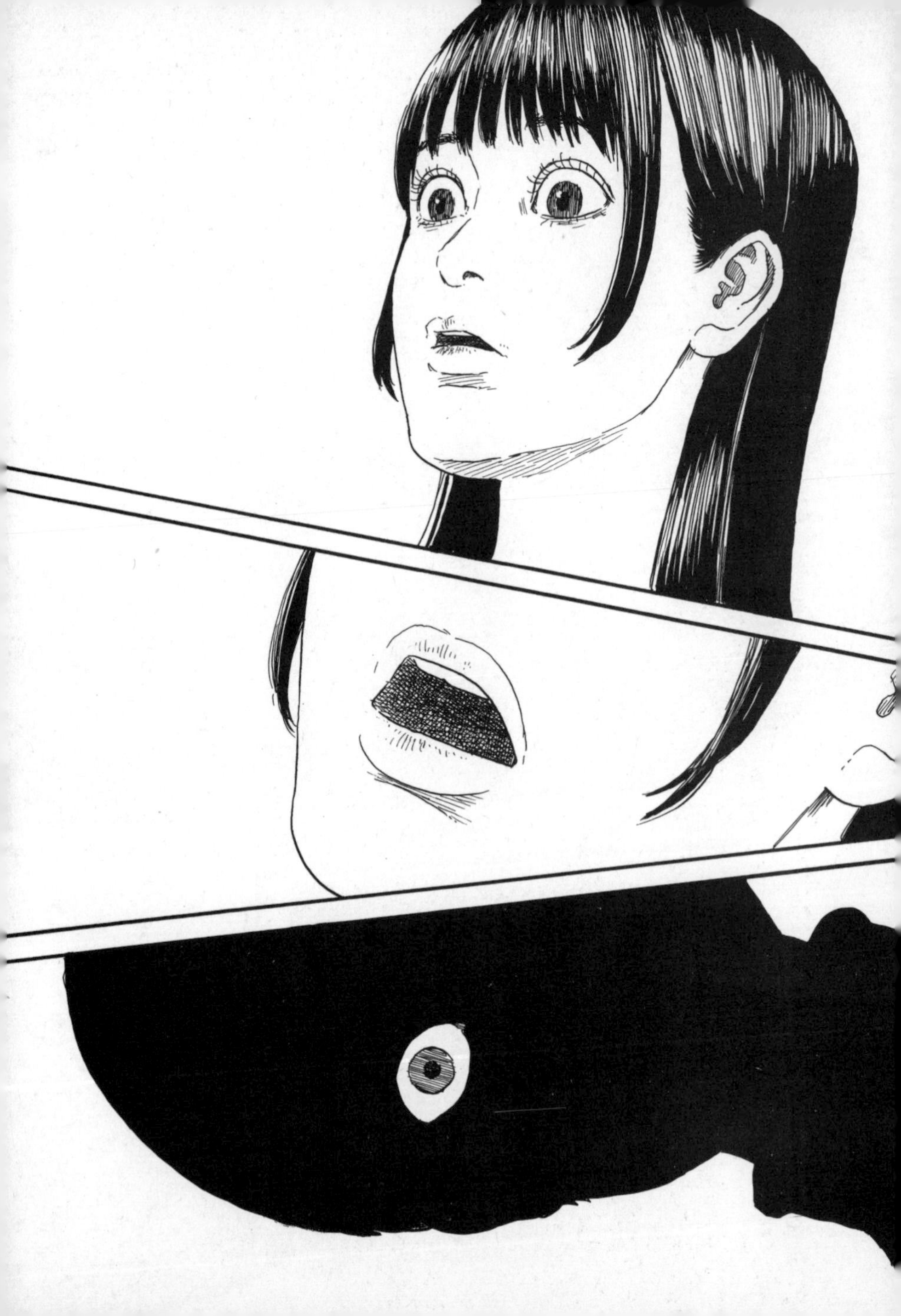

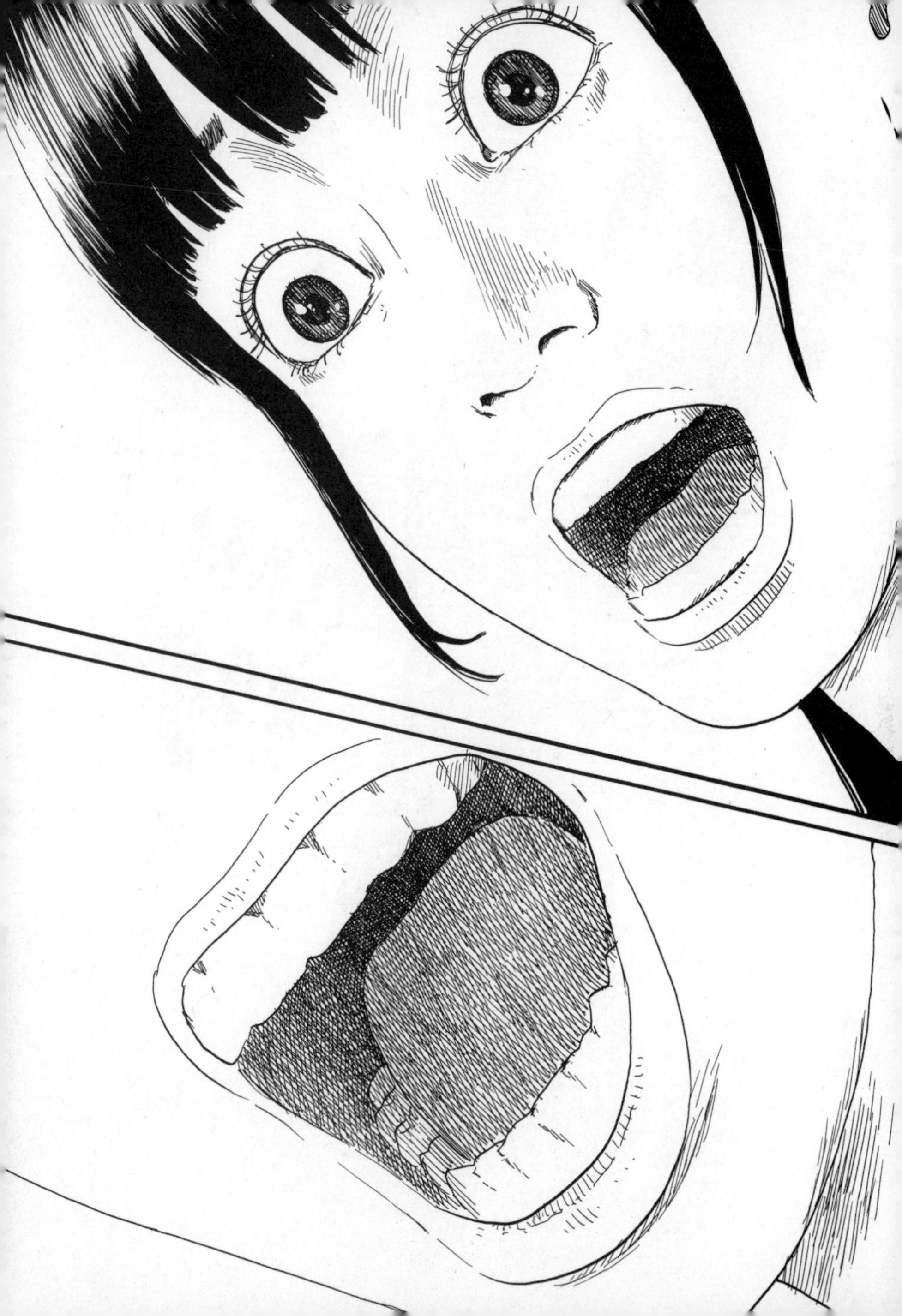

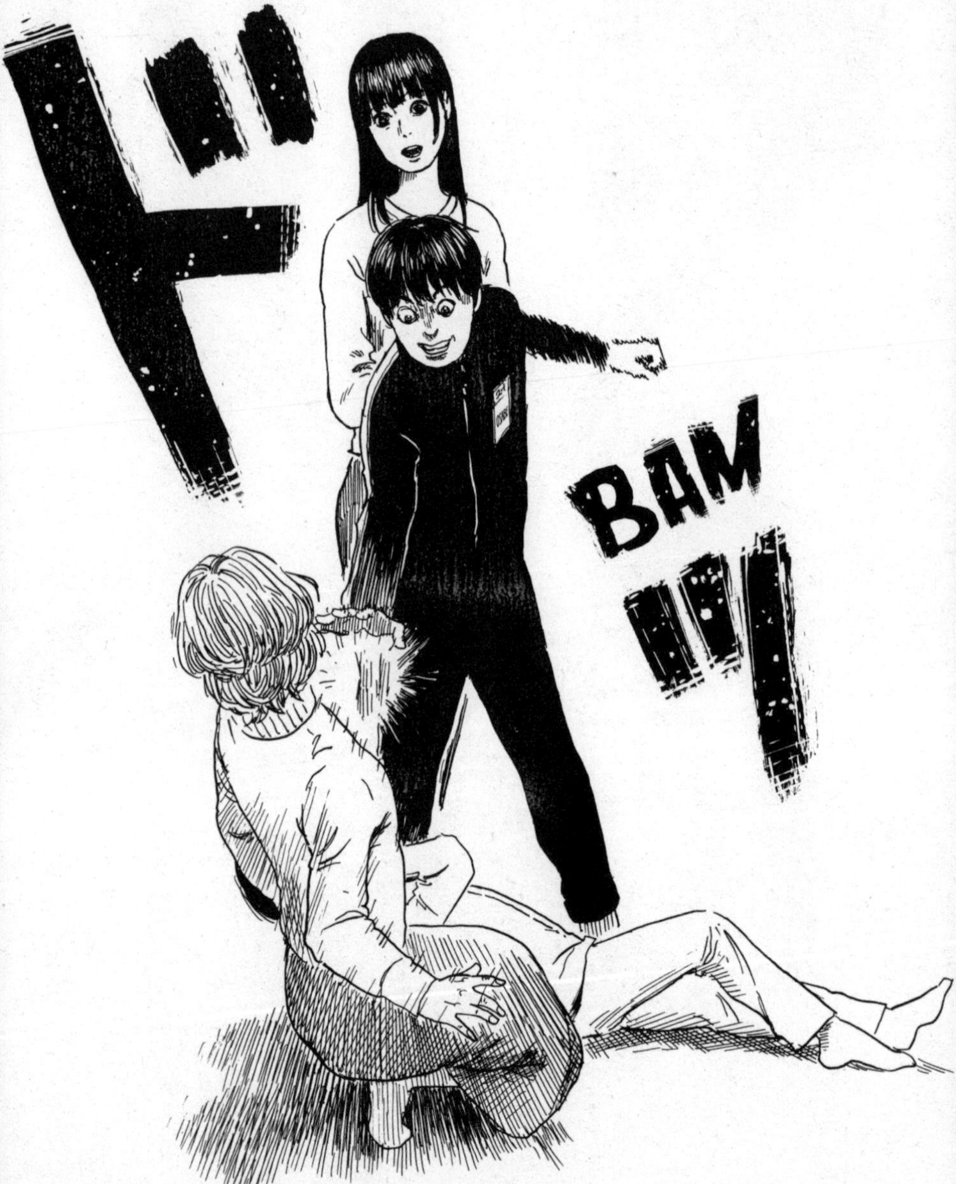
ド
BAM

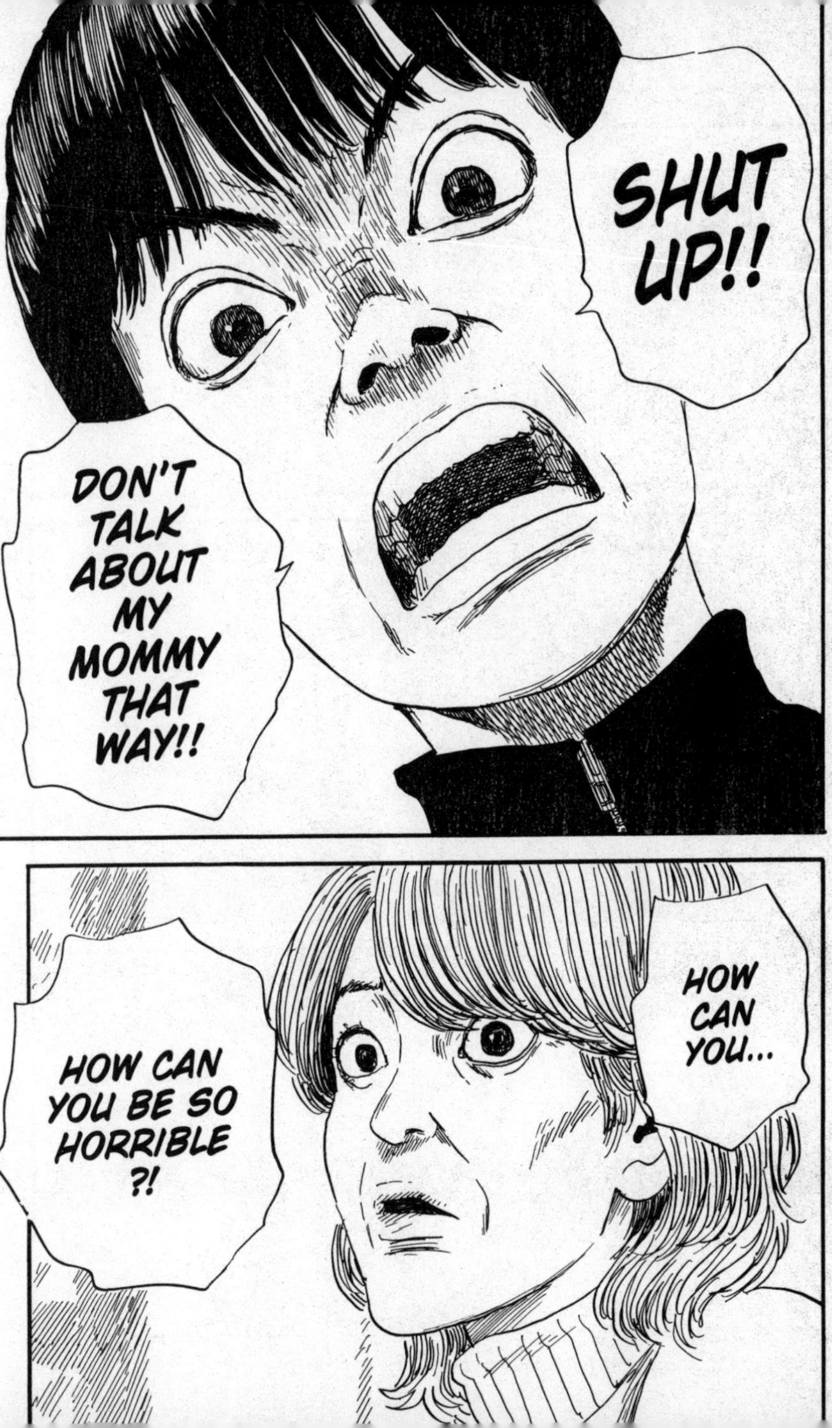
SHUT UP!!
DON'T TALK ABOUT MY MOMMY THAT WAY!!
HOW CAN YOU...
HOW CAN YOU BE SO HORRIBLE ?!

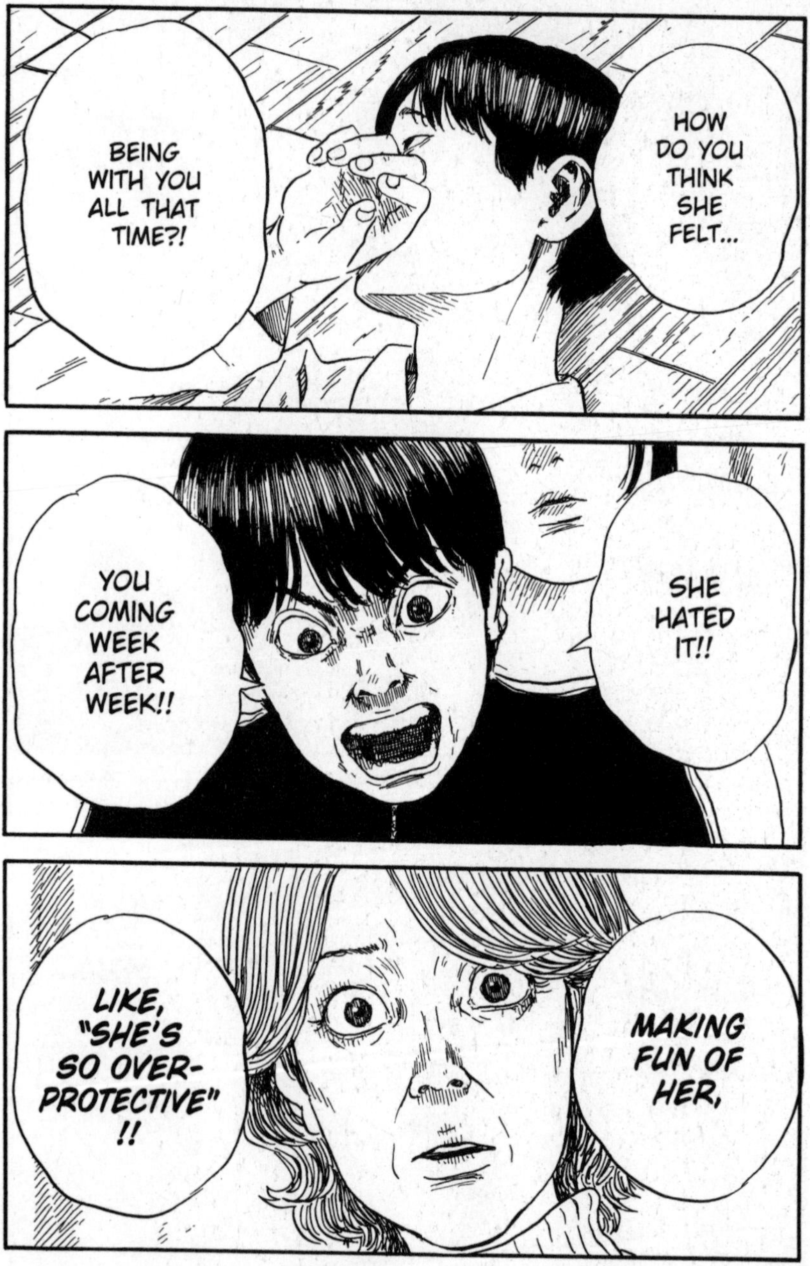
HOW DO YOU THINK SHE FELT...
BEING WITH YOU ALL THAT TIME?!
SHE HATED IT!!
YOU COMING WEEK AFTER WEEK!!
MAKING FUN OF HER,
LIKE, "SHE'S SO OVER-PROTECTIVE" !!

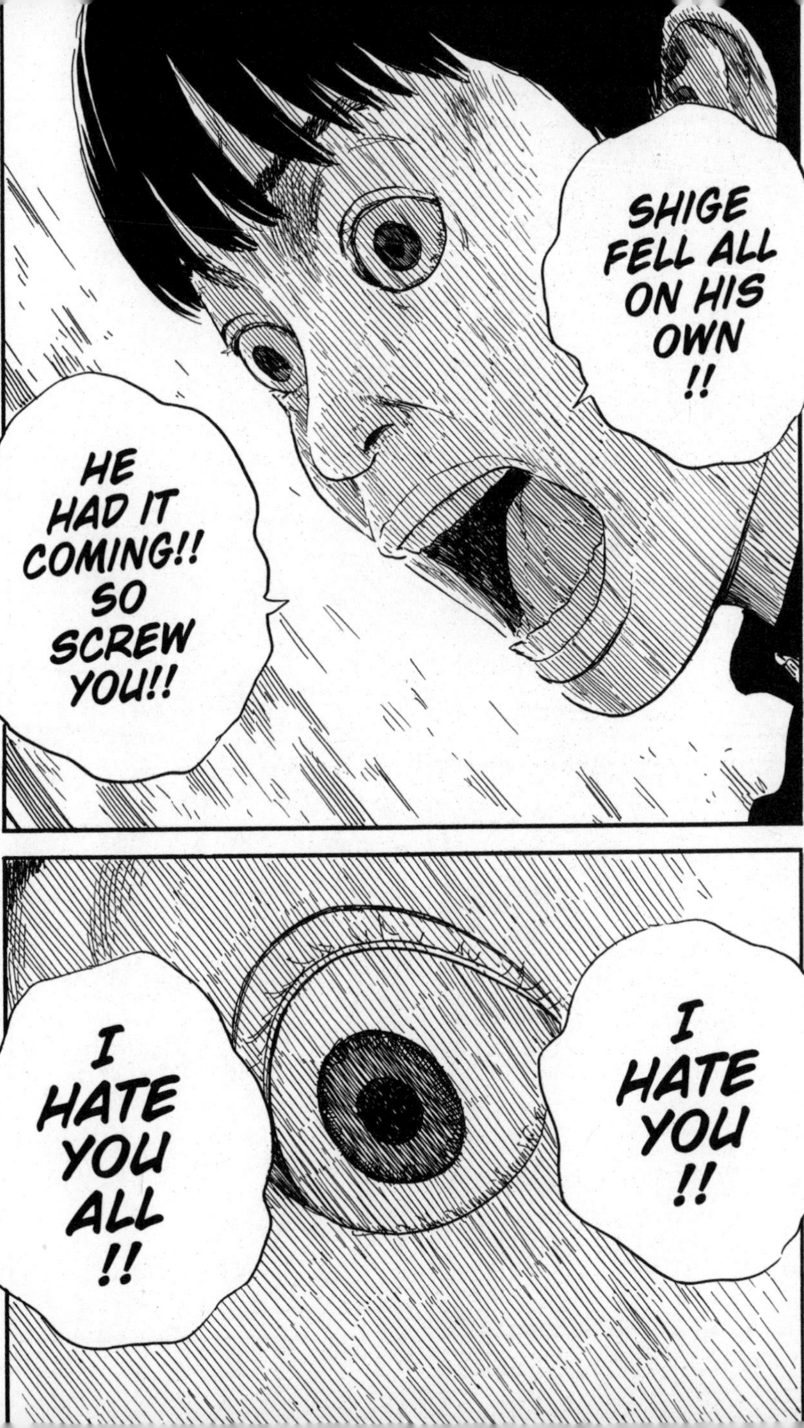
SHIGE FELL ALL ON HIS OWN!!
HE HAD IT COMING!! SO SCREW YOU!!
I HATE YOU!!
I HATE YOU ALL!!

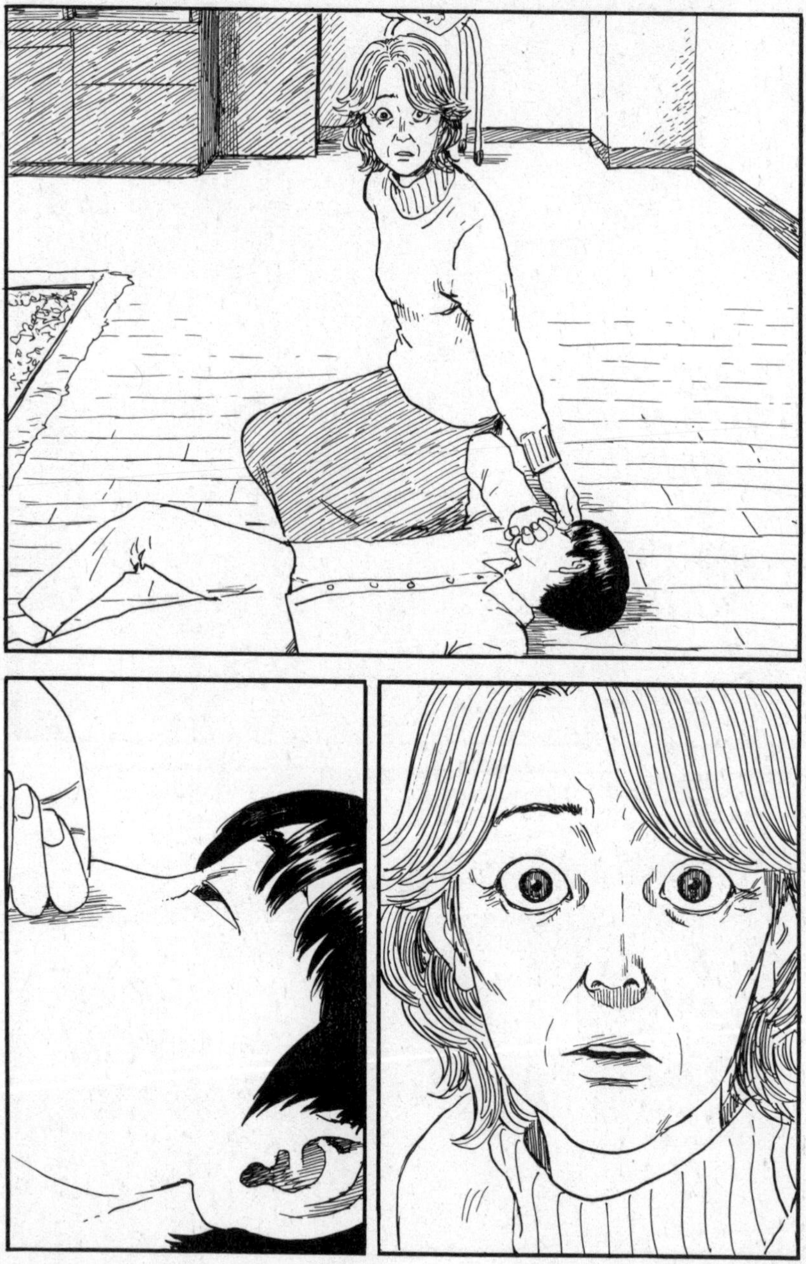

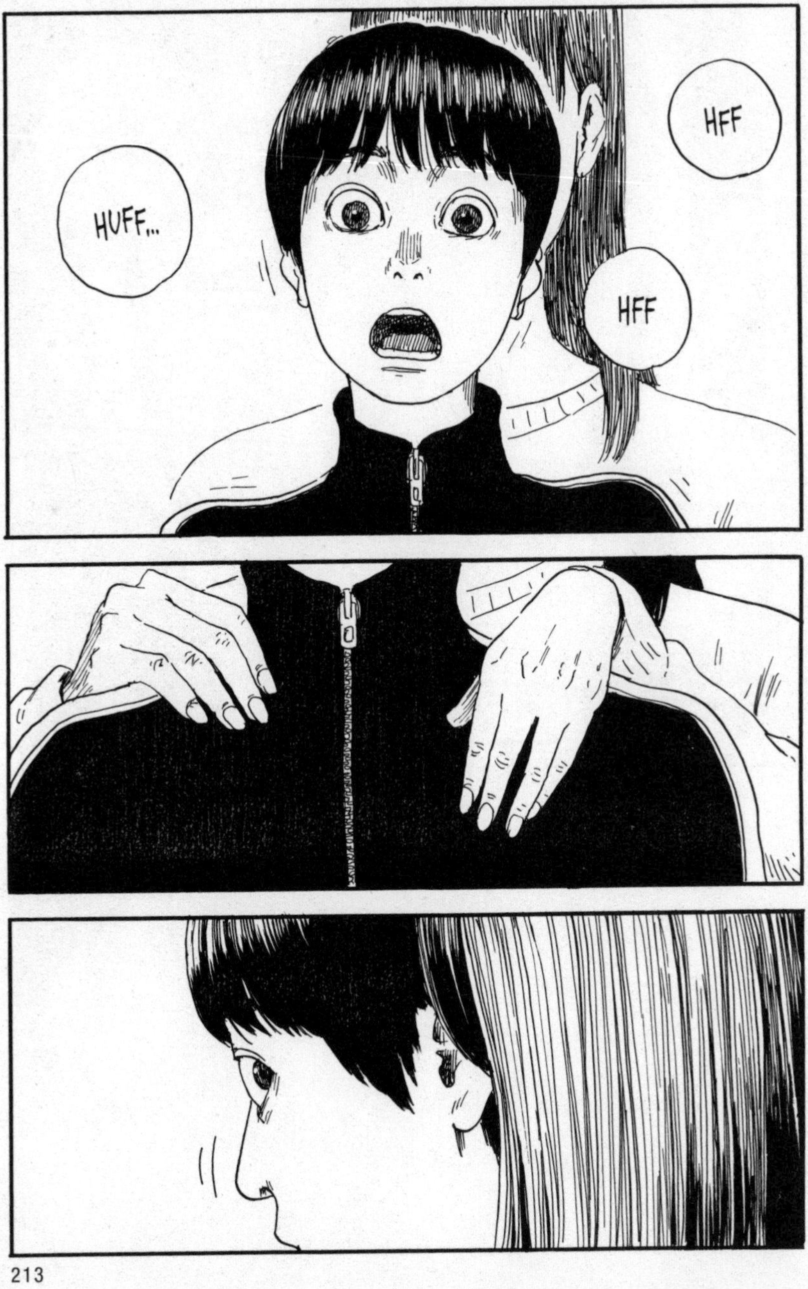
HFF
HUFF...
HFF

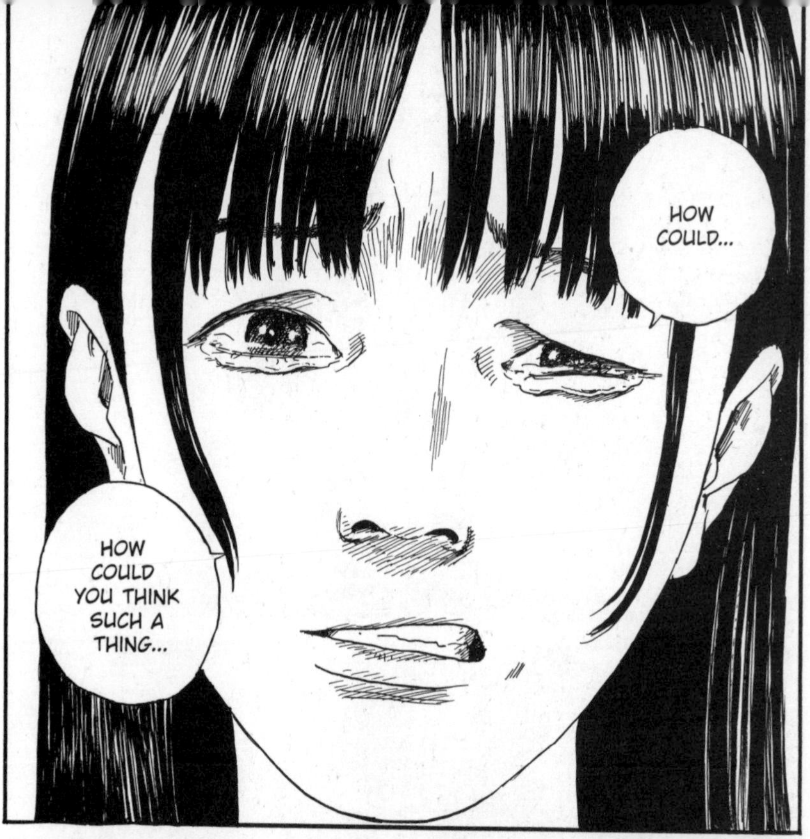
HOW COULD...
HOW COULD YOU THINK SUCH A THING...
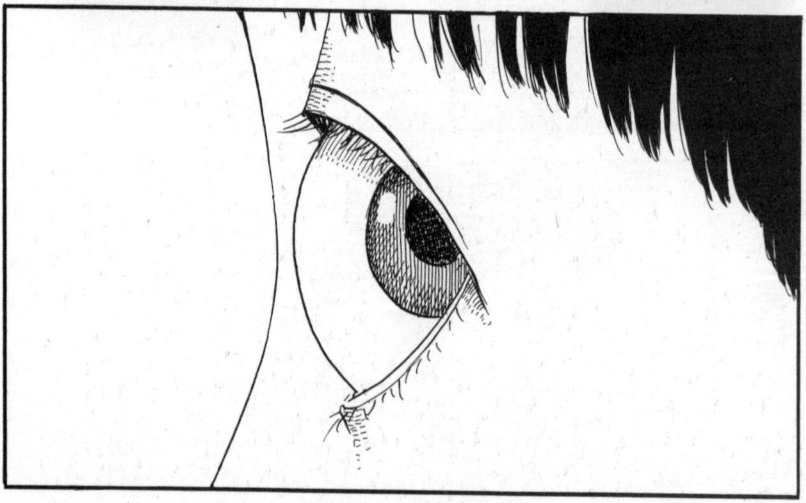

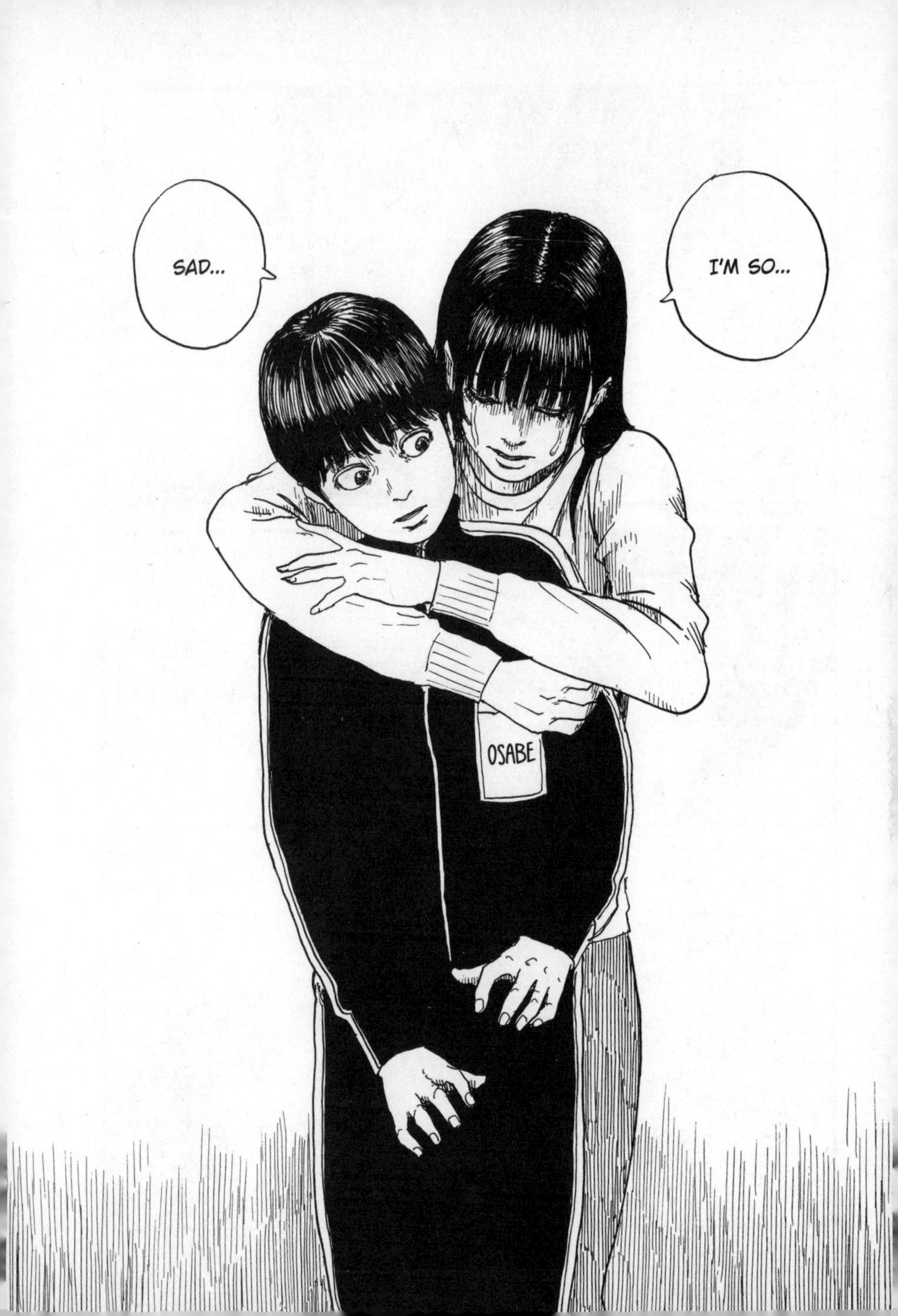
I'M SO...
SAD...
OSABE

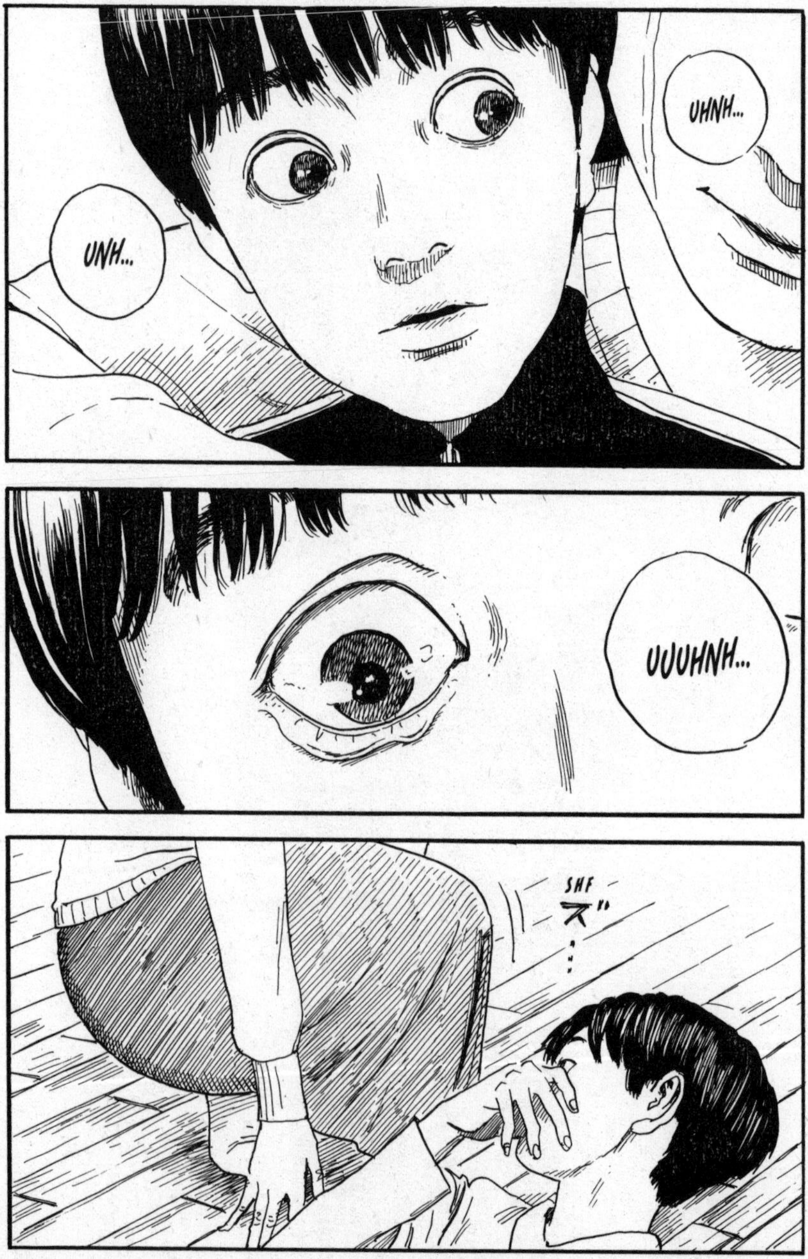
UHNH...
UNH...
UUUHNH...
SHF

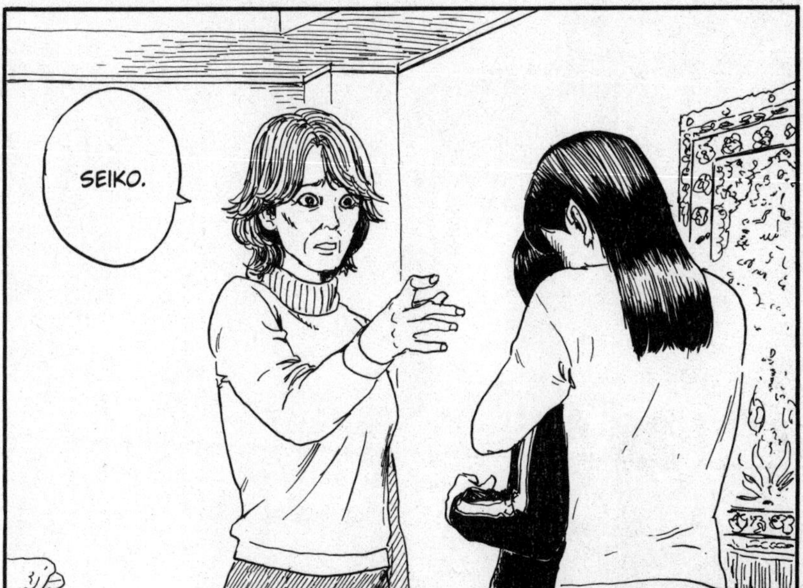
SEIKO.
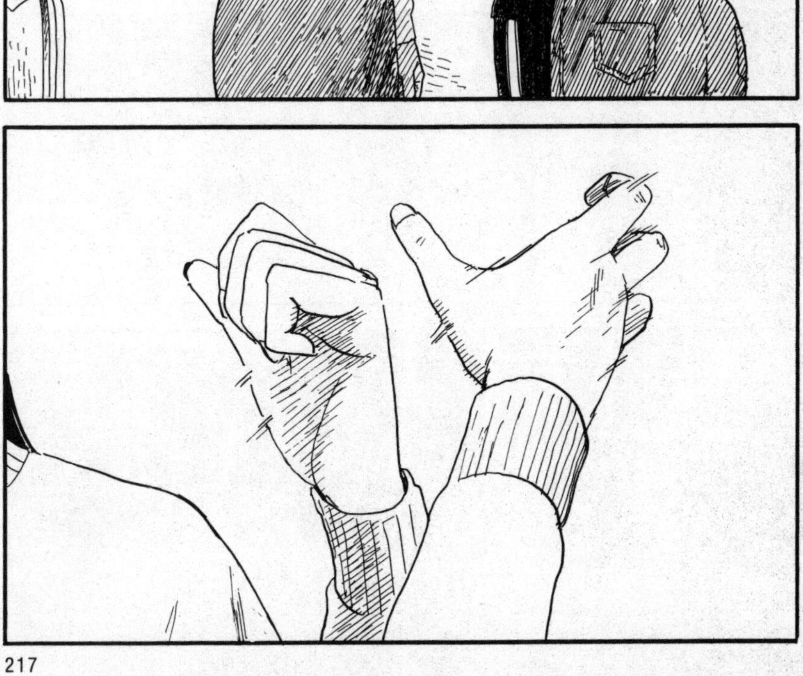

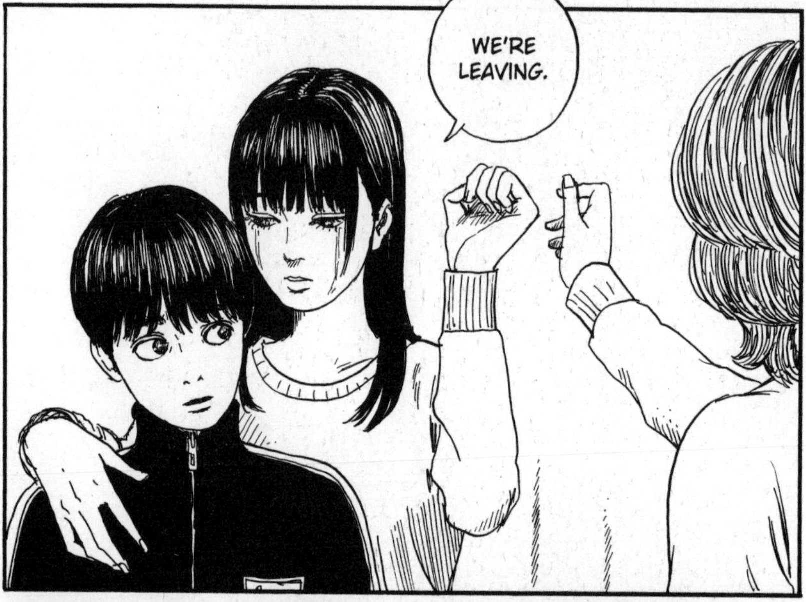
WE'RE LEAVING.
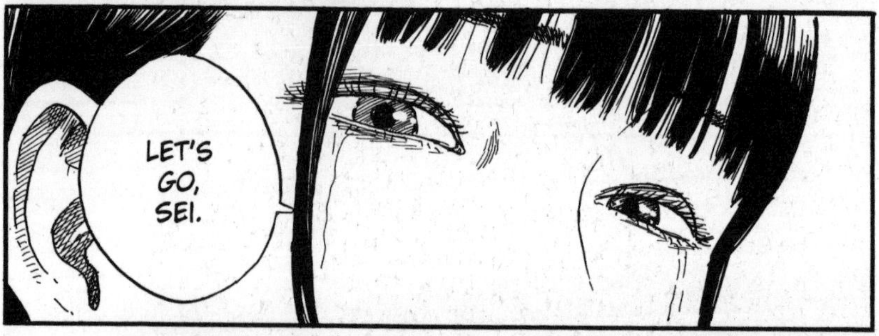
LET'S GO, SEI.
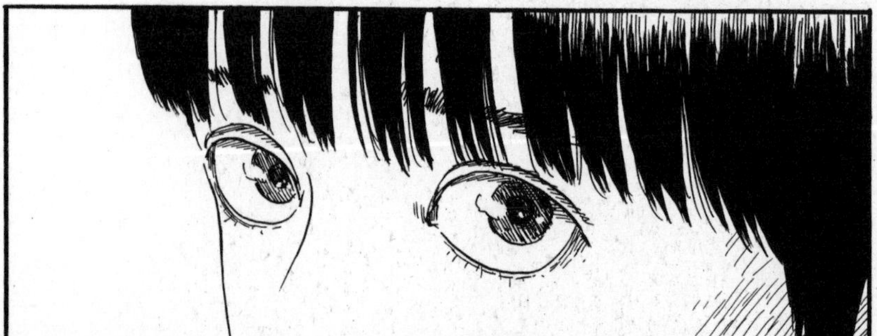

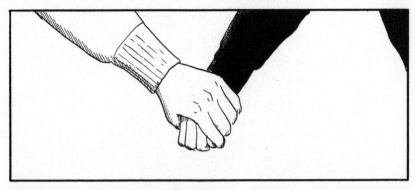

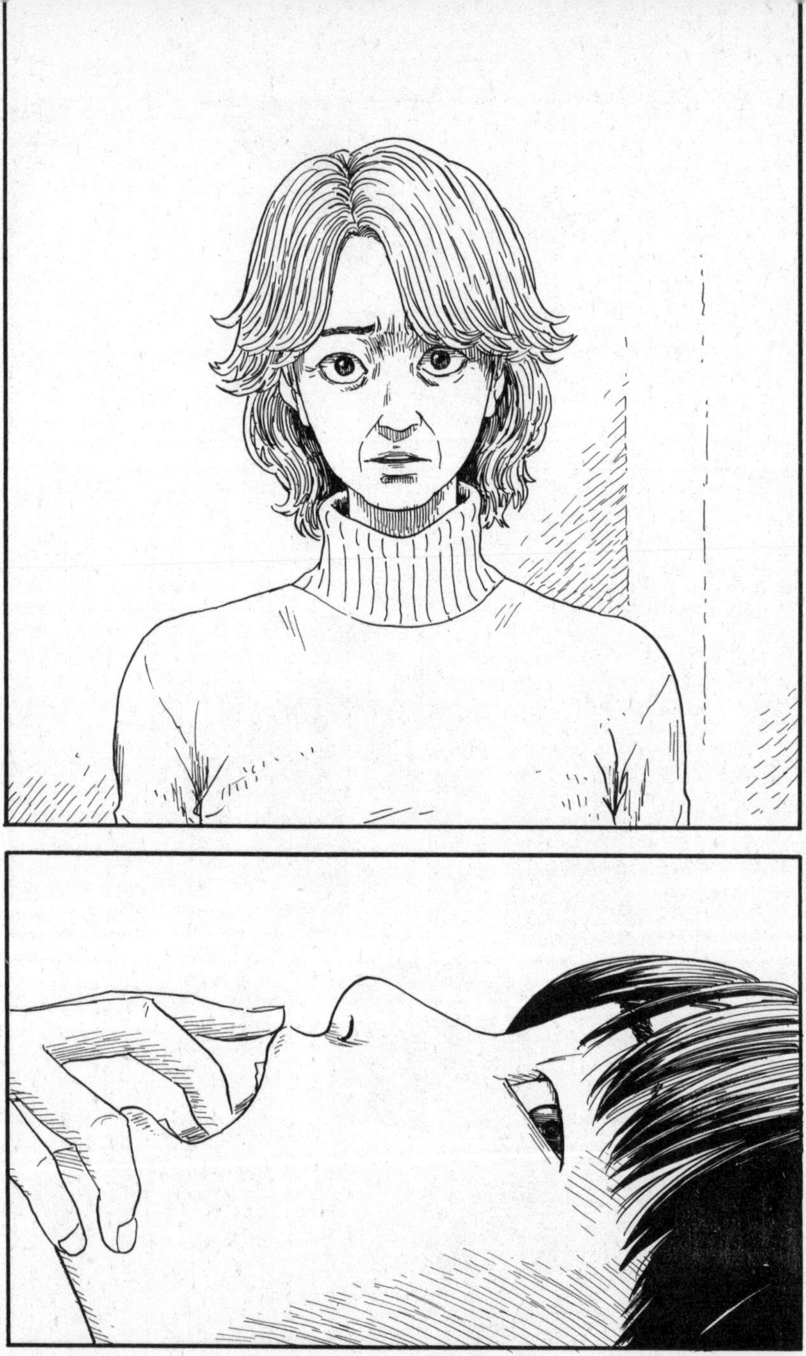

Blood on the Tracks VOLUME 7 • END

Blood
on
the
Tracks

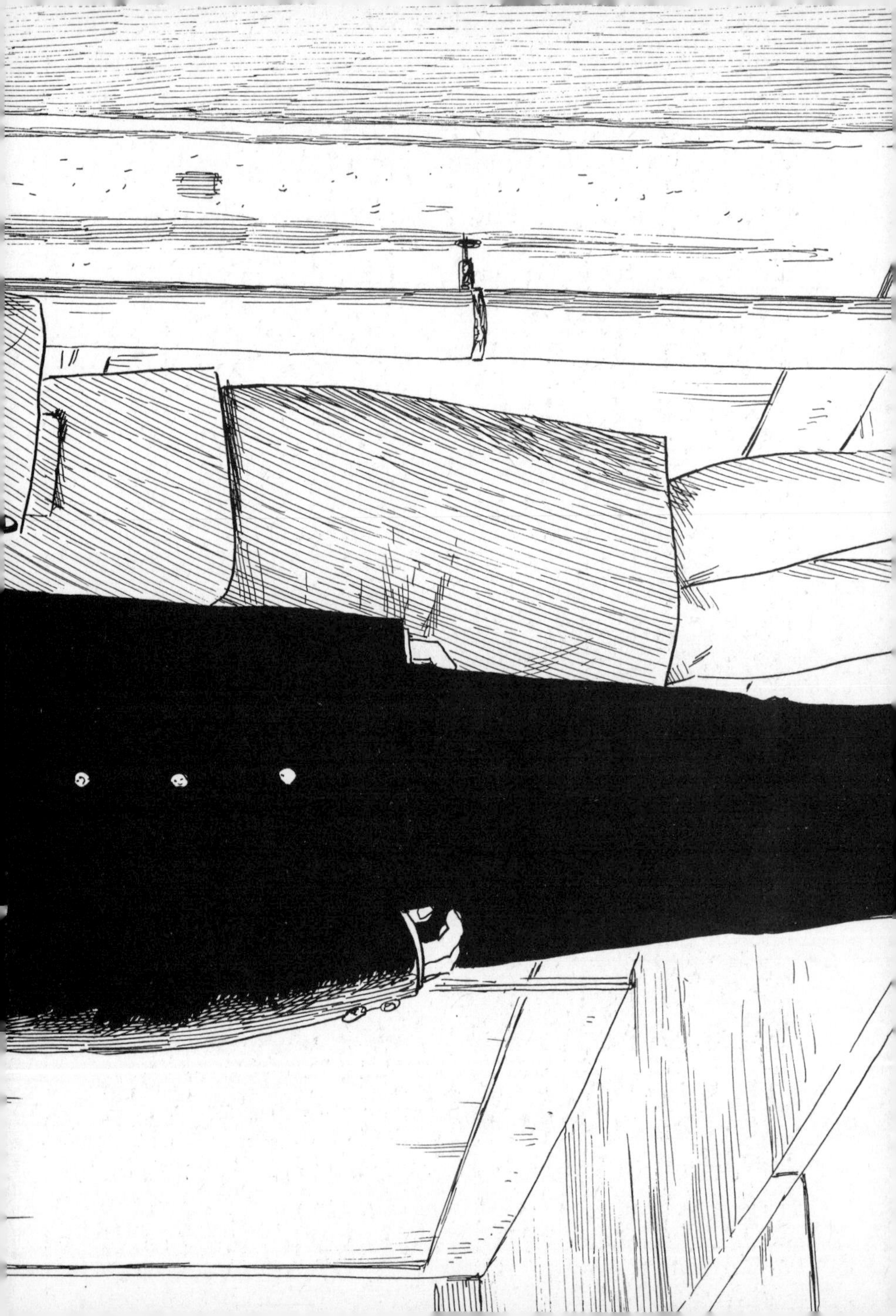

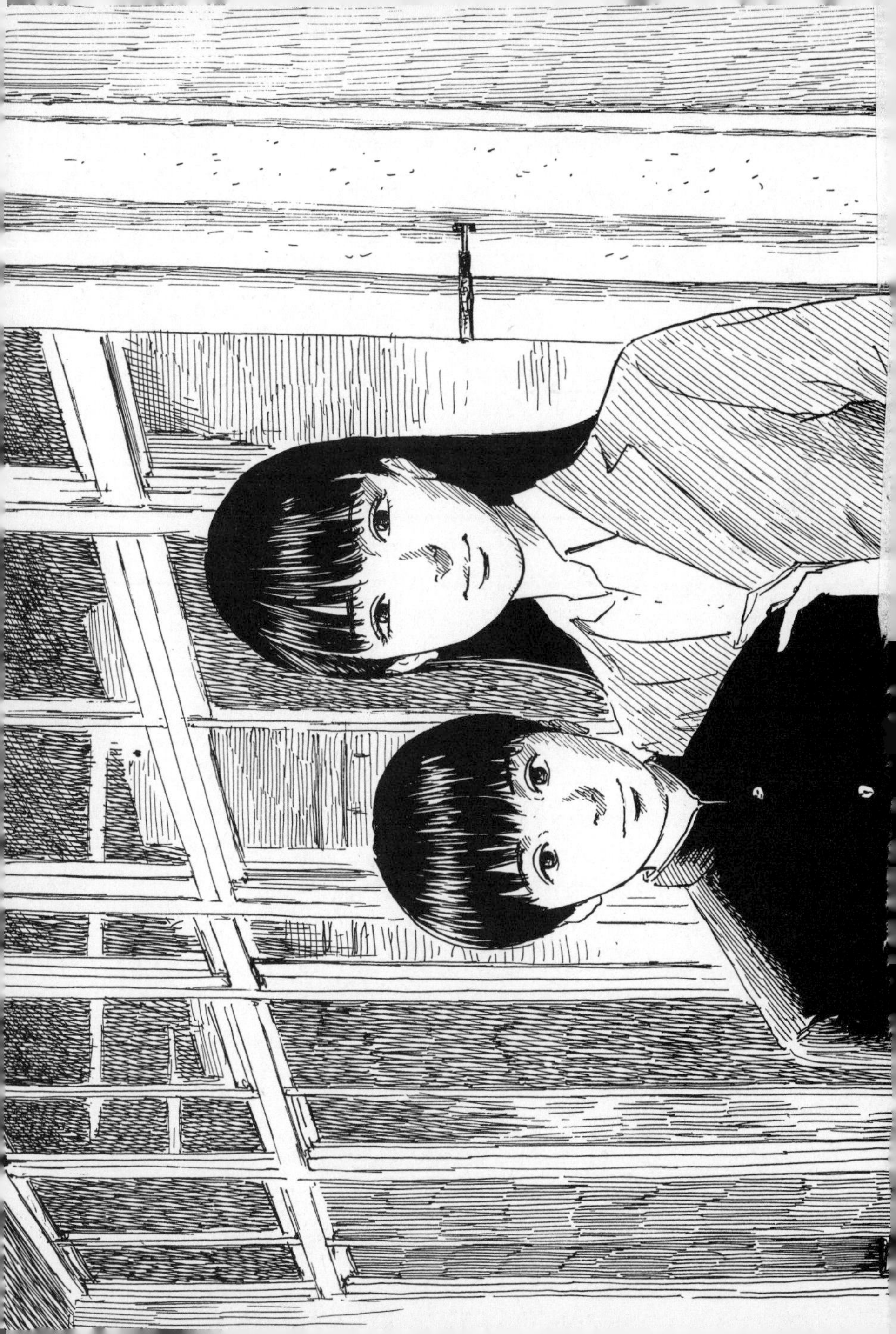

# Blood on the Tracks 7

A Vertical Comics Edition

Editor:        Daniel Joseph
Translation: Daniel Komen
Production: Risa Cho
               Evan Hayden

CHI NO WADACHI 7
by Shuzo OSHIMI

Translation provided by Vertical Comics, 2021
Published by Vertical Comics, an imprint of Kodansha USA Publishing, LLC, New York

Originally published in Japanese as *Chi no Wadachi 7* by Shogakukan, 2019
*Chi no Wadachi* serialized in *Big Comic Superior*, Shogakukan, 2017-

This is a work of fiction.

ISBN: 978-1-64729-070-2

Manufactured in the United States of America

First Edition

Kodansha USA Publishing, LLC
451 Park Avenue South
7th Floor
New York, NY 10016
www.kodansha.us

Vertical books are distributed through Penguin-Random House Publisher Services.